Dedicated to
the CLPA Library
In honour of
MR. JAMES HILL

-Class of 2008

GREAT JEWS ON STAGE AND SCREEN

GREAT JEWS ON STAGE AND SCREEN

★★★★★★★★★★★★★★★★★★★★★★★★★★★★★★★★★★★★

Darryl Lyman

Jonathan David Publishers, Inc.
Middle Village, New York 11379

**GREAT JEWS ON
STAGE AND SCREEN**

Jonathan David Publishers, Inc.
68-22 Eliot Avenue
Middle Village, New York 11379

10 9 8 7 6 5 4 3 2

Library of Congress Cataloging-in-Publication Data

Lyman, Darryl, 1944-
Great Jews on stage and screen.

"A companion to Great Jews in sports . . . and Great Jews in music"—
Includes index.
1. Jewish entertainers—Biography—Dictionaries.
2. Jewish entertainers—Israel—Biography—Dictionaries. I. Title.
PN1583.L94 1987 790.2'089924 87-4214
ISBN 0-8246-0328-1

Book design by Arlene Schleifer Goldberg

Printed in the United States of America

To the memory of my father,

LYNN LYMAN

★★

Contents

Major Biographies

★★

Thumbnail Sketches

★★★

Acknowledgments

I would like to thank Alfred J. Kolatch and David Kolatch of Jonathan David Publishers, Inc., for their encouragement and suggestions.

The following institutions and individuals helped me in my search for photographs: the bookstores Larry Edmunds Bookshop (Hollywood) and Eddie Brandt's Saturday Matinee (North Hollywood); the film studios Columbia, Metro-Goldwyn-Mayer, Orion, Paramount, Republic, Twentieth Century-Fox, United Artists, Universal, and Warner Bros.; the television networks ABC, CBS, NBC, and PBS; the magazines *International Musician* and *Musical America*; the staffs of the American Jewish Archives, the Bob Dylan Office, Herbert H. Breslin, Inc., ICM Artists, Ltd., and the William Morris Agency; and the individuals Jaacov Agor, Clarence S. Bull, Coburn, Shimon Finkel, Roman Freulich, Brian Hamill, Gene Kornman, Dennis Lyman, Newey, Joyce Rudolph, Jack Scagnetti, Barbra Streisand, and Joe Walters.

★★

Introduction

Great Jews on Stage and Screen is a companion to *Great Jews in Sports* (1983) by Robert Slater and *Great Jews in Music* (1986) by the present writer, both also published by Jonathan David Publishers, Inc. This volume focuses on Jewish performers in the theater, in films, and on television.

In the ancient world, pious Jews kept away from all theatrical activity. But many other Jews did attend pagan theaters. By the first century of the Christian Era, Jews were even performing on the pagan stage. In Rome the Jewish actor Aliturus was among Emperor Nero's favorites.

As Jews became increasingly unpopular, however, they tended to conceal their origin. For several centuries Jewish theatrical activity was obscured.

Later, during the Renaissance period, Jews created their own theater. In central Europe, especially in Germany, Yiddish religious plays were performed. In Italy and Holland, comedies and sacred dramas were staged in Hebrew. Italian Jews frequently participated in the gentile theater as well, particularly in Mantua.

However, throughout most of Europe, Jews seldom appeared on the gentile stage up to the mid-1800s. During that time Jewish actors, few in number, faced prejudice and often abuse.

Eventually the emancipation and assimilation movements of the nineteenth century opened doors for Jews on the stage. Among the first Jews to gain prominence in the modern gentile theater were Rudolf Schildkraut in Germany and David Warfield in the United States.

The late nineteenth century also saw the rise of the modern Yiddish theater, beginning in Romania through the efforts of Abraham Goldfaden, an author, composer, producer, manager, and impresario. The movement soon spread throughout Europe and the United States, a strong Yiddish theater thriving for many years in New York City. However, a decline set in between World Wars I and II as more and more American Jews grew up without Yiddish. Many Yiddish actors and actresses tried to switch to the English-language stage. Among the most successful at that adjustment were Paul Muni and Molly Picon.

Jews were emerging not only in the legitimate theater but also in the realm of lighter entertainment. From the early Middle Ages on, Jews had excelled as clowns, mimes, singers, dancers, jugglers, acrobats, storytellers, and wild-animal tamers. Often they were itinerants. From their traditions evolved innumerable modern revue, burlesque, vaudeville, music-hall, and musical-comedy stars. Examples included the escape artist Harry Houdini; the burlesque clown Bert Lahr; the revue performers Fanny Brice, Eddie Cantor, Al Jolson, and Sophie Tucker; and the entertainer-actors Jack Benny, Milton Berle, George Burns, Danny Kaye, Phil Silvers, and Ed Wynn.

In the early twentieth century, Jews found unprecedented opportunities in yet another entertainment medium—film. In Russia, Germany, the United States, and elsewhere, Jews were allowed to play a major role in the development of the motion-picture industry as a business and an art form. Movies were new. They had no traditions or vested interests to be defended by the established powers in the Jews' host countries. Furthermore, moving pictures were widely regarded as a low-grade form of entertainment. Therefore, immigrants, including many Jews, more or less had the budding movie industry dropped into their laps. Aiding them was the fact that early movies, unlike stage entertainments, were silent and did not require a knowledge of vernacular languages. Hence, wandering Jews could go anywhere in the world and set up movie companies with little technical difficulty.

Jews in huge numbers became film executives, producers, and directors. As performing artists, too, they had a major impact. One of the most important silent-screen Jews was the French comic actor Max Linder, who influenced Charles Chaplin. Later film giants of Jewish heritage included Woody Allen, Alan Arkin, Lauren Bacall, Mel Brooks, Tony Curtis, Kirk Douglas, Richard Dreyfuss,

★★★

John Garfield, Dustin Hoffman, Judy Holliday, Leslie Howard, Jerry Lewis, Peter Lorre, Paul Lukas, the Marx Brothers, Walter Matthau, Luise Rainer, Edward G. Robinson, Peter Sellers, Barbra Streisand, Gene Wilder, and Shelley Winters.

Television proved to be a major vehicle for many others, such as Beatrice Arthur, Edward Asner, Gene Barry, Sid Caesar, Peter Falk, Lorne Greene, Goldie Hawn, Jack Klugman, Harvey Korman, Hal Linden, Leonard Nimoy, William Shatner, Dinah Shore, and Henry Winkler.

Who is a Jew? In this book, I have followed the definition established by Jewish law: a Jew is anyone who was born of a Jewish mother or who converted to Judaism. The fact that the person later defected and joined a Christian church would not matter; according to Jewish law the subject is still a Jew.

The above definition forces the exclusion of performers born of a Jewish father and non-Jewish mother, as in the cases of Don Adams, Melvyn Douglas, Carrie Fisher (father, Eddie Fisher; mother, Debbie Reynolds), John Houseman, Michael Landon, Paul Newman, and Simone Signoret. On the other hand, it allows the inclusion of such converts as Sammy Davis, Jr., Marilyn Monroe, Norma Shearer, and Elizabeth Taylor.

Great Jews on Stage and Screen is a compendium of one hundred major biographies supplemented by an appendix of thumbnail sketches. I hope that you, the reader, get as much enjoyment from reading the stories of these diverse and fascinating personalities as I did in researching and writing them.

Darryl Lyman

Whittier, California

★★★

Note on Style

Abbreviations

The following abbreviations are sometimes used in this text:

Fr. = France
G.B. = Great Britain
Ger. = Germany
It. = Italy
Pol. = Poland
U.S. = United States
Yid. = Yiddish

Dates

Film dates, unless otherwise noted, are years of general release, as distinct from years of production, copyright, or limited release.

Selected Performances

In the "Selected performances" lists, television appearances are limited to shows in which the person had a continuing role in a series.

MAJOR BIOGRAPHIES

★★★

Luther Adler

Distinguished Product of American Yiddish Theater

(1903-1984)

Luther Adler was born in New York City, New York, on May 4, 1903. His original name was Lutha Adler. He belonged to a famous family of actors and actresses, including his parents (Jacob and Sarah), his brother Jay, and his sister Stella.

Lutha Adler studied acting under his father; and from 1908 (debuting at the age of five) to 1921, the youth appeared in plays with his father's Yiddish theater company. He then entered the English-language theater, working in New York City in *The Hand of the Potter* (1921) and touring in *Sonya* (1922).

Changing his first name to Luther, Adler made his Broadway debut by playing Leon Kantor, a young violinist with a self-sacrificing mother, in *Humoresque* (1923). Throughout the rest of the 1920s he worked steadily on the English-language stage. In 1929 he replaced Horace Braham as Samuel Kaplan, the law student, in *Street Scene*.

After spending 1930-31 on the Yiddish stage, Adler joined the Group Theater, where he began with a minor role in *Night over Taos* (1932). Then, over the next several years, he gave a number of performances through which he rose to become one of the most distinguished stage actors of his time.

He played the ambitious, vicious Sam Ginsburg in *Success Story* (1932), the radical professor Julian Vardaman in *Alien Corn* (1933), the steadfast physician Dr. Gordon in *Men in White* (1933), and the crippled war veteran Moe Axelrod in *Awake and Sing!* (1935). Perhaps the most important role of his career was as Joe Bonaparte, who abandons a promising career as a violinist to earn money as a boxer, in *Golden Boy* (1937).

Among his roles over the next several years were those of Charleston in *Thunder Rock* (1939); Mr. Robinson in *Jane Eyre* (1943), which he also directed; and the title character in *Uncle Harry* (1944).

The Holocaust prompted Adler and others to participate in stage works that focused the general public's attention on the plight of Jews. In 1943 he appeared in Ben Hecht's pageant *We Will Never Die.* The program consisted of three parts: "The Roll Call," a recitation of great Jewish names in the arts and sciences from ancient times to the modern era; "Jews in the War," a dramatization of the contributions of American Jewish war heroes; and "Remember Us," a presentation of reports about the slaughters in Nazi Europe.

In 1946 Adler directed Hecht's drama-pageant *A Flag Is Born,* which was produced to aid and explain the cause of Zionism. Among the performers whom Adler directed in the play were Paul Muni, Celia Adler (his half sister), and the young non-Jew Marlon Brando.

Adler devoted the late 1940s and early 1950s primarily to film work. He had made his movie debut in *Lancer Spy* (1937). But it was his role as a belligerent Dutch tycoon in *Wake of the Red Witch* (1949) that firmly established him as an important movie character actor.

His heavy features often led filmmakers to cast him as a villain. He played a crime boss in *D.O.A.* (1950). In *The Desert Fox* (1951) he portrayed Adolf Hitler. In *The Magic Face* (1951) he played Janus the Great, a vaudeville star who kills, and then impersonates, Hitler. Adler was never fully appreciated in Hollywood, and his acting was frequently much better than the poor movies in which he was cast.

From the early 1950s on, he divided his time among stage, TV, and movie projects. On the stage his roles included Shylock in *The Merchant of Venice* (1953), Eddie Carbone in *A View from the Bridge* (1957), Willy Loman in *Death of a Salesman* (1960), Henry Drummond in *Inherit the Wind* (1961), Chebutykin in *The Three Sisters* (1964), and, as a replacement for Zero Mostel, Tevye in *Fiddler on the Roof* (1965).

Adler contributed fine performances to a number of live productions during TV's Golden Age. Among the plays that he appeared in were "Hedda Gabler" on *The U.S. Steel Hour* (1954), "Man with a Vengeance" on *General Electric Theater* (1955), and "The Plot to Kill Stalin" on *Playhouse Ninety* (1958). He later guest-starred on many TV dramatic series, including *Twilight Zone* (1965), *Ben Casey* (1965), and *Hawaii Five-O* (1972). In 1971 he had a regular role in the series *The Psychiatrist*.

Adler appeared in the films *The Girl in the Red Velvet Swing* (1955) and *The Last Angry Man* (1959). In *Cast a Giant Shadow* (1966) he played Jacob Zion in a story about the Arab-Israeli War of 1948-49. In *The Man in the Glass Booth* (1975) he was the judge in the trial of a Jew who claims that he is a Nazi war criminal and who becomes obsessed with the idea that he can absorb Nazi guilt and Israeli hatred. Adler's later films included *Voyage of the Damned* (1976) and *Absence of Malice* (1981).

He was married twice. In 1938 he wedded the actress Sylvia Sidney. She appeared with him in *We Will Never Die*. They had a son, Jacob, before they divorced in the late 1940s. In 1959 he married Julia Hadley Roche.

Adler died at his home in Kutztown, Pennsylvania, on December 8, 1984.

Selected performances:

Stage

The Hand of the Potter (1921)
Sonya (1922)
Humoresque (1923)
The Monkey Talks (1925)
Monkey Business (1926)
We Americans (1926)
John (1927)
Red Rust (1929)
Street Scene (1929)
Millions (1930)
The Wild Man (1930)
Night over Taos (1932)
Success Story (1932)
Alien Corn (1933)
Men in White (1933)
Gold Eagle Guy (1934)
Awake and Sing! (1935)
Waiting for Lefty (1935)
Paradise Lost (1935)
The Case of Clyde Griffiths (1936)
Johnny Johnson (1936)
Golden Boy (1937)
Rocket to the Moon (1938)
Thunder Rock (1939)
Two on an Island (1940)
No Time for Comedy (1940)
Accent on Youth (1941)
The Russian People (1942)
Jane Eyre (1943)
Uncle Harry (1944)
Common Ground (1945)
The Beggars Are Coming to Town (1945)
Dunnigan's Daughter (1945)
Tovarich (1952)
The Play's the Thing (1952)
The Merchant of Venice (1953)
The Time of the Cuckoo (1954)
Angel Street (1955)
A Month in the Country (1956)
Reclining Figure (1956)
A View from the Bridge (1957)
Death of a Salesman (1960)
Inherit the Wind (1961)
The Happy Time (1962)
Anna Christie (1962)
Tchin-Tchin (1963)
Brecht on Brecht (1963)
The Passion of Josef D. (1964)
The Three Sisters (1964)
Fiddler on the Roof (1965)
The Tenth Man (1966)

Films

Lancer Spy (1937)
Cornered (1945)
Saigon (1948)
The Loves of Carmen (1948)
Wake of the Red Witch (1949)
House of Strangers (1949)
South Sea Sinner (1950)
Under My Skin (1950)
D.O.A. (1950)
Kiss Tomorrow Goodbye (1950)
M (1951)
The Magic Face (1951)
The Desert Fox (1951)
Hoodlum Empire (1952)
The Tall Texan (1953)
The Miami Story (1954)
Crashout (1955)
The Girl in the Red Velvet Swing (1955)
Hot Blood (1956)

The Last Angry Man (1959)
Cast a Giant Shadow (1966)
The Brotherhood (1968)
The Sunshine Patriot (TV, 1968)
The Psychiatrist: God Bless the Children (TV, 1970)
Crazy Joe (1974)
The Man in the Glass Booth (1975)
Murph the Surf (1975)
Voyage of the Damned (1976)
The Three Sisters (1977)
Absence of Malice (1981)

TV

The Psychiatrist (1971)

★★

Woody Allen

Comic Neurotic

(1935-   )

Woody Allen was born of Orthodox Jewish parents in New York City, New York, on December 1, 1935. His original name was Alan Stewart Konigsberg.

While growing up in the Flatbush section of Brooklyn, he spent as little time as possible at schoolwork. He preferred to play sports (especially baseball), watch stage shows, and perform magic tricks.

After graduating from Midwood High School in Brooklyn, he was pressured by his parents into going to college. He briefly attended New York University and then City College of the City University of New York, both of which expelled him within a few months because of his low marks and poor attendance.

Meanwhile, however, the real direction of his life had already been set into motion. In his early teens he began to sell gags to newspapers. Later, still in his teens, he wrote material for radio and TV performers, including Sid Caesar. By then he had taken the name Woody Allen.

In 1954 he married Harlene Rosen, a teacher. They had known each other since their high-school days.

For the next several years he earned a good living as a TV comedy writer. His material was used on *The Tonight Show, The Garry Moore Show,* and other programs.

But in the late 1950s and early 1960s his life and career took sharp turns. One change was the dissolution of his marriage.

Woody Allen (far right)

He also decided to become a performer, beginning as a stand-up comic in Greenwich Village nightclubs. Of a basically shy nature, he found performing to be difficult at first. But he settled down and became a tremendous success after he created his now well-known fictional persona: an intelligent contemporary urban man struggling feebly against the alienation and anxieties of the cold, mechanized modern world—in comic terms, a klutzy neurotic. By 1963 Allen, through nightclub dates and TV appearances, had established a national reputation.

In 1964 he was asked to write and costar in his first film, *What's New, Pussycat?* (1965), a broad, episodic sex farce. In *Casino Royale* (1967) he played Jimmy Bond, a spoof of the he-man spy James Bond.

Allen wrote, but did not appear in, the light comedy play *Don't Drink the Water,* which was staged in 1966 and released as a film in 1969. He both wrote and starred in *Play It Again, Sam,* staged in 1969 and released as a film in 1972. The story centers on a neurotic film critic trying to recover from the defection of his wife. He drifts back and forth between the worlds of reality and fantasy, in the latter of which he often confers with the ghost of the macho Humphrey Bogart.

Allen drew some of the subject matter of *Play It Again, Sam* from his personal experience. Having divorced his first wife, Allen, in 1966, married the actress Louise Lasser, who had appeared in *What's New, Pussycat?* Within a few years, however, that marriage, too, ended in divorce.

Allen and Lasser appeared together in several films, even after they split up. Among them were *Take the Money and Run* (1969), *Bananas* (1971), and *Everything You Always Wanted to Know about Sex* (*but Were Afraid to Ask)* (1972). Besides starring in those films, he directed them and had a major hand in preparing the scripts. *Take the Money and Run* is a mock documentary of a young man who aspires to become public-enemy number one but who fails to make even the top ten. *Bananas* parodies Latin American revolutions, while *Everything You Always Wanted to Know about Sex* spoofs the popular sex manual of that name.

He coscripted, directed, and starred in *Sleeper* (1973). Set two hundred years in the future, the film satirizes sophisticated modern life. Allen also played clarinet (at which he is very proficient) in the jazz background score for the movie. *Sleeper* is generally regarded as the first of Allen's truly great motion pictures, in which a witty script blends with a visual complexity and continuity to create a rich comic-film artistry.

Love and Death (1975), set in czarist Russia during the Napoleonic wars, is a mock epic in which the protagonist (Allen) is a self-professed "militant coward." Allen also wrote and directed the film, which may be viewed as a spoof of nineteenth-century Russian novels.

The evils of blacklisting during the McCarthy era are the principal subject of *The Front* (1976), starring Allen. With *Annie Hall* (1977) he returned to his triple role as coscriptwriter, director, and star. While telling the tender, introspective story of the breakup of a love affair, the film provides subtle insight into modern relationships.

After writing and directing, but not appearing in, the movie *Interiors* (1978), Allen made *Manhattan* (1979), a romanticized paean to his beloved city. Besides cowriting and directing the film, he starred as Isaac Davis, a successful comedy writer who quits his TV job to write a novel. Though imbued with much humor, the story is also a serious study of "selling out," both personally and artistically.

Allen then wrote, directed, and starred (as Sandy Bates, a comedy-film director) in *Stardust Memories* (1980). In it, he directs acid humor at both himself and overly serious movie fans.

Allen's mature writing has extended beyond films. Besides writing pieces for major periodicals, including *Playboy* and *The New Yorker,* he has published the books *Getting Even* (1971), *Without Feathers* (1975), and *Side Effects* (1980). His play *The Floating Light Bulb* was staged, without him performing or directing, in 1981.

A Midsummer Night's Sex Comedy (1982), which he wrote, directed, and starred in, is a light, sunny movie set near the turn of the century. In *Zelig* (1983) Allen spliced himself into newsreel clips from the 1920s and 1930s. Besides playing the role of the human chameleon in the picture, Allen wrote and directed this "mockumentary."

He then wrote, directed, and starred in *Broadway Danny Rose* (1984). It is the story of a small-time talent agent who falls in love with the girlfriend of a second-rate nightclub singer, the agent's own client.

Allen wrote and directed, but did not appear in, *The Purple Rose of Cairo* (1985), a fantasy about a housewife and her movie hero, who walks off the screen and into her gray life.

In *Hannah and Her Sisters* (1986), which he wrote, directed, and starred in, Allen dealt with some of his familiar topics: adultery, upscale New York City life, and the modern existential crisis—cast in a humorous mold. But he also incorporated new elements: the celebrating of family and the finding of love.

Radio Days (1987), which Allen wrote, directed, and narrated (but did not appear in), is a nostalgic story about the effect of radio on people's lives during the medium's golden era (1930s and 1940s).

In recent years Allen has had a romantic liaison with Mia Farrow, star of several of his films. In the spring of 1987 it was announced that Allen and Farrow were expecting a baby.

Selected performances:

Stage

Play It Again, Sam (1969)

Films

What's New, Pussycat? (1965)
Casino Royale (1967)
Take the Money and Run (1969)
Bananas (1971)
Play It Again, Sam (1972)
Everything You Always Wanted to Know about Sex (*but Were Afraid to Ask)* (1972)
Sleeper (1973)
Love and Death (1975)
The Front (1976)
Annie Hall (1977)
Manhattan (1979)
Stardust Memories (1980)
A Midsummer Night's Sex Comedy (1982)
Zelig (1983)
Broadway Danny Rose (1984)
Hannah and Her Sisters (1986)
Radio Days (narrator, 1987)

★★

Alan Arkin

Versatile Actor

(1934-)

Alan Arkin was born in New York City, New York, on March 26, 1934. Early in his childhood he became interested in entertaining others. Already showing signs of the great versatility that would mark his later career, he was overheard telling his friends, "Let's play circus. I'll be everything."

Later he moved with his parents to the Highland Park section of Los Angeles, California, where he attended Benjamin Franklin High School. There he won a talent contest by imitating another versatile performer, Danny Kaye.

After graduating from high school in 1951, Arkin studied drama at Los Angeles City College (1951-52) and Los Angeles State College (1952-53). In 1953 he enrolled at Bennington College for women in Vermont, having received a special drama scholarship created to have men available for male roles in school plays. In 1955 he left Bennington without a degree.

Arkin settled in New York City and began a career as a songwriter and folksinger. In the late 1950s he sang in nightclubs in the United States and Europe with a folk trio called the Tarriers.

But he turned increasingly toward the theater. In 1958 he had a small part in the off-Broadway play *Heloise.* Then he joined an improvisational group in Saint Louis, returned briefly to New York City, and joined another improvisational group in Chicago. It was in Chicago that he finally found himself as an actor. Through the improvisational method, he learned how to mold characters and shape scenes.

With the Chicago troupe, called the Second City, Arkin made his Broadway debut, in a revue entitled *From the Second City* (1961). He then appeared in *Man Out Loud, Girl Quiet* (1962), for which he also composed the music.

The big step upward in his career came with his role as a Jewish adolescent in the Broadway farce *Enter Laughing* (1963). Originally listed as a minor supporting actor, he gave such a brilliant performance as the stage-struck Bronx delivery boy that he stole the show and was soon raised to star billing.

After another successful role in a Broadway comedy, as a would-be suicide in *Luv* (1964), Arkin won his first part in a movie. In his spectacular film debut, he played the wacky leader of a landing party of Russian sailors whose submarine is grounded on a New England island in the hilarious comedy *The Russians Are Coming, the Russians Are Coming* (1966).

Arkin, refusing to be typecast, followed with movie roles that allowed him to exercise his versatility. In *Wait Until Dark* (1967) he played a diabolic thug. In *The Heart Is a Lonely Hunter* (1968) he starred as a deaf-mute who loses, one by one, the few connections he has with the rest of the world and finally commits suicide.

Returning to comedy, Arkin played the title role in *Inspector Clouseau* (1968), as the bumbling French detective previously (and subsequently) portrayed by Peter Sellers. In *Popi* (1969) Arkin was a Puerto Rican father. In the black-humor story of *Catch-22* (1970) he played Yossarian, who loses control of his life and mind when he is trapped in the madness of wartime military service.

Arkin had the title role in *The Defection of Simas Kudirka* (TV, 1978), based on the true story of a Lithuanian seaman who leaped from a Russian ship to the deck of an American Coast Guard cutter in an abortive bid for freedom in 1970. *The In-Laws* (1979) was a spoof of international crime dramas, while *The Last Unicorn* (1982) was an animated children's film for which he skillfully recorded the voice of Schmendrick the Magician. In the fact-based *A Deadly Business* (TV, 1986) he played Harold Kaufman, who goes undercover for the Federal Bureau of Investigation (FBI) to expose organized crime's involvement in illegal toxic-waste dumping.

In the fact-based *Escape from Sobibor* (TV, 1987) Arkin had one of his most powerful roles, as Leon Feldhendler, leader of the most daring and successful mass escape from a Nazi death camp during World War II. In the spring of 1987 he starred in the TV comedy series *Harry,* as Harry Porschak, a schemer working in a hospital purchasing department.

Arkin's versatility has shown up in other areas of his career as well. Besides performing as a folksinger, he has been involved in children's music. He composed "Cuddle Bug," "That's Me," and other children's songs, and he recorded children's albums, including *The Babysitters* (1958) and *The Family Album* (1965). His work as a director has included the stage (1969) and film (1971) versions of *Little Murders*. In addition, he is a gifted writer, having published the juvenile books *Tony's Hard Work Day* (1972) and *The Lemming Condition* (1976) and the adult book *Halfway through the Door* (1979), an account of his experiences with yoga.

Arkin married the actress Barbara Dana in 1964. They had met the previous year when she was his leading lady in *Enter Laughing*. Later they costarred together in a series of spots for the children's TV series *Sesame Street* and in the comedy series *Harry*. They had a son: Anthony.

From a previous marriage, to a Bennington girl, Arkin had two sons: Adam and Matthew. Both boys have become actors, and each has appeared with their father; examples are Alan and Adam in *Chu Chu and the Philly Flash* (1981) and Alan and Matthew in *The Defection of Simas Kudirka*.

Selected performances:

Stage

Heloise (1958)
From the Second City (1961)
Man Out Loud, Girl Quiet (1962)
Enter Laughing (1963)
Luv (1964)
The White House Murder Case (1970)
The Opening (1972)

Films

The Russians Are Coming, the Russians Are Coming (1966)
Wait Until Dark (1967)
Woman Times Seven (1967)
The Heart Is a Lonely Hunter (1968)
Inspector Clouseau (1968)
The Monitors (1969)
Popi (1969)
Catch-22 (1970)
Little Murders (1971)
Last of the Red Hot Lovers (1972)
Freebie and the Bean (1974)
Rafferty and the Gold Dust Twins (1975)
Hearts of the West (1975)
The Seven-Per-Cent Solution (1976)
The Other Side of Hell (TV, 1978)
The Defection of Simas Kudirka (TV, 1978)
The In-Laws (1979)
The Magician of Lublin (1979)
Simon (1980)
Improper Channels (1981)
Chu Chu and the Philly Flash (1981)
The Last Unicorn (1982)
Joshua Then and Now (1985)
Bad Medicine (1985)
Big Trouble (1986)
A Deadly Business (TV, 1986)
Escape from Sobibor (TV, 1987)

TV

Harry (1987)

★★★

Beatrice Arthur

Maude

(1926-)

Beatrice Arthur was born in New York City, New York, on May 13, 1926. Her original name was Bernice Frankel.

At about the age of eleven she moved with her family to Cambridge, Maryland. While attending Cambridge High School, she amused her friends with imitations of Mae West. Later she graduated from Linden Hall High School in Liberty, Pennsylvania, and studied for two years at Blackstone College, a junior college in Virginia.

Then, at the Franklin Institute of Science and Arts, she earned a degree as a medical-lab technician. But after working for a short time at a hospital in her hometown of Cambridge, she decided to go into show business.

Arthur went to New York City, where she studied acting for two years under Erwin Piscator at the Dramatic Workshop of the New School for Social Research. Among her fellow students were Marlon Brando and Gene Saks. Because of her height (5′9½″) and her deep, powerful voice, she was cast in the title role, a classic heroine, of the Dramatic Workshop's production of *Lysistrata* (1947), her first stage appearance.

Later in 1947, at the Cherry Lane Theater in Greenwich Village, she made her professional debut, as a member of the speaking chorus in *The Dog beneath the Skin*. Over the next couple of years, at the same theater, she played many important roles, including Inez in *No Exit* (1948), Kate in *The Taming of the Shrew* (1948), and Hesione in *Heartbreak House* (1949).

Also at Cherry Lane was Gene Saks, whom Arthur married in 1950. It was largely through her encouragement that Saks later turned to directing, at which he became very successful. They adopted two sons, Matthew and Daniel, before they divorced.

In 1951 Arthur joined the stock company at Atlantic City's Circle Theater, where she appeared in several productions, including *The Voice of the Turtle* (1951). In 1953 she worked as the resident comedienne at the Tamiment Theater in Pennsylvania. She sang and acted as Lucy Brown in the off-Broadway production of Kurt Weill's *The Threepenny Opera* (1954). In 1955 she was a comedienne in *Shoestring Revue*. And in 1957 she appeared in her first Broadway comedy, *Nature's Way*.

Early in her career, when her theater work was sporadic, Arthur occasionally sang in major New York City nightclubs, such as the Blue Angel and the Number One Fifth Avenue.

She also made tentative ventures into TV. In 1948 she sang in a TV production of *Once upon a Time*. And in the 1950s she had guest bits on TV variety series hosted by Steve Allen, Sid Caesar, Ed Sullivan, and others.

In 1959 Norman Lear, who had been a fan of Arthur's since he saw her in *Shoestring Revue,* asked her to join the cast of George Gobel's TV show, of which Lear was the producer-director. Arthur went to Hollywood for the show, but after making two episodes she returned to New York City.

In the early 1960s Arthur went into semiretirement from the theater. She appeared in *Gay Divorce* (1960) and *A Matter of Position* (1962), but she spent much of her time encouraging her husband through his first assignments as a director. In 1964 she returned to the stage in the role of Yente, the matchmaker, in *Fiddler on the Roof.* She then won her greatest Broadway acclaim with her performance in *Mame* (1966), as Vera Charles, Aunt Mame's friend and severest critic. Arthur's husband, Gene Saks, directed the show.

In the late 1960s Arthur went into semiretirement again. This time her purpose was simply to enjoy the country home that she and Saks had purchased forty miles outside Manhattan. In the early 1970s Lear tried to induce her to appear on the new TV series *All in the Family.* Arthur was reluctant, partly because she did not want to travel to Hollywood and partly because she was simply not attracted to TV.

Finally she agreed to do a guest part in *All in the Family.* Her performance, aired in late 1971, was electric. The series was dominated by the character Archie Bunker (played by Carroll O'Connor, with whom Arthur had appeared in the 1958 stage work *Ulysses in Nighttown),* a reactionary, bigoted loudmouth. Arthur created the new character Maude, cousin of Archie's wife, Edith (played by Jean Stapleton). Maude, an outspoken liberal, proved to be more than a match for Archie and gave him his long-overdue comeuppance.

Arthur's performance was so well received that the following year she was given her own TV comedy series, *Maude,* which ran till 1978. The character Maude, an aggressive libertarian and women's libber, made the country laugh at her own human foibles as she tackled such controversial topics as abortion, race relations, and pornography. Maude remains the role by which Arthur is most popularly identified.

Arthur has been in only a few movies. Her first film appearance was a small part in *That Kind of Woman* (1959). She also had roles in the filmed version of *Mame* (1974) and in Mel Brooks's comedy *History of the World, Part I* (1981).

Since 1985 Arthur has played Dorothy, one of four women living together, in the hit TV comedy series *The Golden Girls.*

Selected performances:

Stage

The Dog beneath the Skin (1947)
Gas (1947)
Yerma (1947)
No Exit (1948)
The Taming of the Shrew (1948)
Six Characters in Search of an Author (1948)
The Owl and the Pussycat (1948)
Yes Is for a Very Young Man (1949)
The Creditors (1949)
Heartbreak House (1949)
Personal Appearance (1951)
Candle Light (1951)
Love or Money (1951)
The Voice of the Turtle (1951)
The New Moon (1953)
Gentlemen Prefer Blondes (1953)
The Threepenny Opera (1954)
Shoestring Revue (1955)
Seventh Heaven (1955)
What's the Rush? (1956)
Mistress of the Inn (1957)
Nature's Way (1957)
Ulysses in Nighttown (1958)
Gay Divorce (1960)
A Matter of Position (1962)
Fiddler on the Roof (1964)
Mame (1966)
A Mother's Kisses (1968)
The Floating Light Bulb (1981)

Films

That Kind of Woman (1959)
Lovers and Other Strangers (1970)
Mame (1974)
History of the World, Part I (1981)

TV

Maude (1972-78)
The Golden Girls (1985-)

★★

Edward Asner

Lou Grant

(1929-)

Edward Asner was born of Russian immigrants in Kansas City, Missouri, on November 15, 1929. While in his teens, he performed on a local radio station as part of a class that he took at Wyandotte High School. Later he attended the University of Chicago, where he was active in dramatics.

After two years of college (1947-49) he dropped out and began to do odd jobs. In 1951 he was drafted into the army and sent to Europe. There he managed a highly rated army basketball team.

Released from military service in 1953, Asner was invited to join the Playwrights Theater Club in Chicago, where he performed in plays for two years. In 1955 he moved to New York City and began to act in off-Broadway productions, notably the Brecht-Weill musical *The Threepenny Opera* (1956). He also did numerous Shakespearean roles, such as Bardolph in *The Merry Wives of Windsor* (1959) and the Duke of Exeter in *Henry V* (1960).

In 1959 Asner married the literary agent Nancy Lou Sykes, an Episcopalian. They had delayed the marriage for two years for fear that an intermarriage would anger his Orthodox parents. The wedding ceremony was civil, and their three children—Matthew, Liza, and Kathryn—were raised in the Jewish faith.

In 1961 Asner moved to Los Angeles and began to appear in guest roles on TV dramas, such as *Naked City*. In 1964-65 he was a regular on the series *Slattery's People*. Over the next several years he acted in a number of movies and TV dramas, often as a policeman or a criminal.

His big break came in 1970 when he became a regular member of the cast on the new TV comedy series *The Mary Tyler Moore Show*. Though he had had very little experience in comedy, he auditioned for, and won, the role of Lou Grant, the irascible but lovable boss of the fictitious WJM-TV newsroom in Minneapolis. For seven seasons (1970-77) the show was one of the most popular series on TV.

During the run of *The Mary Tyler Moore Show*, Asner frequently used his free time to continue his career as a dramatic actor, especially in made-for-TV movies. For example, in *Hey, I'm Alive!* (TV, 1975) he played an airplane pilot who crashes in a frozen Yukon forest and, with his female passenger, somehow finds the physical and psychological strength to survive forty-nine days till rescued. In *Rich Man, Poor Man* (TV, 1976) he was the patriarch of the Jordache family. In *Roots* (TV, 1977) he was a captain of a slave ship. In the biopic *The Life and Assassination of the Kingfish* (TV, 1977) he portrayed Huey Long, Louisiana's Depression-era governor and United States senator.

When *The Mary Tyler Moore Show* went off the air in 1977, Asner's role became the basis for a new series, *Lou Grant* (1977-82). In that show he played the hard-hitting but compassionate city editor of a Los Angeles newspaper.

The Lou Grant character closely resembled Asner himself. Like Grant, Asner became identified with important public issues about which he had strong opinions. That identification became a source of great controversy during his term as the elected president of the Screen Actors Guild (1981-85). He used his visibility to voice his liberal viewpoint on a number of political and social issues, such as his stand, in 1982, in opposition to American involvement in El Salvador and in favor of the rebels there. When his *Lou Grant* series was dropped from that fall's lineup, it was widely assumed that the reason for the cancellation was his controversial status.

Asner also lent his name to a wide variety of Jewish causes. In 1979, for example, he hosted a Public Broadcasting Service (PBS) series on Jewish holidays. In early 1985 he received a medal from the Jewish Theological Seminary of America for his service in promoting "human rights and interfaith understanding."

Meanwhile, Asner's professional career continued. In *Anatomy of an Illness* (TV, 1984) he portrayed Norman Cousins in the true story of the latter's efforts to cure himself of a debilitating spinal disorder after the medical community had given up hope. Asner narrated the TV documentary *Battered Wives, Shattered Lives* (1985).

There followed appearances in the TV movies *Kate's Secret* (TV, 1986) and *The Christmas Star* (TV, 1986). In the spring of 1987 he began to star in the new TV drama series *The Bronx Zoo*, as Joe Danzig, the tough but lovable principal of an inner-city high school.

Selected performances:

Stage

Venice Preserv'd (1955)
The Threepenny Opera (1956)
Romeo and Juliet (1959)
The Merry Wives of Windsor (1959)
All's Well That Ends Well (1959)
Legend of Lovers (1959)
The Tempest (1959)
Henry V (1960)
Face of a Hero (1960)

Films

The Satan Bug (1965)
The Slender Thread (1965)
The Doomsday Flight (TV, 1966)
El Dorado (1967)
Gunn (1967)
The Venetian Affair (1967)
Change of Habit (1969)
Daughter of the Mind (TV, 1969)
The House on Greenapple Road (TV, 1970)
The Old Man Who Cried Wolf! (TV, 1970)
Halls of Anger (1970)
They Call Me MISTER Tibbs (1970)
The Last Child (TV, 1971)
They Call It Murder (TV, 1971)
Skin Game (1971)
Haunts of the Very Rich (TV, 1972)
The Police Story (TV, 1973)
The Girl Most Likely to . . . (TV, 1973)
The Impostor (TV, 1975)
Death Scream (TV, 1975)
Hey, I'm Alive! (TV, 1975)
Rich Man, Poor Man (TV, 1976)
Gus (1976)
Roots (TV, 1977)
The Life and Assassination of the Kingfish (TV, 1977)
The Gathering (TV, 1977)
Family Man (TV, 1979)
A Small Killing (TV, 1981)
Fort Apache, the Bronx (1981)
Daniel (1983)
Anatomy of an Illness (TV, 1984)
Kate's Secret (TV, 1986)
The Christmas Star (TV, 1986)
Cracked Up (TV, 1987)

TV

Slattery's People (1964-65)
The Mary Tyler Moore Show (1970-77)
Lou Grant (1977-82)
The Bronx Zoo (1987-)

★★★

Lauren Bacall

Elegant Lady

(1924-)

Lauren Bacall was born in New York City, New York, on September 16, 1924. Her original name was Betty Perske. Her mother had been born in Romania with the surname Weinstein-Bacal (*Weinstein* is German, and *Bacal* Romanian, for "wineglass"). When the Weinstein-Bacals arrived in the United States, immigration officials dropped the second half of the hyphenated name and the family became simply the Weinsteins.

Later Betty's mother married a man surnamed Perske. But when Betty was six years old, her parents split up; and after the divorce, her mother took the name Bacal. Lauren Bacall, then, grew up as Betty Bacal.

At an early age she made up her mind to become a Hollywood actress. As a preteenager she did some modeling, and while attending Manhattan's Julia Richman High School she took Saturday-morning drama lessons at the New York School of the Theater.

After graduating from high school in 1940, Betty studied at the American Academy of Dramatic Arts in New York City for one year. She then worked as a model and a theater usher.

Her professional acting debut came in the Broadway show *Johnny 2 x 4* (1942), in which she had a walk-on part. At about that time she added another *l* to her surname to avoid such mispronunciations as "Backle."

Later in 1942 she had a speaking role in *Franklin Street,* but it closed out of town.

The big break in her career came when her picture appeared on the cover of the March 1943 issue of *Harper's Bazaar* magazine. The photo was seen by the movie director Howard Hawks, and soon Bacall was on her way to Hollywood.

Hawks changed her first name to Lauren and gave her an important role opposite Humphrey Bogart in *To Have and Have Not* (1944). The movie saw the birth of what came to be called The Look, a Bacall pose with her chin down and her eyes insinuatingly up. She has said that the pose originated merely as a way of controlling her nerves in her earliest scenes with her famous costar.

Bacall soon began a romance with Bogart. They married in 1945 and appeared together in *The Big Sleep* (1946), *Dark Passage* (1947), and *Key Largo* (1948). Bogart and Bacall also did the radio series *Bold Venture* (1950-51) together. They had a son (Stephen) and a daughter (Leslie).

Bacall made a tremendous impact in her early movies, usually cast as a tough, sultry woman of the world. Later her roles widened, as in *How to Marry a Millionaire* (1953), in which she played one of three models (with Betty Grable and Marilyn Monroe) in search of rich husbands. The part allowed her to show her great talent as a comedienne.

In 1957 Bogart died. Bacall, devastated, had difficulty redefining herself.

But her work since then has shown a steady maturing and deepening of her skills. In 1959 she returned to the Broadway stage in *Goodbye, Charlie,* as a callous philanderer whose punishment after death is to be sent back to earth as a woman.

In 1961 she married the actor Jason Robards, Jr. They had a son (Sam) before divorcing in 1969.

During the 1960s she appeared in several movies, including *Sex and the Single Girl* (1964) and *Harper* (1966). In 1965 she stole the show in the Broadway comedy *Cactus Flower,* as a dentist's secretary who wins her boss after posing as his wife to get him out of a sticky situation with a younger woman.

Lauren Bacall

In the 1970 Broadway show *Applause,* a musical version of the famous movie *All about Eve,* Bacall gave an electric performance in her portrayal of a fading film star. Her 1970s movies included the mystery *Murder on the Orient Express* (1974) and the comedy *Perfect Gentlemen* (TV, 1978).

In 1981 Bacall hit the New York City stage as a high-powered lady newscaster in the musical *Woman of the Year.* In the movie *The Fan* (1981) she played a high-strung Broadway star preparing for her first musical and becoming a homicidal maniac's object of attention. During 1983-84 she toured with *Woman of the Year,* and in 1985 she starred in a London production of *Sweet Bird of Youth,* which later moved to the United States.

In her autobiography, *Lauren Bacall by Myself* (1979), she shows her real-life qualities of humor, perception, and straightforwardness. Those qualities also characterize her work. Even during her early years, as a sexpot, she exuded a rare kind of elegance in her performances. With added years, she has refined and enriched her stage and screen presence, so that she now virtually dominates every project that she touches.

Selected performances:

Stage

Johnny 2 x 4 (1942)
Franklin Street (1942)
Goodbye, Charlie (1959)
Cactus Flower (1965)
Applause (1970)
Woman of the Year (1981, 1983-84)
Sweet Bird of Youth (1985-86)

Films

To Have and Have Not (1944)
Confidential Agent (1945)
The Big Sleep (1946)
Dark Passage (1947)
Key Largo (1948)
Young Man with a Horn (1950)
Bright Leaf (1950)
How to Marry a Millionaire (1953)
Woman's World (1954)
The Cobweb (1955)
Blood Alley (1955)
Written on the Wind (1956)
Designing Woman (1957)
The Gift of Love (1958)
Flame over India (1960)
Sex and the Single Girl (1964)
Shock Treatment (1964)
Harper (1966)
Murder on the Orient Express (1974)
The Shootist (1976)
Perfect Gentlemen (TV, 1978)
The Fan (1981)
Health (1982)

Radio

Bold Venture (1950-51)

★★★

Martin Balsam

Archie Bunker's Partner

(1919-)

Martin Balsam was born in New York City, New York, on November 4, 1919, He made his stage debut by appearing as a villain in an amateur production of *Pot Boiler* (1935). After graduating from DeWitt Clinton High School in 1937, he worked at odd jobs for a few years.

In 1941 he made his professional acting debut by portraying Johann in a Locust Valley, New York, production of *The Play's the Thing.* His New York City debut came later that year, as Mr. Blow in *Ghost for Sale.*

From 1941 to 1945 he was in the army, first with the combat engineers and then, from 1943 on, with the air force.

Returning to civilian life, he studied acting under Erwin Piscator at the Dramatic Workshop of the New School for Social Research from 1946 to 1948. Since 1948 he has been a member of the famed Actors Studio of New York City.

Balsam renewed his stage career in 1947, playing Sizzi in *Lamp at Midnight.* Over the next several years he made a powerful impression as a versatile character actor in a variety of plays, including *Macbeth* (1948), *Home of the Brave* (1949), *The Rose Tattoo* (1951), *Camino Real* (1953), and *Detective Story* (1953).

He also began to make guest appearances on TV. His early TV credits included the comedy series *The Goldbergs* and *Mr. Peepers,* the drama series *Inner Sanctum,* and the anthology series *Playhouse Ninety.*

Balsam's successes on the stage and on TV resulted

in his getting film offers. He made a good impression in his movie debut, as a crime investigator in *On the Waterfront* (1954). In *Twelve Angry Men* (1957) he played the foreman of the jury. He was the private investigator who was attacked by a madman with a knife in a classic scene from the Hitchcock masterpiece *Psycho* (1960).

Balsam played the presidential press secretary in *Seven Days in May* (1964). In one of his finest performances, he portrayed Arnold Burns, the conventional brother of an offbeat New Yorker (played by Jason Robards, Jr.), in *A Thousand Clowns* (1965). In the black comedy *Catch-22* (1970) he played the ridiculous Colonel Cathcart.

Balsam performed well as the son who misjudges his father (portrayed by Edward G. Robinson) in *The Old Man Who Cried Wolf!* (TV, 1970). In *The Taking of Pelham One Two Three* (1974) Balsam played a member of a gang of subway-train hijackers.

He was one of the Jewish passengers in *Raid on Entebbe* (TV, 1977), a recounting of the true story of a planeload of people who were kidnapped by terrorists, held at the Entebbe Airport in Uganda, and finally rescued in a daring raid by Israeli commandos. In *The House on Garibaldi Street* (TV, 1979) he portrayed Isser Harel, the author of the book serving as the basis for the film, which tells the story of the capture of the real-life Nazi war criminal Adolf Eichmann by Israeli agents in Argentina in 1960.

While Balsam was building a fine movie career, he also continued to appear onstage. He won high praise for playing three roles in *You Know I Can't Hear You When the Water's Running* (1967). His later stage work included *Death of a Salesman* (1974).

From 1979 to 1981 Balsam had a regular role as Murray Klein on the TV comedy series *Archie Bunker's Place.* He played the liberal, Jewish business partner of the reactionary, super-WASP bigot Archie Bunker.

Balsam's later movies included *Little Gloria . . . Happy at Last* (TV, 1982), *I Want to Live!* (TV, 1983), and *The Delta Force* (1986).

He has had three marriages. In 1952 he wedded the actress Pearl L. Somner, whom he divorced in 1954. In 1959 he married the actress Joyce Van Patten, with whom he had a daughter, Talia, before obtaining a divorce in 1962. He married Irene Miller, a TV production assistant, in 1963. Talia Balsam became an actress, appearing on her own in numerous films and with her father in *The Millionaire* (TV, 1978).

Martin Balsam

Selected performances:

Stage

The Play's the Thing (1941)
Ghost for Sale (1941)
Lamp at Midnight (1947)
The Wanhope Building (1947)
Macbeth (1948)
Sundown Beach (1948)
The Closing Door (1949)
Three Men on a Horse (1949)
Home of the Brave (1949)
A Letter from Harry (1949)
The Rose Tattoo (1951)
Camino Real (1953)
The Country Girl (1953)
Detective Story (1953)
Thirteen Clocks (1954)
Wedding Breakfast (1955)
Middle of the Night (1956)
With Respect to Joey (1957)
A View from the Bridge (1958)
The Iceman Cometh (1961)
Nowhere to Go but Up (1962)
The Porcelain Year (1965)
You Know I Can't Hear You When the Water's Running (1967)
Death of a Salesman (1974)
Cold Storage (1977)

Films

On the Waterfront (1954)
Twelve Angry Men (1957)
Time Limit (1957)
Marjorie Morningstar (1958)
Al Capone (1959)
Middle of the Night (1959)
Psycho (1960)
Ada (1961)
Breakfast at Tiffany's (1961)
Cape Fear (1962)
Everybody Go Home! (1962)
Who's Been Sleeping in My Bed? (1963)
The Carpetbaggers (1964)
Seven Days in May (1964)
The Bedford Incident (1965)
Conquered City (1965)
Harlow (1965)
A Thousand Clowns (1965)
After the Fox (1966)
Hombre (1967)
The Good Guys and the Bad Guys (1969)
Me, Natalie (1969)
Trilogy (1969)
Catch-22 (1970)
Little Big Man (1970)
Tora! Tora! Tora! (1970)
Hunters Are for Killing (TV, 1970)
The Old Man Who Cried Wolf! (TV, 1970)
The Anderson Tapes (1971)
Night of Terror (TV, 1972)
The Man (1972)
The Stone Killer (1973)
Summer Wishes, Winter Dreams (1973)
A Brand New Life (TV, 1973)
The Six-Million-Dollar Man (TV, 1973)
Trapped beneath the Sea (TV, 1974)
Confessions of a Police Captain (1974)
The Taking of Pelham One Two Three (1974)
Murder on the Orient Express (1974)
Mitchell (1975)
Miles to Go before I Sleep (TV, 1975)
Death among Friends (TV, 1975)
The Lindbergh Kidnapping Case (TV, 1976)
All the President's Men (1976)
Two Minute Warning (1976)
The Sentinel (1977)
Raid on Entebbe (TV, 1977)
Contract on Cherry Street (TV, 1977)
The Storyteller (TV, 1977)
Siege (TV, 1978)
Rainbow (TV, 1978)
The Millionaire (TV, 1978)
The Silver Bears (1978)
Cuba (1979)
The Seeding of Sarah Burns (TV, 1979)
The House on Garibaldi Street (TV, 1979)
Aunt Mary (TV, 1979)
The Love Tapes (TV, 1980)
The People vs. Jean Harris (TV, 1981)
Little Gloria . . . Happy at Last (TV, 1982)
I Want to Live! (TV, 1983)
Space (TV, 1985)
St. Elmo's Fire (1985)
The Delta Force (1986)
Second Serve (TV, 1986)
Queenie (TV, 1987)

TV

Archie Bunker's Place (1979-81)

★★

Gene Barry

Debonair TV Star

(1922-   )

Gene Barry was born in New York City, New York, on June 4, 1922. His original name was Eugene Klass. While attending New Utrecht High School in Brooklyn, he participated in school dramatic productions and studied music.

Soon after leaving high school, he began to appear on the professional stage. In 1942 he made his Broadway debut by performing in the musical *The New Moon*. He also sang in revivals of classic operettas, such as *The Merry Widow* (1943).

In 1944 he married Betty Claire Kalb. They had three children: Michael, Fredric, and Liza.

In the early 1950s Barry made his first movies, beginning with *The Atomic City* (1952). In the science-fiction picture *The War of the Worlds* (1953) he starred as a scientist. There followed a number of other films in the 1950s, including the western musical *Red Garters* (1954).

But it was on TV that Barry had his greatest success. In the revised format of the *Our Miss Brooks* (1955) comedy series, he played the elementary-school gym instructor Gene Talbot, a suitor to the English teacher Connie Brooks (played by Eve Arden).

The major break in Barry's career, shooting him to stardom, was his title role in the TV western series *Bat Masterson* (1958-61). As Bat Masterson, famed real-life lawman of the Old West, Barry was finally able to apply his dignified, debonair manner—which distinguishes all of his best work—to a character of great popular appeal.

There followed several other TV series starring Barry. In *Burke's Law* (1963-65) he was a Los Angeles police captain. That series spun off a sequel, *Amos Burke, Secret Agent* (1965-66). He also starred in the crime drama *The Name of the Game* (1968-71) and the adventure series *The Adventurer* (1972).

Barry has also acted in many TV movies. In *Prescription: Murder* (TV, 1968) he became the first killer to be captured by Lieutenant Columbo (played by Peter Falk), later the principal character in the now legendary TV series *Columbo*. Other movies featuring Barry included *The Devil and Miss Sarah* (TV, 1971), *Aspen* (TV, 1977), and *The Adventures of Nellie Bly* (TV, 1981).

Barry retains his early interest in music. He has for many years done a song-and-dance act in nightclubs.

In 1983 Barry starred in the New York City stage production of the musical *La Cage aux Folles,* as the owner of a homosexual nightclub of that name. In early 1986 he gave a striking performance in an episode of the TV series *Crazy like a Fox,* as an aging but flamboyant actor whose eccentric behavior prompts his daughter to seek a competency hearing against him.

Selected performances:

Stage

The New Moon (1942)
Rosalinda (1942)
The Merry Widow (1943)
Catherine Was Great (1944)
The Would-Be Gentleman (1946)
Bless You All (1950)
The Perfect Setup (1962)
La Cage aux Folles (1983)

Films

The Atomic City (1952)
The Girls of Pleasure Island (1953)
The War of the Worlds (1953)
Those Redheads from Seattle (1953)
Alaska Seas (1954)
Red Garters (1954)
Naked Alibi (1954)
Soldier of Fortune (1955)
The Purple Mask (1955)
Back from Eternity (1956)
China Gate (1957)
Thunder Road (1958)
Maroc 7 (1966)
Subterfuge (1968)
Prescription: Murder (TV, 1968)
Istanbul Express (TV, 1968)
Do You Take This Stranger? (TV, 1971)
The Devil and Miss Sarah (TV, 1971)
Ransom for Alice! (TV, 1977)
Aspen (TV, 1977)
Guyana, Cult of the Damned (1980)
A Cry for Love (TV, 1980)
The Girl, the Gold Watch, and Dynamite (TV, 1981)
The Adventures of Nellie Bly (TV, 1981)
Perry Mason: The Case of the Lost Love (TV, 1987)

TV

Our Miss Brooks (1955)
Bat Masterson (1958-61)
Burke's Law (1963-65)
Amos Burke, Secret Agent (1965-66)
The Name of the Game (1968-71)
The Adventurer (1972)

Gene Barry

★★★

Richard Benjamin

Mild-mannered Actor

(1938-)

Richard Benjamin was born in New York City, New York, on May 22, 1938. He was educated at the High School of Performing Arts in New York City and at the Northwestern University drama school in Evanston, Illinois.

As a teenager in the 1950s he played some bit parts in movies, such as *Thunder over the Plains* (1953). But it was on the New York City stage that he first made a name for himself. He appeared in a number of plays, including Shakespeare's *As You Like It* (1963), before making his Broadway debut in *The Star-spangled Girl* (1966).

During the 1967-68 TV season he costarred with his wife, Paula Prentiss (whom he had married in 1961), in the comedy series *He and She*. He followed that with his adult movie debut in *Goodbye, Columbus* (1969), as an aimless Jewish youth.

In the early 1970s Benjamin gained fame for his performances in several black comedies. His boyish image, pleasant manner, and clean-cut appearance sharply contrasted with the weird inner natures of his characters. In *Catch-22* (1970) he portrayed Major Danby, who cheerfully accepts the madness and slaughter going on around him in World War II and does his job in a pleasant, businesslike fashion. In *Portnoy's Complaint* (1972) he played a model Jewish youth who seethes within. Other fine performances by Benjamin during those years were in *Diary of a Mad Housewife* (1970) and *The Marriage of a Young Stockbroker* (1971).

Later he became a reliable light-comedy supporting actor in such films as *The Sunshine Boys* (1975), *House Calls* (1978), and *The Last Married Couple in America* (1980). In the movie *Packin' It In* (TV, 1983) he costarred with his wife in a back-to-nature comedy.

Benjamin has also shown an interest in directing. In 1969 he directed his wife in two New York City plays, and he won acclaim for his direction of the films *My Favorite Year* (1982) and *City Heat* (1984).

Selected performances:

Stage

As You Like It (1963)
The Star-spangled Girl (1966)
The Little Black Book (1972)
The Norman Conquests (1975)

Films

Thunder over the Plains (1953)
Crime Wave (1954)
Goodbye, Columbus (1969)
Catch-22 (1970)
Diary of a Mad Housewife (1970)
The Marriage of a Young Stockbroker (1971)
The Steagle (1971)
Portnoy's Complaint (1972)
The Last of Sheila (1973)
Westworld (1973)
The Sunshine Boys (1975)
House Calls (1978)
Scavenger Hunt (1979)
The Last Married Couple in America (1980)
How to Beat the High Cost of Living (1980)
First Family (1980)
Saturday the Fourteenth (1982)
Packin' It In (TV, 1983)

TV

He and She (1967-68)
Quark (1978)

★★

Jack Benny

Beloved Comedian

(1894-1974)

Jack Benny was born in Chicago, Illinois, on February 14, 1894. His original name was Benjamin (or Benny) Kubelsky.

He was raised in Waukegan, Illinois, where he began to take violin lessons at the age of six. Later he studied at the Chicago School of Music. When he was fourteen he began to play in local dance bands and theater orchestras. He also played in the Waukegan Township High School Orchestra till he flunked out of school after his second term.

Benny never went back to school. Having little formal education profoundly affected him in later life. He became an avid reader and made a conscious effort to learn the ways of the world. He also developed a sincere humility and simplicity that endeared him to his audiences.

After leaving school he got a job playing the violin at a local vaudeville house. In 1911 Waukegan was visited by the zany Marx Brothers in their popular vaudeville act. The boys' mother liked Benny's playing and offered him a job as their musical accompanist, traveling with them on the vaudeville circuit. Benny's parents refused to let the seventeen-year-old go. But the episode did give him confidence and did allow him to meet Zeppo Marx, who became a good friend of Benny's.

In 1912, however, Benny turned eighteen and decided to make a serious attempt at a show-business career. He joined the pianist Cora Salisbury to form a musical duo, Salisbury and Kubelsky, that played classical and popular pieces on vaudeville stages. Soon the established violinist Jan Kubelik complained to officials of the vaudeville circuit that the value of his name was being jeopardized by the young upstart's use of the name Kubelsky. After futilely arguing that his name really was Kubelsky, the teenager adopted the stage name Ben K. Benny, and the billing became Salisbury and Benny.

In 1913 he changed the spelling to Ben K. Bennie ("I thought it looked much classier," he later explained) and joined a pianist named Lyman Woods. The billing became Bennie and Woods, but they performed much the same material as the earlier duo had.

In 1917 the act broke up, and the violinist, once again as Benjamin Kubelsky, enlisted in the navy. There he began to play the violin in regular Saturday-night entertainments put on by and for the sailors. One night he was playing "The Rosary" when the audience started booing him. In desperation, he began, haltingly at first, to ad-lib a navy joke: "You see, I claim the Swiss navy is bigger than the Irish navy . . . but that the *Jewish* navy is bigger than both of them put together." It was the first time that he had ever talked onstage, and he brought the house down. Later he acted a comedy part in a service revue. In late 1918 he left the navy.

The following year he created a new vaudeville act as a single, billed as Ben K. Benny. He told jokes, performed comic bits on the violin, and even sang a little. Again, however, he faced a complaint from someone with a similar name, this time the vaudeville star Ben Bernie. In January 1921 the future great entertainer billed himself for the first time as Jack (after the vaudeville comic Jack Osterman) Benny (after his own original first name).

Over the next several years he became a star vaudevillian. Also during that time he had a four-year love affair with Mary Kelly, a vaudeville dancer. They planned to marry, but in early 1926 she called off the engagement when her strongly Catholic family, objecting to Benny's being Jewish, threatened to disown her if she married him.

In early 1927 he married Sadie Marks. They had first met in Vancouver, Canada, in 1922 when her parents invited the Marx Brothers to Passover dinner, and Zeppo Marx showed up not with his brothers but with Jack Benny. Sadie was only twelve at the time. In 1926 they met again, when her family was living in Los Angeles and Benny was appearing there at the Orpheum Theater.

Benny soon invited his wife to help him in his vaudeville act. Later they also worked together on radio, in movies, and on TV. For her professional work she changed her name to Marie Marsh and then to Mary Livingstone.

The Bennys had no children of their own. But in 1934 they adopted a baby girl: Joan.

When Benny got married, he was working in the stage revue *The Great Temptations.* He later appeared in the revue *Earl Carroll Vanities of 1930.* In 1934 he was on the legitimate stage for the play *Bring On the Girls,* a political satire.

During the late 1920s and early 1930s, he continued

to be a vaudeville star, notably at New York City's Palace Theater (1927-29, 1931).

Simultaneously he was making his early films, including *The Hollywood Revue* (1929) and *Chasing Rainbows* (1930). He later appeared in such light film fare as *The Big Broadcast of 1937* (1936), *Artists and Models* (1937), and *Buck Benny Rides Again* (1940). In *Charley's Aunt* (1941) Benny, cast in the title role, had audiences rolling with laughter in the aisles. Benny's finest screen work was in *To Be or Not to Be* (1942), as a Shakespearean actor who dresses up as a Nazi and outwits the Gestapo. He also gave fine comedy performances in *George Washington Slept Here* (1942) and *The Horn Blows at Midnight* (1945).

However, Benny gained his greatest fame through the medium of radio. *The Jack Benny Program* was phenomenally successful for over twenty years (1932-55). The basis for his long-lived popularity was that ordinary people could identify with him. He portrayed a consistent, realistic character involved in simple but carefully planned comedic situations; he was not just a voice telling a string of unrelated jokes. Moreover, he allowed himself to be the target of most of the humor, especially through the themes of his being "the world's worst violin player" and "the stingiest man in show business." (In reality he was a fine violinist and a gentle, generous person.) In Jack Benny's radio character, audiences found a forgivably fallible average guy confidently making plans only to have them explode in his face.

Benny was renowned for his comic timing. But it was not instinctive; he had to work to develop it. The classic example of this aspect of his artistry was on those occasions when, after being insulted, he paused before coming out with a perfectly timed "Well!"

The famous "feud" between Benny and comedian Fred Allen started in 1937 when Allen, on his own radio show, poked fun at Benny's violin playing. Thereafter, they took turns hurling insults at each other. Allen, for example, on Benny: "When Jack Benny plays the violin, it sounds as if the strings are still back in the cat." Benny, for example, on Allen: "Listening to Fred Allen is like listening to two Abbotts and no Costello." Actually Benny and Allen were close friends who deeply admired each other's work.

Benny's radio show made his theme song, "Love in Bloom," one of the most familiar tunes in America. In the early 1930s he was in a supper club when the orchestra asked him to join them on the violin in the next number. By chance, the tune was "Love in Bloom." A writer mentioned the performance in a newspaper column, and soon so many others began to associate him with the melody that he decided to adopt it as his theme.

The same tune introduced each episode of his TV series, which ran from 1950 to 1965. The TV programs were immensely popular and followed the same basic format as the radio shows.

Jack Benny (right) and Mary Livingstone (left)

After the series went off the air, he returned to TV for many specials. In his later years he also played small roles in a number of motion pictures, including *Gypsy* (1962); *It's a Mad, Mad, Mad, Mad World* (1963); and *A Guide for the Married Man* (1967).

Besides appearing on TV and in films, Benny continued to give live performances at hotels and elsewhere right up to his final illness. He was ready to begin filming *The Sunshine Boys* (in the role later taken by George Burns, one of Benny's closest friends) when it was discovered that he had terminal cancer of the pancreas.

Benny died at his home in Beverly Hills, California, on

December 26, 1974. He was universally mourned as the most beloved comedian of his time. One of the provisions in his will was that one red rose be delivered to his wife, Mary, every day for the rest of her life. Mary, with Hilliard Marks (her brother) and Marcia Borie, wrote *Jack Benny* (1978), the definitive book on the great entertainer.

Selected performances:

Stage

The Great Temptations (1926)
Earl Carroll Vanities of 1930 (1930)
Bring On the Girls (1934)
Jack Benny (1963)

Films

The Hollywood Revue (1929)
Chasing Rainbows (1930)
The Medicine Man (1930)
Transatlantic Merry-Go-Round (1934)
Broadway Melody of 1936 (1935)
It's in the Air (1935)
The Big Broadcast of 1937 (1936)
College Holiday (1936)
Artists and Models (1937)
Artists and Models Abroad (1938)
Man about Town (1939)
Buck Benny Rides Again (1940)
Love Thy Neighbor (1940)
Charley's Aunt (1941)
To Be or Not to Be (1942)
George Washington Slept Here (1942)
The Meanest Man in the World (1943)
Hollywood Canteen (1944)
The Horn Blows at Midnight (1945)
It's in the Bag (1945)
Somebody Loves Me (1952)
Gypsy (1962)
It's a Mad, Mad, Mad, Mad World (1963)
A Guide for the Married Man (1967)

Radio

The Jack Benny Program (1932-55)

TV

The Jack Benny Program (1950-65)

★★★

Milton Berle

Mr. Television

(1908-)

Milton Berle was born in New York City, New York, on July 12, 1908. His original name was Milton Berlinger.

When he was five years old, he won a Charles Chaplin contest. Soon his mother was able to get parts for him in silent movies, beginning with an episode in the serial *The Perils of Pauline* (1914). He went on to play juvenile parts in many films, both in the New York-New Jersey area and in California. Among the movies that he appeared in were *Tillie's Punctured Romance* (1914), with Charles Chaplin; *Rebecca of Sunnybrook Farm* (1917), with Mary Pickford; and *The Mark of Zorro* (1920), with Douglas Fairbanks, Sr.

After playing in some vaudeville kid acts in Philadelphia, he returned to New York City to appear in the Broadway musical *Florodora* (1920). Then he changed his stage name to Milton Berle and began to do comic routines in big-time vaudeville. Meanwhile, he finished his formal education through the Professional Children's School, doing his homework on the road and mailing it in. In 1931 he added nightclubs to his schedule.

The major break in his career came when he was asked to act as master of ceremonies at vaudeville's famous Palace Theater in New York City early in 1932. Later that year he hit Broadway as a star comedian in the *Earl Carroll Vanities* revue. He returned to Broadway in several more shows, including *See My Lawyer* (1939) and *Ziegfeld Follies of 1943* (1943).

BERLE

In the late 1930s Berle began to make movies. His early films included *New Faces of 1937* (1937), *Sun Valley Serenade* (1941), and *Always Leave Them Laughing* (1949).

He also entered radio, heading several different shows from 1939 to 1949. But his essentially visual brand of humor did not fare well on radio.

Television, however, was a different matter. Berle was among the first to perform on TV, with appearances in experimental broadcasts in 1929 and 1933. Then, from 1948 to 1953, he hosted the most popular variety series in TV history, *The Texaco Star Theater* (also known as *The Milton Berle Show*). His slapstick and buffoonery, largely based on outlandish costumes and other sight gags, helped to spur the purchase of TV sets by lower-income families all over the United States.

Berle was known affectionately as Uncle Miltie and respectfully as Mr. Television, TV's first superstar. Other comedians, however, because of his reputation for using other performers' material, called him the Thief of Badgags.

He hosted several later TV variety shows, but with decreasing popular success. Among them were *The Buick-Berle Show* (1953-55) and *The Kraft Music Hall* (1958-59).

Berle has been married to two women. His first wife was the showgirl Joyce Mathews, with whom he had two marriages, 1941-47 and 1949-50, both ending in divorce. They adopted a baby girl: Victoria (or Vicki). In 1953 he married the film publicist Ruth Cosgrove, with whom he adopted William (or Billy).

Before his marriage to Ruth, he had had love affairs with many women. In his candid book *Milton Berle: An Autobiography* (with Haskel Frankel, 1974), he discusses those affairs, including romances with the evangelist Aimee Semple McPherson and the actress Marilyn Monroe.

After he left his regular TV series, Berle continued to return to the small screen for numerous specials. He also acted onstage in *Last of the Red Hot Lovers* (1970), *The Sunshine Boys* (1976), and other plays. And he appeared in many movies, including *It's a Mad, Mad, Mad, Mad World* (1963); *The Oscar* (1966); *Lepke* (1975); and *Broadway Danny Rose* (1984). He surprised most observers by showing a remarkable talent for straight dramatic acting, notably in the movies *Seven in Darkness* (TV, 1969) and *Family Business* (TV, 1983).

In 1984 Berle was among the first seven people inducted into the Television Academy Hall of Fame. In June 1985 he had quadruple bypass heart surgery. The operation was a success, and soon he was making public appearances again.

In 1986 he returned to TV on a regular basis, starring in his first situation comedy, *Moscow and Vine,* as an ex-vaudevillian who owns a Hollywood music store.

Selected performances:

Stage

Florodora (1920)
Earl Carroll Vanities of 1932 (1932)
Saluta (1934)
Lost Paradise (1934)
See My Lawyer (1939)
Ziegfeld Follies of 1943 (1943)
The Goodbye People (1968)
Last of the Red Hot Lovers (1970)
Two by Two (1971)
Norman, Is That You? (1973)
The Sunshine Boys (1976)

Films

New Faces of 1937 (1937)
Radio City Revels (1938)
Tall, Dark, and Handsome (1941)
Sun Valley Serenade (1941)
Rise and Shine (1941)
A Gentleman at Heart (1942)
Whispering Ghosts (1942)
Over My Dead Body (1942)
Margin for Error (1943)
Always Leave Them Laughing (1949)
Let's Make Love (1960)
The Bellboy (1960)
It's a Mad, Mad, Mad, Mad World (1963)
The Sound of Laughter (1963)
The Loved One (1965)
The Oscar (1966)
The Happening (1967)
Who's Minding the Mint? (1967)
For Singles Only (1968)
Seven in Darkness (TV, 1969)
Can Heironymus Merkin Ever Forget Mercy Humppe and Find True Happiness? (1969)
Evil Roy Slade (TV, 1972)
The Legend of Valentino (TV, 1975)
Lepke (1975)
The Muppet Movie (1979)
Cracking Up (1983, originally released as *Smorgasbord*)
Family Business (TV, 1983)
Broadway Danny Rose (1984)

TV

The Texaco Star Theater (or *The Milton Berle Show*, 1948-53)
The Buick-Berle Show (1953-55)
The Milton Berle Show (1955-56)
The Kraft Music Hall (1958-59)
Jackpot Bowling (1960-61)
The Milton Berle Show (1966-67)
Moscow and Vine (1986)

★★

Theodore Bikel

"General Practitioner" Actor

(1924-)

Theodore Bikel was born in Vienna, Austria, on May 2, 1924. He learned Hebrew and Yiddish in his parents' home, and German in the Vienna public schools.

After Nazi Germany took over Austria in 1938, the family fled to Palestine. There young Bikel attended agricultural college for one year and worked as a laborer on a collective farm, or kibbutz. But he also studied linguistics and showed a flair for the theater. Consequently he was reassigned to direct the staging of pageants for his community.

After several years on the kibbutz he went to Tel Aviv to become an apprentice actor at the Habimah, the Hebrew national theater. He left the Habimah and helped to found the Tel Aviv Chamber Theater (1944), where he acted in plays for two years.

In 1946 Bikel left Palestine to study acting at the Royal Academy of Dramatic Art in London, from which he graduated in 1948. He soon began to appear in plays on the London stage, debuting in *You Can't Take It with You* (1948). The following year he played Pablo Gonzales in *A Streetcar Named Desire,* and in 1950 he toured as Harold Mitchell in the same play.

Bikel moved to the United States in 1954 and became a naturalized American citizen in 1961. He made his American stage debut with his performance as Inspector Massoubre in *Tonight in Samarkand* (1955).

Also in the United States he began to give powerful performances on TV anthology series, as in "The Bridge of San Luis Rey" (1958) for *The Du Pont Show of the Month* and "The Dybbuk" (1960) for *The Play of the Week.* In the late 1950s he wrote and performed material for *The Eternal Light* and *Look Up and Live,* spiritually oriented TV programs. Later he guest-starred in many TV series, such as *All in the Family, Cannon,* and *Twilight Zone.*

Bikel made his movie debut in the American picture *The African Queen* (1951), as a German soldier. That part was followed by supporting roles in numerous British and American films throughout the 1950s, highlighted by his performance as a humane Southern sheriff in *The Defiant Ones* (1958).

Bikel went on to appear in many films, but he never became a movie "star." He preferred to remain a character actor in supporting roles to avoid being stereotyped. Combining his great linguistic skills with his acting talent, he played characters of many different nationalities, such as a German in *The African Queen,* an American South-

erner in *The Defiant Ones,* and a Russian in *The Russians Are Coming, the Russians Are Coming* (1966). In *Victory at Entebbe* (TV, 1976), based on a true story, he was one of the Jews captured by terrorists, imprisoned at Uganda's Entebbe Airport, and then rescued by a daring Israeli raid on July 4, 1976.

Often overlooked by critics and audiences, Bikel nevertheless impressed careful observers with his dependability, no matter how much his characters varied in age, nationality, or personality. Comparing actors with doctors, he said he preferred to be not a specialist but a "general practitioner" so that he could acquire a wide range of experiences.

Meanwhile, his career expanded beyond just acting. Since 1955 he has been a folksinger, accompanying himself on the guitar, in annual concert tours throughout the United States, Canada, and Europe. From 1958 to 1963 he had his own radio show, *At Home with Theodore Bikel.* His albums include *Israeli Folk Songs* (1955), *Jewish Folk Songs* (1958), *Bravo Bikel* (1959), *Folk Songs from Just about Everywhere* (1959), *From Bondage to Freedom* (1961), *The Best of Bikel* (1962), and *Theodore Bikel Is Tevye* (1968). Bikel's album *Silent No More* (1972) consists of Soviet underground songs. He collected folksongs from a variety of languages and published some of them with comments in the book *Folksongs and Footnotes* (1960).

Singing also led to Bikel's first great leading role, as Captain Georg Von Trapp in the original Broadway production of the Rodgers and Hammerstein musical *The Sound of Music* (1959). In recent years the stage has been his principal working place. Since 1967 he has starred many times as Tevye in the Bock and Harnick musical *Fiddler on the Roof,* a story about Jews in a 1905 Russian village. His other stage appearances included roles in *The Rothschilds* (1972), *Zorba* (1976), and *The Threepenny Opera* (1983).

In 1967 Bikel married Rita Weinberg. Some years earlier he had been married for a time to Ofra Ichilov, an Israeli.

Bikel has long been active in politics and Jewish affairs. He founded the arts chapter of the American Jewish Congress in 1961. In 1968 he was a delegate to the Democratic National Convention. And from 1973 to 1982 he served as president of the Actors Equity Association. In December 1984 Bikel, along with two other leaders of the American Jewish Congress, was arrested at the South African Embassy in Washington, D.C., while protesting South Africa's policy of racial segregation.

Selected performances:

Stage

Tevye the Milkman (1943)
Charley's Aunt (1945)
You Can't Take It with You (1948)
A Streetcar Named Desire (1949)
A Streetcar Named Desire (1950)
The Love of Four Colonels (1951)
Dear Charles (1954)
Tonight in Samarkand (1955)
The Lark (1955)
The Rope Dancers (1957)
The Sound of Music (1959)
Brecht on Brecht (1962)
Café Crown (1964)
Pousse-Café (1966)
Fiddler on the Roof (1967 and many times since then)
The Rothschilds (1972)
The Sunshine Boys (1973)
The Good Doctor (1975)
Zorba (1976)
The Inspector General (1978)
The Threepenny Opera (1983)

Films

The African Queen (1951)
Never Let Me Go (1953)
Melba (1953)
Desperate Moment (1953)
The Little Kidnappers (1954)
Chance Meeting (1955)
The Vintage (1957)
The Pride and the Passion (1957)
The Enemy Below (1957)
The Defiant Ones (1958)
I Want to Live! (1958)
Woman Obsessed (1959)
The Angry Hills (1959)
A Dog of Flanders (1960)
My Fair Lady (1964)
Sands of the Kalahari (1965)
The Last Chapter (1966)
The Russians Are Coming, the Russians Are Coming (1966)
Festival (1967)
The Desperate Ones (1968)
Sweet November (1968)
My Side of the Mountain (1969)
Darker Than Amber (1970)
Killer by Night (TV, 1972)
Murder on Flight 502 (TV, 1975)
Victory at Entebbe (TV, 1976)
Testimony of Two Men (TV, 1977)
Loose Change (TV, 1978)

★★

Claire Bloom

Outstanding Dramatic Actress

(1931-)

Claire Bloom was born in North Finchley, a suburb of London, England, on February 15, 1931. Her original name was Patricia Claire Blume. She had early acting ambitions, which were encouraged by the well-known actress Mary Grew, Claire's mother's sister.

In 1941 Claire, her brother, and her mother moved to the United States to get away from World War II. While in America, Claire took dancing lessons and began to sing and act on both stage and radio.

The family traveled to Portugal in 1943 and arrived in England in early 1944. Claire soon began to take dancing and acting lessons in London, first at the Cone School and then at the Guildhall School of Music and Drama (1944-45) and the Central School of Speech Training and Dramatic Art (1945-46), the latter being the training ground for players at London's famed Old Vic theater.

In 1946 she began her professional career by performing in plays with the British Broadcasting Corporation (BBC) radio repertory. Her stage debut came with the Oxford Repertory Theater in *It Depends What You Mean* (1946). In 1947 she made her London debut when she appeared as a walk-on in *The White Devil*. She also made her first movie that year, *The Blind Goddess* (released 1948).

Bloom then spent a season performing Shakespearean roles in Stratford-upon-Avon, including Ophelia in *Hamlet* (1948). Returning to London, she proved herself in modern plays, such as Christopher Fry's *The Lady's Not for Burning* (1949) and Jean Anouilh's *Ring round the Moon* (1950).

Then Charles Chaplin hired her to costar with him in his last great film: *Limelight* (1952). As the struggling, wistful young ballet dancer in the movie, Bloom made a tremendous impression. Overnight she became an international film star.

At the same time, 1952, she hit her full stride as a stage actress by making her debut at the Old Vic, as Juliet in Shakespeare's *Romeo and Juliet*. Many critics regarded Bloom as the greatest Juliet of her time.

She continued to play Shakespearean roles at the Old Vic through the 1953-54 season. In 1956 she gave her first New York City performances, again in Shakespearean roles with the Old Vic company.

From the 1950s on, Bloom continually alternated her film and stage work between England and the United States. Her early movies included *Richard III* (1955), *The Brothers Karamazov* (1958), and *Look Back in Anger* (1959). Her stage appearances included many of Shakespeare's plays, as well as a New York City production of *Rashomon* in 1959.

Her costar in *Rashomon* was Rod Steiger. They married in 1959 and sometimes acted together, as in the film *The Illustrated Man* (1969). They had one child, Anna, before divorcing in 1969. In that year she also began an unsuccessful marriage to the producer-director Hillard Elkins.

In the 1960s Bloom turned increasingly away from

plays and toward films so that she could spend as much time as possible with her daughter. Among her movies during that time were *The Haunting* (1963), as a bohemian of lesbian leanings and ESP powers; *The Spy Who Came In from the Cold* (1965), as a mild-mannered Communist librarian; and *Charly* (1968), as a scientist who falls in love with a man who is the object of her experiments.

In 1971 Bloom returned to the stage and was highly praised for her New York City performances as Nora in Ibsen's *A Doll's House* and as the title character in the same playwright's *Hedda Gabler*. In 1974 she played Blanche DuBois (her favorite role) in a London production of Tennessee Williams's *A Streetcar Named Desire*. In 1981-82 she toured the United States in *These Are Women,* a portrait of Shakespeare's heroines.

After her return to the stage in the early 1970s, she continued to appear in films. They included *A Doll's House* (1973), *Islands in the Stream* (1977), *Clash of the Titans* (1981), and *Déjà Vu* (1985).

Bloom has appeared frequently on TV, in both England and America, since the early 1950s. Among her many performances for American TV anthologies were those as Roxane in "Cyrano de Bergerac" (1956) on *Producers' Showcase* and as Queen Anne in "Soldier in Love" (1967) on *Hallmark Hall of Fame*. She was a member of the cast in the BBC-TV series *The Legacy* (1975) and *Brideshead Revisited* (1981). And she gave extraordinarily rich and mature performances for the BBC-TV series of Shakespeare films, including her roles as Katharine in *Henry VIII* (TV, 1979), Gertrude in *Hamlet* (TV, 1980), and Constance in *King John* (TV, 1983).

Bloom is the author of the autobiographical book *Limelight and After: The Education of an Actress* (1982).

Though possessing great physical beauty, she has never relied on that for getting by with soft roles. On the contrary, she has deliberately sought the most arduous roles available and interpreted them with rare depth and intensity.

Selected performances:

Stage

It Depends What You Mean (1946)
The White Devil (1947)
He Who Gets Slapped (1947)
The Wanderer (1947)
King John (1948)
Hamlet (1948)
The Winter's Tale (1948)
The Damask Cheek (1949)
The Lady's Not for Burning (1949)
Ring round the Moon (1950)
Romeo and Juliet (1952)
The Merchant of Venice (1953)
Hamlet (1953)
Twelfth Night (1954)
Coriolanus (1954)
The Tempest (1954)
King Lear (1955)
Richard II (1956)
Romeo and Juliet (1956)
Duel of Angels (1958)
Rashomon (1959)
Altona (1961)
The Trojan Women (1963)
Ivanov (1965)
A Doll's House (1971)
Hedda Gabler (1971)
Vivat! Vivat Regina! (1972)
A Doll's House (1973)
A Streetcar Named Desire (1974)
The Innocents (1976)
Rosmersholm (1977)
The Cherry Orchard (1981)
These Are Women (1981)

Films

The Blind Goddess (1948)
Limelight (1952)
The Man Between (1953)
Richard III (1955)
Alexander the Great (1956)
The Brothers Karamazov (1958)
The Buccaneer (1958)
Look Back in Anger (1959)
Brainwashed (1961)
The Chapman Report (1962)
The Wonderful World of the Brothers Grimm (1962)
The Haunting (1963)
The Outrage (1964)
The Spy Who Came In from the Cold (1965)
Charly (1968)
The Illustrated Man (1969)
Three into Two Won't Go (1969)
A Severed Head (1971)
Red Sky at Morning (1971)
A Doll's House (1973)
Islands in the Stream (1977)
Backstairs at the White House (TV, 1979)
Henry VIII (TV, 1979)
Hamlet (TV, 1980)
Clash of the Titans (1981)
King John (TV, 1983)
Déjà Vu (1985)
Promises to Keep (TV, 1985)
Liberty (TV, 1986)
Anastasia: The Mystery of Anna (TV, 1986)
Queenie (TV, 1987)

TV

The Legacy (1975)
Brideshead Revisited (1981)

★★

Fanny Brice

Queen of Comediennes

(1891-1951)

Fanny Brice was born in New York City, New York, on October 29, 1891. Her original name was Fannie Borach.

At an early age she began to develop show-business skills. Her parents were saloon owners, and as a tiny tot she was encouraged by her father, Charles Borach (a happy-go-lucky gambler known as Pinochle Charlie), to sing for his customers.

Fannie's acting talents were honed through numerous childhood pranks. For example, she and one of her siblings often went to Coney Island, where they would stop passersby and tearfully pretend to be stranded far from home. That ploy nearly always induced the strangers to offer carfare, which the youngsters proceeded to spend on hot dogs and amusement-park rides.

Fannie, determined to make a career in show business, quit school before she turned fourteen. She entered many amateur-night contests as a singer, and soon she was averaging thirty dollars a week in prize money. It was during that period that she changed her name to Fannie (later Fanny) Brice, after John Brice, a friend of her mother's. The young entertainer made the change because she was tired of having her name punned by friends, as in "More-Ache" and "Bore-Act."

At fifteen she was hired as a chorus girl for a Broadway revue, George M. Cohan's *The Talk of New York*. Cohan fired her during rehearsals when he found out that she could not dance. Soon, however, she got a job for the 1906-1907 season, touring Pennsylvania in a show called *A Royal Slave*, in which she played the part of an alligator.

After a few years of struggling, she got a big break as a singer in *Transatlantic Burlesque* (1910) in New York City and on the road. Also in 1910 she toured in the burlesque show *The College Girl*. While on that tour, she impulsively married Frank White, a Springfield, Massachusetts, barber. The marriage was soon annulled on the grounds that she was underage.

Her comic performances in *The College Girl* attracted the attention of the great Broadway producer Florenz Ziegfeld, who quickly signed her for the 1910 edition of his *Follies* revue. Brice went on to appear in many of the annual *Ziegfeld Follies* productions throughout the 1910s and early 1920s, specializing in humorous songs and skits in which she frankly made a virtue of her plainness.

In 1918 Brice married Jules W. ("Nick") Arnstein (also known by several other names). She remained loyal to him through his imprisonment in Sing Sing for fraud (1915-17) and in Leavenworth for theft (1924-25). But she finally divorced him in 1927 for infidelity.

Their two children, Frances and William, were raised by servants while Brice worked. Her own parents had separated when she was a child, and she learned from her mother, who went into the real-estate business, how to be a strong, independent woman. But Brice missed having a family life. "I didn't want my daughter to have a career," she said. "Because if a woman has a career, she misses an awful lot. . . . If you have a career, then the career is your life."

Meanwhile, her own career flourished. Besides appearing in seven editions of Ziegfeld's *Follies* from 1910 through 1923, she worked in other shows, including the Broadway musical comedy *The Honeymoon Express* (1913). She headlined at the Palace Theater, New York City's prestigious vaudeville house, in 1923.

Brice then appeared in *The Music Box Revue* (1924) and toured in vaudeville (1925-26). Her only stage failure came when she played a serious dramatic role in David Belasco's production of Willard Mack's *Fanny* (1926), a story unrelated to the star's own life. She then successfully returned to her natural comedic genre by appearing in the musical *Fioretta* (1929).

In 1929 Brice married the Broadway producer Billy Rose (originally William Samuel Rosenberg). Soon she was featured in two of his shows: *Sweet and Low* (1930) and *Crazy Quilt* (1931). Her stage career reached its peak in the 1934 and 1936 editions of the *Ziegfeld Follies*. In 1938 she divorced Rose for (as with Arnstein) infidelity.

In her stage work Brice displayed a large, varied repertory, both as a singer and as an actress. Her vocal techniques included her satiric "concert-room vocalizing," her broadly humorous specialties (such as "I'm an Indian"), and her comic Yiddish-accented renditions of songs (such as "Sadie Salome, Go Home"). But she could also wring tears from her audiences by singing sad ballads, notably "My Man," whose lyrics echoed the

Fanny Brice

story of Brice's unhappy marriage to Arnstein. On November 21, 1927, in her first public appearance after her divorce from Arnstein, she stood silent for fifteen minutes onstage in the Palace Theater, refusing audience demands for the song.

As an actress-clown, Brice was a pioneer in proving that women could create brilliant comedy without exploiting their sexuality and without relying on home-making topics. She was famed for her lampoons of fan dancers, tap dancers, lady evangelists, and silent-screen vamps (her vamp skits ended with the wonderful line, "I may be a bad woman, but I'm awful good company"). Her comic performances of *The Dying Swan* ballet and of modern dance were hilarious, as were her burlesque of Camille (with W. C. Fields as the maid) and her Yiddish-dialect monologues. But she was never cruel; she always poked fun with sensitivity and human understanding.

Brice explained her approach to humor: "You must set up your audience for the laugh you are working for. So you go along and everything is fine, like any other art, and then—boom! You give it to them. Like there is a beautiful painting of a woman and you paint a mustache on her."

Brice made six movies, beginning with *My Man* (1928), in which she played a poor girl who becomes a star. She portrayed herself in *The Great Ziegfeld* (1936) and performed, with a heavy Yiddish accent, in the comic skit "A Sweepstakes Ticket" in *Ziegfeld Follies* (1946). But she was never really comfortable around cameras: "Making pictures is like making love in public," she said. "You can't be at ease when somebody is watching." Her wild ethnic humor was more at home in the raucous atmosphere of burlesque and vaudeville theaters than in the comparatively bland and rigid atmosphere of motion-picture studios.

She did, however, influence the films of others. Twentieth Century-Fox, without her permission, based the 1939 movie *Rose of Washington Square* on her life. Brice thereupon brought a $750,000 defamation suit against the studio. The suit was settled out of court, Brice receiving $30,000 in December 1940. Many years later Barbra Streisand made her greatest impact by sensitively portraying Brice in the Broadway musical *Funny Girl* (1964) and in its movie adaptation in 1968, as well as in a film sequel, *Funny Lady* (1974).

Radio proved to be a good medium for Brice's talents. In 1932 she performed as a straight singer with George Olsen's orchestra in a short-lived radio series. But she became best known to millions of listeners for her creation of the impish little-girl character Baby Snooks. Brice had invented the character, modeled after the real-life child star Baby Peggy, as part of her vaudeville act in 1912. At a party in 1921 Brice revived the character to perform the burlesque song "Poor Pauline" as a six-year-old child might sing it. Baby Snooks then appeared on the stage in *Sweet and Low* in 1930, as well as in the 1934 and 1936 editions of the *Ziegfeld Follies.* Also in 1936 the precocious brat was introduced to radio listeners on *The Ziegfeld Follies of the Air.* She then made regular appearances on *Good News* from 1937 to 1940, when the program changed its name to *Maxwell House Coffee Time,* where she remained a fixture for the next several years. In 1944 the enfant terrible (who constantly badgered her father with the question, "Why-y-y, Daddy?") was given her own radio series, *The Baby Snooks Show,* which remained on the air for the rest of Brice's life.

As Baby Snooks became increasingly established as an individual entity, Brice almost completely abandoned her natural voice in public, preferring to speak in Snooks's mischievous-little-girl tones. In interviews, the entertainer often referred to "Schnooks" as if the child were a real person.

In her own real life, Brice was interested in far more than just show business. She was an art collector, an oil painter, a dress designer (she designed the costumes for *Crazy Quilt),* and a gifted interior decorator (she decorated the homes of Eddie Cantor, Ira Gershwin, Dinah Shore, and others).

Brice had red hair, green eyes, and a large mouth. Her nose-straightening surgery in August 1923 received wide publicity.

At the age of fifty-nine she suffered a massive cerebral hemorrhage at her home in Beverly Hills, California. She died five days later, on May 29, 1951. Brice left the bulk of her $2 million estate to her two children.

Selected performances:

Stage

Follies of 1910 (1910)
Ziegfeld Follies of 1911 (1911)
The Honeymoon Express (1913)
Nobody Home (1915)
Ziegfeld Follies of 1916 (1916)
Ziegfeld Follies of 1917 (1917)
Ziegfeld Follies of 1920 (1920)
Ziegfeld Follies of 1921 (1921)
Ziegfeld Follies of 1923 (1923)
The Music Box Revue (1924)
Fanny (1926)
Fioretta (1929)
Sweet and Low (1930)
Crazy Quilt (1931)
Ziegfeld Follies of 1934 (1934)
Ziegfeld Follies of 1936 (1936)

Films

My Man (1928)
Night Club (1929)
Be Yourself! (1930)
The Great Ziegfeld (1936)
Everybody Sing (1938)
Ziegfeld Follies (1946)

Radio

The Ziegfeld Follies of the Air (1932, 1936)
Good News (1937-40)
Maxwell House Coffee Time (1940-44)
The Baby Snooks Show (1944-51)

★★

Mel Brooks

Wild Parodist

(1926-   )

Mel Brooks was born in New York City, New York, on June 28, 1926. His original name was Melvyn Kaminsky.

When Mel was 2½ years old, his father died, leaving the boy with a permanent sense of loss and anger. While growing up in the tough Williamsburg section of Brooklyn, he learned to clothe his anger in comedy to protect himself. "I'm sure that a lot of my comedy is based on anger and hostility," the adult Brooks has admitted.

His mother also contributed to Mel's future. "My mother had this exuberant joy of living, and she infected me with that," he has said. "She really was responsible for the growth of my imagination."

In his teens he earned money by playing the drums after school and during the summer vacations. After graduating from high school in 1943, he attended Brooklyn College of the City University of New York for one year.

He then went into the army, where he was trained as a combat engineer whose specialty was to deactivate land mines. His first action was in the Battle of the Bulge in December 1944. No wonder his later show-business career came to be marked by fearless risk-taking.

After leaving the army in 1946, he returned to the drums, which he played in nightclubs and on the borscht circuit. He began as Mel Kaminsky, but he soon changed his name to Mel Brooks to avoid confusion with the well-known jazz trumpeter Max Kaminsky. Gradually Brooks turned to comedy, beginning when he substituted for an ailing comic at a small Catskills hotel.

While working on the borscht circuit, he became friends with Sid Caesar. In 1949 Caesar asked Brooks to help write comic sketches for Caesar's TV series *The Admiral Broadway Revue*. A year later Brooks joined Caesar, Carl Reiner, Imogene Coca, and others in writing for the extremely successful TV variety series *Your Show of Shows*. Brooks occasionally appeared on the program as a performer. When that show went off the air in 1954, he continued to work with Caesar, notably in *Caesar's Hour* (1954-57).

Brooks also wrote for TV specials starring Andy Williams and Victor Borge. Later he helped to create the TV spy-spoof series *Get Smart* (1965) and the Robin Hood comedy *When Things Were Rotten* (1975).

Brooks worked on several Broadway shows. He wrote and acted in the sketch "Of Fathers and Sons," a parody of *Death of a Salesman,* for the revue *New Faces of 1952* (1952). He also worked on the books for the musical comedies *Shinbone Alley* (1957) and *All American* (1962).

In 1960 Brooks made the first of a series of comedy records with Carl Reiner, in which Brooks played a two-thousand-year-old man with a Yiddish accent. The old man had seen everything but been impressed by nothing. The series culminated in a three-disc album entitled *The Incomplete Works of Carl Reiner and Mel Brooks* (1973).

Brooks reached the peak of his success when he turned to filmmaking. He conceived, wrote, and narrated the highly praised cartoon short *The Critic* (1963).

In his full-length films he has functioned in one or more capacities (producer, writer, director, actor) to stamp each work with his unique brand of wild, manic humor. His principal technique is to parody established film genres, with such knowledge of, and obvious affection for, the originals that the spoofs can quite accurately be called homages.

Brooks's first major film was *The Producers* (1967), which he wrote and directed. It parodies the old putting-on-the-show musical films popular in the 1930s. Here, however, the show is called *Springtime for Hitler,* which surprisingly becomes a camp hit.

After playing a bit part in *Putney Swope* (1969), Brooks wrote and directed *The Twelve Chairs* (1970), a comedy about greed in early Communist Russia. A highlight of the film is Brooks's own small role as Tikon, an ex-serf who yearns for his former master's beatings.

With *Blazing Saddles* (1974), a parody of Hollywood westerns, Brooks reached his full stride as a filmmaking artist and simultaneously became a cult hero to many of his fans. Besides coscripting and directing the movie, he played a villainous governor and a Yiddish-speaking Indian chief.

In *Young Frankenstein* (1974), a takeoff on 1930s

horror movies, Brooks served as cowriter and director. He coscripted, directed, and starred in *Silent Movie* (1976), an affectionate spoof about a director trying to make a present-day silent picture.

High Anxiety (1977) parodies Alfred Hitchcock's thrillers. Brooks coscripted, produced, and directed the film. He also starred as Dr. Richard H. Thorndyke, a Nobel Prize-winning psychiatrist who suffers from "high anxiety."

After making a guest appearance in *The Muppet Movie* (1979), Brooks wrote, produced, and directed *History of the World, Part I* (1981). He played several roles in the film, including that of Moses. Brooks produced and starred in a remake of the classic 1942 comedy *To Be or Not to Be* (1984), in which a troupe of actors outwit the German Nazis during the latter's occupation of Warsaw in World War II. *Spaceballs* (1987), which he cowrote, directed, and starred in, is a spoof of space epics.

Through the years, Brooks has developed close associations with a number of actors and actresses who have appeared regularly in his works. Those performers include Dom DeLuise *(The Twelve Chairs; Blazing Saddles; Silent Movie; History of the World, Part I)*, Marty Feldman *(Young Frankenstein, Silent Movie)*, Madeline Kahn *(Blazing Saddles; Young Frankenstein; High Anxiety; History of the World, Part I)*, Harvey Korman *(Blazing Saddles; High Anxiety; History of the World, Part I)*, Cloris Leachman *(Young Frankenstein; High Anxiety; History of the World, Part I)*, and Gene Wilder *(The Producers, Blazing Saddles, Young Frankenstein)*.

Brooks established his own film company, Brooksfilms. It has produced some of his own movies, including both *History of the World, Part I* and *To Be or Not to Be*. But it has also created some serious dramatic pictures, notably *The Elephant Man* (1980).

Brooks is married to the famed actress Anne Bancroft, whom he wedded in 1964. They had one child: Maximilian. From an earlier marriage, to Florence Baum, he had three children: Stefanie, Nick, and Edward. Bancroft appeared with Brooks in *Silent Movie* and *To Be or Not to Be* and was featured in *The Elephant Man*.

Selected performances:

Stage

New Faces of 1952 (1952)

Putney Swope (1969)
The Twelve Chairs (1970)
Blazing Saddles (1974)
Silent Movie (1976)
High Anxiety (1977)
The Muppet Movie (1979)
History of the World, Part I (1981)
To Be or Not to Be (1984)
Spaceballs (1987)

★★★

George Burns
Show-Biz Methuselah
(1896-)

George Burns was born in New York City, New York, on January 20, 1896. His original name was Nathan Birnbaum.

When Nathan was seven, his father died. The boy immediately went to work at part-time odd jobs, often instilling them with his already-developing love of show business. For example, he would sing as he sold crackers up and down the streets of his home neighborhood, the Lower East Side of Manhattan.

A few years later he quit school and organized himself and three other children into a singing quartet. The boys sang wherever they found a crowd of people, passing a hat to collect whatever they could.

Striking out on his own, Nathan developed a variety of routines, including trick roller-skating, and in his early teens began to play the vaudeville stage. When he was fourteen, a case of stage fright led him to search for a prop that he could hold on to for security; he chose the cheapest thing he could think of—a cigar.

Meanwhile, his name changed in two stages. First he became Nathan Burns, having acquired the new surname from neighbors who knew that he regularly stole coal from the Burns Brothers coal company. Later he himself adopted the first name George because it was the nickname for one of his older brothers, Isadore, whom Nathan admired.

Even after becoming George Burns, he often performed under a variety of pseudonyms. According to Burns himself, he changed his name over and over again because his early acts were so bad that he feared he would not be able to get jobs if managers knew who he really was.

He also went through a succession of partners, including a trained seal. Another partner was Hannah Siegal, with whom Burns developed a Latin dance act. After working for a while in the New York City area, they were offered a contract for a long tour. But Hannah's parents refused to let her go unless Burns married her. The youngsters married, made their thirty-six-week tour, and then, returning to New York City, amicably divorced.

Burns continued to labor in small-time vaudeville for several more years. He has since admitted that his problem was that he could not deliver material as well as he could create it. That problem was solved in 1923 when he met Gracie Allen.

She was a young unemployed Irish-American Catholic trying to break into show business. Hearing that Burns was looking for a partner in his new comedy act, she asked for the job and got it. At first she played the straight part, while Burns told the jokes. But audiences tended to laugh at her questions more than at his jokes. Burns and Allen switched roles and soon became a hit act.

In 1926 they married. Later that year they hit the big time by signing with the B. F. Keith chain of theaters.

In 1929 they began to make one-reel movies. A few years later they entered the feature-film market. Eventually they played supporting or cameo roles together in more than a dozen pictures, including *College Humor* (1933), *The Big Broadcast of 1936* (1935), and *Honolulu* (1939).

But a better medium for them was radio. Their first work over the air occurred in 1930 in London. Later that year they began to make guest appearances on American radio programs. Their own series, *The George Burns and Gracie Allen Show* (1932-50), was one of the most popular in radio history. At first they drew from their episodic vaudeville routines. But in 1942 they changed the format to a situation comedy, with a sustained story line in each program.

In 1950 they switched over to the new medium of television. Their series, *The George Burns and Gracie Allen Show* (1950-58), was a domestic situation comedy in which they played under their own names, with him as a professional entertainer and her as his scatterbrained wife. The show concerned itself primarily with their home life and with the simple situations that she somehow managed to make unbelievably complex. Burns, the only character aware of the audience, would make explanations and comments to viewers between scenes.

Burns has credited Allen with being the principal figure in their success. She had an uncanny genius for delivering non sequiturs, malapropisms, and other zany remarks with absolute faith in their believability. A fine and intelligent dramatic actress, Allen sometimes tired of

playing the fool, but she went along with it because the team was so successful.

Burns and Allen had no children of their own. But they adopted a daughter (Sandra) and a son (Ronald).

In 1955 Burns published his autobiography: *I Love Her, That's Why!* (with Cynthia Hobart Lindsay). In 1958 his wife retired. With a slightly revised format, he tried to continue on TV with *The George Burns Show* (1958-59).

In 1960, at the age of sixty-four, he launched a whole new career for himself by developing a solo nightclub act, consisting of songs and patter (often based on recollections). His trademarks were his cigar, his unfinished songs (actually performed as a low murmuring), and his self-deprecation. After Allen's death in 1964, Burns added another element to his act: his preoccupation with being around very young women.

The period 1964-74 was active yet not spectacular. He was a regular on the TV series *Wendy and Me* (1964-65), and he continued his nightclub and concert work.

However, 1974 saw another big change in his career. The year began badly: he was not in great demand; he had open-heart surgery; and his best friend, Jack Benny, died. But Burns recovered quickly from his operation, and soon he was offered an important movie part that had originally been scheduled for Benny. Reluctant at first to take the job for fear of being disloyal to his friend, Burns was finally convinced by Benny's agent that the late comedian would have wanted Burns to play the role.

The part was that of Al Lewis in *The Sunshine Boys* (1975). Lewis and Willie Clark (played by Walter Matthau) are retired entertainers who used to form a great vaudeville comedy team but who have not spoken to each other in twelve years. Brought together for a one-shot TV special, they resume old battles and open old wounds. In *The Sunshine Boys* Burns surprised both filmmakers and audiences with his acting skills, which had never really been tested in his routines with Allen or in his solo nightclub acts.

Since then he has made a number of movies. The best known is the satirical fantasy *Oh, God!* (1977), in which Burns played the title role. Others include *Sgt. Pepper's Lonely Hearts Club Band* (1978); *Just You and Me, Kid* (1979); and *Oh, God! Book II* (1980). In *Two of a Kind* (TV, 1982) he starred as a senior citizen who becomes lethargic after he is put into a nursing home by his son; but the elderly man's interest in life is rejuvenated by his retarded grandson. In *Oh, God! You Devil* (1984) he played both the Deity and the Prince of Darkness.

Burns remains active in other spheres as well. He continues to give live performances. In 1983, for example, he worked at New York City's Palace Theater, where he had first performed in 1924.

He also appears regularly on TV commercials, talk shows, and comedy series. In 1983 he was honored in the TV special *George Burns Celebrates Eighty Years in Show Business*. In the autumn of 1985 he hosted *George Burns Comedy Week*, an anthology. His ninetieth birthday was celebrated in a TV special in January 1986.

He has also branched out into making records and writing books. In the early 1980s he released the albums *I Wish I Was Young Again* and *George Burns in Nashville*. He has authored the books *Living It Up; or, They Still Love Me in Altoona!* (1976); *The Third Time Around* (1980); *How to Live to Be One Hundred—or More: The Ultimate Diet, Sex, and Exercise Book* (*at My Age, Sex Gets Second Billing)* (1983); *Dr. Burns' Prescription for Happiness* (1984); and *Dear George: Advice and Answers from America's Leading Expert on Everything from A to B* (1985).

Selected performances:

Films

International House (1933)
College Humor (1933)
Six of a Kind (1934)
We're Not Dressing (1934)
Many Happy Returns (1934)
Love in Bloom (1935)
The Big Broadcast of 1936 (1935)
Here Comes Cookie (1935)
The Big Broadcast of 1937 (1936)
College Holiday (1936)
A Damsel in Distress (1937)
College Swing (1938)
Honolulu (1939)
The Sunshine Boys (1975)
Oh, God! (1977)
Sgt. Pepper's Lonely Hearts Club Band (1978)
The Comedy Company (TV, 1978)
Just You and Me, Kid (1979)
Going in Style (1979)
Oh, God! Book II (1980)
Two of a Kind (TV, 1982)
Oh, God! You Devil (1984)

Radio

The George Burns and Gracie Allen Show (1932-50)

TV

The George Burns and Gracie Allen Show (1950-58)
The George Burns Show (1958-59)
Wendy and Me (1964-65)
George Burns Comedy Week (1985)

★★★

Red Buttons

Little Guy with Troubles

(1919-)

Red Buttons was born in New York City, New York, on February 5, 1919. His original name was Aaron Chwatt. He grew up in the Lower East Side of Manhattan and later in the Bronx.

At the age of twelve he won an amateur-night contest, under the name Little Skippy, by singing "Sweet Jennie Lee." In 1935 he became a bellboy and singer at Dinty Moore's tavern in the Bronx. Because of his red hair and his bellboy uniform loaded with buttons, customers nicknamed him Red Buttons. Also in 1935 he gave his first performances on the borscht circuit.

Buttons graduated from the Bronx's Evander Childs High School in 1937. In 1938 he worked on the borscht circuit again. After that, he became a burlesque comic.

In 1941 Buttons was invited to Hollywood for a part in the movie *The Admiral Takes a Wife,* a musical comedy about peacetime naval life in Hawaii. The Japanese attack on Pearl Harbor, precipitating the entry of the United States into World War II, occurred just three days before the scheduled release of the film. The movie was shelved.

In 1942 Buttons was back in New York City, where he performed onstage in the farce *Vickie.* After he left the show, he worked for a few months in vaudeville-burlesque.

In 1943 Buttons was drafted into the army and cast in the service play *Winged Victory* (1943), which was staged for the Army Emergency Relief. After a long run in New York City, the show, with Buttons, was filmed (1944). He then toured in the production. In 1945 Buttons was transferred to another entertainment unit, which performed at the Potsdam Conference.

Following his discharge from the army in 1946, he had a one-word part in the movie *13 Rue Madeleine* (1946) and appeared in the New York City stage musicals *Barefoot Boy with Cheek* (1947) and *Hold It!* (1948). Through his stage performances, he began to develop a wide reputation as a comic, and he was invited to perform as a guest on TV shows, including Milton Berle's.

In 1947 Buttons married a burlesque performer known as Roxanne. They divorced in 1951, and later that year he married Helayne McNorton.

Buttons finally reached stardom when he was given his own TV series, *The Red Buttons Show,* in 1952. At first it was a musical-variety show, centering on little comic sketches in which he played several recurring characters, such as Buttons the Bellboy, Muggsy (a juvenile delinquent), and Rocky Buttons (a punch-drunk prizefighter). His low-key humor was much appreciated by audiences, and the show became very popular. However, by the end of the 1953-54 season it had become a situation comedy and its ratings began to drop. The show left the air in 1955.

The next two years were difficult for Buttons. He worked very little, chiefly in nightclubs. A highlight of that period was his portrayal of Bottom in Shakespeare's *A Midsummer Night's Dream* in the summer of 1956.

Then came a great turning point in his career: he was given an important role in the movie *Sayonara* (1957). Buttons played Sergeant Joe Kelly, an American serviceman based in post-World War II Japan. Kelly and his Japanese bride, hounded by prejudice and military red tape against mixed marriages, commit double suicide.

For his sensitive tragicomic portrayal of Kelly, Buttons won universal praise.

After that success, he began to work steadily as a character actor in films, often in serious dramatic roles. His early movies included *The Big Circus* (1959); *The Longest Day* (1962); *Stagecoach* (1966); *They Shoot Horses, Don't They?* (1969); and *The Poseidon Adventure* (1972).

However, Buttons did not abandon comedy. He starred in the short-lived TV situation-comedy series *The Double Life of Henry Phyfe* (1966), and much of his time in recent years has been spent as a first-rate night-club comic. He once described his basic comedy persona as "a little guy and his troubles."

His later films included *Pete's Dragon* (1977), *The Dream Merchants* (TV, 1980), and *Reunion at Fairborough* (TV, 1985). In *Alice in Wonderland* (TV, 1985) he played the White Rabbit.

Selected performances:

Stage

Vickie (1942)
Winged Victory (1943)
Barefoot Boy with Cheek (1947)
Hold It! (1948)
A Midsummer Night's Dream (1956)

Films

Winged Victory (1944)
13 Rue Madeleine (1946)
Sayonara (1957)
Imitation General (1958)
The Big Circus (1959)
One, Two, Three (1961)
Five Weeks in a Balloon (1962)
Gay Purr-ee (1962)
Hatari! (1962)
The Longest Day (1962)
A Ticklish Affair (1963)
Your Cheatin' Heart (1964)
Harlow (1965)
Up from the Beach (1965)
Stagecoach (1966)
They Shoot Horses, Don't They? (1969)
Breakout (TV, 1970)
The Poseidon Adventure (1972)
The New, Original Wonder Woman (TV, 1975)
Louis Armstrong—Chicago Style (TV, 1976)
Gable and Lombard (1976)
Viva Knievel (1977)
Pete's Dragon (1977)
Telethon (TV, 1977)
Vega$ (TV, 1978)
The Users (TV, 1978)
Movie Movie (1978)
When Time Ran Out (1980)
Power (TV, 1980)
The Dream Merchants (TV, 1980)
Leave 'Em Laughing (TV, 1981)
Side Show (TV, 1981)
Reunion at Fairborough (TV, 1985)
Alice in Wonderland (TV, 1985)

TV

The Red Buttons Show (1952-55)
The Double Life of Henry Phyfe (1966)

★★

James Caan

Dynamic Actor

(1939-)

James Caan was born in New York City, New York, on March 26, 1939. The spelling of his surname is a Dutch variant of *Cahn*. His maternal grandparents fled to the United States from Germany in the early stages of the Nazi era. Some of their relatives who stayed behind ended up in death camps.

In his youth Caan was interested mostly in sports. After graduating from Manhattan's Rhodes School at the age of sixteen, he enrolled at Michigan State University so that he could be part of its celebrated football team. When he failed to make the team, he transferred to Hofstra University in Hempstead, New York. But the academic life did not suit him, and he soon dropped out.

After holding a series of odd jobs, Caan enrolled at the Neighborhood Playhouse in New York City, where he studied acting for one year. Then he studied for two years under the drama coach Wynn Handman.

In 1960, billed as Jimmy Caan, he appeared in an off-Broadway production of the play *La Ronde.* After serving as an understudy in a Broadway play the following year, he moved to California. There he soon found work as a guest performer on *Route 66, Ben Casey,* and other TV drama series.

Caan found his true métier when he won a supporting role in the movie *Lady in a Cage* (1964), in which he played the leader of a trio of violent hoodlums. He followed that up by making a good impression in *The Glory Guys* (1965). His first starring role came in *Red Line 7000* (1965), as a racing-car driver. His work over the next several years was highlighted by his performance as a gentle, brain-damaged ex-football player in *The Rain People* (1969).

Caan finally reached stardom and gained a large following when he played the wisecracking, fun-loving football player Brian Piccolo in the movie *Brian's Song* (TV, 1971). The film recounts the true story of the young running back's rivalry and friendship with Gale Sayers. Caan movingly portrayed Piccolo's last days before the latter's early death from cancer.

In *The Godfather* (1972) Caan further enhanced his reputation through his performance as a volatile young gangster. Though he was surrounded with major talents in that picture, including Marlon Brando, Caan, with his characteristic dynamism, held his own.

To avoid being typecast as a violent criminal, Caan purposely began to select roles to show his versatility. In *Slither* (1973), for example, he played an offbeat comedy role. In *Cinderella Liberty* (1973) he was a sailor who becomes involved with a prostitute and her child. In *The Gambler* (1974) he portrayed a compulsive gambler.

Caan's later films included *Rollerball* (1975) and *Thief* (1981). After a five-year layoff he returned in *Gardens of Stone* (1987).

He has had two marriages. In 1961 he married Dee Jay Mattis, then the lead dancer on the *Sing Along with Mitch* TV series. They had a daughter, Tara, before divorcing in 1966. Later he wedded Sheila Ryan, with whom he had a son, Scott, before divorcing again.

Selected performances:

Stage

La Ronde (1960)

Films

Lady in a Cage (1964)
The Glory Guys (1965)
Red Line 7000 (1965)
El Dorado (1967)
Games (1967)
Countdown (1968)
Journey to Shiloh (1968)
The Rain People (1969)
Submarine X-1 (1969)
Rabbit, Run (1970)
Brian's Song (TV, 1971)
T. R. Baskin (1971)
The Godfather (1972)
Slither (1973)
Cinderella Liberty (1973)
Freebie and the Bean (1974)
The Gambler (1974)
The Godfather, Part II (1974)
Funny Lady (1975)
Rollerball (1975)
The Killer Elite (1975)
Harry and Walter Go to New York (1976)
Silent Movie (1976)
A Bridge Too Far (1977)
Another Man, Another Chance (1977)
Comes a Horseman (1978)
Chapter Two (1979)
Hide in Plain Sight (1980)
Thief (1981)
Bolero (1982)
Kiss Me Goodbye (1982)
Gardens of Stone (1987)

★★★

Sid Caesar

Brash Comedian

(1922-)

Sid Caesar (full name, Isaac Sidney Caesar) was born in Yonkers, New York, on September 8, 1922. His father owned a luncheonette, where the boy learned to mimic the languages of Italian, Russian, Hungarian, Polish, French, Spanish, and other factory workers.

While attending Hawthorne Junior High School, he earned money by playing the saxophone in a little band at dances and weddings. During his years at Yonkers High School, he played in a band at school events and in restaurants and bars.

After graduating from high school in 1939, he moved to New York City, where he soon found work as a theater usher and doorman. Meanwhile, he studied to become a serious musician, taking saxophone lessons from Frank Chase of the National Broadcasting Company (NBC) Symphony Orchestra and auditing theory courses at the Juilliard School of Music.

In 1940, to earn money, he began to play in dance bands at hotels, casinos, and elsewhere. He rapidly became known as an excellent musician.

Simultaneously, however, another career was also opening for him. In the summers of 1939 and 1940, while performing principally as a saxophonist, he helped to create and perform comic sketches on the borscht circuit. His reputation as a comic grew as fast as his reputation as a saxophonist. In the summer of 1941 he worked as a comic in Monticello, while that autumn he returned to saxophone playing in New York City.

In the summer of 1942 he performed as a comic at the Avon Lodge in the Catskills. The niece of the owner was Florence Levy, whom Caesar married in 1943. They had three children: Michele (called Shelly), Rick, and Karen.

Late in 1942 Caesar entered the Coast Guard. There he helped to stage revues for the service personnel. Later he was part of the revue *Tars and Spars,* which toured many American cities. In that show Caesar performed his now famous war-movie routine, a monologue in which he played several characters and created many sound effects. The tour culminated in Los Angeles, where the show was made into a movie that was released in early 1946.

Meanwhile, World War II had ended and Caesar had left the Coast Guard. He stayed in Los Angeles and appeared in another movie, *The Guilt of Janet Ames* (1947), in which he played a nightclub comic.

Then he went to New York City and did some nightclub and theater work before spending a year with the Broadway revue *Make Mine Manhattan* (1948). After that, he entered the exciting new medium of television.

In 1949 he hosted the TV variety show *The Admiral Broadway Revue.* That was followed by *Your Show of Shows* (1950-54), *Caesar's Hour* (1954-57), and *Sid Caesar Invites You* (1958). Unlike many other early TV comedy-variety shows, which used stand-up comedy or slapstick vaudeville routines, Caesar's utilized some of the best comedy writers of the time (including Woody Allen, Mel Brooks, and Neil Simon) to create well-rounded sketches and a host of zany characters (notably the Professor) played by Caesar himself. He became famous for his ability to ape a wide variety of accents and human types.

Offstage, Caesar was shy and intellectual, a lover of history, literature, and classical music. But onstage, he hid behind a comedy persona that was brash and aggressive. When his TV series was canceled in 1958, he fell apart. In his autobiography, *Where Have I Been?* (with Bill Davidson, 1982), he confessed that between 1958 and 1978 his sense of insecurity and his difficulty in facing the pressure of success led him to a dependence on alcohol and pills. Periods of despair alternated with periods of rage and violence.

"I worked," he wrote in his autobiography, "and I was there, but I really wasn't there." He was still effective in the Broadway musical *Little Me* (1962), playing seven roles. But, as he admitted, he was working with "residual" capabilities.

Through the rest of the 1960s and most of the 1970s, he went through the motions in nightclubs, on TV, on the stage, and in films, such as *The Busy Body* (1967) and *Silent Movie* (1976).

In 1978 he finally hit rock bottom and began to turn himself around, largely on his own initiative. By the early 1980s he felt fully recovered in mind and body.

In 1981 Caesar toured in the stage production *A Touch of Burlesque,* which was taped for release over cable TV in 1982. Since then he has appeared in several

Sid Caesar (left) and Janet Blair (right)

films, including *Grease II* (1982) and *Over the Brooklyn Bridge* (1984). In *Alice in Wonderland* (TV, 1985) he played the Gryphon, and in 1986 he was seen in a TV play called *Christmas Show,* in which he portrayed a Scrooge-like landlord.

Selected performances:

Stage

Make Mine Manhattan (1948)
Little Me (1962)
Last of the Red Hot Lovers (1972)
The Prisoner of Second Avenue (1973)
A Touch of Burlesque (1981)

Films

Tars and Spars (1946)
The Guilt of Janet Ames (1947)
It's a Mad, Mad, Mad, Mad World (1963)
The Busy Body (1967)
A Guide for the Married Man (1967)
The Spirit Is Willing (1967)
Flight to Holocaust (TV, 1973)
Airport 1975 (1974)
Silent Movie (1976)
Curse of the Black Widow (TV, 1977)
Grease (1978)
The Cheap Detective (1978)
The Fiendish Plot of Dr. Fu Manchu (1980)
History of the World, Part I (1981)
The Munsters' Revenge (TV, 1981)
Grease II (1982)
Found Money (TV, 1983)
Over the Brooklyn Bridge (1984)
Alice in Wonderland (TV, 1985)
Love Is Never Silent (TV, 1985)

TV

The Admiral Broadway Revue (1949)
Your Show of Shows (1950-54)
Caesar's Hour (1954-57)
Sid Caesar Invites You (1958)
The Sid Caesar Show (1963-64)

★★

Dyan Cannon

Versatile Actress

(1937-)

Dyan Cannon was born in Tacoma, Washington, on January 4, 1937. Her original name was Samille Diane Friesen, daughter of a Baptist father and Jewish mother.

After briefly attending the University of Washington, she moved to Los Angeles and worked as a model. In the late 1950s she began to find some acting jobs. She made guest appearances on TV series, such as *Playhouse Ninety* and *Bat Masterson,* and had a minor role in the movie *The Rise and Fall of Legs Diamond* (1960).

During 1960-61 Cannon played a regular role in the TV soap opera *Full Circle,* as a young widow. Then, in New York City, she studied acting with Sanford Meisner and appeared in the Broadway plays *The Fun Couple* (1962) and *The Ninety Day Mistress* (1967).

In the early 1960s Cannon began to live with the actor Cary Grant. They finally married in 1965 and had one child, Jennifer, before divorcing in 1968.

Cannon then resumed her film career by taking a role in *Bob and Carol and Ted and Alice* (1969). Among her movies over the next few years were *Doctors' Wives* (1971), *Such Good Friends* (1971), and *Death Scream* (TV, 1975).

After directing the movie *Number One* (1976), Cannon returned to acting with outstanding performances in *Lady of the House* (TV, 1978) and *Heaven Can Wait* (1978). In the former, based on fact, she played a San Francisco madam of the 1930s and 1940s who retired in 1950 to open a restaurant in nearby Sausalito, where, despite severe local opposition, she served as mayor during 1976-78. In the comedy *Heaven Can Wait* Cannon portrayed a scheming would-be murderess.

Among her later films were *Honeysuckle Rose* (1980), *Author! Author!* (1982), and *Master of the Game* (TV, 1984). In 1985 she had the title role in the well-publicized two-part TV movie *Jenny's War,* as an American woman searching for her son in Nazi Germany just before World War II.

At one time in danger of being typecast as a floozy, Cannon has carefully chosen her roles since the late 1970s to show her versatility.

Selected performances:

Stage

The Fun Couple (1962)
The Ninety Day Mistress (1967)

Films

The Rise and Fall of Legs Diamond (1960)
Bob and Carol and Ted and Alice (1969)
Doctors' Wives (1971)
The Anderson Tapes (1971)
The Love Machine (1971)
Such Good Friends (1971)
The Burglars (1972)
Shamus (1973)
The Last of Sheila (1973)
Death Scream (TV, 1975)
Lady of the House (TV, 1978)
Heaven Can Wait (1978)
Revenge of the Pink Panther (1978)
Honeysuckle Rose (1980)
Coast to Coast (1980)
Deathtrap (1982)
Author! Author! (1982)
Having It All (TV, 1982)
Master of the Game (TV, 1984)
Jenny's War (TV, 1985)

TV

Full Circle (1960-61)

★★★

Eddie Cantor

Banjo Eyes

(1892-1964)

Eddie Cantor was born of Russian immigrants in New York City, New York, on January 31, 1892. His parents died when he was a toddler, and the orphan, originally named Isidore Itzkowitz, was raised in Manhattan's Lower East Side by his maternal grandmother, Esther Kantrowitz, a warmhearted woman who greatly influenced the future entertainer's gentle, kindly character.

She was also responsible, inadvertently, for his eventual name and career. When she was enrolling the six-year-old in school, she mistakenly began to give the registrar her own name, Kantrowitz, but never finished it. The registrar wrote down "Isidore Kanter." Later the boy himself changed the spelling of his new surname to Cantor. Still later he changed the Isidore to Eddie because his girlfriend, Ida Tobias, liked the name Eddie.

Grandma Esther's ability as a mimic gave Cantor the idea of performing for others. His sentimental recitations kept him in school for several years after he had stopped earning passing grades. And he often sang and performed comic impersonations for his friends, sometimes combining the two skills, as when he pretended to be Anna Held singing "I Just Can't Make My Eyes Behave."

Soon after leaving school at the age of thirteen, Cantor teamed up with a friend to perform a variety act at weddings and other events. In 1907 they made their first appearance on a real stage, at the Clinton Music Hall; but the act fell flat because they spoke in English, not realizing that they were in a Yiddish theater. On his own, Cantor won some money in amateur-night contests with his comedy-dialect routines.

He then got a job with a touring burlesque show, his first professional engagement. When the tour folded four weeks later, he became a singing waiter in a Coney Island saloon. The pianist at the saloon became Cantor's lifelong friend and a world-famous entertainer in his own right—Jimmy Durante.

In 1909 Cantor was hired as a comedian on a small vaudeville circuit. There he was praised for his ability to repeat the same act in various ethnic accents, including one in blackface. He continued his blackface role from 1910 to 1912 as an assistant to the comedy juggling team of Bedini and Arthur. The trio burlesqued the famous stars of the day. An important step forward came when Cantor was allowed to sing Irving Berlin's "Ragtime Violin" as part of the act. He was so nervous that he skipped back and forth on the stage, clapping and gyrating his hands and rolling his eyes as he sang. Those gestures later became his trademarks.

From 1912 to 1914 Cantor toured with Gus Edwards's *Kid Kabaret* revue. There he met George Jessel, who, like Durante, became a lifelong friend and a well-known entertainer.

In 1914 Cantor married Ida Tobias. He had met her in 1905, and she encouraged him through his early struggles. Their marriage was widely regarded as one of the most harmonious in show business. It also became one of the best-known marriages because Cantor later incorporated numerous anecdotes about his wife and five daughters (Marjorie, Natalie, Edna, Marilyn, and Janet) in his routines. He adopted "Ida, Sweet As Apple Cider" as his theme song.

The Cantors honeymooned in London. While there, he appeared in the revue *Not Likely,* in which he scored his first major success. Until then he had relied on imitations and dialects. In *Not Likely* he sang and performed comedy routines as himself.

Back in the United States later in 1914, Cantor renewed his vaudeville work as a blackface comedian and singer. Breaking blackface tradition, however, he performed without dialect and without comedy clothes. In 1916 he appeared in his first musical: a Los Angeles production of *Canary Cottage.*

Then he worked in a cabaret format for twenty-seven weeks at Florenz Ziegfeld's New York City supper club, the Midnight Frolic. That engagement led to Cantor's Broadway debut when he appeared in the *Ziegfeld Follies of 1917,* followed by the 1918 and 1919 editions of the show.

He then appeared in the revues *The Midnight Rounders* (1920) and *Make It Snappy* (1922). In a famous skit in the latter show, he played Max, a mousy tailor whose customer demanded a coat with a belt in the back; the "belt" he received was not the type he expected.

The musical comedy *Kid Boots* (1923) was one of Cantor's greatest hits. In the *Ziegfeld Follies of 1927* he broke precedent by being the only star in the whole revue. That show was followed by the musical comedy

Eddie Cantor (center)

Whoopee (1928). His last stage work was in *Banjo Eyes* (1941), the title coming from his nickname, which referred to his wide, expressive eyes.

In his stage appearances, Cantor did some of his routines with, and some without, blackface. As was true of many other white entertainers of the time, such as Al Jolson and Sophie Tucker, Cantor's use of blackface was intended not as a racial slur but simply as a theatrical convention that helped performers overcome inhibitions. After their confidence was built, they could come out from behind the "mask" and perform without the black makeup.

The development of sound movies in the late 1920s doomed vaudeville and hurt the live theater in general. Cantor quickly jumped into the new medium. His first film appearance was in a silent-movie version of *Kid Boots* (1926). Among his musical talkies were *Glorifying the American Girl* (1929), a filmed version of *Whoopee* (1930), *Palmy Days* (1931), *Roman Scandals* (1933), *Ali Baba Goes to Town* (1937), *Thank Your Lucky Stars* (1943), and *If You Knew Susie* (1948). Cantor played a nonmusical comedic role in *Forty Little Mothers* (1940). He appeared briefly in, and sang for the music track of, the biopic *The Eddie Cantor Story* (1953), in which he was portrayed by Keefe Brasselle.

However, it was through radio that Cantor reached the peak of his popularity. He made some guest appearances during the 1920s, but his first great impact came on Rudy Vallee's *Fleischmann Hour* in February 1931. In September of that year Cantor took over as host of *The Chase and Sanborn Hour,* soon also known as *The Eddie Cantor Show.* He had his own radio variety show, under various titles, almost continuously for the next two decades. Cantor, beginning in 1932, pioneered the use of live-audience response on radio, where studio visitors had previously been admonished to remain silent.

Besides offering his own performances on his radio programs, Cantor provided audiences with such new talents as the comedian Harry Einstein (famous as Parkyakarkus) and the singers Deanna Durbin and Dinah Shore. (In 1949 he helped to get Eddie Fisher's career under way by taking the young singer on a live tour.)

In 1950, at Cantor's own suggestion, the National Broadcasting Company (NBC) established the TV series *The Colgate Comedy Hour,* in which Cantor and several other comedians rotated in hosting their own variety programs. *The Eddie Cantor Show* (1950-54) was part of that series. In 1955 he hosted and occasionally starred in *The Eddie Cantor Comedy Theater,* a series of variety programs and comedy plays. Later he made guest appearances on many TV programs. In 1956 he won critical acclaim for a dramatic role in "Seidman and Son" on the *Playhouse Ninety* TV anthology series.

Cantor's enormous popularity as a comic actor and singer during his lifetime was due to his unique manner of performing with an irresistible energy and cheerfulness, a dignified yet boyish charm, and a sincere human warmth. His friend George Jessel called Cantor "the most resourceful comic figure that there ever was in America."

Cantor was extremely active in raising funds for many causes. In 1920 he began to give benefits for Surprise Lake Camp for underprivileged youngsters. The project was especially dear to him because it was while he himself was at the camp in his own childhood that he had first realized what a great morale boost such kindness can give to people living in bleak circumstances. In the late 1930s he helped to raise money for sending refugee children, whose parents had been killed or interned by the Nazis, to Palestine. He raised hundreds of millions of dollars for other causes, including hospitals, veterans, Catholic and Protestant projects, and the United Jewish Appeal. Much of his work was done for the state of Israel, where he was affectionately referred to in Yiddish as the *schnorrer* ("beggar"). When President Franklin D. Roosevelt asked Cantor to organize a drive to raise money for fighting infantile paralysis, the entertainer suggested a plan in which each donor would be asked for only ten cents, calling it a "march of dimes." Roosevelt immediately adopted that slogan for the program. When Dr. Jonas Salk developed his polio vaccine in the 1950s, the money had come from the March of Dimes.

Cantor wrote several books, including the autobiographical *My Life Is in Your Hands* (with David Freeman, 1928) and *Take My Life* (with Jane Kesner Ardmore, 1957). *As I Remember Them* (1963) is a book of recollections.

After a 1952 heart attack, Cantor was forced into semiretirement. In 1962 his life changed even more drastically with the death of his beloved Ida. His own death, in Los Angeles, California, came on October 10, 1964.

Selected performances:

Stage

Kid Kabaret (1912)
Not Likely (1914)
Canary Cottage (1916)
Ziegfeld Follies of 1917 (1917)
Ziegfeld Follies of 1918 (1918)
Ziegfeld Follies of 1919 (1919)
The Midnight Rounders (1920)
Broadway Brevities of 1920 (1920)
Make It Snappy (1922)
Kid Boots (1923)
Ziegfeld Follies of 1923 (1923)
Ziegfeld Follies of 1927 (1927)
Whoopee (1928)
Banjo Eyes (1941)

Films

Kid Boots (1926)
Special Delivery (1927)
Glorifying the American Girl (1929)
Whoopee (1930)
Palmy Days (1931)
The Kid from Spain (1932)
Roman Scandals (1933)
Kid Millions (1934)
Strike Me Pink (1936)
Ali Baba Goes to Town (1937)
Forty Little Mothers (1940)
Thank Your Lucky Stars (1943)
Hollywood Canteen (1944)
Show Business (1944)
If You Knew Susie (1948)
The Story of Will Rogers (1952)
The Eddie Cantor Story (1953)

Radio

The Eddie Cantor Show (also known as *The Chase and Sanborn Hour,* 1931-34; *The Eddie Cantor Pabst Blue Ribbon Show,* 1935-39; and *Time to Smile,* 1940-49)

TV

The Eddie Cantor Show (1950-54, part of *The Colgate Comedy Hour*)
The Eddie Cantor Comedy Theater (1955)

★★

Morris Carnovsky

Distinguished Shakespearean

(1897-)

Morris Carnovsky was born in Saint Louis, Missouri, on September 5, 1897. He made his stage debut by performing the title role in *Disraeli* (1914) at Teatman High School in his hometown. Later he appeared in more plays in Saint Louis, earned a B.A. degree (1920) at Washington University in the same city, and then performed with stock companies in Boston. He studied acting under Emanuel Reacher in 1922 and Michael Chekhov in 1935.

Carnovsky made his New York City debut by taking the role of Reb Aaron in *The God of Vengeance* in 1922. From 1924 to 1930 he was one of the Theater Guild members, with whom he performed many important roles. Among them were Kublai the Great Khan in *Marco Millions* (1928), the title role in *Uncle Vanya* (1929), and Francis Bacon in *Elizabeth the Queen* (1930).

His later stage roles included Dr. Levine, the unhappy physician, in *Men in White* (1933); Jacob, the self-sacrificing grandfather, in *Awake and Sing!* (1935); Mr. Bonaparte, the father whose son becomes a boxer instead of a violinist, in *Golden Boy* (1937); and Ben Stark, the dentist with a shrewish wife, in *Rocket to the Moon* (1938).

Carnovsky made his film debut by portraying the author Anatole France in *The Life of Emile Zola* (1937), in which he made a beautiful speech at Zola's bier. Throughout the 1940s and early 1950s Carnovsky appeared in numerous movies. In *Rhapsody in Blue* (1945) he played George Gershwin's father. In *Cyrano de Bergerac* (1950) he was the hero's friend Le Bret. Among his other films were *Edge of Darkness* (1943), *Our Vines Have Tender Grapes* (1945), and *Dead Reckoning* (1947).

Carnovsky's life took a dramatic turn in the early 1950s when he was blacklisted for his refusal to cooperate with the House Committee on Un-American Activities. Consequently his movie career came to an abrupt halt.

But the stage was still open to him. He played Aaron Katz and the Presiding Angel in *The World of Sholom Aleichem* (1953) and Tzaddik in *The Dybbuk* (1954).

From 1956 on, Carnovsky frequently appeared at the

American Shakespeare Festival in Stratford, Connecticut. He became one of the most distinguished Shakespearean actors of his time, especially noted for his title role in *King Lear* and for his powerful, moving portrayal of the Jewish usurer Shylock in *The Merchant of Venice*.

Carnovsky's affinity for Shakespeare stemmed at least in part from his love of language. "I began by adoring words," he said in 1970. "I've always liked to learn words, and as an actor I've learned how to use them for all their juiciness and malleability."

He continued to play non-Shakespearean parts as well. In 1961 he was the Logician in *Rhinoceros* and Mr. Baker in *Come Blow Your Horn*. He was highly praised for two portrayals of the scientist Galileo, in *Galileo* (1966) and in *Lamp at Midnight* (1969).

Carnovsky also made a few returns to movies and some memorable appearances on TV. He acted in the films *A View from the Bridge* (1962) and *The Gambler* (1974), and he narrated *The City* (1977). On TV he played three roles (the Presiding Angel, Mr. Katz, and the Rabbi) in "The World of Sholom Aleichem" (1961) for *The Play of the Week,* and he was Judge Julius Hoffman in *The Chicago Eight Conspiracy Trial* (1970).

Carnovsky was widely admired, especially by knowledgeable theatrical people, for the range of his character-acting skills. He was particularly effective as troubled, thoughtful men.

In 1941 Carnovsky married the actress Phoebe Brand, with whom he had a son. It was his second marriage, his first having been to Florence Lasersohn from 1922 to 1933, when it ended in divorce.

Selected performances:

Stage

The God of Vengeance (1922)
The Failures (1923)
Saint Joan (1923)
The Creaking Chair (1926)
Juarez and Maximilian (1926)
The Brothers Karamazov (1927)
The Doctor's Dilemma (1927)
Marco Millions (1928)
Volpone (1928)
Uncle Vanya (1929)
Hotel Universe (1930)
Elizabeth the Queen (1930)
Night over Taos (1932)
Both Your Houses (1933)
Men in White (1933)
Awake and Sing! (1935)
Paradise Lost (1935)
The Case of Clyde Griffiths (1936)
Johnny Johnson (1936)
Golden Boy (1937)
Rocket to the Moon (1938)
Thunder Rock (1939)
Night Music (1940)
My Sister Eileen (1940)
Café Crown (1942)
An Enemy of the People (1950)
The World of Sholom Aleichem (1953)
The Dybbuk (1954)
The Three Sisters (1955)
King John (1956)
Measure for Measure (1956)
The Taming of the Shrew (1956)
The Merchant of Venice (1957 and several times since then)
Hamlet (1958)
Twelfth Night (1958)
Romeo and Juliet (1959)
The Merry Wives of Windsor (1959)
Twelfth Night (1960)
The Tempest (1960)
Antony and Cleopatra (1960)
Rhinoceros (1961)

Come Blow Your Horn (1961)
Twelfth Night (1961)
Richard III (1961)
A Family Affair (1962)
The Caucasian Chalk Circle (1962)
King Lear (1963 and several times since then)
Galileo (1966)
Antigone (1967)
Lamp at Midnight (1969)
Hamlet (1969)
A Swan Song (1972)
Awake and Sing! (1976)

Films

The Life of Emile Zola (1937)
Tovarich (1937)
Edge of Darkness (1943)
Address Unknown (1944)
The Master Race (1944)
Rhapsody in Blue (1945)
Our Vines Have Tender Grapes (1945)
Cornered (1945)
Miss Susie Slagle's (1946)
Dead Reckoning (1947)
Dishonored Lady (1947)
Saigon (1948)
Siren of Atlantis (1949)
Thieves' Highway (1949)
Gun Crazy (1950)
Cyrano de Bergerac (1950)
The Second Woman (1951)
A View from the Bridge (1962)
The Gambler (1974)
The City (narrator, 1977)

★★★

Jeff Chandler

Action Hero

(1918-61)

Jeff Chandler was born in New York City, New York, on December 15, 1918. His original name was Ira Grossel. He was raised in Brooklyn by his mother after his parents had separated when he was very young.

As a boy he acted in school plays. After graduating from Erasmus Hall High School, he spent one year in an art school and then went to work as a layout artist.

But he soon realized that what he really wanted to do was to act. He studied for less than one year at a New York City drama school before leaving to perform with a Long Island stock company. In the summer of 1941 he and a friend started their own stock company, called the Shady Lane Playhouse, in Illinois.

Soon, however, World War II came, and Chandler entered the army. He fought as an infantryman in the Pacific theater and rose from the rank of private to that of first lieutenant.

Released from the army in 1946, Chandler soon began to get roles on radio. Over the next several years he earned a growing reputation by playing the title roles in the medical-drama series *The Private Practice of Dr. Dana* (1947-48) and the private-detective series *Michael Shayne* (1948). He was also in the original radio version of the series *Our Miss Brooks* (1948-49), playing the bashful biology teacher Philip Boynton (a rare comedy role for him).

His success on radio led to offers for film work. Chandler's first movie role was a bit part as a surly gambler in *Johnny O'Clock* (1947). In *Sword in the Desert* (1949) he played an underground leader of Jews fighting the British in Palestine. That role helped him to become regarded as a legitimate leading man.

But Chandler's rise to stardom came when he was cast as Cochise, a chief of the Chiricahua Indians in the American Southwest, in the western movie *Broken Arrow* (1950). He played the same character in *The Battle at Apache Pass* (1952).

For the next decade he starred as a popular hero in

western and other action dramas. His prematurely gray hair and gaunt features led to his frequently playing parts actually designed for men older than he was, as in his Cochise role.

In *Two Flags West* (1950) he portrayed a tough cavalry commandant. In *Deported* (1950) he played a gangster sent from the United States back to his native Italy, where he becomes reformed through love. *Yankee Pasha* (1954) is an adventure movie set in Morocco.

In *Away All Boats* (1956) Chandler starred as the captain of a ship carrying American troops to the Pacific theater during World War II. In *Jeanne Eagels* (1957) he was a carnival barker.

Chandler gave a particularly strong performance as a lawman in the western *Man with a Shadow* (1958). *Raw Wind in Eden* (1958) is an adventure story set on a Mediterranean island. In the war drama *Merrill's Marauders* (1962) he played Brigadier General Frank Merrill, the courageous, inspirational leader of an American unit behind Japanese lines during World War II.

In 1956 he established, with his agent, Meyer Mishkin, his own film company, Earlmar Productions. Chandler also wrote and recorded popular songs, publishing them through his own firm, Chandler Music.

He was an active supporter of Israel. As a result, in 1960 his films were banned from all Arab countries.

Chandler married the former actress Marjorie Hoshelle in 1946. They separated in 1954, later reunited, separated again in 1957, and finally divorced in 1960. They had two daughters: Jamie and Dana.

On June 17, 1961, Chandler died in Culver City, California, of complications, specifically blood poisoning, following spinal surgery. He was only forty-two.

Selected performances:

Films

Johnny O'Clock (1947)
The Invisible Wall (1947)
Roses Are Red (1947)
Sword in the Desert (1949)
Abandoned Woman (1949)
Broken Arrow (1950)
Two Flags West (1950)
Deported (1950)
Bird of Paradise (1951)
Smuggler's Island (1951)
Iron Man (1951)
Flame of Araby (1951)
The Battle at Apache Pass (1952)
Red Ball Express (1952)
Because of You (1952)
East of Sumatra (1953)
The Great Sioux Uprising (1953)
Yankee Pasha (1954)
Sign of the Pagan (1955)
Foxfire (1955)
Female on the Beach (1955)
The Spoilers (1955)
Toy Tiger (1956)
Away All Boats (1956)
Pillars of the Sky (1956)
The Tattered Dress (1957)
Jeanne Eagels (1957)
Man with a Shadow (1958)
The Lady Takes a Flyer (1958)
Raw Wind in Eden (1958)
Stranger in My Arms (1959)
Thunder in the Sun (1959)
Ten Seconds to Hell (1959)
Return to Peyton Place (1961)
Merrill's Marauders (1962)

Radio

The Private Practice of Dr. Dana (1947-48)
Michael Shayne (1948)
Our Miss Brooks (1948-49)

★★★

Jill Clayburgh

Conveyer of Emotional Complexity

(1944-)

Jill Clayburgh was born in New York City, New York, on April 30, 1944. She came from an affluent, cultured Upper East Side family, and she was educated at the exclusive Brearley School. At Sarah Lawrence College she concentrated on philosophy, religion, and literature.

One of her college friends persuaded Clayburgh to spend a vacation as an apprentice in summer stock at the Williamsburg Theater Festival in Massachusetts. There she painted scenery, had a one-line part in Shaw's *Man and Superman,* and became hooked on acting. While still in college, she had a role in the film *The Wedding Party* (released several years later, in 1969).

After graduating from Sarah Lawrence College (B.A., 1966), Clayburgh studied acting in Manhattan with Uta Hagen and John Lehne, from whom she learned a modified form of the Method technique. Soon she became a member of the Charles Playhouse in Boston, where she met the young actor Al Pacino.

Clayburgh and Pacino became romantically involved, and they moved back to New York City together. There she appeared in off-Broadway plays, including *Calling In Crazy* (1969), in which she played a half-hearted nonconformist. During that time she also acted in some TV shows, such as *N.Y.P.D.* and *Search for Tomorrow.*

Clayburgh's Broadway debut came as the beautiful, spirited Hannah Cohen in the musical *The Rothschilds* (1970). The following year she appeared in a Los Angeles production of *Othello.* While there, she was given the role of Naomi in the film *Portnoy's Complaint* (1972). She also had small parts in the movies *The Thief Who Came to Dinner* (1973) and *The Terminal Man* (1974).

The turning point of her career came with her sensitive performance as the prostitute Wanda in *Hustling* (TV, 1975). That role gave her the prominence to win important leading parts in other films.

In *Griffin and Phoenix* (TV, 1976) she costarred with Peter Falk as two terminally ill people who have a last love affair. In *Gable and Lombard* (1976) she portrayed the 1930s actress Carole Lombard. In *An Unmarried Woman* (1978) she played a woman traumatized by her husband's desertion after many years of marriage. In the Italian-made picture *La Luna* (1979, *Luna* in the United States) she was a self-centered mother with an unhealthy attachment to her son.

In 1979 Clayburgh appeared onstage in a Long Beach, California, production of *In the Boom Boom Room,* as a vulnerable, morally wounded go-go dancer. In that year she also married the play's author, David Rabe.

In the film *I'm Dancing As Fast As I Can* (1982) she played an edgy career woman living with a man who resents her success. In *Hanna K.* (1983) she portrayed a lawyer defending an Arab in a land dispute. In *Miles to Go* (TV, 1986) she was a woman dying of cancer and worrying about the coming void in her husband's and children's lives.

Clayburgh is renowned for her ability to convey a complex interplay of emotional impulses. Her generally intelligent, vulnerable characters have provided her with many opportunities for quick, subtle contrasts in emotion.

Selected performances:

Stage

It's Called the Sugar Plum (1968)
The Sudden and Accidental Re-education of Horse Johnson (1968)
Calling In Crazy (1969)
The Nest (1970)
The Rothschilds (1970)
The Devil's Disciple (1970)
Othello (1971)
Pippin (1972)
Jumpers (1974)
In the Boom Boom Room (1979)
Design for Living (1984)

Films

The Wedding Party (1969)
Portnoy's Complaint (1972)
The Snoop Sisters (TV, 1972)
The Thief Who Came to Dinner (1973)
The Terminal Man (1974)
Hustling (TV, 1975)
The Art of Crime (TV, 1975)
Griffin and Phoenix (TV, 1976)
Gable and Lombard (1976)
Silver Streak (1976)
Semi-Tough (1977)
An Unmarried Woman (1978)
La Luna (1979, It.; U.S., *Luna*)
Starting Over (1979)
It's My Turn (1980)
First Monday in October (1981)
I'm Dancing As Fast As I Can (1982)
Hanna K. (1983)
Miles to Go (TV, 1986)

★★★

Lee J. Cobb

Gravel-voiced Actor

(1911-76)

Lee J. Cobb was born in New York City, New York, on December 8, 1911. His original name was Leo Jacoby.

After a wrist injury ended his early hopes to become a concert violinist, he looked to the theater to fulfill his craving for the performing arts. He graduated from high school in New York City and then went to California, where he became associated with the Pasadena Playhouse in 1929.

However, he soon returned to New York City. While working as a salesman during the day, he studied accounting at night at City College of the City University of New York (1929-31).

In 1931 he went back to the Pasadena Playhouse and worked there for two years as an actor-director. After two more years as a freelance actor on tour and in New York City, he made his Broadway debut by playing Koch and the Saloon Keeper in *Crime and Punishment* in 1935. In that year he also became a member of the famed Group Theater players, with whom he performed a series of character roles over the next few years. Notable among his parts were those of Mr. Carp in *Golden Boy* (1937) and Lammanawitz in *The Gentle People* (1939).

In 1939 he appeared in the movie version of *Golden Boy*. For the next several years he alternated working in Hollywood films and on the New York City stage.

From 1943 to 1945 Cobb served in the United States Army Air Forces, for whom he acted in the stage show *Winged Victory* (1943). He also appeared in the filmed version (1944).

After his discharge, he returned to Hollywood and continued his career as a character actor in a wide variety of supporting roles. In *Anna and the King of Siam* (1946) he played a Siamese prime minister, in *Boome-*

rang (1947) a police chief, in *Captain from Castile* (1947) a Spanish buccaneer, in *Call Northside 777* (1948) a newspaper editor, and in *The Dark Past* (1948) a scientist.

He finally reached star status when he played the lead in Arthur Miller's *Death of a Salesman* (1949) on Broadway. As Willy Loman, the salesman whom life has defeated, Cobb had an opportunity to portray a well-rounded character and to carry an entire show on his own shoulders.

He returned to the stage several more times, notably as Mr. Bonaparte in a revival of *Golden Boy* (1952). Cobb also made guest appearances in numerous TV series, such as *Playhouse Ninety, Studio One,* and *Zane Grey Theater*. In the long-running TV western series *The Virginian* (1962-70), he played Judge Henry Garth; and he was David Barrett in the courtroom drama *The Young Lawyers* (1970-71).

But Cobb spent most of his mature years making movies. Next to his role as Willy Loman in *Death of a Salesman,* his most famous part was as the vicious gangster Johnny Friendly in the film *On the Waterfront* (1954). He played a Chinese war lord in *The Left Hand of God* (1955) and a country judge in *The Man in the Gray Flannel Suit* (1956).

In the mid-1950s Cobb testified before the House Un-American Activities Committee. He admitted that he had briefly been a member of the Communist party in the 1930s. Shortly after his testimony, he suffered a massive heart attack that nearly killed him.

But soon he returned to work and gave outstanding performances as a hard-line jurist in *Twelve Angry Men* (1957) and, in one of his most memorable roles, as the father in *The Brothers Karamazov* (1958). In *Exodus* (1960), a story about the liberation of Israel in 1947-48, he played a Jewish conservative.

Among his later movies were *Come Blow Your Horn* (1963), *Mackenna's Gold* (1969), and *The Exorcist* (1973). Many critics agreed that Cobb's gravel-voiced performances enhanced, even salvaged, countless films. He was widely regarded as one of the finest character actors of his time.

Near the end of his life he starred in several TV movies. For example, in *Dr. Max* (TV, 1974), based on the same story as that used in the 1959 movie *The Last Angry Man* (starring Paul Muni), Cobb played a curmudgeonly big-city doctor who has a genuine concern for his poverty-stricken patients.

Cobb was married twice. In 1940 he wedded the actress Helen Beverly, with whom he had two children: Vincent and Julie. They divorced in 1952, and in 1957 he married Mrs. Mary Hirsch (née Brako), a Los Angeles schoolteacher. They raised two children, one from her previous marriage and one of their own: Tony and Jerry.

Cobb died in the Woodland Hills section of Los Angeles, California, on February 11, 1976.

Selected performances:

Stage

Crime and Punishment (1935)
Waiting for Lefty (1935)
Till the Day I Die (1935)
The Mother (1935)
Bitter Stream (1936)
Happy Valley, Limited (1936)
Golden Boy (1937)
The Gentle People (1939)
Thunder Rock (1939)
The Fifth Column (1940)
Clash by Night (1941)
Winged Victory (1943)
Death of a Salesman (1949)
Golden Boy (1952)
The Emperor's Clothes (1953)
King Lear (1968)

Films

Golden Boy (1939)
This Thing Called Love (1941)
Men of Boys Town (1941)
Paris Calling (1942)
The Moon Is Down (1943)
Tonight We Raid Calais (1943)
The Song of Bernadette (1944)
Winged Victory (1944)
Anna and the King of Siam (1946)
Boomerang (1947)
Johnny O'Clock (1947)
Captain from Castile (1947)
Call Northside 777 (1948)
The Miracle of the Bells (1948)
The Luck of the Irish (1948)
The Dark Past (1948)
Thieves' Highway (1949)
The Man Who Cheated Himself (1951)
Sirocco (1951)
The Fighter (1952)
The Tall Texan (1953)
Yankee Pasha (1954)
Gorilla at Large (1954)
On the Waterfront (1954)
The Racers (1955)
The Left Hand of God (1955)
The Man in the Gray Flannel Suit (1956)
Twelve Angry Men (1957)
The Garment Jungle (1957)
The Three Faces of Eve (1957)
The Brothers Karamazov (1958)
Man of the West (1958)
Party Girl (1958)
The Trap (1959)
Green Mansions (1959)
But Not for Me (1959)
Exodus (1960)
The Four Horsemen of the Apocalypse (1962)
Come Blow Your Horn (1963)
How the West Was Won (1963)
Our Man Flint (1966)
In like Flint (1967)

Coogan's Bluff (1968)
Mackenna's Gold (1969)
The Liberation of L. B. Jones (1970)
Macho Callahan (1970)
Lawman (1971)
Heat of Anger (TV, 1972)
Double Indemnity (TV, 1973)
The Man Who Loved Cat Dancing (1973)
The Exorcist (1973)
Dr. Max (TV, 1974)
Trapped beneath the Sea (TV, 1974)
The Great Ice Rip-off (TV, 1974)
That Lucky Touch (1975)

TV

The Virginian (1962-70)
The Young Lawyers (1970-71)

★★★

Tony Curtis

Popular Leading Man

(1925-)

Tony Curtis was born in New York City, New York, on June 3, 1925. His original name was Bernard Schwartz.

His father had been an actor in Hungary. But after immigrating to the United States, the elder Schwartz found English to be difficult and had to change professions; he became a tailor.

Bernard grew up in a tough neighborhood, faced anti-Semitism, and became a gang member. A truant officer took the boy to the Jones Memorial Settlement House, where Bernard developed an interest in acting in plays.

He also attended Seward Park High School. But his homelife had been miserable for years, his mother being a child abuser. Before finishing high school, Bernard ran away from home and joined the navy. After his discharge he went back to Seward Park and graduated in 1946.

His interest in acting had grown, and he used the GI bill to study for one year at the Dramatic Workshop of the New School for Social Research in New York City. After touring the borscht circuit with a stock company, he began to make stage appearances in the New York City area, notably in the title role in *Golden Boy* with the Cherry Lane players in Greenwich Village. He was seen by a talent scout and signed to a Hollywood film contract.

In his early days at Universal-International Pictures, he changed his name to Anthony Curtis and began to take courses in voice, dramatics, gymnastics, horsemanship, and pantomime. Meanwhile, he performed bit parts in several movies, including *City across the River* (1949) and *Francis* (1950). Beginning with *Kansas Raiders* (1951) he shortened his name to Tony Curtis.

His first leading role was in *The Prince Who Was a Thief* (1951). He soon became enormously popular with audiences for his athleticism, good looks, and genial personality in such movies as *Houdini* (1953) and *Trapeze* (1956).

Critics, however, remained cool toward Curtis for many years. In 1953 he began psychoanalysis, which he claimed helped him both as a person and as an actor.

In the late 1950s Curtis finally began to win critical acceptance as a major actor. He gave a series of excellent performances in such films as *Sweet Smell of Success* (1957), as an overly ambitious publicist; *Kings Go Forth* (1958), as a spoiled rich youth; *The Defiant Ones* (1958), as an embittered escaped convict; and *Some Like It Hot* (1959), as a bogus female saxophonist and as a phony millionaire.

In later years he continued to expand his range as a leading man. He portrayed a stereotyped hero and daredevil in the comedy *The Great Race* (1965), a homicidal maniac in the mystery *The Boston Strangler* (1968), and a gangster in *Lepke* (1975). Curtis won high praise for his starring role in *Moviola: The Scarlett O'Hara War* (TV,

1980), as the producer David O. Selznick searching for a leading lady for his 1939 movie *Gone with the Wind.*

However, by the early 1980s his roles were getting fewer and fewer as he became increasingly incapacitated by a long addiction to alcohol and drugs. He began taking barbiturates in the early 1960s, and from the mid-1970s to the early 1980s he used cocaine. Finally in 1984 he entered the Betty Ford Center in Rancho Mirage, California, where he received help in overcoming his addictions.

Curtis then campaigned for, and won, the role of the crime boss Salvatore ("Sam") Giancana in the fact-based movie *Mafia Princess* (TV, 1986). He gave a powerful performance and rejuvenated his career. In *Murder in Three Acts* (TV, 1986) he played a retired film star surrounded by memorabilia of better days; Curtis shipped many of his own photos, awards, and other objects from his Palm Springs, California, home to Acapulco, Mexico, for location shooting.

Curtis has had three marriages. In 1951 he married the actress Janet Leigh, with whom he appeared in the films *The Vikings* (1952), *Houdini, The Black Shield of Falworth* (1954), *The Perfect Furlough* (1959), and *Who Was That Lady?* (1960). In 1962 Curtis and Leigh divorced. The following year he married the actress Christine Kaufmann, with whom he appeared in *Taras Bulba* (1962) and *Wild and Wonderful* (1964). After they divorced, he wedded Leslie Allen. His third marriage, too, ended in divorce.

Curtis's marriages produced two sons and four daughters (two children with each wife). He and Leigh are the parents of the actress Jamie Lee Curtis, who has become well known principally in horror films, such as *Halloween* (1979).

Selected performances:

Stage

I Ought to Be in Pictures (1980)

Films

Criss Cross (1949)
City across the River (1949)
The Lady Gambles (1949)
Johnny Stool Pigeon (1949)
Francis (1950)
I Was a Shoplifter (1950)
Winchester '73 (1950)
Sierra (1950)
Kansas Raiders (1951)
The Prince Who Was a Thief (1951)
Flesh and Fury (1952)
The Vikings (1952)
No Room for the Groom (1952)
Son of Ali Baba (1952)
Houdini (1953)
Forbidden (1954)
Beachhead (1954)
Johnny Dark (1954)
The Black Shield of Falworth (1954)
Six Bridges to Cross (1955)
So This Is Paris (1955)
The Purple Mask (1955)
The Square Jungle (1955)
Trapeze (1956)
The Rawhide Years (1956)
Mister Cory (1957)
Sweet Smell of Success (1957)
The Midnight Story (1957)
Kings Go Forth (1958)
The Defiant Ones (1958)
The Perfect Furlough (1959)
Some Like It Hot (1959)
Operation Petticoat (1959)
Who Was That Lady? (1960)

The Rat Race (1960)
Spartacus (1960)
The Great Impostor (1961)
The Outsider (1961)
Taras Bulba (1962)
Captain Newman, M.D. (1963)
Forty Pounds of Trouble (1963)
The List of Adrian Messenger (1963)
Goodbye Charlie (1964)
Paris When It Sizzles (1964)
Sex and the Single Girl (1964)
Wild and Wonderful (1964)
Boeing Boeing (1965)
The Great Race (1965)
Arrivederci, Baby! (1966)
Chamber of Horrors (1966)
Not with My Wife, You Don't! (1966)
Don't Make Waves (1967)
The Boston Strangler (1968)
Rosemary's Baby (1968)
On My Way to the Crusades, I Met a Girl Who . . . (1969)
Those Daring Young Men in Their Jaunty Jalopies (1969)
Suppose They Gave a War and Nobody Came (1970)
You Can't Win 'Em All (1970)
The Third Girl from the Left (TV, 1973)
The Count of Monte Cristo (TV, 1975)
The Big Ripoff (TV, 1975)
Lepke (1975)
The Last Tycoon (1976)
The Manitou (1978)
The Bad News Bears Go to Japan (1978)
Vega$ (TV, 1978)
The Users (TV, 1978)
Sextette (1979)
Title Shot (1979)
Little Miss Marker (1980)
The Mirror Crack'd (1980)
Moviola: The Scarlett O'Hara War (TV, 1980)
Inmates: A Love Story (TV, 1981)
The Million Dollar Face (TV, 1981)
Portrait of a Showgirl (TV, 1982)
Where Is Parsifal? (1984)
Insignificance (1985)
Mafia Princess (TV, 1986)
Club Life (1986)
Murder in Three Acts (TV, 1986)

TV

The Persuaders (1971-72)
McCoy (1975-76)
Vega$ (1978-81)

★★

Rodney Dangerfield

Comedian Who Gets "No Respect"

(1921-)

Rodney Dangerfield was born in Babylon, New York, on November 22, 1921. His original name was Jacob Cohen.

He struggled through many difficulties as a child. His father, at one time a vaudeville pantomime comic, ran out on the family when Jacob was just a baby. Later his mother moved the family to the borough of Queens in New York City, in a neighborhood that was actually beyond their means. The boy faced not only poverty but also the embarrassment of having a job that required him to deliver groceries to the homes of the well-to-do children with whom he went to school. He also encountered anti-Semitism, even among his teachers.

At fifteen he began to write jokes as a way of escaping reality. Soon he was working in the Catskills as a stand-up comedian under the name Jack Roy (Roy having been his father's stage name). For the next nine years he struggled as a comic and a singing waiter. He already showed signs of being a good comedy writer, but as yet he lacked a distinct stage character.

When he was twenty-eight he left show business to marry the singer Joyce Indig. For the next dozen years he ran his own business, selling house paint and siding. During those years he continued to write jokes, and he sold some of them to Jackie Mason and Joan Rivers.

In his early forties Cohen/Roy decided to return to

the stage, and he was booked into a Brooklyn nightclub that he had worked years before. To avoid embarrassment, he asked the club's owner, George McFadden, to bill him under a new name. McFadden chose the name Rodney Dangerfield, which the would-be comedian permanently adopted.

His career soon received tremendous boosts from TV appearances on *The Ed Sullivan Show* and *The Tonight Show*. He also began to work in America's top nightclubs.

His success has been based on his creation of a unique comedic appearance and personality. His plaintive bugging eyes have been likened to fried eggs; and his brow-wiping, neck-craning, tie-adjusting, and shoulder-twitching suggest a thoroughly modern neurotic. The basis of his verbal humor is that, in his words, "I don't get no respect." "My mother never breast-fed me," he says; "she told me she liked me as a friend." Life has been going downhill ever since then: "My psychiatrist told me I was going crazy. I said, 'If you don't mind, I'd like a second opinion.' He said, 'Okay. You're ugly, too.' "

In 1969 he opened his own nightclub, Dangerfield's, in New York City so that he could spend more time with his children, Brian and Melanie. He married and divorced his wife, Joyce, twice. After the second divorce, in 1970, Dangerfield raised the children himself.

TV has remained an important vehicle for him. During the 1972-73 season he was a regular on *The Dean Martin Show*. More recently he has often appeared on *The Tonight Show* and has guest-hosted *Saturday Night Live*. He has also recorded comedy albums, such as *The Loser* (1967) and *Rappin' Rodney* (1983), and written books, including *I Don't Get No Respect* (1973).

Dangerfield has appeared in several movies. In the fantasy *The Projectionist* (1971) he played a dual role as a theater manager and as the villainous Bat. In *Caddyshack* (1980) he was the endearing loudmouth Al Czervik, a nouveau-riche boor. In *Easy Money* (1983) he portrayed a cheerful reprobate who, to collect on a multimillion-dollar inheritance, must give up his high-living ways. In *Back to School* (1986) he was a clothing-store tycoon who returns to college.

Dangerfield is now probably best known to most Americans through his recent TV commercials for Miller Lite beer. He appears in the commercials with a number of former athletes, from whom he consistently gets no respect.

Selected performances:

Films

The Projectionist (1971)
Benny and Barney: Las Vegas Undercover (TV, 1977)
Caddyshack (1980)
Easy Money (1983)
Back to School (1986)

TV

The Dean Martin Show (1972-73)

★★

Howard da Silva

Tough-looking Actor

(1909-1986)

Howard da Silva was born in Cleveland, Ohio, on May 4, 1909. His original name was Harold Silverblatt.

After being raised in the Bronx section of New York City, he moved to Pittsburgh, where he financed his way through the Carnegie Institute of Technology by working in steel mills. Then, in 1928, he joined Eva Le Gallienne's Civic Repertory Company in New York City. For the next decade he was extremely active as a character actor on the stage. Among his roles were those of Schumann in *Siegfried* (1930), a Stationmaster in *The Cherry Orchard* (1931), the Cook and the White Knight in *Alice in Wonderland* (1932), Thorvald in *A Doll's House* (1933), Hansy McCulloh in *Black Pit* (1935), Lewis in *Golden Boy* (1937), Larry Foreman in *The Cradle Will Rock* (1937), and Jack Armstrong in *Abe Lincoln in Illinois* (1938).

Da Silva repeated his role in the filmed version of *Abe Lincoln in Illinois* (1940). Throughout the 1940s and early 1950s he spent most of his time making movies. His most important stage appearance during that period was as Jud Fry in the Rodgers and Hammerstein musical *Oklahoma!* (1943).

Da Silva's film appearances gradually increased from bit parts to substantial roles, often as heavies because of his tough-looking facial features. He made a powerful impact as one of the murderous escaped convicts in *They Live by Night* (1948). Among his other films were *The Sea Wolf* (1941), *Sergeant York* (1941), *Keeper of the Flame* (1943), *The Lost Weekend* (1945), *The Blue Dahlia* (1946), *Two Years before the Mast* (1946), and *M* (1951).

He also began to appear on TV. In 1950 he acted in the *Silver Theater* production of "My Heart's in the Highlands."

But then da Silva appeared as an unfriendly witness before the House Un-American Activities Committee and fell victim to the McCarthy-era blacklisting of liberal-leaning entertainers. For the next decade he was barred from movies and TV.

Returning full time to the stage, he increased his theatrical reputation by producing, directing, and acting in plays at theaters all over America. His character-acting abilities were displayed in such works as *The World of Sholom Aleichem* (1953), *Mister Roberts* (1954), *The Adding Machine* (1956), *Volpone* (1957), and *Fiorello!* (1959). He stated that his favorite roles included Ben Marino in *Fiorello!*, Mendele in *The World of Sholom Aleichem,* and the White Knight in *Alice in Wonderland.*

Beginning in the early 1960s da Silva was again

allowed to work in films and on TV. He gave a beautiful performance as Dr. Alan Swinford, a gentle, understanding psychiatrist for disturbed youngsters, in the movie *David and Lisa* (1962). And he began to make guest appearances on such TV series as *Ben Casey, The Defenders, The Man from U.N.C.L.E.,* and *Outer Limits.* In 1965 he had a regular role, as a district attorney, in the series *For the People.*

The highlight of da Silva's work in the late 1960s was his role as Benjamin Franklin in the musical *1776* (1969). He subsequently performed the work at the White House by special invitation of President Richard M. Nixon (an ironic turn of events, considering Nixon's strong support for, and leadership in, the witch-hunting that had caused da Silva to be blacklisted in the 1950s). Da Silva repeated his role in the filmed version of *1776* (1972).

In 1974 he played Nikita Khrushchev in the TV docudrama "The Missiles of October" on *ABC Theater.* Da Silva was also highly praised for his supporting-role performance in the TV play "Verna: USO Girl" (1978) on *Great Performances.* In 1981 he portrayed the film tycoon Louis B. Mayer in the movie *Mommie Dearest.*

Da Silva married Marjorie Nelson in 1950. They divorced in 1960, and the following year he wedded the actress Nancy Nutter. His marriages produced two sons (Peter and Daniel) and three daughters (Rachel, Judith, and Margaret).

Da Silva died on February 16, 1986, in Ossining, New York.

Selected performances:

Stage

The Would-Be Gentleman (1929)
Romeo and Juliet (1930)
Siegfried (1930)
Alison's House (1930)
Camille (1931)
The Cherry Orchard (1931)
Liliom (1932)
The Three Sisters (1932)
Alice in Wonderland (1932)
A Doll's House (1933)
Hedda Gabler (1933)
The Master Builder (1933)
Sailors of Cattaro (1934)
Black Pit (1935)
Golden Boy (1937)
The Cradle Will Rock (1937)
Casey Jones (1938)
Abe Lincoln in Illinois (1938)
Summer Night (1939)
Two on an Island (1940)
Oklahoma! (1943)
Burning Bright (1950)
The World of Sholom Aleichem (1953)
Mister Roberts (1954)
The Adding Machine (1956)
Diary of a Scoundrel (1956)
Volpone (1957)
Compulsion (1957)
Fiorello! (1959)
Romulus (1962)
In the Counting House (1962)
Dear Me, the Sky Is Falling (1963)
Hamlet (1964)
The Unknown Soldier and His Wife (1967)
1776 (1969)
Volpone (1972)
The Caucasian Chalk Circle (1975)
The Most Dangerous Man in America (1976)

Films

Abe Lincoln in Illinois (1940)
I'm Still Alive (1940)
The Sea Wolf (1941)
Strange Alibi (1941)
Sergeant York (1941)
Bad Men of Missouri (1941)
Blues in the Night (1941)
Wild Bill Hickok Rides (1942)
Bullet Scars (1942)
Native Land (1942)
Juke Girl (1942)
The Big Shot (1942)
Reunion in France (1943)
Keeper of the Flame (1943)
Tonight We Raid Calais (1943)
Duffy's Tavern (1945)
The Lost Weekend (1945)
The Blue Dahlia (1946)
Two Years before the Mast (1946)
Blaze of Noon (1947)
Unconquered (1947)
They Live by Night (1948)
The Great Gatsby (1949)
Border Incident (1949)
The Underworld Story (1950)
Wyoming Mail (1950)
Tripoli (1950)
Fourteen Hours (1951)
Three Husbands (1951)
M (1951)
David and Lisa (1962)
It's a Mad, Mad, Mad, Mad World (1963)
The Outrage (1964)
Nevada Smith (1966)
1776 (1972)
The Great Gatsby (1974)
Smile, Jenny, You're Dead (TV, 1974)
Power (TV, 1980)
Mommie Dearest (1981)

TV

For the People (1965)

★★★

Sammy Davis, Jr.

Complete Entertainer

(1925-90)

Sammy Davis, Jr., was born of a Baptist father and Roman Catholic mother in the Harlem section of the borough of Manhattan in New York City, New York, on December 8, 1925. His father was the lead dancer, and his mother a top chorus girl, in Will Mastin's vaudeville troupe. The boy's paternal grandmother took care of him in Harlem while his parents traveled with the show.

When he was two years old, his parents separated and his father took him to join the Will Mastin players. At first little Sammy was used only as a silent prop, bringing laughter by mugging the actions of other performers. Later he learned to sing and dance in the show.

At the age of seven he won the title role in the two-reel movie *Rufus Jones for President* (1933), which starred Ethel Waters and was filmed in Brooklyn. Soon afterward he made another film, *Seasoned Greetings* (1933), with Charles Chaplin, Jr., and Chaplin's mother, Lita Grey, who wanted to adopt Sammy and take him to Hollywood to make him a movie star. But the Davis family decided to stay together.

In 1934 vaudeville was dying out, largely because of competition from sound movies. Will Mastin, a close friend of the Davis family, had to reduce his troupe down to just himself, Sammy Davis, Sr., and Sammy Davis, Jr. The child had already become the main attraction, and the new group was called Will Mastin's Gang, Featuring Little Sammy. After several other name changes, the group was eventually billed as the Will Mastin Trio, Featuring Sammy Davis, Jr. In the late 1930s and early 1940s, the trio worked across the United States and Canada many times. During that period Sammy met the legendary tap dancer Bill ("Bojangles") Robinson and the young singer Frank Sinatra.

When Sammy turned eighteen, he was drafted into the army for World War II service. During basic training, young Davis, a black, encountered, for the first time in his life, blatant, brutal racial prejudice. Then he was transferred into Special Services, where he did shows in camps across the country.

After the war, Sammy rejoined the Will Mastin Trio. But vaudeville was dead, and the act went through some lean years, playing nightclubs in various cities. In 1947-48 they toured in a show starring Mickey Rooney, from whom Sammy learned much about live performing.

Young Davis constantly worked on developing new skills to freshen up the trio's act, which soon became a showcase for him, while the two older men tap-danced and soft-shoed in the background. Besides broadening his singing and dancing repertory, he played various instruments and did impressions of singers, such as Dean Martin, and film stars, such as Humphrey Bogart, Marlon Brando, and James Cagney.

By the early 1950s the trio, because of young Davis's growing talent and reputation, began to receive big-time engagements, notably on *The Eddie Cantor Show* as part of *The Colgate Comedy Hour* TV series. They also performed at the famed Copacabana nightclub in New York City, which a few years earlier had refused, on racial grounds, to allow Sammy even to enter the building.

Then, in November 1954, while driving from Las Vegas to Los Angeles, Sammy was in a horrible car accident, as a result of which he lost his left eye. One of his visitors during his hospital stay was Eddie Cantor, who earlier had given Sammy a mezuzah (a holy Hebrew charm) as a gift and whose depth of understanding in this crisis favorably impressed the young man. Sammy was also visited in the hospital by a rabbi, who was making routine rounds.

After he left the hospital young Davis began to study Judaism seriously. He saw the affinity between the Jews and the blacks as oppressed peoples. Within months his conversion to Judaism was psychologically complete, the formal ceremony coming a few years later, in 1958.

Meanwhile, he made his show-business comeback. Wearing an eye patch (later replaced by a glass eye), he joined his father and Mastin for successful engagements at major American nightclubs. In fact, the publicity surrounding his accident actually increased the demand for the Will Mastin Trio.

In 1956 they hit Broadway with *Mr. Wonderful,* a musical play written especially for Sammy, about a young black nightclub entertainer who becomes successful by virtue of his talent and will in the face of strong racial opposition. The production itself was widely criti-

cized, but the show lasted over a year because of the versatile power of young Davis himself.

Soon after *Mr. Wonderful* closed, the trio broke up, both Mastin and Sammy Davis, Sr., retiring. But the career of Sammy Davis, Jr., skyrocketed. Besides continuing as a major attraction in nightclubs, he went back to Broadway for the musical *Golden Boy* (1964) and the one-man show *Sammy* (1974). He also starred in *Stop the World—I Want to Get Off* (1978) at the New York State Theater in Lincoln Center.

In the late 1950s Davis began to be active in movies. He sang for the soundtrack of, but did not appear in, *Meet Me in Las Vegas* (1956). In *Anna Lucasta* (1959) he had a straight dramatic role as a jive-talking sailor. Perhaps his most memorable film role was Sportin' Life in the movie version of George Gershwin's black opera *Porgy and Bess* (1959).

Davis went on to appear in many films, showing his versatility by successfully performing in dramas and comedies, musicals and nonmusicals. *Convicts Four* (1962) was a prison drama. *Sergeants Three* (1962) was a western comedy. In *A Man Called Adam* (1966) he played a jazzman who falls from greatness. In the musical *Sweet Charity* (1969) he played the hip revivalist Big Daddy.

Davis became a member of a famous Hollywood group of entertainers and friends called the Rat Pack or the Clan, led by Frank Sinatra and including Joey Bishop, Dean Martin, and Peter Lawford. Various members of the Rat Pack appeared with Davis in the movies *Ocean's Eleven* (1960), *Johnny Cool* (1963), *Robin and the Seven Hoods* (1964), *One More Time* (1970), and others.

His association with the Rat Pack led to fast living, heavy smoking, and hard drinking. Eventually he developed liver and kidney ailments, and early in 1974 he was hospitalized with chest pains. After that, he moderated his habits.

Beginning in the late 1950s Davis made numerous TV appearances. He hosted his own musical-variety specials and series, including the series *The Sammy Davis, Jr., Show* (1966) and *Sammy and Company* (1975-77). He also guest-hosted *The Tonight Show* and guest-starred in the anthology series *General Electric Theater*, the drama series *Mod Squad*, the comedy series *All in the Family*, and many other TV programs.

Davis was a major recording artist. The songs with which he was closely identified include "The Candy Man," "Mr. Bojangles," "That Old Black Magic," and "What Kind of Fool Am I?"

Singer, dancer, actor, comedian, impressionist—Sammy Davis, Jr., was one of the last great examples of the "complete entertainer" nurtured in vaudeville.

He had three marriages. In the late 1950s he wedded

Loray White, a black dancer; but they divorced after only one year together. Shortly thereafter he married the white Swedish actress May Britt. They had a natural daughter (Tracey) and two adopted sons (Mark and Geoff). Because of their racially mixed marriage, Davis and Britt were subjected to many ugly remarks and incidents. In 1968 that marriage, too, ended in divorce. In 1970 he married Altovise Gore, another black dancer.

Davis authored the autobiographical books *Yes, I Can: The Story of Sammy Davis, Jr.* (with Jane and Burt Boyar, 1965) and *Hollywood in a Suitcase* (1980).

He provided a voice for the soundtrack of the animated film *Heidi's Song* (1982). In 1983 he appeared onstage in *Two Friends.* And he played the Caterpillar in the movie *Alice in Wonderland* (TV, 1985).

Davis died on May 23, 1990.

Selected performances:

Stage

Mr. Wonderful (1956)
Golden Boy (1964)
Sammy (1974)
Stop the World—I Want to Get Off (1978)
Two Friends (1983)

Films

Anna Lucasta (1959)
Porgy and Bess (1959)
Pepe (1960)
Ocean's Eleven (1960)
Sergeants Three (1962)
Convicts Four (1962)
Johnny Cool (1963)
Nightmare in the Sun (1964)
Robin and the Seven Hoods (1964)
A Man Called Adam (1966)
Salt and Pepper (1968)
Sweet Charity (1969)
The Pigeon (TV, 1969)
One More Time (1970)
The Trackers (TV, 1971)
Poor Devil (TV, 1973)
Sammy Stops the World (1978)
The Cannonball Run (1981)
Heidi's Song (1982)
Cracking Up (1983, originally released as *Smorgasbord*)
Cannonball Run II (1984)
Alice in Wonderland (TV, 1985)

TV

The Sammy Davis, Jr., Show (1966)
Sammy and Company (1975-77)

★★

Kirk Douglas

Rugged, Intelligent Actor

(1918-)

Kirk Douglas was born of Russian immigrants in Amsterdam, New York, on December 9, 1918 (some sources give 1916 or 1920). His original name was Issur Danielovitch. Later he changed it to Isadore Demsky before settling on his present name.

Interested in acting from his earliest youth, he performed in school productions. After graduating from high school, he attended Saint Lawrence University in Canton, New York, where he studied dramatics, served as president of the student body, and became an outstanding intercollegiate wrestler. He also wrestled in carnivals to earn extra money.

After graduating from college with a B.A. degree in 1938, he moved to New York City, where he studied at the American Academy of Dramatic Arts from 1939 to 1941. In the latter year he made his Broadway debut by performing a minor role in *Spring Again.*

Following some other work as a bit player, Douglas joined the navy and saw World War II action in the Pacific. He received internal injuries and was discharged

in 1944. Returning to New York City, he resumed his work in minor stage roles.

Then an old acting-school friend, Lauren Bacall, recommended him to the film producer Hal B. Wallis, and Douglas was invited to Hollywood. He made his movie debut with a supporting part in *The Strange Love of Martha Ivers* (1947). That was followed by supporting roles in several other films.

Douglas finally reached stardom with his leading role in *Champion* (1949), as a ruthless, egotistical boxer. Over the next several years he proved his ability to handle a wide variety of roles. In *The Glass Menagerie* (1950), for example, he was the sensitive "gentleman caller" who encourages a handicapped girl.

But in his early years as a star, Douglas was renowned primarily for his roles as a neurotic villain. He created characters that displayed realistic, clearly motivated, often self-destructive obsessiveness. In *Ace in the Hole* (1951) he played an amoral newspaper reporter. In *Detective Story* (1951) he was a New York City police detective destroyed through his hatred of lawbreakers. In *The Bad and the Beautiful* (1952) he portrayed a ruthless Hollywood producer.

Less villainous but still destroyed by obsessiveness were his characters in *The Juggler* (1953) and *Lust for Life* (1956). In the former, Douglas played an ex-vaudevillian who arrives in the haven of Israel but, demented by his experiences in Nazi concentration camps, imagines that he is still surrounded by brutes. In the biopic *Lust for Life* he portrayed the painter Vincent van Gogh, who drives himself mad through overwork.

Meanwhile, Douglas was turning increasingly toward heroic or high-principled roles. A midpoint in that turn was his role in Disney's adventure film *Twenty Thousand Leagues under the Sea* (1954), as the harpooner Ned Land, who has some of the abrasive characteristics of Douglas's earlier roles but who also fulfills the heroic function of saving himself and his companions from Captain Nemo's submarine prison. Douglas had the title role in the Italian adventure movie *Ulysses* (1955), a recounting of the ancient Greek's heroic struggles to return home after the Trojan War.

Of his roles as high-principled men, the most outstanding early example was his part in *Paths of Glory* (1957). He played an outraged colonel trying to prevent the execution of three innocent World War I French soldiers, who are selected at random, charged with cowardice, and sentenced to die merely to salve a general's vanity.

Douglas was a battler in real life as well. In the 1950s he fought the Hollywood blacklist, notably by insisting that Dalton Trumbo be credited for the screenplay to Douglas's *Spartacus* (1960), at a time when other banned writers had to work under assumed names. Douglas also fought the Hollywood studio system by becoming the first major actor to establish his own film-making company, called Bryna Productions, after his mother (whose original name was Bryna Sanglel).

In *Lonely Are the Brave* (1962) he portrayed a contemporary itinerant cowboy who refuses to give up his individualism despite his clashes with modern life. In *Seven Days in May* (1964) he was an American military officer who reveres a general but opposes him when the latter plans a military coup in the United States. In *Cast a Giant Shadow* (1966) he played an American colonel who aids in the defense of modern Israel during its early days.

Douglas is one of the most highly accomplished actors of his time. Throughout his career—as a villain, a hero, or a complex somewhere between the two—he has infused his best work with a unique combination of ruggedness and intelligence.

His later films have covered a wide range of genres, including the bitter modern-life drama *The Arrangement* (1969), the adventure *The Light at the Edge of the World* (1971), the space story *Saturn 3* (1980), and the light-hearted western *Draw!* (TV, 1984). In *Victory at Entebbe* (TV, 1976) he played an Israeli who pleads with his government to negotiate with terrorists who have hijacked a plane carrying his daughter.

Douglas has also served as a producer and director. For example, he produced and starred in the Broadway play *One Flew over the Cuckoo's Nest* (1963). He produced, directed, and starred in the movie *Posse* (1975).

Douglas has had two marriages. In 1943 he married Diana Dill, whom he had met when both were students at the American Academy of Dramatic Arts. They had two children: Michael and Joel. Michael became an actor-producer, best known for his costarring role in the TV crime-drama series *The Streets of San Francisco*. Joel became a film producer.

In the early 1950s Douglas's first marriage dissolved. In 1954 he wedded the movie publicist Anne Buydens, with whom he had his children Peter and Eric. Anne became deeply involved with Kirk's professional life, long serving as president of his corporation and producing, for example, the movie *Scalawag* (1973), which he directed and starred in. Peter became a movie producer, while Eric became an actor and appeared in films with his father, notably *Remembrance of Love* (TV, 1982). In that movie the elder Douglas played a middle-aged widower, a Holocaust survivor who unexpectedly meets a woman he loved, and separated from, when both were teenagers in the Polish ghetto during World War II; Eric played his father as a youth.

Douglas has aged gracefully. Still athletic in appearance and movement, he also still infuses his roles with ruggedness and intelligence. In *Amos* (TV, 1985; produced by his son Peter) he played an elderly man who is injured in an auto accident and has to retire to a nursing home, where he literally gives his life to restore dignity to the abused patients.

In real life, Douglas publicly spoke out for legislation to protect senior citizens from physical, financial, and emotional abuse. Now in his own senior years, he has lost none of the intensity that has made him one of the giants in film history.

Selected performances:

Stage

Spring Again (1941)
The Three Sisters (1942)
Alice in Arms (1945)
The Wind Is Ninety (1945)
Woman Bites Dog (1946)
One Flew over the Cuckoo's Nest (1963)

Films

The Strange Love of Martha Ivers (1947)
Mourning Becomes Electra (1947)
Out of the Past (1947)
I Walk Alone (1948)
The Walls of Jericho (1948)
A Letter to Three Wives (1949)
My Dear Secretary (1949)
Champion (1949)
Young Man with a Horn (1950)
The Glass Menagerie (1950)
Along the Great Divide (1951)
Ace in the Hole (1951)
Detective Story (1951)
The Big Trees (1952)
The Vikings (1952)
The Big Sky (1952)
The Bad and the Beautiful (1952)
The Juggler (1953)
Act of Love (1954)
Twenty Thousand Leagues under the Sea (1954)
The Racers (1955)
Man without a Star (1955)
Ulysses (1955)
The Indian Fighter (1955)
Lust for Life (1956)
Top Secret Affair (1957)
Gunfight at the O.K. Corral (1957)
Paths of Glory (1957)
Last Train from Gun Hill (1959)
The Devil's Disciple (1959)
Strangers When We Meet (1960)
Spartacus (1960)
The Last Sunset (1961)
Town without Pity (1961)
Lonely Are the Brave (1962)
Two Weeks in Another Town (1962)
For Love or Money (1963)
The Hook (1963)
The List of Adrian Messenger (1963)
Seven Days in May (1964)
In Harm's Way (1965)
Cast a Giant Shadow (1966)
The Heroes of Telemark (1966)
Is Paris Burning? (1966)
The War Wagon (1967)
The Way West (1967)
The Brotherhood (1968)
A Lovely Way to Die (1968)
The Arrangement (1969)
There Was a Crooked Man . . . (1970)
The Light at the Edge of the World (1971)
Scalawag (1973)
Mousey (TV, 1974)
Posse (1975)
The Moneychangers (TV, 1976)
Victory at Entebbe (TV, 1976)
The Fury (1978)
The Chosen (1978)
The Villain (1979)
Saturn 3 (1980)
Home Movies (1980)
The Final Countdown (1980)
The Man from Snowy River (1982)
Remembrance of Love (TV, 1982)
Eddie Macon's Run (1983)
Draw! (TV, 1984)
Amos (TV, 1985)
Tough Guys (1986)
Queenie (TV, 1987)

★★★

Richard Dreyfuss

Master of "Humanity Expressing Humanity"

(1947-)

Richard Dreyfuss was born in New York City, New York, on October 29, 1947. In 1956 he moved with his parents to Los Angeles.

At the age of nine he decided that he wanted to be an actor. Soon he joined an acting group at Los Angeles's West Side Jewish Community Center, where he made his first stage appearances.

While attending Beverly Hills High School, Dreyfuss used to sneak into a local movie studio and absorb the atmosphere. During that time he also began to work on the professional stage at the Gallery Theater in Los Angeles.

After graduating from high school, Dreyfuss studied at San Fernando Valley State College (1965-67). His schooling was interrupted when he was called up by the military draft. Refusing induction on the grounds that he was a conscientious objector, he performed two years of alternative service as a file clerk at Los Angeles County General Hospital.

During that time, however, his career began to move forward. In the late 1960s and early 1970s he appeared in a few minor movies, such as *The Young Runaways* (1968); performed guest roles on TV series, such as *Mod Squad;* and did stage work in Los Angeles and in New York City, his Broadway debut coming in *But Seriously . . .* (1969).

In 1972 he toured nationally in the play *The Time of Your Life,* starring Henry Fonda. Dreyfuss's first important screen role was as the gangster Baby Face Nelson in *Dillinger* (1973).

But the major turning point in his career came when he was offered an important part in the movie *American Graffiti* (1973), a nostalgic evocation of one summer night in the lives of teenagers in a California city in 1962. In his role as Curt Henderson, Dreyfuss portrayed a witty intellectual apprehensive about leaving his hometown to attend an Ivy League college.

Having shown promise in *American Graffiti,* Dreyfuss was then given the leading role in *The Apprenticeship of Duddy Kravitz* (1974). In that film he played a poor young Jew whose aggressive pursuit of success blinds him to the hurt that he often inflicts on others. In

the thriller *Jaws* (1975) he portrayed a wisecracking scientist involved in a terrifying shark hunt.

In 1976 he had an important role in the TV movie *Victory at Entebbe,* based on a true story. He played the Israeli colonel who was killed while leading the July 4, 1976, raid on the Entebbe Airport in Uganda to rescue Jewish hostages held by terrorists.

Two 1977 releases moved Dreyfuss up to the category of superstar: the science-fiction fantasy *Close Encounters of the Third Kind* and the comedy *The Goodbye Girl*. Special praise went to his performance in the latter film, in which he played an egocentric young actor.

He then turned to the classical stage, playing Cassius in *Julius Caesar* (1978) and Iago in *Othello* (1979).

In the movie *The Competition* (1980) Dreyfuss portrayed a young pianist trying to establish himself. *Whose Life Is It Anyway?* (1981) posed a new problem for him. Usually a very physical actor, he had to play a bedridden sculptor who has been paralyzed from the neck down following a car crash. Feeling that his life is useless now, the character challenges the doctors and nurses to let him die. Dreyfuss's performance showed a new maturity in his skills.

In the movie *The Buddy System* (1984) he played a would-be novelist. Later he costarred with Bette Midler in the film comedy *Down and Out in Beverly Hills* (1986) and with Danny DeVito in *Tin Men* (1987).

In late 1985 he discussed his craft on the *Actors on Acting* TV series. He said that he is difficult to cast and that he looks forward to the day when audiences will become bored with perfect biceps and come to admire "short, slightly overweight Jewish neurotics."

Dreyfuss has a wide range of friends and interests, including liberal politics. He has expressed a desire to run for political office someday. His sociopolitical viewpoint is reflected in his definition of acting: "humanity expressing humanity."

In 1983 he married the actress-writer Jeramie Rain (also known as Susan Davis).

Selected performances:

Stage

But Seriously . . . (1969)
Line (1971)
And Whose Little Boy Are You? (1971)
The Time of Your Life (1972)
Major Barbara (1972)
Miss Julie (1976)
A Man of Destiny (1976)
The Tenth Man (1977)
Julius Caesar (1978)
Othello (1979)
Whose Life Is It Anyway? (1980)
A Day in the Life of Joe Egg (1981)
Total Abandon (1983)
The Hands of Its Enemy (1984)

Films

The Young Runaways (1968)
Hello Down There (1969)
Two for the Money (TV, 1972)
Dillinger (1973)
American Graffiti (1973)
The Apprenticeship of Duddy Kravitz (1974)
Jaws (1975)
Victory at Entebbe (TV, 1976)
Inserts (1976)
Close Encounters of the Third Kind (1977)
The Goodbye Girl (1977)
The Big Fix (1978)
The Competition (1980)
Whose Life Is It Anyway? (1981)
The Buddy System (1984)
Down and Out in Beverly Hills (1986)
Tin Men (1987)
Stakeout (1987)

★★★

Peter Falk

Columbo

(1927-   )

Peter Falk was born in New York City, New York, on September 16, 1927. He was raised in Ossining, New York. At the age of three he developed a malignant tumor in his right eye, which had to be removed. Since then he has used a glass eye. At first he was self-conscious about the artificial eye; but after he started playing games with neighborhood children, he and they simply joked about it.

Falk first appeared onstage when he was twelve, in a summer-camp production of *The Pirates of Penzance.* At Ossining High School he was an excellent student, a star athlete, and the president of his class.

After graduating from high school in 1945, he spent 1½ years in the merchant marine. He then studied at Hamilton College in Clinton, New York, for two years before transferring to the New School for Social Research in New York City, where he earned a B.A. in political science (1951). Then, at Syracuse University, he obtained a master's degree in public administration (1953).

After applying unsuccessfully for a job with the Central Intelligence Agency (CIA), Falk became a management analyst (or efficiency expert) with the Connecticut State Budget Bureau in Hartford. In his spare time he performed with the Mark Twain Maskers in Hartford and studied acting under Eva Le Gallienne at the White Barn Theater in Westport (1955).

At the age of twenty-eight Falk quit his job and moved to New York City, where he studied acting under various teachers, notably Sanford Meisner in 1957. Falk made his professional debut by appearing in an off-Broadway production of Molière's *Don Juan* (1956). For the next two years he performed in numerous plays on the New York City stage, notably as the bartender in an acclaimed production of Eugene O'Neill's *The Iceman Cometh* (1956).

A theatrical agent advised Falk that his glass eye would prevent him from ever getting good parts in movies. Indeed, Harry Cohn, head of Columbia Pictures, after initially expressing an interest in Falk, rejected the young actor specifically because of the glass eye.

But other studios recognized Falk's talent and did not let the glass eye bother them. His film debut came with a small part in *Wind across the Everglades* (1958). Over the next few years he came close to being permanently typecast as a gangster because of his solid performances in that role in several TV programs and movies, especially *Murder, Inc.* (1960), in which he portrayed a vicious assassin for a crime syndicate.

A big breakthrough in his career came with his performance in *Pocketful of Miracles* (1961), in which he again played a gangster, but this time with a touch of comedy. Many critics felt that Falk had outshone the film's stars, including Bette Davis and Glenn Ford.

Falk further enhanced his reputation with excellent performances in the late 1950s and early 1960s in TV anthology and drama series, such as *Omnibus, Studio One,* and *The Untouchables.* He won special acclaim in the episode "Cold Turkey" (1961) of *The Law and Mr. Jones,* as a drug addict, and in the episode "The Price of Tomatoes" (1962) of *The Dick Powell Show,* as a truck driver who picks up a pregnant hitchhiker. He also starred in the lighthearted TV series *The Trials of O'Brien* (1965-66), as an untidy, disorganized criminal attorney.

Meanwhile, Falk continued to appear in a variety of movie roles. He was a comic stooge to the villain in *The Great Race* (1965), a police lieutenant in the comedy *Penelope* (1966), and a Mafia leader in *Machine Gun McCain* (Italy, 1968; United States, 1970).

The TV movies *Prescription: Murder* (TV, 1968) and *Ransom for a Dead Man* (TV, 1971) served as pilots for the TV crime-drama series *Columbo* (1971-77). Falk's role as the Los Angeles Police Department homicide detective Lieutenant Columbo became one of the most popular characters in TV history. Disheveled in appearance, slurred in speech, and fumbling in manner, Columbo seems to be no match for the intelligent murderers whom he pursues. The villains themselves underestimate him till they gradually become aware of his truly sharp mind and forceful nature. In the end, his unrelenting pursuit pays off and he pounces on the criminals.

In recent years Falk has performed mostly comedy roles. In *Murder by Death* (1976), for example, he was Sam Diamond, a satirical imitation of Humphrey Bogart's private-detective persona Sam Spade. In *The In-Laws* (1979) he played a bizarre CIA man. In *. . . All the Marbles* (1981) he gave a fine comic performance as the manager of women wrestlers. In the 1985 Los Angeles stage production of the cynical comedy *Glengarry Glen Ross,* he played the salesman Shelly Levene.

Though he is still best known as Columbo, Falk has proven himself to be a solid performer in a wide variety of roles. Rather than regarding his glass eye as a liability, he uses it to advantage—squinting with it to create effects of menace, humor, detachment, and so on, depending on the dramatic situation.

Falk has been married twice. In 1960 he wedded Alyce Mayo, whom he had met when both were students at Syracuse University. They had two daughters, Katherine and Jacqueline, before divorcing in 1976. The following year he married Shera Danese, an actress.

Selected performances:

Stage

Don Juan (1956)
The Iceman Cometh (1956)
Saint Joan (1956)
Diary of a Scoundrel (1956)
The Lady's Not for Burning (1957)
The Bonds of Interest (1958)
The Passion of Josef D. (1964)
The Prisoner of Second Avenue (1971)
Glengarry Glen Ross (1985)
Light Up the Sky (1987)

Films

Wind across the Everglades (1958)
The Bloody Brood (1959)
Murder, Inc. (1960)
Pocketful of Miracles (1961)

Peter Falk

Pressure Point (1962)
The Balcony (1963)
It's a Mad, Mad, Mad, Mad World (1963)
Robin and the Seven Hoods (1964)
The Great Race (1965)
Penelope (1966)
Luv (1967)
Anzio (1968)
Machine Gun McCain (1968)
Prescription: Murder (TV, 1968)
Castle Keep (1969)
Husbands (1970)
A Step out of Line (TV, 1971)
Ransom for a Dead Man (TV, 1971)
A Woman under the Influence (1974)
Mikey and Nicky (1976)
Murder by Death (1976)
Griffin and Phoenix (TV, 1976)
The Cheap Detective (1978)
The Brink's Job (1978)
The In-Laws (1979)
. . . All the Marbles (1981)
Big Trouble (1986)

TV

The Trials of O'Brien (1965-66)
Columbo (1971-77)

★★

Marty Feldman

Popeyed Comic

(1934-82)

Marty Feldman was born in London, England, on July 8, 1934. He grew up in the rough East End section of the city, and at the age of fifteen he quit school.

His great dream at that time was to become a jazz trumpeter. In his late teens he led his own jazz band.

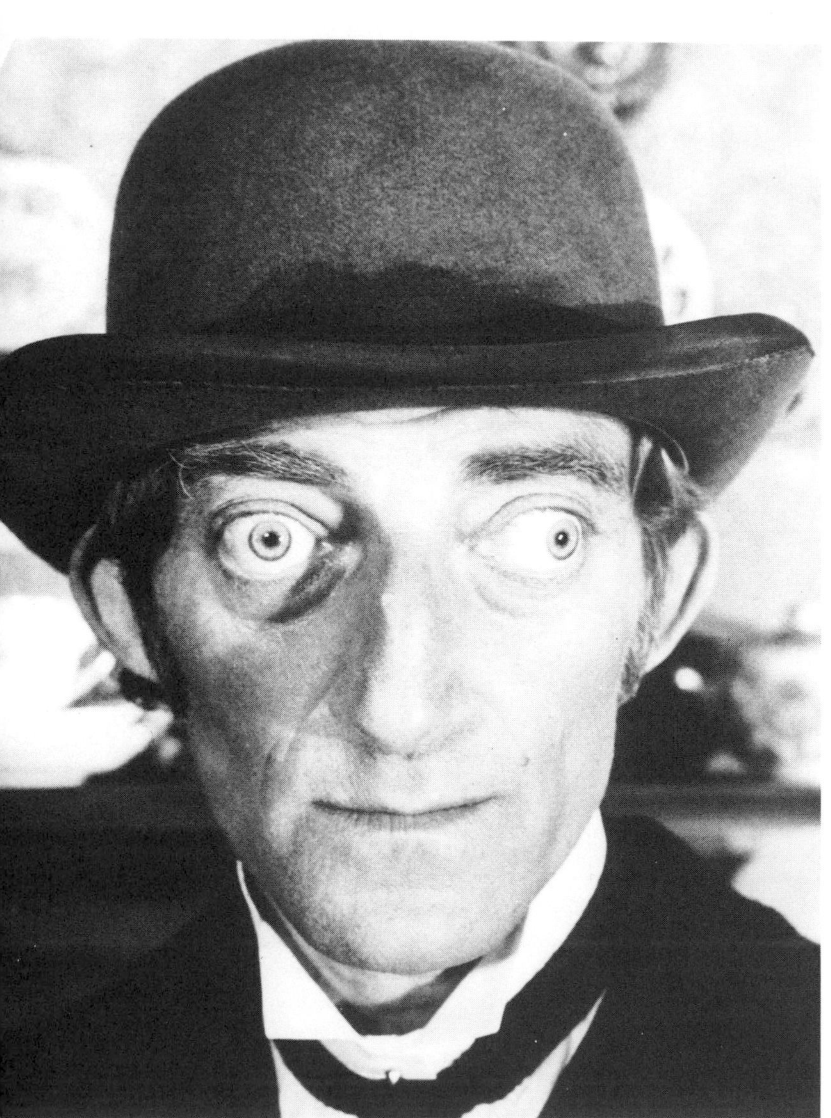

When his music career did not move forward, Feldman turned to acting and writing. He toured England's carnival circuit as an assistant to an Indian fakir, and he sold jokes.

Eventually he graduated to writing comedy sketches for British radio and TV. Among those for whom he wrote was David Frost, who later asked Feldman to be one of the writer-performers, along with the future Monty Python members Graham Chapman and John Cleese, on the TV series *At Last the 1948 Show* (1967). Feldman then had his own TV series, *Marty* (1968-69). He became one of the most popular entertainers in England, developing his own cult following.

In the late 1960s Feldman appeared in his first film, the allegory *The Bed Sitting Room* (1969), in which he had a small part as a male nurse. He then coscripted and starred in the comedy *Every Home Should Have One* (1970; American title, *Think Dirty*).

In 1970 he performed on the American TV musical-variety series *The Golddiggers in London. The Marty Feldman Comedy Machine* (1971-72) was a comedy series taped in London and then shown on American TV.

However, Feldman's reputation today rests principally on a handful of American films in which his unique comic gifts were featured. In Mel Brooks's *Young Frankenstein* (1974) Feldman played Igor (which he pronounced "eye-gore"), assistant to Dr. Frankenstein (played by Gene Wilder), a brain surgeon who follows in his ancestor's footsteps by creating a manlike creature. In Gene Wilder's *The Adventure of Sherlock Holmes' Smarter Brother* (1975) Feldman took the role of Orville Sacker, a retired London detective who assists Sigerson Holmes (played by Wilder) just as Dr. Watson helped the more famous Holmes brother. *Silent Movie* (1976) was another Brooks film. In it Feldman portrayed Marty Eggs, who aided Mel Funn (played by Brooks) in an attempt to make a modern silent movie.

Feldman then set out to make his own films. He cowrote, directed, and starred in *The Last Remake of Beau Geste* (1977), a spoof of old foreign-legion adventure yarns. He also cowrote, directed, and starred in the biting satire *In God We Tru$t* (1980), subtitled *Gimme That Prime Time Religion*. In it Feldman played Brother Ambrose, a monk who, at the request of his superior, leaves his cloister to perform an errand in the big city, where he becomes involved with religious hucksters.

Feldman was a master of zany slapstick. He performed most of his own pratfalls and movie stunts.

In private life he was literate, sensitive, and reflective. "I see life as absurd," he said. "And there's dignity in the absurd."

Feldman's bulging eyeballs, his trademark, were the result of a thyroid condition brought on by a childhood accident. He was short, with frizzy hair and a large, askew nose. "Physically," he admitted, "I am basically equipped to be a clown." Feldman developed unique facial expressions to go along with his natural appearance, so that he became one of the few comedians who could make audiences roar with laughter just by looking at them.

On December 2, 1982, the world was deprived of one of its greatest comics when Feldman suddenly died of a massive heart attack in Mexico City, Mexico, where he had just finished his role in the film *Yellowbeard* (1983), a spoof of pirate pictures. He also appeared in the posthumously released movie *Slapstick of Another Kind* (1984).

Feldman was survived by Lauretta, his wife of twenty-three years. She had served as associate producer of *In God We Tru$t.*

Selected performances:

Films

The Bed Sitting Room (1969)
Every Home Should Have One (1970, G.B.; U.S., *Think Dirty*)
Young Frankenstein (1974)
The Adventure of Sherlock Holmes' Smarter Brother (1975)
Silent Movie (1976)
The Last Remake of Beau Geste (1977)
In God We Tru$t (1980)
Yellowbeard (1983)
Slapstick of Another Kind (1984)

TV

At Last the 1948 Show (1967)
Marty (1968-69)
The Golddiggers in London (1970)
The Marty Feldman Comedy Machine (1971-72)

★★★

John Garfield

Young Loner

(1913-52)

John Garfield was born of Russian immigrants in New York City, New York, on March 4, 1913. His father was a factory worker during weekdays, but on weekends and holidays he served as a cantor. The boy's original name was Jacob Garfinkle (with no middle name). But in his early childhood his parents informally added the name Julius in front of his given name and began to call him Julie.

He spent part of his youth in Manhattan's Lower East Side and in Brooklyn's Brownsville section, where he became involved in the street life of the urban poor. His experiences there helped to form his social consciousness and his mannerisms as an actor.

At the time, however, he came close to becoming a real hoodlum. He averted that fate through the help of Angelo Patri, the principal of the Bronx junior high school that Garfield attended. Patri encouraged the boy to enter amateur boxing, at which he did fairly well. More importantly, Patri led him into an interest in debate and dramatics.

After Garfield graduated from junior high school in 1928, Patri helped him to get a scholarship with the drama workshop of the Heckscher Foundation. Garfield also began high school but dropped out in 1929.

With Patri's financial help, Garfield studied acting at the American Laboratory Theater. He also did odd jobs backstage for Theater Guild productions and made his Broadway debut with a one-night-only appearance in *The Camel through the Needle's Eye* (1929).

Garfield's first big break came when he was given a part in the Guild's production of *Red Rust* (1929). He was billed as Julian Garfield.

Soon afterward he joined the Civic Repertory Theater as an apprentice. There he billed himself as Jules Garfield, the name that he continued to use till 1938.

In 1930 he entered a Golden Gloves boxing tournament. The following year he hitchhiked to California, where he worked as a migrant farm worker.

Returning to New York in 1932, he worked for a while as an assistant social director at a Jewish resort in the Catskills. He then played in *Counsellor-at-Law* in New York City and on the road.

In 1933 he had one day's unbilled work in the film musical *Footlight Parade.* Also in 1933 he had a minor part in the play *Peace on Earth,* produced by the radically based Theater Union.

In 1934 Garfield became an apprentice with the Group Theater, with the members of whom he shared leftist attitudes. His first Group Theater play was *Gold Eagle Guy* (1934).

With some degree of financial security at that point (1934), Garfield was able to marry Roberta Seidman, whom he had met when both were teenagers in the Bronx. They had three children: Katherine, who died in early childhood; David Patton, who became an actor in the early 1960s under the name John Garfield, Jr., later known as John David Garfield; and Julie Roberta, who became an actress.

In 1935 Garfield was given an important role in *Awake and Sing!* The play had been written by Clifford Odets, who had helped Garfield get into the Group Theater. The young actor then followed with minor parts in two other plays.

Early in 1937 he won the lead in *Having Wonderful Time,* a romantic comedy staged in Catskills resorts. That autumn he rejoined the Group Theater to appear in Odets's *Golden Boy.* The playwright had promised Garfield the lead, Joe Bonaparte, a young man torn in a career choice between boxing and violin playing. However, Garfield was actually given the supporting role of the protagonist's brother-in-law.

He then turned to films, signing with Warner Bros. in 1938. The studio pressured him into selecting a new stage name to replace Jules, the final choice being John.

In his first movie, *Four Daughters* (1938), he played a young loner and loser who is cynical but appealing. The role created his basic screen image for the rest of his career. He became the forerunner of the new-style heroes—flawed and vulnerable—who have included Marlon Brando, Montgomery Clift, James Dean, Dustin Hoffman, Paul Newman, Steve McQueen, and Al Pacino.

After making several more films, including *They Made Me a Criminal* (1939) and *Dust Be My Destiny* (1939), he returned to Broadway in 1940 to appear in *Heavenly Express.*

A heart condition kept Garfield out of military service during World War II. But he frequently entertained troops overseas, and he made several war-related movies, highlighted by *Pride of the Marines* (1945), in which he portrayed a real-life blind American military hero.

During that period, in 1942, he also officially changed his legal name from Jacob Garfinkle to John Jules Garfield.

Immediately after the war, Garfield began to make some of his most memorable films, including *The Postman Always Rings Twice* (1946), *Humoresque* (1946), and *Force of Evil* (1948). A landmark in his career was his opportunity to show the real depth and range of his acting talent in *Body and Soul* (1947), in which he evolved from an arrogant youthful boxer into a disillusioned middle-aged champ.

In *Gentleman's Agreement* (1947) he played the part of a young Jewish friend of the principal character, who pretends to be a Jew so that he can get material for a magazine article on anti-Semitism. It was unusual for a star of Garfield's stature to take such a small role, but it was something that he felt he "had to do." His performance won high praise.

In 1947 he was offered the part of Stanley Kowalski in the Broadway production of Tennessee Williams's *A Streetcar Named Desire.* Garfield turned it down because he wanted more money than the producer offered. It became the role that shot young Marlon Brando to stardom.

Soon, however, Garfield did return to Broadway, as Joris Kuiper, a Dutch sea captain attempting to rescue Jewish refugees, in *Skipper Next to God* (1948).

He continued to be active on both stage and screen for the next few years. But in 1951 he was called before the House Un-American Activities Committee to answer questions about his association with, and support of, various liberal causes and organizations. He succeeded in convincing the committee that he had never belonged to the Communist party but not that he was unaware of others as party members. As bizarre and un-American as it now seems, the committee's attitude toward Garfield actually cast a shadow over him and dampened his career.

Early in 1952 he appeared in a Broadway revival of *Golden Boy,* this time in the lead. It was to be his final role.

Garfield had a long history of heart trouble. He had minor attacks in 1944, 1947 during the filming of *Body and Soul,* and 1950. But he ignored his condition and constantly overdid tennis, alcohol, and sex (he had affairs with numerous women, including many of his film costars).

After his appearance before the House committee, he began to worry about his career. That stress, plus the neglect of his illness, was too much for his heart. He died in his sleep at the New York City apartment of a woman friend on May 21, 1952, at the age of only thirty-nine.

Selected performances:

Stage

Red Rust (1929)
Counsellor-at-Law (1932)
Lost Boy (1932)
Peace on Earth (1933)
Gold Eagle Eye (1934)
Waiting for Lefty (1935)
Awake and Sing! (1935)
Weep for the Virgins (1935)
The Case of Clyde Griffiths (1936)
Johnny Johnson (1936)
Having Wonderful Time (1937)
Golden Boy (1937)
Heavenly Express (1940)
Skipper Next to God (1948)
The Big Knife (1949)
Peer Gynt (1951)
Golden Boy (1952)

Films

Four Daughters (1938)
They Made Me a Criminal (1939)
Blackwell's Island (1939)
Juarez (1939)
Daughters Courageous (1939)
Dust Be My Destiny (1939)
Castle on the Hudson (1940)
Saturday's Children (1940)
Flowing Gold (1940)
East of the River (1940)
The Sea Wolf (1941)
Out of the Fog (1941)
Dangerously They Live (1942)
Tortilla Flat (1942)
Air Force (1943)
The Fallen Sparrow (1943)
Thank Your Lucky Stars (1943)
Destination Tokyo (1944)
Between Two Worlds (1944)
Hollywood Canteen (1944)
Pride of the Marines (1945)
The Postman Always Rings Twice (1946)
Nobody Lives Forever (1946)
Humoresque (1946)
Body and Soul (1947)
Gentleman's Agreement (1947)
Force of Evil (1948)
We Were Strangers (1949)
Under My Skin (1950)
The Breaking Point (1950)
The Difficult Years (narrator, 1950)
He Ran All the Way (1951)

John Garfield

★★★

Jack Gilford

Wistful Comic Actor

(1907-90)

Jack Gilford was born in New York City, New York, on July 25, 1907. His original name was Jacob Gellman.

He began his career by performing as a comedian in amateur-night contests in 1934. Having difficulty getting a professional show-business career underway, he became the manager of a cosmetics store. One day the entertainer Milton Berle entered the store, and Gellman began to do comic imitations of famous personalities, including Laurel and Hardy. Berle later auditioned Gellman and gave him a job touring in vaudeville with the *Milton Berle Revue* (1935-38).

It was Berle who suggested that Gellman change his surname, perhaps to Guilford. The youth chose Jack Gilford.

During his association with Berle, Gilford also began to make vaudeville appearances on his own. Soon he added work on the borscht circuit and in nightclubs, especially New York City's Café Society Downtown and Café Society Uptown, where he performed off and on for many years.

In 1940 he made his Broadway debut by appearing in *Meet the People.* Over the next few years he returned to the New York City stage in other shows, including *They Should Have Stood in Bed* (1942).

Gilford was turned down for World War II service because he was in psychotherapy. But he toured the Pacific theater as an entertainer with the United Service Organizations (USO). He also appeared in his first films, including *Hey, Rookie* (1944).

After the war, he continued to work as a comedian in vaudeville, in nightclubs, and on the borscht circuit. In the late 1940s and early 1950s he began to perform in the new medium of television, as on the variety shows hosted by Garry Moore and Milton Berle. He also resumed his movie work, in *Main Street to Broadway* (1953).

But Gilford's TV and movie appearances were interrupted when he was blacklisted during the McCarthy-era Communist witch-hunts. He did, however, continue his other activities. Most important was his new emphasis on stage roles.

In 1950, for example, he portrayed Frosch, a nonsinging comic part, in the operetta *Die Fledermaus* at the Metropolitan Opera. He played the same role many times in the future. In *The World of Sholom Aleichem* (1953) he was the painfully shy Bontche Schweig, while in *The Diary of Anne Frank* (1955) he played the fussy, frightened Mr. Dussel. Gilford was the mute king Sextimus in *Once upon a Mattress* (1959), and in *A Funny Thing Happened on the Way to the Forum* (1962) he portrayed the timid slave Hysterium.

In the mid-1960s the blacklist lost its effectiveness, and Gilford began to get TV and movie assignments again. During the 1960s and 1970s he appeared as a guest on many TV series, including *All in the Family, The Defenders, Get Smart,* and *Rhoda.* He was a regular on *The David Frost Revue* (1971) and *Apple Pie* (1978). His films during that period included *Mister Buddwing* (1966), *Enter Laughing* (1967), *Catch-22* (1970), *Save the Tiger* (1973), and *Seventh Avenue* (TV, 1977).

However, he did not neglect the stage, where he acted in *The Sunshine Boys* (1973), *The Seven Year Itch* (1975), and other plays.

In the 1980s Gilford continued to be active in a variety of outlets. On the stage, he played four roles in a revival of *The World of Sholom Aleichem* (1982). Among his films were *Wholly Moses!* (1980), *Happy* (TV, 1983), and *Hostage Flight* (TV, 1985). And he appeared in TV commercials.

Gilford married the entertainer Madeline Lederman (stage name, Madeline Lee) in 1949. She brought with her a daughter, Lisa, from a previous marriage. They also had two children together: Joseph and Sam.

The book *170 Years of Show Business* (1978) was written by Kate Mostel and Madeline Gilford, with help from their husbands, the actor Zero Mostel and Jack Gilford. Mostel and Gilford, close friends for many years, liked working together, as in the stage show *Once Over Lightly* (1955) and in the stage (1962) and film (1966) versions of *A Funny Thing Happened on the Way to the Forum.*

Gilford played all sorts of roles—comic, dramatic; singing, nonsinging. He was principally known, however, as a straight comic actor with a uniquely wistful quality. Gilford died on June 6, 1990.

Selected performances:

Stage

Meet the People (1940)
They Should Have Stood in Bed (1942)
It's All Yours (1942)
The New Meet the People (1943)
Alive and Kicking (1950)
The Live Wire (1950)
Die Fledermaus (1950 and many times since then)
The World of Sholom Aleichem (1953)
The Passion of Gross (1955)
Once Over Lightly (1955)
The Diary of Anne Frank (1955)
Romanoff and Juliet (1957)
Drink to Me Only (1958)
Look After Lulu (1959)
Once upon a Mattress (1959)
The Tenth Man (1959)
The Policeman (1961)
A Funny Thing Happened on the Way to the Forum (1962)
Cabaret (1966)
Three Men on a Horse (1969)
No, No, Nanette (1971)
The Sunshine Boys (1973)
Anything Goes (1973)
The Seven Year Itch (1975)
Sly Fox (1976)
The Supporting Cast (1981)
The World of Sholom Aleichem (1982)

Films

Hey, Rookie (1944)
Reckless Age (1944)
Main Street to Broadway (1953)
The Daydreamer (1966)
A Funny Thing Happened on the Way to the Forum (1966)
Mister Buddwing (1966)
Enter Laughing (1967)
The Incident (1967)
Who's Minding the Mint? (1967)
Catch-22 (1970)
They Might Be Giants (1971)
Save the Tiger (1973)
Harry and Walter Go to New York (1976)
Seventh Avenue (TV, 1977)
Wholly Moses! (1980)
Caveman (1981)
Cheaper to Keep Her (1981)
Goldie and the Boxer Go to Hollywood (TV, 1981)
Happy (TV, 1983)
Hostage Flight (TV, 1985)
Cocoon (1985)

TV

The David Frost Revue (1971)
Apple Pie (1978)

★★

Hermione Gingold

Revue Comedienne and Character Actress (1897-1987)

Hermione Gingold was born in London, England, on December 9, 1897. She attended private school and studied acting at the Rosina Filippi School of the Theater in London.

Her first stage appearance came in a kindergarten production of *Henry VIII*. She made her professional debut by playing a herald in *Pinkie and the Fairies* (1908). Over the next several years the child continued to gain professional stage experience. Soon she was performing Shakespeare at London's Old Vic theater and in the Bard's hometown of Stratford-upon-Avon. Gingold also performed in other plays, such as *Little Lord Fauntleroy* (1931).

She opened a new phase of her career in the late 1930s when she began to appear in musical revues. Her work in that direction was climaxed by performances in the most popular British revues of the 1940s: *Sweet and Low* (1943), *Sweeter and Lower* (1944), and *Sweetest*

and Lowest (1946). By then she had become an expert comedienne.

Gingold's American debut came in the revue *It's about Time,* produced in Cambridge, Massachusetts, in 1951. Her first New York City performance was in *John Murray Anderson's Almanac* (1953). An American critic called her "one of the funniest women in the world."

She continued to perform onstage in both England and America. Her most memorable role was as Madame Armfeldt, an elderly once-famous courtesan, in the Broadway production of Stephen Sondheim's musical *A Little Night Music* (1973).

Gingold began her film career with an appearance in the British picture *Someone at the Door* (1936). After moving to the United States in the 1950s, she made American films. Gingold soon became a greatly loved comedy character actress, especially for her roles as haughty eccentrics. In the comedy *Bell, Book, and Candle* (1958) she played a modern-day witch. In *Gigi* (1958) she portrayed a woman who grooms her granddaughter to be a courtesan. For the animated film *Gay Purr-ee* (1962) she supplied the voice of the jaded Madame Rubens-Chatte. She was the wild wife of the mayor in *The Music Man* (1962). And she repeated her stage role in the filmed version of *A Little Night Music* (1977).

Gingold had performed on British radio and TV before her arrival in the United States. In the mid-1950s she began to appear on American TV. She performed on *The Ed Sullivan Show, The Jack Benny Program, The Steve Allen Show,* and other comedy-variety series. But she also worked in straight dramatic roles, as in *Alfred Hitchcock Presents.*

Gingold's talents extended beyond the stage and the screen. She made a number of recordings, including *La Gingold* (1956), which is a collection of specialty songs and revue material. And she authored many works, including articles, humorous essays, short stories, and the books *The World Is Square: My Own Unaided Work* (1945) and *Sirens Should Be Seen and Not Heard* (1963).

Gingold's first marriage was to the British publisher Michael Joseph. They had two sons: Stephen, who became director of London's Theater-in-the-Round, and Leslie, who became a businessman. Gingold and Joseph divorced, and she later married Eric Maschwitz, an author and broadcasting program director. That marriage, too, ended in divorce.

In her late years Gingold made many appearances on American TV talk shows, including *The Merv Griffin Show* and *The Mike Douglas Show.* Her deep, expressive voice and her devastating wit made her an entertaining guest.

She was also active offstage. In June 1984 she cut the ribbon at the official opening of the Harrods store on the liner *Queen Elizabeth II.*

Gingold died in New York City on May 24, 1987.

Selected performances:

Stage

Pinkie and the Fairies (1908)
The Merry Wives of Windsor (1909)
The Marriage Market (1913)
The Merchant of Venice (1914)
If (1921)
The Dippers (1922)
Little Lord Fauntleroy (1931)
From Morn to Midnight (1932)
This World of Ours (1935)
Spread It Abroad (1936)
Laura Garrett (1936)
The Gate Revue (1938)
Swinging the Gate (1940)
Rise above It (1941)
Sky High (1942)
Sweet and Low (1943)
Sweeter and Lower (1944)
Sweetest and Lowest (1946)
Slings and Arrows (1948)
Fumed Oak (1949)
Fallen Angels (1949)
It's about Time (1951)
John Murray Anderson's Almanac (1953)
The Sleeping Prince (1956)
First Impressions (1959)
From A to Z (1960)
Abracadabra (1961)
Milk and Honey (1961)
Oh, Dad, Poor Dad, Mamma's Hung You in the Closet and I'm Feelin' So Sad (1963)
Dumas and Son (1967)
Charley's Aunt (1968)
Highly Confidential (1969)
A Little Night Music (1973)
Side by Side by Sondheim (1978)

Films

Someone at the Door (1936)
Meet Mr. Penny (1938)
The Pickwick Papers (1952)
Around the World in Eighty Days (1956)
Gigi (1958)
Bell, Book, and Candle (1958)
The Naked Edge (1961)
Gay Purr-ee (1962)
The Music Man (1962)
I'd Rather Be Rich (1964)
Harvey Middleman, Fireman (1965)
Munster, Go Home! (1966)
Promise Her Anything (1966)
Jules Verne's Rocket to the Moon (1967, G.B.; U.S., *Those Fantastic Flying Fools*)
Banyon (TV, 1971)
A Little Night Music (1977)

★★★

Elliott Gould

The Original Trapper John

(1938-)

Elliott Gould was born in New York City, New York, on August 29, 1938. His original name was Elliott Goldstein. He lived in Brooklyn till he moved to West Orange, New Jersey, with his parents when he was an adolescent.

His mother encouraged him to enter show business, and when he was eight she enrolled him in speech, singing, dance, and drama classes at Charles Lowe's Broadway school for youngsters in Manhattan. With other children from the school, little Elliott performed in vaudeville acts at temples, bar mitzvahs, weddings, and so on. They also hit television. For his first TV appearance, his mother changed his stage name to Gould because she thought it sounded better. At the age of eleven he danced in an act with an adult professional vaudevillian at the famed Palace Theater.

Gould completed his formal scholastic studies at the Professional Children's School in Manhattan. During his years there, he spent summer vacations performing on the borscht circuit and in summer stock. He graduated in 1955.

For the next several years Gould struggled, getting occasional small parts in Broadway shows and on TV but often having to take odd jobs. In 1960 things began to improve when he made a favorable impression in the New York City stage musical *Irma La Douce*. He began by playing an Usher, a Priest, and a Warder; but later he was promoted to the role of Polyte-le-Mou.

Gould then won the lead in the Broadway musical comedy *I Can Get It for You Wholesale* (1962). However, his work in that show was eclipsed by the explosive performance of the newcomer Barbra Streisand, who had a supporting role in the production.

Gould and Streisand soon developed a romance, and they were married in 1963. They had one child, Jason, before separating in 1969 and divorcing in 1971.

One reason for the tension in the marriage was that Gould's career was floundering at that time, while Streisand's was flourishing. He did some more musical-comedy stage and TV work in the mid-1960s, but nothing that significantly improved his reputation.

However, he found a new direction when he began to undergo psychoanalysis and to study with Lee Strasberg at the Actors Studio. Gould played an apathetic antihero in the short-lived Broadway play *Little Murders* (1967). In the movie *The Night They Raided Minsky's* (1968) he appeared as the harried manager of a 1920s burlesque house.

The big break in his career came with his performance in the highly successful film *Bob and Carol and Ted and Alice* (1969). Playing Ted, an easygoing conventional man who has difficulty adjusting to the new sexual morality, Gould showed a surprising gift for light comedy. He soon became one of the most popular actors of the early 1970s.

His next major success was in the movie *M*A*S*H* (1970), in which he played Trapper John, a hip young surgeon who undermines army bureaucracy. It is probably the role by which he is best known, a role later taken by others in the TV series *M*A*S*H* and *Trapper John, M.D.* In Ingmar Bergman's initial English-language film, *The Touch* (1971), Gould had his first noncomic role, as a man who falls in love with a married woman.

At about that time, however, Gould suffered a nervous breakdown. For the next two years he was unable to work.

In 1973 he made a comeback with his performance as the private detective Philip Marlowe in *The Long Goodbye*. Later he had a role in the spy comedy *S*P*Y*S* (1974), while in *California Split* (1974) he played one of a pair of compulsive gamblers.

In 1973 Gould married Jennifer Bogart. They divorced in 1975 but remarried in 1978. Their two children are Jennifer and Sam.

In the late 1970s and early 1980s Gould went through a downswing in his career as he appeared in a succession of films that added little to his prestige. Among them were *Harry and Walter Go to New York* (1976), *Capricorn One* (1978), and the Disney pictures *The Last Flight of Noah's Ark* (1980) and *The Devil and Max Devlin* (1981).

However, in the mid-1980s his career took a new lease on life. In *Over the Brooklyn Bridge* (1984) he played a Jewish restaurateur whose money is tied to an uncle who disapproves of the nephew's Catholic girlfriend. In *Vanishing Act* (TV, 1986) he was an idiosyncratic police chief trying to solve a baffling mystery.

Selected performances:

Stage

Rumple (1957)
Say, Darling (1958)
Irma La Douce (1960)
I Can Get It for You Wholesale (1962)
Drat! The Cat! (1965)
Little Murders (1967)
A Way of Life (1969)

Films

The Night They Raided Minsky's (1968)
Bob and Carol and Ted and Alice (1969)
Getting Straight (1970)
I Love My Wife (1970)
*M*A*S*H* (1970)
Move (1970)
Little Murders (1971)
The Touch (1971)
The Long Goodbye (1973)
Busting (1974)
*S*P*Y*S* (1974)
California Split (1974)
I Will, I Will . . . for Now (1976)
Whiffs (1976)
Harry and Walter Go to New York (1976)
A Bridge Too Far (1977)
Capricorn One (1978)
Matilda (1978)
The Silent Partner (1979)
Escape to Athena (1979)
The Lady Vanishes (1979)
The Muppet Movie (1979)
The Last Flight of Noah's Ark (1980)
Falling in Love Again (1980)
The Devil and Max Devlin (1981)
The Rules of Marriage (TV, 1982)
The Naked Face (1984)
Over the Brooklyn Bridge (1984)
Vanishing Act (TV, 1986)
Conspiracy: The Trial of the Chicago Eight (TV, 1987)

TV

Together We Stand (1986)

★★

Lee Grant

Actress Who Overcame Blacklisting

(1931-)

Lee Grant was born in New York City, New York, on October 31, 1931. (The date is so listed in *Who's Who in America*. Other sources give every year from 1926 through 1930.) Her original name was Lyova Rosenthal.

She was encouraged by her mother (a model and actress from Odessa, Russia) to enter the performing arts. In 1933 the child made her stage debut by appearing in a Metropolitan Opera production, and soon she was dancing in the Metropolitan Opera Ballet. Later she studied voice and violin at the Juilliard School of Music.

After graduating from George Washington High School, she studied acting at the Neighborhood Playhouse and soon made her adult professional debut while touring the nation as an understudy to Celeste Holm for the role of Ado Annie in *Oklahoma!* She then gained experience with a number of other stage engagements, including her Broadway debut, in *Joy to the World* (1948).

In 1949 she became a member of the Actors Studio. That same year saw the first major break in her career as she stole the show in the Broadway drama *Detective Story,* in a small role as a neurotic young shoplifter.

In 1950 she performed in *All You Need Is One Good Break* by the playwright Arnold Manoff, whom she married. They had one child: Dinah.

Grant appeared in the filmed version of *Detective Story* (1951). Returning to Broadway, she won praise for her work in *Lo and Behold!* (1951).

In 1952 Grant became a victim of the political blacklisting inspired by the Communist witch-hunts of Senator Joseph McCarthy. She was placed on the blacklist simply because her husband was on the list for alleged Communist connections. For more than a decade after that, she was allowed very little movie and television work.

During that period, Grant spent most of her time as a homemaker for her husband, their daughter, and his children from a previous marriage. When family funds ran short, she worked in summer stock and occasionally on Broadway, as in *Wedding Breakfast* (1954) and *A Hole in the Head* (1957).

Finally, in the mid-1960s, after years of fighting the whole idea of blacklisting, she got her name cleared. One of her first projects after that was an episode in the TV series *Peyton Place.* That appearance helped to reestablish her in the mass media.

In 1965 her husband died. In 1967 she married the independent filmmaker Joseph Feury, with whom she had her daughter Belinda.

Since her return to major commercial films, Grant has been one of America's busiest and most successful actresses. She quickly appeared in three popular movies: *Divorce American Style* (1967), *In the Heat of the Night* (1967), and *Valley of the Dolls* (1967). In *The Landlord* (1970) she was devastatingly funny as the hero's mother. In *Portnoy's Complaint* (1972) she played a caricatured Jewish mother. In *Shampoo* (1975) she gave a powerful performance as a devouring rich woman. In *Voyage of the Damned* (1976) she was one of a shipload of Jews sent by German Nazis to Cuba in 1939. Among her later theater films were *Damien: Omen II* (1978) and *Visiting Hours* (1982).

Grant has been particularly active in made-for-TV movies, beginning with *Night Slaves* (TV, 1970). In *Ransom for a Dead Man* (TV, 1971) she costarred with Peter Falk in the second of the two pilots for the *Columbo* series, as a lady lawyer who executes an intricate plan to murder her husband. Grant's later TV movies included *What Are Best Friends For?* (TV, 1973), *The Spell* (TV, 1977), *Backstairs at the White House* (TV, 1979), and *Thou Shalt Not Kill* (TV, 1982). In the biopic *Will There Really Be a Morning?* (TV, 1983) she played the mother of actress Frances Farmer. In *Mussolini: The Untold Story* (TV, 1985) she portrayed the dictator's wife.

Selected performances:

Stage

Joy to the World (1948)
Detective Story (1949)
All You Need Is One Good Break (1950)
Arms and the Man (1950)
Lo and Behold! (1951)
Wedding Breakfast (1954)
A Hole in the Head (1957)
The Captains and the Kings (1962)
The Maids (1963)

Electra (1964)
Love's Labour's Lost (1965)
Saint Joan (1966)
Plaza Suite (1968)
The Prisoner of Second Avenue (1971)
The Little Foxes (1975)

Films

Detective Story (1951)
Storm Fear (1955)
Middle of the Night (1959)
An Affair of the Skin (1963)
The Balcony (1963)
Terror in the City (1966)
Divorce American Style (1967)
In the Heat of the Night (1967)
Valley of the Dolls (1967)
The Big Bounce (1969)
Buona Sera, Mrs. Campbell (1969)
Marooned (1969)
The Landlord (1970)
There Was a Crooked Man . . . (1970)
Night Slaves (TV, 1970)
The Neon Ceiling (TV, 1971)
Ransom for a Dead Man (TV, 1971)
Plaza Suite (1971)
Portnoy's Complaint (1972)
Lieutenant Schuster's Wife (TV, 1972)
Partners in Crime (TV, 1973)
What Are Best Friends For? (TV, 1973)
Shampoo (1975)
Voyage of the Damned (1976)
Perilous Voyage (TV, 1976)
The Spell (TV, 1977)
Airport '77 (1977)
Damien: Omen II (1978)
When You Comin' Back, Red Ryder? (1979)
Backstairs at the White House (TV, 1979)
Little Miss Marker (1980)
Charlie Chan and the Curse of the Dragon Queen (1981)
The Million Dollar Face (TV, 1981)
For Ladies Only (TV, 1981)
Visiting Hours (1982)
Thou Shalt Not Kill (TV, 1982)
Bare Essence (TV, 1982)
Will There Really Be a Morning? (TV, 1983)
Mussolini: The Untold Story (TV, 1985)

TV

Fay (1975)

★★★

Lorne Greene

Ben Cartwright
(1915-87)

Lorne Greene was born in Ottawa, Canada, on February 12, 1915. He early developed a booming voice, and in high school he was cast in a play as one of two deaf people shouting at each other. While attending Queen's University in Kingston (1932-37), he produced, directed, and acted in plays. He even changed his major from chemical engineering to languages (French and German) so that he would have more time for theater activities.

After receiving his B.A. (1937) from Queen's University, Greene spent two years (1937-39) in New York City, studying acting at the Neighborhood Playhouse School of the Theater and stage movement at Martha Graham's School of Contemporary Dance.

Returning to Canada in 1939, he found acting jobs scarce. But because of his strong baritone voice, he was hired to read national news nightly over the Canadian Broadcasting Corporation radio network. Greene soon came to be called the Voice of Canada. He also read parts in radio plays.

After a World War II tour of duty in the Canadian army abroad, Greene returned to radio work in Toronto. There he founded the Academy of Radio Arts to train broadcasting students. Still interested in stage work, he also helped to establish the Jupiter Theater in Toronto, a repertory group with which he directed or acted in dozens of plays. His occasional work in the new medium of television was as an announcer for commercials or as a narrator for documentaries.

In the course of his radio broadcasting work, Greene experienced the problem of trying to determine how much time remained near the end of a program. To solve that problem, he developed a stopwatch that ran backward from 60 to 0. The device was produced and widely used.

In 1953 he flew to New York City to demonstrate his stopwatch for a TV executive. While there he met Fletcher Markle, who had taught at Greene's Academy of Radio Arts. Markle induced Greene to appear on the American TV series *Studio One,* which Markle produced.

After doing two episodes of *Studio One,* Greene made his American stage debut by acting in the Broad-

way play *The Prescott Proposals* (1953). His first film was *The Silver Chalice* (1954), followed by several more movies through the late 1950s, including *Peyton Place* (1957) and *The Buccaneer* (1958). He also began to appear in guest roles on other American TV shows, such as the anthology series *Alfred Hitchcock Presents, Omnibus,* and *Playhouse Ninety.*

In a 1959 episode of the TV western series *Wagon Train,* Greene played a particularly forceful character. His performance greatly impressed the National Broadcasting Company (NBC) executives who were planning a new western series called *Bonanza.* NBC had two unusual purposes in mind with the new show. First, to help sell RCA (NBC's parent company) color TV sets, the series would be one of the earliest TV shows to be filmed in color. Second, the series would feature an especially strong father-son relationship because of widespread concern about American soldiers' defections in Korea being traced by some psychologists to momism.

In *Bonanza* Greene—a 6′1½″, heavily built man with a rugged, expressive face—was cast as the father, Ben Cartwright, originally conceived as a stern, Bible-reading, gun-toting patriarch. But Greene changed the role into, in his words, a "loving father who commands respect through the force of his own personality, a good man, a strong man, a decent man." Drawing on his own happy childhood, Greene modeled Ben Cartwright after his own father, Daniel Greene, a maker of orthopedic boots and shoes.

Ben Cartwright's sons were Adam, the intellectual (played by Pernell Roberts, who left the show in 1965); Hoss, or Eric, the buffoon (played by Dan Blocker, who died in 1972); and Little Joe, the charmer (played by Michael Landon). The stories, usually set on or near the Cartwright's cattle range, the Ponderosa, centered on Ben's efforts to get his sons out of various difficulties. The series ran from 1959 to 1973.

After that Greene starred in several other series, including *Battlestar Galactica* (1978-79) and *Code Red* (1981-82). Of special significance to him was his hosting the TV series *Last of the Wild* (or *Lorne Greene's Last of the Wild,* 1974-79). He was chairman of the National Wildlife Foundation, and he was a member of the board of directors of the American Horse Protection Association. (Another activity was his work as the chairman of the American Freedom from Hunger Foundation.)

In addition, he appeared in many films, mostly TV movies and miniseries. Among them were *Tidal Wave* (1975), *Roots* (TV, 1977), *The Bastard* (TV, 1978), and *A Time for Miracles* (TV, 1980). In the animated film *Heidi's Song* (1982) he supplied the grandfather's voice.

In 1986 he appeared in TV commercials for Alpo dog food, and he acted in the made-for-TV film *The Alamo: Thirteen Days to Glory* (telecast in 1987).

Greene married Rita Hands, of Toronto, in 1940. They had twins, Belinda and Charles, before divorcing in 1960. In 1961 he wedded Nancy Anne Deale, with whom he had one child.

Greene died in Santa Monica, California, on September 11, 1987.

Selected performances:

Stage

The Prescott Proposals (1953)
Julius Caesar (1955)
The Merchant of Venice (1955)
Speaking of Murder (1956)
Edwin Booth (1958)

Films

The Silver Chalice (1954)
Tight Spot (1955)
Autumn Leaves (1956)
Peyton Place (1957)
The Gift of Love (1958)
The Buccaneer (1958)
The Trap (1959)
The Errand Boy (1961)
Waco (1966)
Destiny of a Spy (TV, 1969)
The Harness (TV, 1971)
Tidal Wave (1975)
Nevada Smith (TV, 1975)
Man on the Outside (TV, 1975)
Roots (TV, 1977)
SST—Death Flight (TV, 1977)
The Trial of Lee Harvey Oswald (TV, 1977)
The Bastard (TV, 1978)
A Time for Miracles (TV, 1980)
Code Red (TV, 1981)
Heidi's Song (1982)
The Alamo: Thirteen Days to Glory (TV, 1987)

TV

Sailor of Fortune (1957)
Bonanza (1959-73)
Griff (1973-74)
Last of the Wild (or *Lorne Greene's Last of the Wild,* 1974-79)
Battlestar Galactica (1978-79)
Galactica 1980 (1980)
Code Red (1981-82)

★★★

Joel Grey

Master of Ceremonies

(1932-)

Joel Grey was born in Cleveland, Ohio, on April 11, 1932. His original name was Joel Katz, son of Mickey Katz, the popular comic musician of the American Yiddish musical theater. Mickey directed a vaudeville troupe in which his wife, Grace, performed and in which little Joel soon learned to sing and dance. The boy made his formal dramatic debut by playing the role of Pud in *On Borrowed Time* (1941) at the Cleveland Playhouse.

The family later moved to Los Angeles, where Joel attended Alexander Hamilton High School and continued to work in his father's show. After graduating, the young man left his father's troupe, changed his stage name from Katz to Kaye and finally to Grey, and built a solo nightclub career.

In 1951, while working in Miami, he was spotted by Eddie Cantor and booked on Cantor's TV show. After that exposure, Grey was engaged at some of the best-known nightclubs in the country, including the Copacabana in New York City. His fast-paced act—singing, dancing, patter—was likened to the style of Danny Kaye.

Grey yearned to perform roles in theatrical productions, but pressure from his parents and agents kept him in nightclub work, where he felt increasingly unhappy. By the age of nineteen he had already developed a bleeding ulcer.

In the mid-1950s Grey finally dropped nightclub work and began to study acting at the Neighborhood Playhouse in New York City. He made his Broadway debut by appearing in *The Littlest Revue* (1956) and then played the title role in the TV special *Jack and the Beanstalk* (1956). Soon he was making guest appearances on TV variety shows, including Ed Sullivan's.

In 1958 Grey married Jo Wilder, an actress. They had two children: Jennifer and Jimmy. Jo was a stabilizing force in his life and career. "Before I was married I was scattered," he admitted, "but afterwards I was able to zero in on my acting projects."

In the early 1960s Grey had a part in the movie *Come September* (1961), understudied several roles on Broadway, and played in the off-Broadway black comedy *Harry, Noon, and Night* (1965). He began to build a reputation among theater people for his dynamism and versatility.

The big break in Grey's career came when he was cast in the Broadway musical *Cabaret* (1966). As the heavily made up, hollow-eyed master of ceremonies at Berlin's Kit Kat cabaret, he personified the decadence that set the stage for Hitler's takeover of Germany. *Cabaret* finally shot Grey into star status, and his part as the master of ceremonies is still the one by which he is best known.

In 1968 he appeared in the title role of *George M!,* a Broadway musical about the famous entertainer George M. Cohan. In 1972 Grey returned to nightclub work on an occasional basis.

His next few stage vehicles were not popular successes. He appeared in the Broadway musical *Goodtime Charley* (1975); the off-Broadway play *Marco Polo Sings a Solo* (1977); and the Broadway show *The Grand Tour* (1979), a musical adaptation of a play about a Polish Jew, Jacobowsky (played by Danny Kaye in the 1958 movie version entitled *Me and the Colonel),* who is escaping from the Nazis during World War II. *The Grand Tour* had a limited run, but Grey's role was personally meaningful to him. "I've never played a Jewish person before," he said. "I've played Nazis and Irishmen and WASPs—but never a Jew. It feels good."

Grey has, in fact, been a Jewish activist outside the theater. In 1974 he served as West Coast chairman of the Committee to Free the Panovs. Valery Panov, a Jew, and his wife, Galina, were famed ballet dancers in the Soviet Union. The Panovs, who wanted to move to Israel, had been denied permission to leave Russia; they had also been forbidden to perform. Pressure from Western countries finally forced the Soviet government to let the Panovs leave. For his efforts, Grey received the Israel Cultural Award in 1974.

His movies are few. He was impressive in the filmed version of *Cabaret* (1972), and in the murder mystery *Man on a Swing* (1974) he played a straight dramatic role as a clairvoyant. In 1976 he appeared in two films: *Buffalo Bill and the Indians* and *The Seven-Per-Cent Solution.*

In the 1980s Grey has opened up new fields for himself. He made his opera debut by performing in the New York City Opera production of the American premiere of Kurt Weill's *Silverlake* in 1980. He showed fine operetta skills in a TV production of Gilbert and Sullivan's

The Yeoman of the Guard (TV, 1984). And in the movie *Remo Williams: The Adventure Begins* (1985) he played a martial-arts master.

Selected performances:

Stage

On Borrowed Time (1941)
The Littlest Revue (1956)
Come Blow Your Horn (1961)
Stop the World—I Want to Get Off (1963)
Half a Sixpence (1965)
Harry, Noon, and Night (1965)
Cabaret (1966)
George M! (1968)
1776 (1972)
Goodtime Charley (1975)
Marco Polo Sings a Solo (1977)
The Grand Tour (1979)
Silverlake (1980)
Cabaret (1987)

Films

About Face (1952)
Come September (1961)
Cabaret (1972)
Man on a String (TV, 1972)
Man on a Swing (1974)
Buffalo Bill and the Indians; or, Sitting Bull's History Lesson (1976)
The Seven-Per-Cent Solution (1976)
The Yeoman of the Guard (TV, 1984)
Remo Williams: The Adventure Begins (1985)
Queenie (TV, 1987)

★★★

Buddy Hackett

Rubber Face

(1924-)

Buddy Hackett was born in New York City, New York, on August 31, 1924. His original name was Leonard Hacker.

While growing up in Brooklyn, he spent some of his summer vacation time on the borscht circuit as a waiter, bellhop, and toomler (that is, a creator of comic tumult). Soon after graduating from New Utrecht High School he joined the army, where he spent three years of World War II service.

Returning to civilian life, he changed his name to Buddy Hackett and began to work in East Coast cafés and nightclubs as a comedian. His progress was slow,

Buddy Hackett (right) and Alan King (left)

however, till he tried California in the early 1950s and scored in big-time nightclubs. One of his funniest routines was his impersonation of a Chinese waiter. Soon he was getting engagements with major nightclubs and hotels throughout the country.

Bigger fields also began to open for him. He appeared in the movies *Walking My Baby Back Home* (1953) and *Fireman, Save My Child* (1954); the Broadway farce *Lunatics and Lovers* (1954); and the TV series *Stanley* (1956-57), in which he starred as the owner of a hotel-lobby newsstand.

In 1955 he married the ex-dancer Sherry Cohen (stage name, Sherry Dubois). They had three children: Sandy, Ivy, and Lisa.

The first role that really gave him a chance to show what he could do was that of Pluto, the lovelorn rustic, in the film *God's Little Acre* (1958). Hackett endowed the comic character with surprising depth and poignancy.

Another milestone in his career was his appearance in 1960 on David Susskind's TV talk show *Open End.* On that program Hackett showed the wit and the ad-libbing skills that had brought him stardom on the nightclub circuit. After his *Open End* performance, he began to appear on many TV talk shows and variety programs.

In the 1960s Hackett created delightful characters in a number of movies. In *The Music Man* (1962), for example, he was a stableboy who helps a con man to bilk a town. Other films included *The Wonderful World of the Brothers Grimm* (1962); *It's a Mad, Mad, Mad, Mad World* (1963); and *The Love Bug* (1969).

From 1974 to 1976 he was a regular panelist on TV's *Celebrity Sweepstakes*. In 1978 he gave one of his most memorable performances, as the famed comedian Lou Costello in the TV biopic *Bud and Lou*.

Hackett's humor tends to be based on an endearing combination of helplessness and craftiness. His comic delivery is aided by his chubby elastic visage, which has been referred to as a "rubber face."

In the 1980s Hackett's work has centered on the nightclub circuit, where his inclination toward the risqué can be freer than on TV. But he does make occasional guest appearances on TV, as in a dramatic role (as an egocentric comedian) on an episode of *Quincy, M.E.* In the Canadian film *Hey, Babe!* (1984) he played a washed-up entertainer who befriends a twelve-year-old orphan.

Selected performances:

Stage

Lunatics and Lovers (1954)
Viva Madison Avenue (1960)
I Had a Ball (1964)

Films

Walking My Baby Back Home (1953)
Fireman, Save My Child (1954)
God's Little Acre (1958)
All Hands on Deck (1961)
Everything's Ducky (1961)
The Wonderful World of the Brothers Grimm (1962)
The Music Man (1962)
It's a Mad, Mad, Mad, Mad World (1963)
Muscle Beach Party (1964)
The Good Guys and the Bad Guys (1969)
The Love Bug (1969)
Bud and Lou (TV, 1978)
Hey, Babe! (1984)

TV

Stanley (1956-57)
Celebrity Sweepstakes (1974-76)

★★★

Laurence Harvey

Perfect Scoundrel

(1928-73)

Laurence Harvey was born in Yonishkis, Lithuania (now in the Soviet Union), on October 1, 1928. His original name was Larushka Mischa Skikne.

In 1934 he moved with his parents to Johannesburg, South Africa, where he improved his English by attending movies. In 1943 he made his stage debut by appearing in *Cottage to Let* with the Johannesburg Repertory Company. In that same year he ran away from home, lied about his age, and joined the South African military service. He saw World War II action in North Africa and Italy before being assigned to an entertainment unit.

After being discharged, he moved to England and entered the Royal Academy of Dramatic Art in London (1946). He was there only briefly, but he did act in the graduation show. Soon he had offers from the American film studio Warner Bros. and from the classical-theater company in Manchester, England. He chose the latter, where, during 1947-51, he developed a mastery of language and style. Eventually he adopted his new surname from the fashionable Harvey Nichols department store in London.

Meanwhile, he also began to appear in British movies. (He became a South African national and a British subject in 1947.) Harvey wanted to become a comedian, but directors guided him into leading-man dramatic roles. His screen debut came in *House of Darkness* (1948), followed by many other second features.

Simultaneously he continued his stage career. His London debut came in *Hassan* (1951). He then joined the Royal Shakespeare Company in Stratford-upon-Avon, where he performed in many of the Bard's plays in 1952 and 1954. It was there that he first attracted serious critical attention, when he played Romeo in *Romeo and Juliet* (1954). He repeated his performance in a filmed version of the play (1954).

For several more years he alternated work on the stage and in films. He made his Broadway debut by playing Angelo, an eccentric stranger who becomes involved with three lonely women, in *The Island of Goats* (1955). But from the late 1950s on, he concentrated mostly on movies, both in England and in the United States.

Harvey reached international stardom with his performance in the British movie *Room at the Top* (1959), as Joe Lampton, an ambitious, self-serving young schemer. There followed a series of pictures in which he played other scoundrels, a type by which he came to be most closely identified. In *Butterfield 8* (1960) he portrayed a philandering husband whose behavior toward his mistress drives her to suicide. He played a dissolute young doctor in *Summer and Smoke* (1961) and a brainwashed assassin in *The Manchurian Candidate* (1962). In *The Ceremony* (1963), which he also produced and directed, he was the leader of a holdup gang. In *Life at the Top* (1965) he re-created his Joe Lampton character in a sequel to *Room at the Top*.

Harvey's typical screen image was that of a bored, coldly impudent young man. But with his classical training and his native intelligence (though having little formal education, he could speak Dutch, English, French, German, and Italian), Harvey was able to give his villains depth and roundness. He was one of the screen's perfect scoundrels.

There were, however, changes of pace. For example, in *The Wonderful World of the Brothers Grimm* (1962) Harvey portrayed a heartwarmingly sincere collector of fairy tales. He played Philip Carey, the clubfooted, tormented lover in *Of Human Bondage* (1964). And on the New York City stage he had the role of King Arthur in the musical *Camelot* (1964), in which he made a stylish singer-dancer.

In real life Harvey's arrogant manner made him unpopular among many in his profession. He was also noted for his strange antics. For example, during the gasoline rationing in London in 1956, he rode about the city on a chauffeur-driven motor scooter.

Harvey had three marriages. In 1957 he married the actress Margaret Leighton. They had met when both were working at Stratford-upon-Avon. Later they appeared together in the movie *The Good Die Young* (1955). Harvey and Leighton divorced in 1961.

In 1968 he wedded Joan Cohn, widow of Harry Cohn, head of Columbia Pictures. That marriage ended in divorce in 1972.

He then married the young fashion model Paulene Stone. They had a daughter: Domino.

Harvey's third marriage was less than a year old when he died of cancer in London on November 25, 1973, at the age of only forty-five.

Laurence Harvey

Selected performances:

Stage

Cottage to Let (1943)
The Man Who Ate the Popomack (1943)
Hassan (1951)
Coriolanus (1952)
As You Like It (1952)
Macbeth (1952)
Volpone (1952)
Romeo and Juliet (1954)
Troilus and Cressida (1954)
The Island of Goats (1955)
The Rivals (1956)
The Country Wife (1956)
Simply Heavenly (1958)
Henry V (1958)
Camelot (1964)

Films

House of Darkness (1948)
Man on the Run (1949)
The Black Rose (1950)
I Believe in You (1952)
Women of Twilight (1952, G.B.; U.S., *Twilight Women*)
King Richard and the Crusaders (1954)
Romeo and Juliet (1954)
Innocents in Paris (1955)
The Good Die Young (1955)
I Am a Camera (1955)
Storm over the Nile (1955)
Three Men in a Boat (1956)
The Truth about Women (1958)
The Silent Enemy (1958)
Room at the Top (1959)
Expresso Bongo (1959)
Butterfield 8 (1960)
The Alamo (1960)
The Long and the Short and the Tall (1961, G.B.; U.S., *Jungle Fighters*)
Summer and Smoke (1961)
Two Loves (1961)
A Girl Named Tamiko (1962)
The Manchurian Candidate (1962)
Walk on the Wild Side (1962)
The Wonderful World of the Brothers Grimm (1962)
The Ceremony (1963)
The Running Man (1963)
Of Human Bondage (1964)
The Outrage (1964)
Darling (1965)
Life at the Top (1965)
The Spy with a Cold Nose (1966)
A Dandy in Aspic (1968)
The Magic Christian (1970)
Escape to the Sun (1972)
Night Watch (1973)
Welcome to Arrow Beach (1974, G.B.; U.S., *Tender Flesh* or *Cold Storage*)

★★

Goldie Hawn

Kooky Comedienne

(1945-)

Goldie Hawn was born of a Jewish mother and Protestant father in Washington, D.C., on November 21, 1945. She was raised in Maryland.

At the age of three she began to study tap dancing and ballet, and at eleven she added modern dance to her lessons. Her father, who played violin, clarinet, and saxophone in society dance bands, gave her voice lessons.

As a teenager she appeared in school and community dramatic productions. After graduating from Montgomery Blair High School in Silver Spring, Maryland, she studied drama at American University in Washington, D.C., for a year and a half.

Hawn then went to work as a professional dancer. She danced in summer-stock musicals, performed as a go-go dancer in a Manhattan discotheque, and appeared in a variety of other outlets.

While dancing in the chorus on an Andy Griffith TV special in 1967, she was spotted by Art Simon, who

Goldie Hawn

became her agent. He helped her to get a small role as the wacky neighbor in the TV situation comedy *Good Morning, World* (1967-68).

Hawn then shot to stardom with her regular appearances on TV's *Laugh-in* (1968-70). Combining sexiness and innocence, she created a character who was childlike but not stupid. Traces of her offbeat persona in *Laugh-in* can be found in many of her other roles as well.

In her first movie, *The One and Only, Genuine, Original Family Band* (1968), she played a small part as a giggly girl. Then, in *Cactus Flower* (1969), she had one of the leading roles and won great praise for her comic portrayal of the young mistress of a middle-aged dentist.

In *There's a Girl in My Soup* (1970) she played a mistress again. In *$* (1971) she was a call girl and amateur bank robber. Her performance as the eccentric neighbor who falls in love with a young blind man in *Butterflies Are Free* (1972) firmly established her reputation as a fine comedienne. Among her other movies in the 1970s were *Shampoo* (1975) and *Foul Play* (1978).

In *Private Benjamin* (1980) she played the title role of a pampered young woman who has difficulty adjusting to life as a soldier. Hawn skillfully blended slapstick and romantic comedy in her performance.

In *Swing Shift* (1984) she portrayed a lonely wife who finds work and romance in an aircraft plant during World War II. In *Protocol* (1984) she played a cocktail waitress who shakes up the State Department. In *Wildcats* (1986) she was a teacher who becomes the boys' football coach at a tough high school.

Hawn has been married and divorced twice. In 1969 she wedded the actor and film director Gus Trikonis. Later she was married for a time to Bill Hudson. Those marriages produced two children: Oliver and Kate. In recent years she has lived with the actor Kurt Russell, her *Swing Shift* costar, with whom she had a child in July 1986.

Selected performances:

Films

The One and Only, Genuine, Original Family Band (1968)
Cactus Flower (1969)
There's a Girl in My Soup (1970)
$ (1971)
Butterflies Are Free (1972)
The Sugarland Express (1974)
The Girl from Petrovka (1974)
Shampoo (1975)
The Duchess and the Dirtwater Fox (1976)
Foul Play (1978)
Private Benjamin (1980)
Seems like Old Times (1980)
Best Friends (1982)
Swing Shift (1984)
Protocol (1984)
Wildcats (1986)

TV

Good Morning, World (1967-68)
Laugh-in (1968-70)

★★★

Dustin Hoffman

Antihero

(1937-)

Dustin Hoffman was born in Los Angeles, California, on August 8, 1937. At the age of twelve he played Tiny Tim in a school production of Dickens's *A Christmas Carol.*

But for the next several years his attention was focused on becoming a classical pianist. After graduating from Los Angeles High School in 1955, he enrolled at Santa Monica City College, where he majored in music but also took an acting class. He then studied classical and jazz piano for a while at the Los Angeles Conservatory of Music.

However, early in 1957 he decided to turn to acting. He began to study the fundamentals of his new art at the Pasadena Playhouse.

In 1958 Hoffman left for New York City, working in various community theaters along the way. After arriving at his destination, he auditioned and failed several times to enter Lee Strasberg's famous Actors Studio. Finally he was accepted at the Studio, where his roommates were Robert Duvall and Gene Hackman.

For quite a while in New York City Hoffman earned his living by doing odd jobs. In 1959 he got a nonpaying role in a Sarah Lawrence College production of *Yes Is for a Very Young Man.* In 1961 he made his Broadway debut with a one-word line in *A Cook for Mr. General.*

An important turning point in Hoffman's career came when he joined the Theater Company of Boston as a character actor. He appeared in a number of plays but made his greatest impression as Pozzo in Beckett's *Waiting for Godot* (1964).

Hoffman was then given his first significant Broadway job: assistant director of a revival of *A View from the Bridge* (1965). There followed a series of acting roles that brought him a growing reputation, culminating in his comedy performance as an inept factory-machine operator in *Eh?* (1966).

Hoffman's first movie role was a bit part as a beatnik lover in *The Tiger Makes Out* (1967). He then had a leading role in the low-budget Italian-Spanish detective comedy *Madigan's Millions* (made in 1967 but released in 1969).

The major break in Hoffman's career came when he was cast in the title role of *The Graduate* (1967). He played Benjamin Braddock, an innocent, confused college graduate who is seduced by an older woman.

That role was the first of many parts that soon turned Hoffman into Hollywood's preeminent antihero, the defenseless character caught in situations reflecting the complexity of the modern world. He played the lame homosexual-hustler Ratso Rizzo in *Midnight Cowboy* (1969); the irritable 122-year-old Jack Crabb, claiming to be the sole survivor of Custer's last stand, in *Little Big Man* (1970); the weak, timid convict Louis Dega in *Papillon* (1973); the controversial real-life comedian Lenny Bruce in *Lenny* (1974); and the student Babe Levy, haunted by memories of his father's suicide (brought on by the McCarthy-era Communist witch-hunts) and trapped in a violent pursuit of diamonds about which he knows nothing, in *Marathon Man* (1976). Hoffman portrayed the real-life Watergate investigative reporter Carl Bernstein, groping his way through a maze of clues and facing possible retribution from the politically powerful, in *All the President's Men* (1976).

In 1969 Hoffman married Anne Byrne, a dancer. She brought with her a daughter, Karina, from an earlier marriage. Later they had another daughter: Jennifer. Anne appeared with Hoffman in *Papillon* as Louis Dega's wife. But the Hoffmans' marriage broke up in the late 1970s. He was particularly worried about the effect of the divorce on his children.

At that point in his life he was offered the role of the divorced parent Ted Kramer in *Kramer vs. Kramer* (1979). Hoffman drew on his personal experience to give one of his most sensitive performances.

In 1980 he married Lisa Gottsegen, a young law-school graduate. They had three children: Jacob, Rebecca, and Max.

Hoffman has a reputation for being obsessive in his research and preparation for his roles. His passion for perfection may be partly related to a desire to compensate for his short stature (only 5′6″). His self-consciousness about his height was a key factor in his decision to go through years of psychoanalysis.

In recent years Hoffman has impressed critics and audiences with the depth and diversity of his performances. In the film comedy *Tootsie* (1982) he played an

Dustin Hoffman

unemployed actor who masquerades as a woman to win a role in a soap opera. In 1984 he starred as Willy Loman in a Broadway revival of Arthur Miller's *Death of a Salesman*. He reprised the role in a filmed version (TV, 1985). In the film comedy *Ishtar* (1987) he sang and danced as one of two (with Warren Beatty) no-talent songwriters on the road.

Selected performances:

Stage

A Cook for Mr. General (1961)
Endgame (1964)
Waiting for Godot (1964)
Three Men on a Horse (1964)
Harry, Noon, and Night (1965)
The Journey of the Fifth Horse (1966)
Eh? (1966)
The Old Jew (1966)
Jimmy Shine (1968)
Death of a Salesman (1984)

Films

The Tiger Makes Out (1967)
The Graduate (1967)
Midnight Cowboy (1969)
John and Mary (1969)
Madigan's Millions (1969)
Little Big Man (1970)
Straw Dogs (1971)
Who Is Harry Kellerman and Why Is He Saying Those Terrible Things about Me? (1971)
Papillon (1973)
Alfredo, Alfredo (1973)
Lenny (1974)
All the President's Men (1976)
Marathon Man (1976)
Straight Time (1978)
Agatha (1979)
Kramer vs. Kramer (1979)
Tootsie (1982)
Death of a Salesman (TV, 1985)
Ishtar (1987)

★★★

Judy Holliday

Dumb-blonde Genius

(1921-65)

Judy Holliday was born in New York City, New York, on June 21, 1921 (some sources give 1922). Her original name was Judith Tuvim.

Judy's parents were of Russian descent, her maternal grandparents having fled their native land to avoid a czarist pogrom. From her father, Abraham, who was a professional fund-raiser for Jewish and socialist organizations, Judy derived her social consciousness. From her mother, Helen, who was a piano teacher, Judy acquired an interest in the arts.

When Judy was six her parents separated. She then began to live with her mother and her grandmother.

In 1938 Judy graduated from Manhattan's Julia Richman High School. Shortly thereafter she worked briefly as a switchboard operator for Orson Welles's Mercury Theater.

Then, with a few friends, including the future great lyricists Betty Comden and Adolph Green, Judy helped to form the Revuers, a topical cabaret act. They worked in nightclubs and had a thirty-two-week run on radio. Judy's gift for comedy showed itself immediately. During her tenure with the Revuers, she changed her name from Judy Tuvim to Judy Holliday (*tuvim* being a Hebrew word for "holiday").

In 1943 the Revuers were in Hollywood, California. While they were there, Holliday played bit parts in the movies *Winged Victory* (1944) and *Something for the Boys* (1944).

Returning to New York City, the Revuers disbanded because Comden and Green had been asked to prepare the book and lyrics for Leonard Bernstein's musical *On the Town.*

Holliday won a small "moronic" part in the Broadway farce *Kiss Them for Me* (1945). She was the hit of the show.

Late in 1945 Jean Arthur was starring in the pre-Broadway performances of *Born Yesterday* when she became ill and had to leave the show. Holliday was called in as a replacement, and in just three days she learned and rehearsed the role of Billie Dawn, a corrupt tycoon's dumb-blonde mistress whose latent sensitivities are awakened, who learns to think for herself, and who finally scores a moral and financial victory in behalf of all "little" people over the wealthy megalomaniac junkman.

In early 1946 *Born Yesterday* hit Broadway and became a tremendous success. During the next few years Holliday played Billie Dawn well over a thousand times.

In 1948 Holliday married David Oppenheim, a clarinetist and later an executive with Columbia Records. They had one child, Jonathan, before divorcing in 1957.

In 1949 she took a leave of absence from *Born Yesterday* to play a similar role in the film *Adam's Rib* (1949). The female star of that movie, Katharine Hepburn, credited Holliday with outshining both Hepburn and the film's male lead, Spencer Tracy.

At about that time, plans were being made to film *Born Yesterday.* But Harry Cohn of Columbia Pictures hesitated to sign Holliday, who wanted a contract calling for her to make only one movie a year. She had made the demand so that she could have time for a personal life with her husband. After a two-year search it became evident to Cohn that no one could match Holliday's brilliant portrayal of Billie Dawn. She was hired, and she subsequently gave a memorable performance in the filmed version of *Born Yesterday* (1950).

In the early 1950s she frequently appeared on TV variety shows. But in 1952 she was called before a Senate subcommittee and questioned about her support of various causes alleged to be fronts for Communist activity. She purposely and skillfully adopted her scatterbrained Billie Dawn persona during her testimony, in which she exonerated herself and avoided naming others. Her ploy beautifully confounded the members of the subcommittee and exemplified the disdain in which level-headed Americans held the extremists among the witch-hunters of the era. Garson Kanin, author of *Born Yesterday,* said, "Her behavior under pressure was a poem of grace."

Nevertheless, the subcommittee did succeed in casting a vague shadow over her. As a result, she was blacklisted from TV for a number of years.

However, her movie career blossomed. Basically continuing her dumb-blonde character, she made outstanding impressions in several films, including *It Should Happen to You* (1954), *Phffft* (1954), and *The Solid Gold Cadillac* (1956).

Judy Holliday

In 1956 she returned to the stage by making her musical debut, as Ella Peterson in *Bells Are Ringing.* Comden and Green had tailored the role to take advantage of Holliday's unique combination of mimic ability, vaudevillian talent, and expressive vulnerability.

While she was enjoying the peak of her success in *Bells Are Ringing,* she had a tempestuous love affair with Sydney Chaplin, son of Charles Chaplin. But Sydney broke off the romance.

In late 1960 she began to perform in the play that she felt would have the greatest impact on her artistic development: *Laurette,* based on the life of the actress Laurette Taylor, Holliday's idol. However, after the New Haven tryouts and just before the scheduled opening in Philadelphia, Holliday became ill and had to leave the show. The official reason given at the time was that she had a throat problem. Indeed, she did have such an affliction. But while the doctor was examining her he also found a lump in her left breast. The lump turned out to be malignant, and the breast had to be removed.

During her subsequent physical and psychological recovery, she was greatly helped by the jazz saxophonist Gerry Mulligan, with whom she had a long-term romantic relationship. She did recover sufficiently to appear in the ill-fated stage musical *Hot Spot* (1963), in which she made her last appearance as an actress.

Holliday had one of the most astonishing careers in show business. She performed in only a small number of plays and movies, most of them unremarkable except for the glow that she gave them. Yet she attained such a rapport with her audiences and created such thoroughly endearing characterizations that her work (through films) continues to win the admiration of each new generation.

In real life Holliday was far from the dumb blonde that she usually portrayed. In fact, she had a genius IQ of 172! Her characterizations, then, were thoroughly artistic creations, and they went much deeper than just the comic surface. With just a tiny inflection in her voice, she could suddenly turn a scene from comedy to tragedy.

Her own life mirrored that same turn. As soon as she reached major success in Hollywood, she was hauled into the Senate hearings. As soon as she found her first big hit (*Bells Are Ringing*) after *Born Yesterday,* she was dropped by her lover. And as soon as she found the great acting vehicle that she had long hoped for, *Laurette,* she became ill and had to leave the show.

Throughout her life she went on periodic eating binges and struggled with the problem of being overweight. Insecure about her looks, she was always shocked when she turned heads in public. She may never have realized that she was actually one of the most appealing and lovable actresses of her time.

Unfortunately for everyone, her time was short. Holliday died of cancer in New York City on June 7, 1965, two weeks short of her forty-fourth birthday.

Selected performances:

Stage

Kiss Them for Me (1945)
Born Yesterday (1946)
Dream Girl (1951)
Bells Are Ringing (1956)
Laurette (1960)
Hot Spot (1963)

Films

Winged Victory (1944)
Something for the Boys (1944)
Adam's Rib (1949)
Born Yesterday (1950)
The Marrying Kind (1952)
It Should Happen to You (1954)
Phffft (1954)
The Solid Gold Cadillac (1956)
Full of Life (1957)
Bells Are Ringing (1960)

★★

Oscar Homolka

Great Screen Heavy
(1898-1978)

Oscar Homolka was born in Vienna, Austria, on August 12, 1898. He studied at the Royal Academy of Dramatic Arts in Vienna and then began his professional stage career in that city.

After spending two years in the Austrian army during World War I, Homolka returned to the stage. In 1918 he went to Berlin, where he became one of the director Max Reinhardt's leading men. Homolka mastered the French and Polish languages and appeared onstage in France and Poland as well as in Austria and Germany. He also began to appear in German-language films in the 1920s.

In the early 1930s he fled Hitler's influence and moved to Great Britain. He made his English-language debut with a performance as Dr. Mesmer in *Mesmer* (1935) in Scotland. Later that year he began to work on the London stage. His first British film appearance was in *Rhodes of Africa* (1936), as President Kruger of the Dutch Transvaal, whose policies led to the Boer War.

In 1937 he made his American film debut in *Ebb Tide,* as a former ship captain who has become a drunken beachcomber. In 1940 came his first performance on the New York City stage, in *Grey Farm.* Homolka became a naturalized American citizen in 1943.

One of his most memorable roles was as the bombastic but benevolent Uncle Chris in *I Remember Mama* (stage, 1944; film, 1948). But for Homolka, one of the greatest heavies in screen history, it was an uncharacteristic part.

His rugged build, heavy facial features, bushy eyebrows, wickedly twinkling eyes, and gravelly voice led to his being typecast as villains. In Alfred Hitchcock's *Sabotage* (1936) Homolka was a saboteur who manufactures bombs in the back room of his theater in London. In *Comrade X* (1940) he portrayed a Russian commissar, while in *Anna Lucasta* (1949) he was a drunken father. In the comedy *The Seven Year Itch* (1955) he played an unsympathetic psychiatrist. In *Funeral in Berlin* (1966), *Billion Dollar Brain* (1967), and *The Tamarind Seed* (1974), he portrayed Russian spies.

Homolka was married five times. His fourth marriage was to Florence Meyer, daughter of Eugene Meyer, publisher of *The Washington Post.* Homolka's two surviving children, Lawrence and Vincent, were products of that marriage, which ended in divorce.

His final and most successful marriage, beginning in 1949, was to the actress Joan Tetzel. They had appeared together on Broadway in *I Remember Mama.*

In the mid-1960s Homolka moved to a rural setting in Sussex, England, after having spent about fifteen years in New York City. He died in Sussex on January 27, 1978. The cause of death was given as pneumonia, but friends said that he was weakened by grief over the loss of his wife, who had died just three months earlier.

Selected performances:

Stage

Pygmalion (1932)
Mesmer (1935)
Close Quarters (1935)
Power and Glory (1938)
Grey Farm (1940)
The Innocent Voyage (1942)
I Remember Mama (1944)
The Last Dance (1948)

Bravo! (1948)
The Broken Jug (1950)
The Master Builder (1955)
Rashomon (1959)

Films

Der Kampf des Donald Westhof (1927, Ger.; U.S., *The Trial of Donald Westhof*)
Dreyfus (1930, Ger.; U.S., *The Dreyfus Case*)
Im Geheimdienst (1931, Ger.; U.S., *In the Employ of the Secret Service*)
Rhodes of Africa (1936, G.B.; U.S., *Rhodes*)
Sabotage (1936, G.B.; U.S., *The Woman Alone*)
Ebb Tide (1937)
Seven Sinners (1940)
Comrade X (1940)
The Invisible Woman (1941)
Rage in Heaven (1941)
Ball of Fire (1941)
Hostages (1943)
Mission to Moscow (1943)
The Shop at Sly Corner (1947, G.B.; U.S., *The Code of Scotland Yard*)
I Remember Mama (1948)
Anna Lucasta (1949)
The White Tower (1950)
Top Secret (1952, G.B.; U.S., *Mr. Potts Goes to Moscow*)
Prisoner of War (1954)
The Seven Year Itch (1955)
War and Peace (1956)
A Farewell to Arms (1957)
The Key (1958)
Mr. Sardonicus (1961)
Boys' Night Out (1962)
The Wonderful World of the Brothers Grimm (1962)
The Long Ships (1964)
Joy in the Morning (1965)
Funeral in Berlin (1966)
Billion Dollar Brain (1967)
The Happening (1967)
The Strange Case of Dr. Jekyll and Mr. Hyde (TV, 1968)
Assignment to Kill (1969)
The Madwoman of Chaillot (1969)
The Executioner (1970)
Song of Norway (1970)
The Tamarind Seed (1974)
One of Our Own (TV, 1975)

★★★

Harry Houdini

Legendary Magician and Escape Artist

(1874-1926)

Harry Houdini was born in Budapest, Hungary, on March 24, 1874. His original name was Erik Weisz.

Shortly after his birth, his parents moved with him to the United States and settled in Wisconsin, first in Appleton and later in Milwaukee. The boy's name was Americanized to Erich Weiss. Houdini always claimed that he had been born in Appleton on April 6, 1874, probably because he strongly felt himself to be a native American and wanted the world to see him as such.

His father, Rabbi Mayer Weiss, had difficulty adjusting to the New World, and the family was very poor. Young Erich early developed an interest in show business as a means of escaping poverty. His first public performance came at a neighborhood circus, probably in a trapeze act.

On his twelfth birthday he ran away from home to look for work. By 1888 he had rejoined his family, which had moved to New York City. He worked at odd jobs, eventually becoming a cutter at a necktie factory.

Meanwhile, however, he had been cultivating a growing interest in magic and feats of dexterity. He learned the rudiments of those skills by observing acts at sideshows and circuses and by reading books.

When he decided to pursue a serious career in magic, he changed his nickname of Ehrie into Harry, and he derived his new surname of Houdini from the name of his

idol, the magician Robert-Houdin. Harry Houdini and his friend Jacob Hyman, a fellow worker at the necktie factory, put together a magic act and had small-time bookings as the Brothers Houdini. Later Hyman was replaced by one of Houdini's four real-life brothers, Theodore (or Theo, later known as the independent magician Hardeen).

On April 3, 1891, Houdini left his factory job and went into show business full time. He and his brother played dime museums, beer halls, and small-time rural vaudeville theaters. At first they concentrated on magic, but Houdini soon began to add escape tricks to the act.

In 1894 Houdini married the Catholic girl Wilhelmina Beatrice Rahner, known as Bess or Bessie. Theodore left the act, which then became known as the Houdinis, starring Harry with Bess as his assistant.

In 1895 they played briefly at Tony Pastor's famous Music Hall in New York City. But over the next several years they struggled in poverty while appearing mostly in saloons, circuses, and dime museums.

At the turn of the century they traveled to Europe. During their five years there, Houdini developed the art of self-publicity, which he would use to tremendous advantage for the rest of his career. When he returned to the United States in 1905, he was a major celebrity.

In America, Houdini took advantage of a new forum, big-time urban vaudeville, to raise himself to an unprecedented level of popularity for a magician and escape artist. His great genius lay in his dramatic escape tricks. In "The Challenge Handcuff Act" he became the first escape artist to invite people from the audience to shackle him with real handcuffs, not the usual fake variety. In "The Chinese Water Torture Cell Escape" Houdini's ankles were padlocked and he was lowered head first into a glass container full of water. "Metamorphosis" was the rapid substitution of one person for another inside a locked and roped trunk. In "The Naked Test Prison Escape" he was stripped and locked in real prison or jail cells. In "The Overboard Box Escape" he was locked in a box, which was then tossed into a river. "The Straitjacket Escape" never ceased to amaze audiences as they watched him squirm out of the binding.

For those and other escapes, Houdini used his knowledge of mechanics, both human and nonhuman. When his escapes depended on sheer strength and physical dexterity, he performed in full view of his audience. But for more difficult tricks, he hid in a cabinet of one kind or another.

After World War I Houdini entered the filmmaking business. He starred in the serial *The Master Mystery* (1918-19) and then made several independent movies. The stories and the acting were not memorable, but the films did have some thrilling adventures featuring Houdini's physical dexterity.

He was also active as a writer. In *The Unmasking of Robert-Houdin* (1908) he exposed the methods and claims of his former idol. *Miracle Mongers and Their Methods* (1921) was an exposé of fire-eaters, gravity-resisters, and other sideshow acts. Many of his essays were collected to form the posthumous *Houdini on Magic* (1953).

Houdini long had an interest in death. That interest was intensified in 1913 when his beloved mother died and then in 1920 when he met Sir Arthur Conan Doyle, creator of the Sherlock Holmes fictional character and champion of spiritualism.

Houdini began to investigate spiritualism as a possible way of communicating with his mother. He soon discovered the tricks used by spiritualists, and by 1922 a strong denunciation of mediums had become a regular part of his own act. His book *A Magician among the Spirits* (1924) was a well-documented exposé of the phony mediums of the day.

On October 21, 1926, while in Montreal, Canada, for a performance, Houdini was approached by two youths from nearby McGill University. They asked if it was true that he had claimed that he could take a punch in the midsection without being affected. He said yes; but before Houdini had time to brace himself, one of the youths threw a vicious blow to the older man's abdomen. Unknown to Houdini, the punch ruptured his appendix. Over the next few days he continued to work, though the pain increased steadily.

On October 24, just after a performance in Detroit, Michigan, he collapsed. An emergency operation was performed on his gangrenous appendix. But he died of advanced peritonitis in Detroit on October 31, 1926. At Houdini's own request he had a Jewish burial service at Mount Zion Temple in New York City.

After his death a furor arose when his widow said that he had promised to try to communicate to her from the "other world," conveying a secret message that he had whispered to her on his deathbed. During a series of séances in 1928-29 the spiritualist Arthur Ford claimed to have received the message. At first Bess agreed with Ford; later she disagreed. Subsequent investigations showed that neither Ford nor Bess was a reliable witness.

Selected performances:

Films

The Master Mystery (1918-19)
The Grim Game (1919)
Terror Island (1920)
The Soul of Bronze (1921)
The Man from Beyond (1922)
Haldane of the Secret Service (1923)

★★★

Leslie Howard

Romantic Intellectual

(1893-1943)

Leslie Howard was born in London, England, on April 3, 1893. His original name was Leslie Howard Steiner (his surname is so indicated on his birth record, though his daughter later spelled it Stainer).

He disliked school, but he enjoyed writing. In his early teens he began to write stories, plays, and short musical comedies. He sold many thrillers to pulp magazines. To encourage him, his mother organized a neighborhood drama club, in whose plays both mother and son appeared.

Howard entered Dulwich College but, at his father's insistence, left at the age of nineteen to become a bank clerk. The outbreak of World War I gave him the opportunity to get away from the bank, where he had never been happy. He enlisted in the military service and was commissioned a second lieutenant in the cavalry in 1915. In the spring of 1916 he was sent to France, where he saw combat action till a case of shellshock caused him to be returned to England in 1917. From his cavalry experience he developed a great love of horses and eventually a passion for polo.

Howard returned to an adoring wife. In 1916, before going to France, he had married Ruth Martin, daughter of a laundry manager. They had two children: a son, Ronald; and a daughter, Leslie Ruth. Each child later wrote a book about their father. Leslie Ruth's was called *A Quite Remarkable Father* (1959), Ronald's *In Search of My Father: A Portrait of Leslie Howard* (1981).

Howard was very close to his children, who were nicknamed Winkie (Ronald, for no particular reason) and Doodie (Leslie Ruth, from her early attempt to say "Daddy"). Basically a shy person, Howard, during parties at his home, would often sneak upstairs to little Doodie's room and doze off on her bed. If he heard his wife coming after him, he would giggle and playfully ask Doodie to hide him.

His wife, Ruth, was a sustaining influence in his career. When he returned from France in 1917, she stood by him in his decision to become an actor. It was for his new career that he dropped his original surname.

In 1917 Howard made his professional debut, touring the provinces in *Peg o' My Heart.* His London debut came in early 1918, with a small part in *The Freaks.*

In 1920, becoming fascinated by movies, he helped to form the small Minerva Films production company, with himself as managing director and leading actor. The company made three short comedies before going out of business.

Returning to the stage, he traveled to the United States, where he made his New York City debut in the fall of 1920 in *Just Suppose.* He spent the next several years in America, often appearing as the juvenile lead in light comedies.

Beginning in 1926, when he returned to England and appeared there in *The Way You Look at It,* he alternated varying lengths of time on stage shows in London and New York City. The British often referred to him as "that American actor."

Indeed, Howard attained stardom, in March 1927, through an American production of *Her Cardboard Lover,* in which he appeared with Jeanne Eagels. In October of that year he solidified his position by making a strong impression in *Escape,* also in New York City.

However, he never really enjoyed acting, and he turned to other activities as much as possible. Still interested in writing, he sold, in the 1920s, several light essays (mostly about acting and the theater) to major American magazines, such as *Vanity Fair* and *The New Yorker*.

He also turned to directing and producing. In 1927 he directed and starred in the New York City production of *Murray Hill,* a farce that he had written. In 1928 he produced a London staging of *Her Cardboard Lover,* in which he again starred. Thereafter, he often served as producer or coproducer of the plays in which he appeared. Highlights of the rest of his stage career included his work in *Berkeley Square* (1929), *The Animal Kingdom* (1932), and *The Petrified Forest* (1935).

In 1930 Howard began to appear in major films. His first performance, as one of a group of ship passengers who slowly realize that they are dead in *Outward Bound* (1930), made a tremendous impression on audiences. He then appeared in a number of light comedies, but he is best remembered for his memorable characterizations of Philip Carey in *Of Human Bondage* (1934), Sir Percy Blakeney in *The Scarlet Pimpernel* (1935), Alan Squier in *The Petrified Forest* (1936), Professor Higgins in *Pygmalion* (which he codirected, 1938), and Ashley Wilkes in *Gone with the Wind* (1939).

Howard typified the romantic intellectual on the screen. Audiences identified him as a thoughtful man of culture and decency fighting against brutality in the world.

In 1939 England entered World War II. Howard, still a British citizen, returned from America to his homeland to aid the war effort. He helped (as producer, director, writer, and/or star) to make propaganda films showing the British viewpoint to American audiences. Outstanding among those films was the biopic *The First of the Few* (1942, released in the United States in 1943 as *Spitfire*), the story of R. J. Mitchell (played by Howard), designer of the Spitfire fighter plane. Howard also made weekly radio broadcasts to North America on the *Britain Speaks* program.

In the spring of 1943, at the request of the British Council, Howard went as a goodwill ambassador to the neutral nations of Spain and Portugal, where he gave a series of lectures. On the return flight, his plane was shot down by German aircraft over the Bay of Biscay on June 1, 1943. His body was never recovered.

Selected performances:

Stage

Peg o' My Heart (1917)
Charley's Aunt (1917)
Under Cover (1917)
The Freaks (1918)
The Title (1918)
Our Mr. Hepplewhite (1919)
Mr. Pim Passes By (1920)
The Young Person in Pink (1920)
East Is West (1920)
Just Suppose (1920)
The Wren (1921)
Danger (1921)
The Truth about Blayds (1922)
A Serpent's Tooth (1922)
The Romantic Age (1922)
The Lady Cristilinda (1922)
Anything Might Happen (1923)
Aren't We All? (1923)
Outward Bound (1924)
The Werewolf (1924)
Isabel (1925)
Shall We Join the Ladies? (1925)
The Green Hat (1925)
The Way You Look at It (1926)
Her Cardboard Lover (1927)
Murray Hill (1927)
Escape (1927)
Her Cardboard Lover (1928)
Berkeley Square (1929)
Candlelight (1929)
The Animal Kingdom (1932)
This Side Idolatry (1933)
The Petrified Forest (1935)
Hamlet (1936)

Films

The Happy Warrior (1917)
The Lackey and the Lady (1919)
Five Pounds Reward (1920)
Bookworms (1920)
Outward Bound (1930)
Never the Twain Shall Meet (1931)
A Free Soul (1931)
Five and Ten (1931)
Devotion (1931)
Service for Ladies (1932, G.B.; U.S., *Reserved for Ladies*)
Smilin' Through (1932)
The Animal Kingdom (1932, U.S.; G.B., *A Woman in His House*)
Secrets (1933)
Captured (1933)
Berkeley Square (1933)
The Lady Is Willing (1934)
Of Human Bondage (1934)
British Agent (1934)
The Scarlet Pimpernel (1935)
The Petrified Forest (1936)
Romeo and Juliet (1936)
It's Love I'm After (1937)
Stand-in (1937)
Pygmalion (1938)
Gone with the Wind (1939)
Intermezzo (1939, U.S.; G.B., *Escape to Happiness*)
From the Four Corners (1940)
Forty-ninth Parallel (1941, G.B.; U.S., *The Invaders*)
Pimpernel Smith (1941, G.B.; U.S., *Mister V*)
The First of the Few (1942, G.B.; U.S., *Spitfire*)

★★★

Sam Jaffe

Gunga Din and Dr. Zorba

(1891-1984)

Sam(uel) Jaffe was born in New York City, New York, on March 10, 1891. He grew up in the Lower East Side section of Manhattan and attended Townsend Harris High School. As a child he occasionally appeared onstage with his mother, Ada Steinberg Jaffe, an actress in the Yiddish theater.

However, his early formal training was in engineering, in which he earned his B.S. degree at City College of the City University of New York (1912). While he pursued his graduate studies at the Columbia School of Engineering, he was a teacher, and then dean (1915-16), of mathematics at the Bronx Cultural Institute, a college-preparatory school. In 1918 he served as an army engineer.

Meanwhile, however, Jaffe was gradually returning to the theater. In 1915-16 he appeared with the Washington Square Players, and in 1917 he worked with a Shakespearean repertory company. His Broadway debut came as Leibush in *The Idle Inn* (1921).

Jaffe gained his first important recognition when he played the comic role of Yudelson in *The Jazz Singer* (1925). Perhaps his greatest stage role was that of Kringelein, a dying, obscure clerk who suddenly experiences luxury for the first time in his life, in *Grand Hotel* (1930).

Jaffe frequently played Jewish roles. Among them were Izzy Goldstein in *The Main Line* (1924), Eli Iskowvitch in *Izzy* (1924), Shylock in *The Merchant of Venice*

(1938), and Jonah Goodman in *The Gentle People* (1939).

In 1943 Jaffe cofounded (with George Freedley) the Equity Library Theater. He himself continued to work on the stage in his later years, but beginning in the early 1930s much of his time was spent in films.

In his first movie, *The Scarlet Empress* (1934), he made a strong impression as the dissolute Grand Duke Peter of Russia. Jaffe soon became one of the all-time great motion-picture character actors. He was the venerable High Lama in *Lost Horizon* (1937) and the title character—the humble, ascetic, noble water-carrier for British soldiers—in *Gunga Din* (1939). In *Gentleman's Agreement* (1947), a story about anti-Semitism, he played a Jewish scientist, while in *The Asphalt Jungle* (1950) he portrayed a coolheaded criminal mastermind. In the science-fiction classic *The Day the Earth Stood Still* (1951) he was the space scientist Jacob Barnhardt, while in *Ben-Hur* (1959) he played a loyal steward in ancient Judea.

From the 1950s on, Jaffe guest-starred on many TV series, such as *Bonanza, The Defenders, Night Gallery,* and *The Untouchables.* He won his widest audience through his regular role as Dr. David Zorba, chief of neurosurgery, in the TV medical-drama series *Ben Casey* (1961-65).

Among his later stage performances, one of his most memorable was as Zero, the anguished bookkeeper who is superseded by automation, in *The Adding Machine* (1956). Jaffe's last stage role was that of a Hindu guru in *A Meeting by the River* (1979).

His later movies included *Born Free* (1966), *The Old Man Who Cried Wolf!* (TV, 1970), and *Gideon's Trumpet* (TV, 1980). In October 1983, at the age of ninety-two, he performed his last film role, as a smuggler of illegal aliens in *On the Line.*

Jaffe was a man of wide-ranging talents and interests. He was an excellent pianist and composer of classical music, and he spoke fluently in at least six languages. He supported many causes, including Israel. A liberal, he had to endure a brief downswing in his career during the McCarthy era in the early 1950s.

Jaffe was married twice. In the mid-1920s he wedded the actress Lillian Taiz, who died in 1941. In 1956 he married the actress Bettye Ackerman, with whom he frequently acted, as in *Ben Casey.*

Jaffe died at the age of ninety-three in Beverly Hills, California, on March 24, 1984.

Selected performances:

Stage

The Clod (1915)
Youth (1918)
Mrs. Warren's Profession (1918)
Samson and Delilah (1920)
The Idle Inn (1921)
The God of Vengeance (1922)
The Main Line (1924)
Izzy (1924)
The Jazz Singer (1925)
Grand Hotel (1930)
Divine Drudge (1933)
The Bride of Torozko (1934)
The Eternal Road (1937)
A Doll's House (1937)
The Merchant of Venice (1938)
The Gentle People (1939)
King Lear (1940)
The King's Maid (1941)
Café Crown (1942)
Thank You, Svoboda (1944)
This Time Tomorrow (1947)
Mademoiselle Colombe (1954)
The Sea Gull (1954)
Saint Joan (1954)
The Adding Machine (1956)
Idiot's Delight (1970)
Storm in Summer (1973)
A Meeting by the River (1979)

Films

The Scarlet Empress (1934)
We Live Again (1934)
Lost Horizon (1937)
Gunga Din (1939)
Stage Door Canteen (1943)
13 Rue Madeleine (1947)
Gentleman's Agreement (1947)
The Accused (1949)
Rope of Sand (1949)
The Asphalt Jungle (1950)
Under the Gun (1951)
I Can Get It for You Wholesale (1951)
The Day the Earth Stood Still (1951)
The Barbarian and the Geisha (1958)
Ben-Hur (1959)
Damon and Pythias (1962)
Born Free (1966)
A Guide for the Married Man (1967)
Guns for San Sebastian (1968)
The Great Bank Robbery (1969)
Night Gallery (TV, 1969)
Quarantined (TV, 1970)
The Old Man Who Cried Wolf! (TV, 1970)
The Dunwich Horror (1970)
Bedknobs and Broomsticks (1971)
QB VII (TV, 1974)
Gideon's Trumpet (TV, 1980)
Battle beyond the Stars (1980)
Nothing Lasts Forever (1983)
On the Line (1983)

TV

Ben Casey (1961-65)

★★

Al Jolson

Jazz Singer
(1886-1950)

Al Jolson was born sometime during the period 1880-86 in Srednike, Lithuania (now in the Soviet Union). Because no birth certificate was made out at the time, the exact date of his birth is not known. Later, however, Jolson himself selected May 26, 1886, as the birth date that he preferred. His original name was Asa Yoelson.

In the early 1890s his father, Moses, moved to the United States. A few years later the elder Yoelson sent for his family, who joined him in Washington, D.C., where he had obtained a post as a cantor.

Moses strictly upheld Orthodox Jewish views and practices, while Asa and his older brother, Hirsch, were lax in such observances. Moreover, Moses taught both boys to sing but he hated popular music, while it was precisely American popular culture that most interested his sons. They sang in the streets to earn money from passersby and often ran away from home to try to break into show business. After Hirsch Americanized his given name to Harry, Asa followed suit by calling himself Al.

Al's first indoor show-business job was singing "Rosie, You Are My Posie" in a Bowery restaurant, where his payment was a meal. At the Bijou Theater in Washington, D.C., he sang from the audience as part of Eddie Leonard's act, later performing the same function there for the burlesque queen Jersey Lil. In 1899 he appeared on a stage for the first time, as an extra in the New York City production of the London Jewish epic *Children of the Ghetto*.

Having Americanized their surname to Joelson (a change initiated by Al), the boys began touring in vaudeville as the Joelson Brothers in a comedy act called *The Hebrew and the Cadet*. Because Al's voice was changing, Harry sang while Al whistled. During the show-business slump following the assassination of President McKinley in 1901, the boys were laid off.

After a couple of years in burlesque, they returned to vaudeville in the comedy team Jolson, Palmer, and Jolson (a printer having suggested the change in spelling because two *Joelsons* were too long for their business card). In their act, entitled *A Little of Everything,* Al used blackface for the first time, finding that with a mask on he could perform with greater abandon.

The team lasted about three years, after which Al developed a solo act. In San Francisco, one week after the great 1906 earthquake there, he made his first significant appearance in his solo vaudeville routine, again in blackface. His first great success, however, came when he performed as one of Lew Dockstader's Minstrels in New York City in 1909.

Jolson then began touring in vaudeville on his own again, still in blackface, and perfected his technique as he went along. Cultivating a style of singing derived from Afro-American music and blackface minstrelsy, he characteristically performed with an intoned declamation that emphasized the text rather than the melodic line. Yet he was also skilled at melodic invention, often improvising whistled choruses in the manner of jazz instrumentalists. In fact, much of his routine was improvised. Besides performing his set numbers, he sang songs on request, sometimes whistled or broke into a buck-and-wing, and kept up a lively extemporaneous monologue consisting of anecdotes, homilies, and confessions.

In 1911 Jolson began his meteoric rise to the position of Broadway's greatest attraction. He appeared that year in *La Belle Paree* and *Vera Violetta.*

In 1912 a runway was built into the orchestra area of the Winter Garden Theater for Jolson's use in the revue *The Whirl of Society,* in which he presented himself as the blackface character Gus. Jolson would use both the runway and the Gus character in many future shows.

In *The Honeymoon Express* (1913) Jolson employed for the first time two gestures that became his hallmark: falling to one knee and extending his arms in a pathetic appeal while singing. He performed those gestures while beseeching his mammy in "Down Where the Tennessee Flows." His original purpose, however, was not theatrical but practical: he was suffering from an ingrown toenail, and he went down to one knee to take pressure off the painful digit; his arms flew out in an instinctive compensation for the sudden immobility of his legs. But the favorable response of the audience induced him to keep the gestures as a regular feature in his performances.

He went on to score big successes in numerous Broadway productions, notably *Robinson Crusoe, Jr.* (1916), *Sinbad* (1918), and *Bombo* (1921). Most of the musicals starring Jolson had little plot interest. He simply

Al Jolson

took over the last segment of each show to work his magic and bring the entertainment to a rousing climax. In his performances, he became closely identified with many songs, including "April Showers," "My Mammy," "Rock-a-bye Your Baby with a Dixie Melody" (his favorite song), "Swanee," and "Toot, Toot, Tootsie."

In the late 1920s, after the successful *Big Boy* (1925), Jolson's popularity began to fade with the changing fashions in the theater public's taste. His last two stage vehicles, *The Wonder Bar* (1931) and *Hold On to Your Hats* (1940), in both of which he performed without blackface, did not fare well.

Jolson, however, proved to be adaptable, and in the late 1920s he turned to films. He debuted, in fact, in the first significant feature-length sound movie: *The Jazz Singer* (1927). Actually the film is not entirely in sound; it is mostly a silent movie, with songs and bits of dialogue audible. The first spoken words in the film occur when Jolson, after singing "Dirty Hands, Dirty Face," says, "Wait a minute! Wait a minute! You ain't heard nothin' yet," and then introduces his next song, "Toot, Toot, Tootsie."

The Jazz Singer was originally a Broadway play in which the main character, Jakie Rabinowitz, was modeled after Jolson himself. Jakie is a cantor's son who runs away from home to become the jazz singer Jack Robin. When his father dies, Jack gives up his big chance on Broadway and goes home to take over his father's cantor duties at the synagogue. For the screen version, a final segment was added showing Jack singing in a Broadway musical entitled *The Jazz Singer*. George Jessel, the original Jakie Rabinowitz on Broadway, had been scheduled to take the screen role; but when he asked for too much money, he was replaced by Jolson.

Among Jolson's later films were *The Singing Fool* (1928); *Mammy* (1930); *Hallelujah, I'm a Bum* (1933); *Swanee River* (1939); and *Rhapsody in Blue* (1945).

Jolson was also a frequent performer on radio, both as the star of his own shows and as a guest on other programs. He hosted several variety series, including *Presenting Al Jolson* (1932-33), *The Kraft Music Hall* (1933-34, 1947-49), and *Shell Chateau* (1935-36). In 1936 he teamed up with two comics, Martha Raye and Parkyakarkas (real name, Harry Einstein), on *The Lifebuoy Program,* a hit show for several seasons.

Jolson's popularity slipped again in the late 1930s and early 1940s. But the semibiographical movies *The Jolson Story* (1946) and *Jolson Sings Again* (1949) revived interest in him. He dubbed in the singing for Larry Parks (as Jolson) in the two films.

Jolson had four marriages. In 1906 he wedded Henrietta Keller, a chorus girl whom he had met in San Francisco; they divorced in 1919. He was then married to the Broadway dancer Alma Osborne, better known by the stage name Ethel Delmar, from 1922 to 1926, when they divorced.

His third marriage, beginning in 1928, was to the famed entertainer Ruby Keeler. In 1929 Keeler starred in the stage work *Show Girl,* in which she was supposed to lead a women's chorus in singing "Liza." In one of Broadway's most famous incidents, Jolson appeared at the theater and sang "Liza" from the audience to calm his young wife. (He returned for several more nights to perform the same function till Keeler felt secure on her own.) They starred together a number of times, as in the film *Go Into Your Dance* (1935) and the program "Burlesque" for *The Lux Radio Theater* (1936).

Al and Ruby adopted a son, whom they named Al Jolson, Jr. But this marriage, too, did not last; they parted in 1939 and divorced in 1940.

In 1945 he married Erle Chenault Galbraith, an X-ray technician and fan from Little Rock, Arkansas. They adopted another son (Asa) and, less formally, a daughter (Alicia).

Jolson was generous with his time for benefit performances, particularly during wartime. He helped to sell World War I Liberty Bonds, and he performed on the United Service Organizations (USO) circuits during World War II and the Korean conflict. Having just returned from a Korean tour, Jolson was stopping over in San Francisco (where his solo career had begun) when he died of a heart attack on October 23, 1950.

His good friend George Jessel delivered the eulogy at Temple Israel in Los Angeles. The bulk of Jolson's estate, estimated at $4 million, was bequeathed to a number of institutions, including Jewish, Catholic, and Protestant charities.

Selected performances:

Stage

La Belle Paree (1911)
Vera Violetta (1911)
The Whirl of Society (1912)
The Honeymoon Express (1913)
Dancing Around (1914)
Robinson Crusoe, Jr. (1916)
Sinbad (1918)
Bombo (1921)
Big Boy (1925)
Artists and Models (1926)
A Night in Spain (1927)
The Wonder Bar (1931)
Hold On to Your Hats (1940)

Films

The Jazz Singer (1927)
The Singing Fool (1928)
Say It with Songs (1929)
Mammy (1930)
Big Boy (1930)
Hallelujah, I'm a Bum (1933)
Wonder Bar (1934)
Go Into Your Dance (1935)
The Singing Kid (1936)
Rose of Washington Square (1939)
Swanee River (1939)
Rhapsody in Blue (1945)
The Jolson Story (voice only, 1946)
Jolson Sings Again (voice only, 1949)

Radio

Presenting Al Jolson (1932-33)
The Kraft Music Hall (1933-34, 1947-49)
Shell Chateau (1935-36)
The Lifebuoy Program (1936-39)

★★★

Madeline Kahn

"Clown with the Face of an Angel"

(1942-)

Madeline Kahn was born in Boston, Massachusetts, on September 29, 1942. Her original name was Madeline Wolfson.

She was raised in New York City. When she was very young, her parents separated. She lived with her mother, who supported the family by working as a secretary, an usherette, a model, and a nightclub singer. When Madeline was about ten, her mother married a man named Kahn. After Mrs. Kahn delivered a baby boy, she gave up her plans for a show-business career.

However, she transferred her hopes to Madeline, who early began to take lessons in piano, dance, and voice. Her first significant public appearance came when she sang on *Children's Hour,* a New York City radio program.

At Martin Van Buren High School in Queens, young Kahn participated in some plays. Then, at Hofstra University in Hempstead, on Long Island, New York, she majored in drama for two years before switching first to music and then to speech, intending to become a speech therapist. Meanwhile, however, she continued her music activities: she took private singing lessons, appeared as a classical singer in university productions, performed in an off-campus opera workshop, and worked as a singing waitress in a German restaurant.

Kahn graduated from Hofstra with a B.A. degree in 1964. She then taught for a while at a public school in Levittown, on Long Island, but soon found that she did not care for the work.

Returning to show business, Kahn performed as a singing waitress in Bellmore, on Long Island, and then as a chorus girl in a City Center revival of *Kiss Me, Kate* (1965). For the next two years she sang opera and light opera with Green Mansions, an upstate New York repertory company.

Kahn's Broadway debut came in the musical comedy *New Faces of 1968* (1968), in which she made a strong impression with her singing of "Das Chicago Song," a parody of the Bertolt Brecht and Kurt Weill musicals. In November 1968 she sang the female lead in Leonard Bernstein's *Candide* at the Lincoln Center, in a performance honoring the composer's fiftieth birthday.

In the late 1960s Kahn began to appear in satirical revues at New York City's Upstairs at the Downstairs club. She also performed onstage in the musicals *Promenade* (1969) and *Two by Two* (1970), and she was a regular on the TV series *Comedy Tonight* (1970). In the stage work *Boom Boom Room* (1973) she gave an impressive acting performance as Chrissy, a shallow, ambitious go-go dancer who is progressively degraded. In addition, during the late 1960s and early 1970s, she made numerous guest appearances on national TV shows hosted by Johnny Carson, Dick Cavett, Mike Douglas, David Frost, and Merv Griffin.

It was in movies, however, that Kahn made her greatest impact on audiences and came to be regarded as one of the outstanding comediennes of her time. Her movie debut came in *What's Up, Doc?* (1972), in which she had the role of Eunice Burns, the shrewish, frustrated fiancée of Howard Bannister (played by Ryan O'Neal). Kahn's comic performance nearly stole the show from the film's star, Barbra Streisand.

In her next picture, *Paper Moon* (1973), Kahn again walked off with high praise for her supporting role. She portrayed Trixie Delight, a Depression-era carnival dancer who teams up with a con man (again played by Ryan O'Neal).

In Mel Brooks's western-movie spoof *Blazing Saddles* (1974) Kahn played the saloon singer Lili von Shtupp, a devastating burlesque of Marlene Dietrich's style in the famous German film *The Blue Angel* (1930) and in the American western *Destry Rides Again* (1939). Kahn gave one of her most hilarious performances as her sexy Lili sneered, sulked, lisped, and pouted through *Blazing Saddles.*

In Brooks's horror-movie spoof *Young Frankenstein* (1974) Kahn took the role of Elizabeth, the primping, finicky fiancée of Dr. Frankenstein (played by Gene Wilder). In Gene Wilder's *The Adventure of Sherlock Holmes' Smarter Brother* (1975), a takeoff on nineteenth-century detective stories, she played Jenny Hill, a music-hall singer (and another sex tease) who constantly changes her identity. In Brooks's *High Anxiety* (1977), a spoof of Alfred Hitchcock thrillers, Kahn portrayed Victoria Brisbane, a glamorous socialite.

Her later films included *The Muppet Movie* (1979),

Brooks's *History of the World, Part I* (1981), and *Yellowbeard* (1983). In 1983 she acted in the play *Blithe Spirit;* starred in her own TV situation-comedy series, *Oh, Madeline;* and made her Carnegie Hall debut by narrating a concert version of Offenbach's operetta *La Perichole.* Then she appeared in the movies *Slapstick of Another Kind* (1984), *City Heat* (1984), and *Clue* (1985).

The film critic Rex Reed has dubbed Kahn "the clown with the face of an angel."

Selected performances:

Stage

Kiss Me, Kate (1965)
Upstairs at the Downstairs (1966)
New Faces of 1968 (1968)
Promenade (1969)
Two by Two (1970)
Boom Boom Room (1973)
Marco Polo Sings a Solo (1977)
She Loves Me (1977)
On the Twentieth Century (1978)
Blithe Spirit (1983)
La Perichole (1983)

Films

What's Up, Doc? (1972)
Paper Moon (1973)
From the Mixed-up Files of Mrs. Basil E. Frankweiler (1973)
Blazing Saddles (1974)
Young Frankenstein (1974)
At Long Last Love (1975)
The Adventure of Sherlock Holmes' Smarter Brother (1975)
High Anxiety (1977)
The Cheap Detective (1978)
The Muppet Movie (1979)
Simon (1980)
Happy Birthday, Gemini (1980)
Wholly Moses! (1980)
First Family (1980)
History of the World, Part I (1981)
Yellowbeard (1983)
Slapstick of Another Kind (1984)
City Heat (1984)
Clue (1985)
My Little Pony, the Movie (1986)

TV

Comedy Tonight (1970)
Oh, Madeline (1983)

★★★

Danny Kaye

Ambassador of Goodwill

(1913-87)

Danny Kaye was born of Russian immigrants in New York City, New York, on January 18, 1913. His original name was David Daniel Kaminski (sometimes spelled Kominski or Kominsky).

He grew up in the Brownsville section of the borough of Brooklyn, the toughest district in all of New York City. Danny, or Duvidl, as his parents called him, survived by being the neighborhood entertainer, singing and clowning around. He always loved to make people laugh.

At Public School 149 and Thomas Jefferson High School, most of his energy went into sports, such as swimming and baseball. His athletic work helped to develop the strength, coordination, and sense of timing that he later applied to his vigorous stage and film routines.

In his early teens he got a job as a messenger boy in the office of a dentist, Dr. Samuel Fine. The doctor's teenage daughter, Sylvia, developed a crush on Danny, but he was so busy that he never paid any attention to her. One day Dr. Fine caught Danny making a sort of needlepoint design on a piece of wood with a dental drill. The doctor fired the boy on the spot.

Shortly after that incident, Danny dropped out of high school and began trying to make his way in show business. His early efforts, such as performing at local parties, did not lead anywhere, and he had to take odd jobs for a while.

In 1929 he went to work on the borscht circuit. There he combined the jobs of waiter, singer, actor, and comedian. His principal task was simply to keep the guests amused, which he often did by falling into the swimming pool—fully clothed, straw hat and all. In the language of the entertainment world, Danny was a toomler, that is, a creator of tumult.

He continued to work as a toomler during the summers of 1930-32. Finally, in the summer of 1933 he got a job as a full-fledged entertainer on the borscht circuit.

Also in 1933 he was asked to join the dancing team of Dave Harvey and Kathleen Young, forming a group called the Three Terpsichoreans. On the opening night, in Utica, New York, Kaye, an inexperienced dancer, accidentally fell during the performance. The audience began to laugh and applaud. Harvey whispered to him, "They love it. Don't get up." Kaye, in a false whisper that could be heard throughout the auditorium, replied, "I can't get up. I've split my pants!" Kaye's clowning became a regular part of the act, which played at vaudeville and burlesque theaters.

Late in 1933 the Three Terpsichoreans joined a revue troupe that worked its way westward across the United States and then sailed for the Orient in February 1934. By then Kaye was singing and monologizing in addition to dancing. To appeal to the non-English-speaking audiences of the Orient, Kaye learned to tell his stories in pantomime, to show emotions by making faces, and to entertain with scat singing, which consists of the expressive vocalizing of meaningless syllables with an occasional recognizable word for emphasis.

After the Oriental tour ended, Kaye found a number of minor engagements in the United States. For a while he toured with the famous fan dancer Sally Rand, holding her fans to assure that she was properly (that is, minimally) covered during her act. In 1938 he was hired for an important engagement at a London cabaret, but he failed to impress the British.

His career was stuck. He simply could not find the right material for his personality.

Then, in 1939, he went to the Keystone Theater on Fifty-second Street in New York City to see about a job. There, seated at the piano was an attractive brunette who looked vaguely familiar. She glanced up, smiled shyly, and said, "I know you, but I bet you don't remember me." It was Sylvia Fine, daughter of Dr. Samuel Fine. She was also the woman destined to change Danny Kaye's entire career and life.

They both got jobs that day, she as a pianist and songwriter and he as a performer, for *The Sunday Night Revue*. The show folded after only one night, but it was the beginning for Danny and Sylvia.

That summer they worked together again, putting on *The Straw Hat Revue* at Camp Tamiment, a Jewish resort camp in the Pocono Mountains of Pennsylvania. In the autumn the show made it to Broadway, where Kaye finally began to develop a reputation and a following.

The new boost to his career can be traced directly to Sylvia Fine's sparkling melodies and absurd lyrics, perfectly tailored to showcase Kaye's personality and talent for dialect singing and for patter (humorous, rapid-fire) songs. There was, for instance, "Anatole of Paris," in which Kaye sang as a schizophrenic modiste with blue hair.

In early 1940 Danny and Sylvia were married. They had one child, Dena, who became a successful writer.

Later in 1940 Kaye was hired at the elite New York City nightclub La Martinique. After a shaky start, he was calmed down and technically advised by Sylvia. Soon he settled into a tremendously successful, now legendary, engagement. His biggest single song success at that time was Sylvia's "Stanislavsky," in which Kaye, in Russian dialect, poked fun at the Soviet artists of the Moscow Theater, where students were taught to "become" inanimate objects.

Thereafter, Sylvia continued to be the most important force in his career, not only writing much of his material but also serving as his personal coach and critic.

Kaye's performances at La Martinique led to a part in the major Broadway musical *Lady in the Dark* in early 1941. Later that year he appeared in another stage show, *Let's Face It*.

When the United States entered World War II, Kaye tried to enlist for military service. But he was rejected because he had a sacroiliac problem. He then aided the war effort by appearing at benefits and rallies to help sell war bonds and by performing at military camps and hospitals. He also appeared in United Service Organizations (USO) tours in Europe.

During the war, Kaye began to make movies, through which his talent became known worldwide. His first film was *Up in Arms* (1944). There followed a series of movies designed as vehicles for Kaye's unique comedic and musical versatility. Through the 1940s there were *Wonder Man* (1945), *The Kid from Brooklyn* (1946), *The Secret Life of Walter Mitty* (1947), *A Song Is Born* (1948), and *The Inspector General* (1949).

One of his most endearing performances came in his portrayal of the title character in the musical film *Hans Christian Andersen* (1952). He also sang in the movies *On the Riviera* (1951), *Knock on Wood* (1954), *White Christmas* (1954), *The Court Jester* (1956), *Merry Andrew* (1958), *The Five Pennies* (1959), *On the Double* (1961), *Pinocchio* (TV, 1976), and *Peter Pan* (TV, 1976).

Kaye proved himself as a straight actor as well, notably in the films *Me and the Colonel* (1958), in which he played a Jewish refugee fleeing 1940 France in the company of an anti-Semitic Polish colonel; *The Man from the Diners' Club* (1963); *The Madwoman of Chaillot* (1969); and *Skokie* (TV, 1981), in which he played a Holocaust survivor confronting resurgent Nazism in contemporary America.

Kaye also performed on radio and TV. He hosted *The Danny Kaye Show* on radio (1945-46) and the very successful TV variety series of the same name (1963-67).

Also notable was his return, after a nearly thirty-year absence, to the Broadway stage in the musical *Two by Two* (1970), based on the biblical story of Noah. But he

Danny Kaye (right) and Laurie Ichino (left)

Danny Kaye conducting the Israel Philharmonic Orchestra

always preferred the freedom of concert appearances, where he could exercise his ability to improvise. Kaye, though he could not read music, frequently appeared on the podium with major orchestras, such as the Israel Philharmonic, conducting them with inspired hilarity.

He maintained his love of sports. In 1976 he became a founder and part owner of the Seattle Mariners professional baseball team. In 1981 he sold most, and in 1983 the remainder, of his interest in the club.

But the dominant factor in his life for many years was his work in behalf of the United Nations International Children's Emergency Fund (UNICEF). From 1953 on he was UNICEF's official ambassador-at-large to the world's children. He went into remote areas of Europe, Asia, Africa, and Latin America to visit children who were undernourished, diseased, or orphaned by war. Exuding an obviously genuine affection for them, he entertained the children while teams of UNICEF workers administered medical and other aid.

In 1957 he hosted the TV program *The Secret Life of Danny Kaye,* in which he presented children of various countries to demonstrate the work of UNICEF. In 1983, while Kaye was recuperating from a successful heart bypass operation, UNICEF saluted him for his thirty years of service by naming him as an honorary delegate to the UNICEF Executive Board.

Kaye did not slow down much after his surgery. On January 1, 1984, he acted as the grand marshal of the Rose Parade. He also continued to make UNICEF tours and to appear as a conductor. In September 1985, for example, he comically conducted the Los Angeles Philharmonic Orchestra at the Hollywood Bowl in a benefit concert for a musicians' fund.

However, complications stemming from his operation finally took their toll, and Kaye died in Los Angeles on March 3, 1987.

Because his humor was never unkind, was always solidly based in humility, was universal in appeal, and was channeled into helping the world's children, Kaye was internationally recognized as one of humanity's greatest treasures and as an independent ambassador of goodwill to people everywhere.

Selected performances:

Stage

The Sunday Night Revue (1939)
The Straw Hat Revue (1939)
Lady in the Dark (1941)
Let's Face It (1941)
Two by Two (1970)

Films

Up in Arms (1944)
Wonder Man (1945)
The Kid from Brooklyn (1946)
The Secret Life of Walter Mitty (1947)
A Song Is Born (1948)
The Inspector General (1949)
On the Riviera (1951)
Hans Christian Andersen (1952)
Knock on Wood (1954)
White Christmas (1954)
Assignment Children (UNICEF short, 1955)
The Court Jester (1956)
Me and the Colonel (1958)
Merry Andrew (1958)
The Five Pennies (1959)
On the Double (1961)
The Man from the Diners' Club (1963)
The Madwoman of Chaillot (1969)
Pinocchio (TV, 1976)
Peter Pan (TV, 1976)
Skokie (TV, 1981)

Radio

The Danny Kaye Show (1945-46)

TV

The Danny Kaye Show (1963-67)

★★★

Jack Klugman

Oscar Madison and Dr. Quincy

(1922-)

Jack Klugman was born in Philadelphia, Pennsylvania, on April 27, 1922. He studied at the Carnegie Institute of Technology in Pittsburgh and at the American Theater Wing in New York City.

After appearing in several stage works, including *Stevedore* (1949) in New York City and *Mister Roberts* (1950-51) on tour, Klugman made his Broadway debut by playing Frank Bonaparte in a revival of *Golden Boy* (1952). In 1954 he performed onstage in *Coriolanus* and began a regular role in the short-lived TV soap opera *The Greatest Gift*.

His film debut came in *Timetable* (1956). The following year he gave a memorable performance as one of the jurors in the movie *Twelve Angry Men* (1957).

During the late 1950s and early 1960s Klugman continued to perform as a solid character actor in various media. He was in the successful stage musical *Gypsy* (1959) and in several films, including *Cry Terror* (1958) and *Days of Wine and Roses* (1962).

But he soon found his greatest successes on TV, making guest appearances on such series as *Ben Casey, Playhouse Ninety, Studio One, Twilight Zone,* and *The Untouchables*. In 1964 he had a regular role in the comedy series *Harris against the World*.

In 1965 an important event in Klugman's career occured when he succeeded Walter Matthau in the role of Oscar Madison in Neil Simon's hit Broadway comedy *The Odd Couple*. Here, at last, was a vehicle that could raise Klugman to star status.

However, it was not till 1970, after he had worked in several other projects, that stardom finally arrived for him. In that year *The Odd Couple* became a TV series, with Klugman as the sloppy, carefree Oscar Madison comically pitted against his roommate, the neurotic fussbudget Felix Unger (played by Tony Randall). The show ran till 1975 and made Klugman a household name.

Many episodes of *The Odd Couple* featured the actress Brett Somers as Oscar's ex-spouse, Blanche. In real life, Klugman and Somers had married in 1956. They had two children, David and Adam, before divorcing.

After *The Odd Couple* ended its TV run, Klugman appeared in the films *Two Minute Warning* (1976) and *One of My Wives Is Missing* (TV, 1976). At that point he was still firmly set in most people's minds as Oscar Madison.

However, he surprised many observers by effectively overcoming that identification when he created a colorful, well-rounded new character in the TV crime-drama series *Quincy, M.E.* (pilot, 1976; series, 1977-83). As a medical examiner in the Los Angeles coroner's office, Dr. Quincy (Klugman) solves crimes and espouses people-helping causes, many of them directly related to current real-life issues, such as pollution, mental health, and "orphan drugs" (medicines for diseases that are too rare to be economically profitable for drug companies to produce). Klugman reached a new peak in his career with his passionate portrayal of the emotionally involved and professionally committed Dr. Quincy.

Since 1983 Klugman has made TV commercials for

Canon home copiers. In 1984 he starred as Lyndon Johnson in a Los Angeles stage production of the one-man show *Lyndon.* During the 1986-87 season he starred in another TV comedy series, *You Again?,* in which he portrayed a father in conflict with his son.

Selected performances:

Stage

Stevedore (1949)
Saint Joan (1949)
Bury the Dead (1950)
Mister Roberts (1950)
Golden Boy (1952)
Coriolanus (1954)
A Very Special Baby (1956)
Gypsy (1959)
The Odd Couple (1965)
The Sudden and Accidental Re-education of Horse Johnson (1968)
Lyndon (1984)

Films

Timetable (1956)
Twelve Angry Men (1957)
Cry Terror (1958)
Days of Wine and Roses (1962)
Act One (1963)
I Could Go On Singing (1963)
The Yellow Canary (1963)
Fame Is the Name of the Game (TV, 1966)
The Detective (1968)
The Split (1968)
Goodbye, Columbus (1969)
Who Says I Can't Ride a Rainbow! (1971)
Poor Devil (TV, 1973)
The Underground Man (TV, 1974)
One of My Wives Is Missing (TV, 1976)
Two Minute Warning (1976)

TV

The Greatest Gift (1954-55)
Harris against the World (1964)
The Odd Couple (1970-75)
Quincy, M.E. (1977-83)
You Again? (1986-87)

★★

Harvey Korman

Master of Sketch Comedy

(1927-)

Harvey Korman was born in Chicago, Illinois, on February 15, 1927. His parents separated when he was four, and he was raised by his mother alone. "My childhood stunk," he later admitted. "We were poor, and there's the no-father bit."

When he was in seventh grade, he joined an after-school theater workshop, which led to his getting some juvenile roles in industrial films. Later he appeared in school productions at Senn High School.

After attending Wright College of the City Colleges of Chicago and serving in the United States Naval Reserve (1945-46), Korman studied for four years (1946-50) at the Goodman School of Drama in Chicago.

In 1950 he moved to New York City, where he shared an apartment with another aspiring young actor, Tom Bosley. In November of that year Korman had a walk-on role in *The Tower beyond Tragedy,* and the following month he played a small part as an Arab in *Captain Brassbound's Conversion.* But soon he found that further advancement would not come easily.

For the next ten years he held a variety of odd jobs while struggling to make it as an actor. Korman went back to the Midwest and performed in stock productions in Chicago and Milwaukee. He then returned to New York City, where he became so despondent over his lack of success that he contemplated suicide. But psycho-

therapy saved him, and he began to work again in Chicago.

During the 1950s Korman also made many trips to California. On one visit he played the title role in a Santa Monica community-theater production of *Hamlet.* His performance was acclaimed by such notables as Bette Davis and Charles Laughton. "The studios got interested in this brilliant young actor," he later explained. "They came out expecting to find a young, blond Adonis and, instead, found a kind of balding, aging Jew." There followed more odd jobs and more stock work.

In 1960 Korman married Donna Ehlert, a fashion model and charm-school teacher whom he had met on a blind date in Milwaukee. They had two children: a daughter (Maria) and a son (Christopher).

In the early 1960s Korman's career finally got a real boost. Seymour Berns, who had directed him in a Chicago production of *Mr. and Mrs.,* invited Korman to California to appear on the TV variety series *The Red Skelton Show,* which Berns directed. Korman performed on that program several times and also made guest appearances on other TV shows, such as *Dennis the Menace, The Donna Reed Show,* and *Dr. Kildare.*

But then yet another slow period came. His wife went back to work as a model.

In 1963 Korman got his big break. Through Berns he won a job as a regular member of the supporting cast in the new TV variety series *The Danny Kaye Show.* Korman soon proved to be a master of sketch comedy on TV. A brilliant straight man for Danny Kaye, he played a Nazi prison-camp commandant, a Gypsy fiddler, and many other roles.

In 1967 that series ended and Korman went to *The Carol Burnett Show,* where for the next ten years he played character roles as one of TV's preeminent comedy-sketch performers. He often appeared as Carol Burnett's husband. Many of the sketches poked fun at specific Hollywood movies or TV soap operas.

While at the peak of his TV fame, Korman described himself as not a comedian but "an actor doing comedy." "I don't look for gags," he said. "I look for characters."

In 1977 he left *The Carol Burnett Show* and made a pilot for *The Harvey Korman Show.* In 1978 the weekly series began, but it lasted only five months.

Korman began to appear in films in the early 1960s. He made especially good impressions in the satire *Lord Love a Duck* (1966), in the romantic comedy *The April Fools* (1969), and, as the phony king, in the musical *Huckleberry Finn* (1974).

His stock as a film actor rose even higher with his performances in three Mel Brooks comedies. In *Blazing Saddles* (1974) Korman was Hedley Lamarr, an unctuous, land-grabbing lawyer. In *High Anxiety* (1977) he again played a villain, the sadomasochistic psychiatrist Dr. Charles Montague. He also appeared in Brooks's *History of the World, Part I* (1981).

Korman showed great dramatic depth in the biopic *Bud and Lou* (TV, 1978), the story of the unhappy private lives of the comedy team of Bud Abbott and Lou Costello. In the role of Abbott, Korman gave a poignant portrayal of the epileptic, heavy-drinking straight man.

Among his other movies were *The Love Boat* (TV, 1976), *Herbie Goes Bananas* (1980), and *Trail of the Pink Panther* (1982). He starred in *Carpool* (TV, 1983) and played the White King in *Alice in Wonderland* (TV, 1985).

In 1986 he returned to TV in the comedy series *Leo and Liz in Beverly Hills.* He played an upstart trying to fit in among the rich and famous.

Selected performances:

Films

Living Venus (1961)
Gypsy (1962)
The Last of the Secret Agents? (1966)
Lord Love a Duck (1966)
The Man Called Flintstone (1966)
Three Bites of the Apple (1967)
Don't Just Stand There (1968)
The April Fools (1969)
Three's a Crowd (TV, 1969)
Suddenly Single (TV, 1971)
Blazing Saddles (1974)
Huckleberry Finn (1974)
The Love Boat (TV, 1976)
High Anxiety (1977)
Bud and Lou (TV, 1978)
Americathon (1979)
Herbie Goes Bananas (1980)
First Family (1980)
History of the World, Part I (1981)
Trail of the Pink Panther (1982)
The Invisible Woman (TV, 1983)
Carpool (TV, 1983)
Alice in Wonderland (TV, 1985)
The Longshot (1986)

TV

The Danny Kaye Show (1963-67)
The Carol Burnett Show (1967-77)
The Harvey Korman Show (1978)
Leo and Liz in Beverly Hills (1986)

★★

Bert Lahr

Cowardly Lion
(1895-1967)

Bert Lahr was born in New York City, New York, on August 13, 1895. His original name was Irving Lahrheim (though his surname was misspelled on his birth certificate as "Laurheim"). His father was German-born and his mother was of German descent. For the first six years of his life Irving Lahrheim spoke only German.

As a youngster he enjoyed making his friends laugh by clowning around, and he often picked up money by street singing in the Bronx. He discovered the thrill of the stage when he performed in an eighth-grade class show, which was a kid act, that is, a satire of classroom life, often couched in familiar but exaggerated dialects.

But he disliked the regimen of school, and he paid little attention to his studies, though he loved to read on his own. When he was ordered to repeat the eighth grade, he simply dropped out of school at the age of fourteen. For six months he did odd jobs.

Then, in 1910, he began to find work in various professional kid acts. Irving Lahrheim became Bert Lahr.

In 1917 he entered burlesque. Soon thereafter he established a common-law marriage with Mercedes Delpino, a chorus girl whom he had met in 1916 and who now had a job with the same burlesque company that employed Lahr. They had one child: Herbert.

In burlesque Lahr began to carve his individual identity as a "Dutch" (that is, German-dialect) comic out of the block of low-comedy stock humor. He experimented with funny gestures and faces; and he learned how to build humorous situations, as opposed to merely telling unrelated jokes. Much of his humor was based on exaggerated dialect and on malapropisms, as in this passage from a song: "Ouououououououch—how dot voman could cook! . . . Her oyshters and fishes were simply—[in sensuous delight] malicious!"

By the early 1920s burlesque was in trouble because of competition from theater revues and silent films. In 1922 Lahr graduated from burlesque to vaudeville. He was the last of America's great comedians who were nurtured in classic burlesque, the genre later degenerating into a peep show.

In vaudeville he teamed up with his wife, Mercedes, for the comedy sketch *What's the Idea?* Mercedes played a sensual woman, while Lahr was a drunken, ill-dressed, wild-spirited policeman. The line "What's the idea?" played a prominent part in the sketch. And when he took his bows, he yelled at the audience, "What's the idea? What's the ideeeeaa?"

In 1927 Lahr made the step up to Broadway by appearing in the revue *Harry Delmar's Revels*, followed by the musical comedy *Hold Everything* (1928). In 1929 he made his first film: *Faint Heart*.

But while his career was skyrocketing, his relationship with Mercedes was disintegrating. She began to suffer from mental illness, and in 1930 she was committed to an institution.

Lahr's stock soon rose so high that the grand Broadway impresario Florenz Ziegfeld picked him to star in the last Ziegfeld extravaganza, *Hot-Cha!* (1932). After Ziegfeld's death in 1932, his competitor George White developed a close association with the young comedian. In *George White's Music Hall Varieties* (1932) Lahr ventured for the first time into satire, spoofing the English matinee idol Clifton Webb. Other 1930s stage shows featuring Lahr included *Life Begins at 8:40* (1934), *George White's Scandals of 1936* (1935), and *Du Barry Was a Lady* (1939).

Hollywood also beckoned. In 1931 he made a filmed version of *Flying High*, in which he had appeared onstage the previous year.

In the late 1930s he made several motion pictures, notably *The Wizard of Oz* (1939), in which he played the Cowardly Lion. The film's lyricist, E. Y. Harburg, had promoted Lahr for the part because "when the Cowardly Lion admits that he lacks courage, everybody's heart goes out to him. He must be somebody who embodies all this pathos and sweetness, yet puts on this comic bravura. Bert had that quality to such a wonderful degree."

Lahr, as the Cowardly Lion, incongruously and hilariously used New York City colloquial pronunciations (such as *noive* for *nerve*) even though the character was set in the imaginary land of Oz. Absolute gems of comic-song interpretation were Lahr's renditions of "If I Only Had the Nerve" and "If I Were King of the Forest." He gave both humor and humanity to his Cowardly Lion. It was the role by which he remained best known for the rest of his life.

In 1940 Lahr married Mildred Schroeder, whom he had met in 1931 when she was a chorus girl. They had two children: John and Jane. John became a drama critic and wrote the definitive biography of his father: *Notes on a Cowardly Lion* (1969).

In the early 1940s Lahr continued to make films, such as *Ship Ahoy* (1942) and *Meet the People* (1944). The later years of that decade were spent mostly on the stage, as in *Burlesque* (1946) and *Make Mine Manhattan* (1948). In the early 1950s he had roles in the play *Two on the Aisle* (1951) and the movies *Mr. Universe* (1951) and *Rose Marie* (1954).

In the 1950s Lahr also began to appear on TV. He frequently performed his old revue routines on Ed Sullivan's variety show.

In 1956 Lahr played Estragon in Samuel Beckett's complex modernistic play *Waiting for Godot*. Lahr's approach was instinctive and theatrical, not intellectual. He saw the play as "two men trying to amuse themselves on earth by playing jokes and little games." His performance was universally praised.

Waiting for Godot opened a whole new chapter in Lahr's career. He began to appear in other great literary plays, such as televised productions of Shaw's *Androcles and the Lion* (1956) and Molière's *The School for Wives* (1956). In 1957 he starred in Feydeau's classic French farce *Hotel Paradiso*. In 1960 he played Bottom in Shakespeare's *A Midsummer Night's Dream* and, without any knowledge of the Bard's writings or traditions, won the Best Shakespeare Actor of the Year Award. In 1964 he starred in *Foxy*, a musical adaptation of Jonson's *Volpone*. His final work in the classics was as Pisthetairos in Aristophanes' *The Birds* (1966).

Lahr's last performance was for the film *The Night They Raided Minsky's* (1968), fittingly a story about burlesque. He died of cancer (not, as reported at the time, pneumonia) in New York City on December 4, 1967.

Selected performances:

Stage

Harry Delmar's Revels (1927)
Hold Everything (1928)
Flying High (1930)
Hot-Cha! (1932)
George White's Music Hall Varieties (1932)
Life Begins at 8:40 (1934)
George White's Scandals of 1936 (1935)
The Show Is On (1936)
Du Barry Was a Lady (1939)
Seven Lively Arts (1944)
Harvey (1945)
Burlesque (1946)
Make Mine Manhattan (1948)
Two on the Aisle (1951)
Waiting for Godot (1956)
Hotel Paradiso (1957)
Visit to a Small Planet (1957)
The Girls against the Boys (1959)
Romanoff and Juliet (1959)
A Midsummer Night's Dream (1960)
The Beauty Part (1962)
Foxy (1964)
The Birds (1966)

Films

Faint Heart (1929)
Flying High (1931)
Happy Landing (1934)
Merry-Go-Round of 1938 (1937)
Love and Hisses (1938)
Just around the Corner (1938)
Josette (1938)
Zaza (1939)
The Wizard of Oz (1939)
Sing Your Worries Away (1942)
Ship Ahoy (1942)
Meet the People (1944)
Always Leave Them Laughing (1949)
Mr. Universe (1951)
Rose Marie (1954)
The Second Greatest Sex (1956)
Androcles and the Lion (TV, 1956)
The School for Wives (TV, 1956)
The Night They Raided Minsky's (1968)

Martin Landau

Gaunt Character Actor

(1934-)

Martin Landau was born in New York City, New York, on June 20, 1934 (some sources give 1928 or 1933). He studied at the Art Students League and worked for a time as a staff artist and cartoonist with the *New York Daily News*. But his interest in acting took him to the Actors Studio in New York City, where he studied dramatics.

In 1951 he made his stage debut by appearing in *Detective Story* at a theater in Maine. His initial New York City performance soon followed in *First Love* (1951). Later he acted in *Goat Song* (1953), *Middle of the Night* (1957), and other plays before turning to movies in the late 1950s.

Gaunt and dark-featured, Landau soon found himself frequently cast in sinister roles. He developed a solid reputation in such films as *Pork Chop Hill* (1959), *North by Northwest* (1959), *Cleopatra* (1963), and *Nevada Smith* (1966).

But he earned his most lasting fame on the TV espionage-adventure series *Mission: Impossible* (1966-69). He played Rollin Hand, a master of disguise.

Also in *Mission: Impossible* was the actress Barbara Bain, whom he had married in 1957. Their two children are Susan and Juliet.

Landau appeared in the popular film *They Call Me MISTER Tibbs* (1970). In *Welcome Home, Johnny Bristol* (TV, 1972) he starred as a Vietnam veteran returning to an imaginary home in the United States.

He also continued to work on TV. In the science-fiction series *Space: 1999* (1975-77) he starred as Commander John Koenig. Landau's wife, Barbara Bain, was also featured in the show.

His later movies included *Meteor* (1979) and *Without Warning* (1980). In *The Fall of the House of Usher* (TV, 1982) Landau starred as Roderick Usher in Edgar Allan Poe's gothic horror story.

Selected performances:

Stage

Detective Story (1951)
First Love (1951)
The Penguin (1952)
Stalag 17 (1952)
Goat Song (1953)
Middle of the Night (1957)

Films

Pork Chop Hill (1959)
North by Northwest (1959)
The Gazebo (1960)
Stagecoach to Dancers' Rock (1962)
Cleopatra (1963)
The Greatest Story Ever Told (1965)
The Hallelujah Trail (1965)
Nevada Smith (1966)
They Call Me MISTER Tibbs (1970)
A Town Called Hell (1971)
Black Gunn (1972)
Welcome Home, Johnny Bristol (TV, 1972)
Savage (TV, 1973)
Strange Shadows in an Empty Room (1977)
Meteor (1979)
The Last Word (1979)
The Death of Ocean View Park (TV, 1979)
Without Warning (1980)
Alien's Return (1980)
The Harlem Globetrotters on Gilligan's Island (TV, 1981)
Alone in the Dark (1982)
The Fall of the House of Usher (TV, 1982)
The Being (1983)
The Return of the Six-Million-Dollar Man and the Bionic Woman (TV, 1987)

TV

Mission: Impossible (1966-69)
Space: 1999 (1975-77)

★★

Louise Lasser

Mary Hartman

(1939-)

Louise Lasser was born in New York City, New York, on April 11, 1939. She studied political science for three years at Brandeis University, where she also appeared in student musicals. After dropping out of Brandeis, she began to study acting under Sanford Meisner in New York City. She also studied philosophy and literature at the New School for Social Research.

In 1962 she made her Broadway debut, as Barbra Streisand's replacement in the musical comedy *I Can Get It for You Wholesale.* The following year Lasser began a promising career as a nightclub singer in New York City. But club work made her excessively nervous, and she dropped it.

In 1964 she appeared in the off-Broadway improvisational revue *The Third Ear.* Her film debut came with a small part in *What's New, Pussycat?* (1965). The movie was written by Woody Allen, who also had a role in the picture.

Lasser and Allen had met in 1961. In 1966 they married, and in 1970 they divorced. She appeared in several of Allen's film comedies, even after their breakup, including *Take the Money and Run* (1969), *Bananas* (1971), and *Everything You Always Wanted to Know about Sex* (*but Were Afraid to Ask)* (1972).

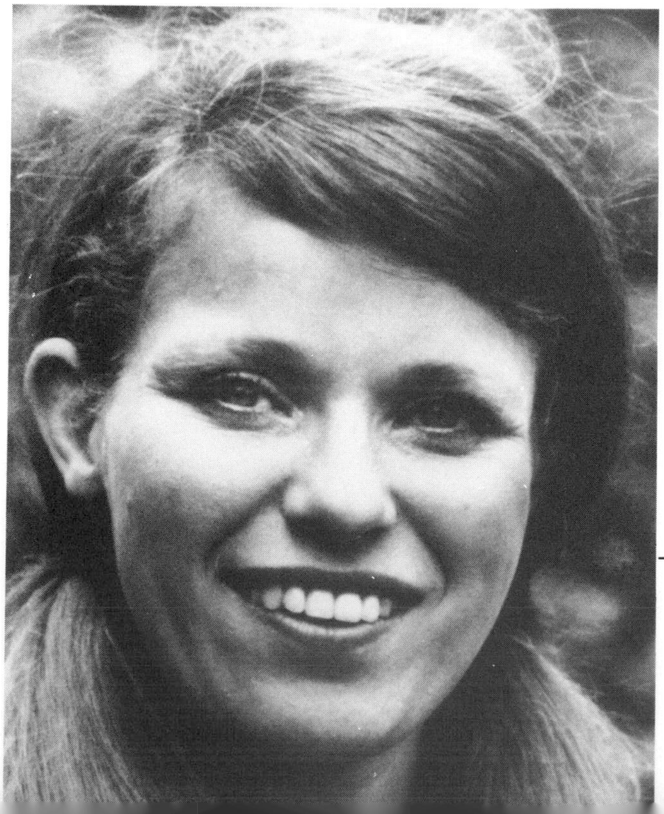

Lasser won her greatest fame for her title role in the TV satirical soap opera *Mary Hartman, Mary Hartman* (1976-77). It was the first serial to deal with such previously taboo subjects as adultery, anti-Semitism, venereal disease, and masturbation. As Mary Hartman, Lasser played a pigtailed, thirtyish, often bewildered housewife trying to face the modern world.

In Marty Feldman's brilliant religious-satire film *In God We Tru$t* (1980) Lasser had the role of a kind-hearted prostitute who helps a monk (played by Feldman) adapt to life in the modern secular city.

She has also appeared in a number of TV movies. Among them were *Just Me and You* (TV, 1978) and *For Ladies Only* (TV, 1981). In the theatrical release *Crimewave* (1985) she portrayed a woman being pursued by killers.

Selected performances:

Stage

I Can Get It for You Wholesale (1962)
The Third Ear (1964)
Henry, Sweet Henry (1967)
Lime Green (1969)
The Chinese (1970)
Marie and Bruce (1980)

Films

What's New, Pussycat? (1965)
Take the Money and Run (1969)
Bananas (1971)
Such Good Friends (1971)
Everything You Always Wanted to Know about Sex (*but Were Afraid to Ask)* (1972)
Slither (1973)
Coffee, Tea, or Me? (TV, 1973)
Isn't It Shocking? (TV, 1973)
Just Me and You (TV, 1978)
Stardust Memories (1980)
In God We Tru$t (1980)
For Ladies Only (TV, 1981)
Crimewave (1985)

TV

Mary Hartman, Mary Hartman (1976-77)

★★★

Sam Levene

Sour-faced Character Actor

(1905-1980)

Sam Levene was born in Russia on August 28, 1905. His original name was Samuel Levine; early in his show-business career he changed the *i* to an *e* in his surname because another actor named Sam Levine was already active at the time.

Brought to the United States when he was two years old, he grew up in New York City. After graduating from Stuyvesant High School in 1923, he went to work in his older brother's dressmaking business.

In 1925, to further his career as a salesman, he attempted to rid himself of his Yiddish accent by enrolling in diction classes at the American Academy of Dramatic Arts. But soon he became a full-time student at the academy, from which he graduated in 1927.

Also in 1927 he made his Broadway debut, in *Wall Street*. For the next eight years he worked steadily on the stage, but his first major recognition came with his role as Patsy, a racing addict, in *Three Men on a Horse* (1935). His movie debut came in a filmed version (1936) of the same story.

Over the next forty-five years Levene stood out as one of the most dependable, respected, and beloved character actors in America. His bushy eyebrows, thick mustache, sour face, and pronounced New York City accent (despite his diction lessons) became familiar to millions through his stage and film appearances.

Among his major theatrical successes were his roles as Gordon Miller, a shoestring producer desperately trying to keep his troupe together, in *Room Service* (1937); Officer Finkelstein, a Jewish policeman who must find the murderer of a Nazi diplomat, in *Margin for Error* (1939); and Sidney Black, an aggressive producer, in *Light Up the Sky* (1948). The role by which he became best known was that of the cocky Nathan Detroit in the Damon Runyon story *Guys and Dolls* (1950). In *Fair Game* (1957), *Make a Million* (1960), and *Paris Is Out!* (1970), Levene literally carried the shows through his great comic sense even though his parts were stereotyped Jewish characters. One of the real plums in his career was the role of Al Lewis, an ex-vaudevillian, in the original Broadway production of Neil Simon's comedy *The Sunshine Boys* (1972). On a deeper level he had important roles in *Heartbreak House* (1959) and *The Royal Family* (1975).

On the screen, too, he kept busy. Among his early films were *After the Thin Man* (1936), *The Shopworn Angel* (1938), and *Golden Boy* (1939). During World War II he appeared in *Action in the North Atlantic* (1943) and *The Purple Heart* (1944). In *The Killers* (1946) he played a detective, in *Boomerang* (1947) a reporter, and in *Brute Force* (1947) a prison inmate. He gave one of his most affecting performances as the gentle Jewish murder victim in *Crossfire* (1947), one of the earliest movies to attack racial intolerance. His later films included *The Babe Ruth Story* (1948), *Sweet Smell of Success* (1957), *Act One* (1963), and *. . . and Justice for All* (1979).

Levene married Constance Hoffmann in 1953. They had one son, Joseph, before divorcing.

In 1980 Levene had his final role, as Samuel Horowitz in *Horowitz and Mrs. Washington*. He performed the part on Broadway and then in Toronto. In December of that year he returned home to New York City. The last time he was seen alive was on Christmas Day. He died sometime between then and December 28, when his body was discovered by his son.

Selected performances:

Stage

Wall Street (1927)
Jarnegan (1928)
Tin Pan Alley (1928)
Solitaire (1929)
Street Scene (1929)
Headquarters (1929)
This Man's Town (1930)
The Up and Up (1930)
Three Times the Hour (1931)
Wonder Boy (1931)
Dinner at Eight (1932)
Yellow Jack (1934)
The Milky Way (1934)
Spring Song (1934)
Three Men on a Horse (1935)
Room Service (1937)
Margin for Error (1939)
A Sound of Hunting (1945)
Light Up the Sky (1948)
Guys and Dolls (1950)
The Matchmaker (1954)

Sam Levene

The Hot Corner (1956)
Fair Game (1957)
Middle of the Night (1958)
Heartbreak House (1959)
The Good Soup (1960)
Make a Million (1960)
Devil's Advocate (1961)
Let It Ride (1961)
Seidman and Son (1962)
Café Crown (1964)
The Last Analysis (1964)
Fidelio (1965)
The Impossible Years (1966)
Don't Drink the Water (1968)
Three Men on a Horse (1969)
Paris Is Out! (1970)
Light Up the Sky (1970)
A Dream out of Time (1970)
Light Up the Sky (1971)
Paris Is Out! (1971)
The Sunshine Boys (1972)
Dreyfus in Rehearsal (1974)
Light Up the Sky (1975)
Sabrina Fair (1975)
The Royal Family (1975)
The Prince of Grand Street (1978)
Goodnight Grandpa (1978)
Horowitz and Mrs. Washington (1980)

Films

Three Men on a Horse (1936)
After the Thin Man (1936)
Yellow Jack (1938)
The Shopworn Angel (1938)
The Mad Miss Manton (1938)
Golden Boy (1939)
Married Bachelor (1941)
Shadow of the Thin Man (1941)
Sunday Punch (1942)
Sing Your Worries Away (1942)
Grand Central Murder (1942)
The Big Street (1942)
Destination Unknown (1942)
Action in the North Atlantic (1943)
I Dood It (1943)
Gung Ho! (1944)
The Purple Heart (1944)
Whistling in Brooklyn (1944)
The Killers (1946)
Boomerang (1947)
Brute Force (1947)
Crossfire (1947)
Killer McCoy (1948)
The Babe Ruth Story (1948)
Guilty Bystander (1950)
With These Hands (1950)
Dial 1119 (1950)
Three Sailors and a Girl (1953)
The Opposite Sex (1956)
Designing Woman (1957)
Sweet Smell of Success (1957)
Slaughter on Tenth Avenue (1957)
Kathy O' (1958)
Act One (1963)
A Dream of Kings (1969)
Last Embrace (1979)
. . . and Justice for All (1979)

★★★

Jerry Lewis

Great Clown

(1926-)

Jerry Lewis was born in Newark, New Jersey, on March 16, 1926. His original name was Joseph Levitch. He came from a show-business family: his father, Daniel Levitch, worked under the name Danny Lewis as one of the last vaudevillians, while Rachel Levitch (née Brodsky) was a pianist.

Young Levitch began experimenting with musical-comedy routines at an early age. When he was fifteen he was expelled from Irvington (New Jersey) High School for punching the principal, who had made an anti-Semitic remark. He was transferred to Irvington Vocational High School, but on his sixteenth birthday he quit school forever and entered show business full time.

He billed himself as Jerry Lewis, taking his father's professional surname and adopting the first name Jerry because he wanted to avoid confusion with comedian Joe E. Lewis and boxer Joe Louis. Soon Jerry Lewis was doing well with a solo act at theaters in Baltimore, Philadelphia, Boston, and elsewhere.

In 1944 he married Patti Palmer (real name, Esther Calonico), a singer whom he had met while both were working at a theater in Detroit. They had six sons: Gary, Ronnie, Scott, Chris, Anthony, and Joseph. Gary became a popular vocalist, led his own band, and appeared a number of times with his father in movies and on TV.

After his marriage Lewis's career went through two years at low ebb. He played on the borscht circuit, in theaters, and in nightclubs—but nothing big and nothing steady.

Then, in 1946 in New York City, he was introduced to the singer Dean Martin by their mutual friend Sonny King, also a singer. Martin and Lewis soon formed a nightclub act. Martin's real name was Paul Dino Crocetti; and privately Lewis always called him Paul, while Martin referred to Lewis as pallie, Jew, or pardner.

The crooning Dean Martin and clowning Jerry Lewis played off each other beautifully. The team quickly became the hottest act in show business, and in 1948 they hit the big time with their appearance at the Copacabana nightclub in New York City.

Also in 1948 they increased their fans enormously when they got in on the ground floor of the new medium of television, appearing on the first show of Ed Sullivan's *Toast of the Town* and on Milton Berle's *The Texaco Star Theater*. From 1949 to 1952 they hosted their own radio show, and from 1950 to 1955 they hosted their own TV show as part of *The Colgate Comedy Hour* series.

But their greatest fame came through films, beginning with *My Friend Irma* (1949). There followed a string of popular movies, including *At War with the Army* (1951), *Sailor Beware* (1952), *The Caddy* (1953), *Three Ring Circus* (1954), *You're Never Too Young* (1955), and, their final picture together, *Hollywood or Bust* (1956).

In 1956, after at least two years of increasing tension

Jerry Lewis

between Martin and Lewis, they split up. The most serious problems between them began when Martin exploded at being relegated to a clearly secondary role in *Three Ring Circus*. Even before then, Martin's contribution to the team's success was largely overlooked by filmmakers, critics, and fans (though not by Lewis). He finally rebelled, stated that he was tired of playing the stooge, and began to psychologically isolate himself from Lewis. The latter, emotionally drained by his efforts to renew the original chemistry between Martin and himself, initiated the formal and legal dissolution of their partnership. Their last performance together was at the Copacabana on July 25, 1956.

Lewis's first film on his own was *The Delicate Delinquent* (1957). Playing the title role, he created one of his most memorable screen moments when, pretending to be a hoodlum, he feigned a knife attack on a woman social worker, warning her that he was "slippin', Baby."

In the title role of *The Bellboy* (1960) he did not speak till the final seconds. It was one of his finest performances, his brilliant slapstick skill equaling that of the masters of silent-film comedy.

The Nutty Professor (1963) was a departure for Lewis. He played the title role without his usual idiot-kid image. The story was a comedy version of *Dr. Jekyll and Mr. Hyde*. The lovable Jekyll-like professor contrasted with the hateful Hyde-like Buddy Love.

The Family Jewels (1965) provided Lewis with a vehicle for a tour-de-force performance. He played seven roles: Willard, the chauffeur; Uncle James, the old ferryboat captain; Uncle Everett, the circus clown; Uncle Eddie, the airline pilot; Uncle Julius, the fashion photographer; Uncle Skylock, the private investigator; and Uncle Bugs, the gangster. Julius was a spinoff of the nutty professor, while the gap-toothed, cheerful, and optimistic—but wholly incompetent—Eddie has to rank as one of Lewis's most inspired creations.

In his post-Martin films, Lewis has often served as producer, director, or writer in addition to star. Examples include *The Delicate Delinquent* (producer), *The Bellboy* (producer, director, writer), *The Ladies' Man* (misspelled without the apostrophe in the film, 1961; producer, director, writer), *The Errand Boy* (1961; director, writer), *The Family Jewels* (producer, director), *The Big Mouth* (1967; producer, director, writer), and *Which Way to the Front?* (1970; producer, director).

In the early 1970s Lewis made *The Day the Clown Cried,* set in Germany during the Nazi era. He played the part of Helmut, once a great clown but now wasted by drinking that was brought on by his abhorrence of the Nazi regime. Helmut is arrested by the Gestapo, interned in a concentration camp, and forced into clowning to help control Jewish children being marched to the ovens. The film remains unreleased, locked up in Stockholm, where it was made, because of ongoing litigation about lack of payments from the producer, Nathan Wachsberger.

After making *The Day the Clown Cried,* Lewis appeared in no more films during the 1970s. In his autobiography, *Jerry Lewis in Person* (with Herb Gluck, 1982), he explained his action. Filmgoers were "crying out for happy entertainment," he wrote, but filmmakers were providing works "tainted by the grime of 'realism' and magnified on celluloid." The industry "was eroding under a heavy flood of X-rated films." Fed up, Lewis stayed away from the screen for a number of years.

During the 1970s he was busy with other projects, notably his volunteer work as national chairman of the Muscular Dystrophy Association (MDA). He had become formally involved with battling the disease in 1950, when he banded together with others to help raise funds to create a muscular dystrophy facility that opened at Columbia University in 1959. In 1966 he gave his first annual *Jerry Lewis Labor Day Telethon* in behalf of MDA. The first two telethons were broadcast in the New York City area only, but since 1968 the show has been networked to many other parts of the country.

Lewis returned to films by writing, directing, and starring in *Hardly Working* (1981). In it he played a circus clown who loses his job and tries various other lines of work, bungling them all. He also cowrote, directed, and starred in *Cracking Up* (1983, originally released as *Smorgasbord*), about a misfit recalling his failures.

In *The King of Comedy* (1983) Lewis played his first straight dramatic role, as a TV talk-show host kidnapped by a deranged would-be comedian. Later he starred in the comedy *Slapstick of Another Kind* (1984). In the fact-based drama *Fight for Life* (TV, 1987) he portrayed Dr. Bernard Abrams, an optometrist who fights to get permission to use a special drug for his daughter's myoclonic epilepsy and then fights to make the drug available to other children as well.

In 1982 Lewis divorced his wife, Patti. In December of that year he suffered a serious heart attack, actually being clinically dead for several seconds. Emergency double-bypass surgery was performed, and he recovered well. In 1983 he married the dancer Sandra ("Sam") Pitnick, whom he had met when he hired her for a part in *Hardly Working*.

Lewis, more than any other comedian of his time, has generated a wide range of opinions about his abilities. Many American critics relegate his "mugging" to the low end of the comic pole, whereas many European critics rank his "clowning antics" as comparable to the genius of the great Charles Chaplin. Some commentators deplore his "sentimentality," yet others see his efforts as reflections of a genuine "social awareness" and concern for the "little guy." Perhaps, as usual in such cases, the truth about the totality of his work lies between the extreme views of his unyielding disparagers and his fanatic followers. However, millions of ordinary viewers around the globe will testify that few other comedians have provided so many hours of uncontrollable belly laughs for so many

Jerry Lewis

years. For that reason alone, completely regardless of whether his work is analyzed as low comedy or high comedy, or sentimental or profound, Lewis deserves to be ranked as one of the greatest clowns and one of the funniest men in film history.

Selected performances:

Films

My Friend Irma (1949)
At War with the Army (1951)
That's My Boy (1951)
Sailor Beware (1952)
Jumping Jacks (1952)
The Stooge (1953)
Scared Stiff (1953)
The Caddy (1953)
Money from Home (1954)
Living It Up (1954)
Three Ring Circus (1954)
You're Never Too Young (1955)
Artists and Models (1955)
Pardners (1956)
Hollywood or Bust (1956)
The Delicate Delinquent (1957)
The Sad Sack (1957)
Rock-a-bye Baby (1958)
The Geisha Boy (1958)
Don't Give Up the Ship (1959)
Visit to a Small Planet (1960)
The Bellboy (1960)
Cinderfella (1960)
The Ladies' Man (1961)
The Errand Boy (1961)
It's Only Money (1962)
The Nutty Professor (1963)
It's a Mad, Mad, Mad, Mad World (1963)
Who's Minding the Store? (1963)
The Patsy (1964)
The Disorderly Orderly (1964)
The Family Jewels (1965)
Boeing Boeing (1965)
Three on a Couch (1966)
Way . . . Way Out (1966)
The Big Mouth (1967)
Don't Raise the Bridge, Lower the River (1968)
Hook, Line, and Sinker (1969)
Which Way to the Front? (1970)
Hardly Working (1981)
Cracking Up (1983, originally released as *Smorgasbord*)
The King of Comedy (1983)
Slapstick of Another Kind (1984)
Retenez-moi ou je fais un malheur (1984, Fr.; English title, *To Catch a Cop*)
Fight for Life (TV, 1987)

Radio

The Martin and Lewis Show (1949-52)

TV

The Dean Martin, Jerry Lewis Show (1950-55, part of *The Colgate Comedy Hour*)
The Jerry Lewis Show (1963, 1967-69)
Will the Real Jerry Lewis Please Sit Down (animated, 1970-72)

★★

Hal Linden

Barney Miller

(1931-)

Hal Linden was born in New York City, New York, on March 20, 1931. His original name was Harold Lipshitz.

He graduated from the High School of Music and Art in New York City (1948), attended Queens College of the City University of New York (1948-50), and graduated with a B.B.A. degree from City College of the City University of New York (1952).

After his college graduation he spent two years in the army (1952-54). There he performed in revues for the special-services division.

Early in his career he was a saxophonist and singer. He performed in the bands of Sammy Kaye, Bobby Sherwood, and Boyd Raeburn.

Linden studied voice in New York City with Lou McCollogh during 1953-56 and John Mace during 1958-64. From 1954 to 1955 Linden studied acting in New York City at the American Theater Wing. In the same city, he studied acting with Paul Mann during 1956-60 and Lloyd Richards during 1962-63.

Linden's stage debut came when he appeared as a member of the chorus in a stock-company production of *Wonderful Town* in Hyannis, Massachusetts, in 1955. His first New York City stage performance came as understudy to Sydney Chaplin (son of Charles Chaplin) as Jeff Moss in *Bells Are Ringing* in 1956; Linden succeeded Chaplin in the lead in 1958. In the filmed version of *Bells Are Ringing* (1960) Linden had a minor role, as the Nightclub Singer performing "The Midas Touch."

During the next dozen years he worked regularly on the stage throughout the United States, particularly in musicals. Among them were *Wish You Were Here* (Massachusetts, 1961), about life at a Jewish summer camp, *The Pajama Game* (New Jersey, 1963), and *The Education of H*Y*M*A*N K*A*P*L*A*N* (New York City, 1968), about the efforts of Jewish immigrants to make themselves at home in America. The culmination of Linden's stage work was his highly praised performance as Meyer Rothschild in the original Broadway production of the musical *The Rothschilds* (1970).

He later appeared as a straight actor in a number of movies, both dramas and comedies. In *Mr. Inside/Mr. Outside* (TV, 1973), for example, Linden played a police detective. He also acted in the farce *How to Break Up a Happy Divorce* (TV, 1976); the disaster picture *Starflight: The Plane That Couldn't Land* (TV, 1983); and the biopic *My Wicked, Wicked Ways: The Legend of Errol Flynn* (TV, 1985), in which he played the film magnate Jack L. Warner.

Early in his career he made some guest appearances on TV series, such as *The Jim Gibbons Show* of Washington, D.C., in 1953 and the nationally telecast *Car 54, Where Are You?* in 1963.

Linden's greatest fame came through his title role in the TV comedy series *Barney Miller* (1975-82). As Captain Miller, chief of detectives at a New York City police precinct, Linden created a strong but compassionate and humanitarian character.

In early 1986 he starred in the TV series *Blacke's Magic*. He played a retired magician who uses his knowledge of magic to solve baffling crimes.

Linden married the actress Frances Martin in 1958. They had four children: Amelia, Jennifer, Nora, and Ian.

Selected performances:

Stage

Wonderful Town (1955)
Strip for Action (1956)
Bells Are Ringing (1958)
Angel in the Pawnshop (1960)
Wildcat (1960)
Wish You Were Here (1961)
Anything Goes (1962)
The Pajama Game (1963)
The Sign in Sidney Brustein's Window (1964)
Something More! (1964)
Remains to Be Seen (1966)
The Boys from Syracuse (1966)
The Apple Tree (1966)
Illya, Darling (1967)
*The Education of H*Y*M*A*N K*A*P*L*A*N* (1968)
The Love Match (1968)
Three Men on a Horse (1969)
The Rothschilds (1970)
Room Service (1983)
I'm Not Rappaport (1986)

Films

Bells Are Ringing (1960)
Mr. Inside/Mr. Outside (TV, 1973)
The Love Boat (TV, 1976)
How to Break Up a Happy Divorce (TV, 1976)
When You Comin' Back, Red Ryder? (1979)
Father Figure (TV, 1980)
Starflight: The Plane That Couldn't Land (TV, 1983)
The Other Woman (TV, 1983)
My Wicked, Wicked Ways: The Legend of Errol Flynn (TV, 1985)

TV

Barney Miller (1975-82)
Blacke's Magic (1986)

★★★

Herbert Lom

Chief Inspector Dreyfus

(1917-)

Herbert Lom was born in Prague, Bohemia (now in Czechoslovakia), on September 11, 1917. His original name was Herbert Charles Angelo Kuchacevich ze Schluderpachern.

He began his stage career in Prague. Moving to England in 1939, Lom studied acting at the Vic-Wells School. From 1940 to 1946 he worked on radio for the European Service of the British Broadcasting Corporation (BBC). He also acted in touring and repertory companies.

Lom made his film debut by portraying Adolf Hitler in *Mein Kampf* (1940). For many years thereafter he was frequently cast as a heavy, aided by his dark hair and eyes and by his sinister use of a Charles Boyer-like Continental accent and manner. Lom played Napoleon

in *The Young Mr. Pitt* (1942) and in *War and Peace* (1956). Among his other parts were those as a Balkan crook in *State Secret* (1950), an impulsive gangster in *The Ladykillers* (1956), and the title role in *The Phantom of the Opera* (1962).

However, Lom was always capable of a wide range of roles. In *The Seventh Veil* (1945), for example, he played a psychiatrist sympathetically treating a woman concert pianist. He later played a similar role in the TV series *The Human Jungle* (1964). Onstage he appeared in London's West End as the King in the musical *The King and I* (1953).

In the 1960s Lom effectively pulled away from being typecast in sinister parts. The single most important step in that direction was his role in the Pink Panther series of comedy films, as the neurotic French policeman Chief Inspector Dreyfus, who is plagued by his subordinate Inspector Clouseau (played by Peter Sellers). Lom played the part in *A Shot in the Dark* (1964), *The Return of the Pink Panther* (1975), *The Pink Panther Strikes Again* (1976), *Revenge of the Pink Panther* (1978), *Trail of the Pink Panther* (1982), and *Curse of the Pink Panther* (1983).

Though he is now best known as Chief Inspector Dreyfus, Lom has continued to appear in films outside the Pink Panther series, such as *And Then There Were None* (1975) and *King Solomon's Mines* (1985).

Selected performances:

Stage

The Seventh Veil (1951)
The Trap (1952)
The King and I (1953)

Films

Mein Kampf (1940)
The Young Mr. Pitt (1942)
The Dark Tower (1943)
The Seventh Veil (1945)
Appointment with Crime (1946)
Night Boat to Dublin (1946)
Dual Alibi (1947)
Good Time Girl (1948)
Night and the City (1950)
The Black Rose (1950)
State Secret (1950)
The Ladykillers (1956)
War and Peace (1956)
I Accuse! (1958)
Chase a Crooked Shadow (1958)
The Roots of Heaven (1958)
I Aim at the Stars (1960)
El Cid (1961)
Mysterious Island (1961)
The Frightened City (1962)
I Like Money (1962)
The Phantom of the Opera (1962)
Tiara Tahiti (1963)
No Tree in the City (1964)
A Shot in the Dark (1964)
Return from the Ashes (1965)
Treasure of Silver Lake (1965)
Bang! Bang! You're Dead! (1966)
Gambit (1966)
Eve (1968)
Villa Rides (1968)
Assignment to Kill (1969)
Journey to the Far Side of the Sun (1969)
Ninety-nine Women (1969)
Uncle Tom's Cabin (1969)
Mister Jerico (TV, 1970)
Asylum (1972)
And Now the Screaming Starts (1973)
And Then There Were None (1975)
The Return of the Pink Panther (1975)
The Pink Panther Strikes Again (1976)
Revenge of the Pink Panther (1978)
The Lady Vanishes (1979)
Peter and Paul (TV, 1981)
Trail of the Pink Panther (1982)
Curse of the Pink Panther (1983)
The Dead Zone (1983)
Memed My Hawk (1984)
Lace (TV, 1984)
King Solomon's Mines (1985)

TV

The Human Jungle (1964)

★★★

Peter Lorre

Neurotic Villain

(1904-1964)

Peter Lorre was born in Rózsahegy (in German, Rosenberg), Hungary (now Ružomberok, Czechoslovakia), on June 26, 1904. His original name was Ladislav Loewenstein (sometimes given as Laszlo Löwenstein).

After moving several times, his family settled in Vienna, Austria. There, in his teens, he changed his name to Peter Lorre and began to appear in plays. In 1924 he went to Breslau and later spent some time in Zurich before returning to Vienna in 1925. For the next three years he labored in obscurity but learned his craft well.

He finally began to receive some recognition when he gave a number of outstanding performances in Berlin, beginning with his role as the village idiot in *Pioniere in Ingolstadt* ("Engineers in Ingolstadt," 1929). In *Dantons Tod* ("Danton's Death," 1929) he portrayed a sadistic "philosopher of terror." In *Frühlings Erwachen* ("Spring's Awakening," 1929) he played a fourteen-year-old boy who, confused by moral conflicts arising from the pangs of puberty, commits suicide.

Soon after his Berlin debut, Lorre began to live with the well-known German actress Cäcilie Lvovsky (who later simplified her name to Celia Lovsky). She introduced him to the great film director Fritz Lang, who cast him in the lead of the movie *M* (1931), a story about a child murderer. Lorre brilliantly caught the weakness, desperation, and self-loathing of the compulsive killer. His sudden shifts from whining and groveling to indignation were to characterize many of his later parts as well.

M brought Lorre worldwide renown, but he initially refused offers from Hollywood. He was afraid that the commercially oriented American filmmakers would typecast him forever as a middle-aged villain. Lorre struggled, at least in his younger years, to force producers to give him a variety of challenging roles. "Acting," he once said, "if money is its only object, is childish and undignified work. There must be some higher motive."

After the release of *M,* Lorre continued to play in German-language films till 1933. That year the Nazis rose to power in Germany, from which he fled to Austria, then to France, and then, in 1934, to England.

Though his English was as yet poor, he soon acted in the British film *The Man Who Knew Too Much* (1934), directed by Alfred Hitchcock. Lorre played one of a band of spies who kidnap a young girl and attempt a political assassination. He gave his character a sad, desperate quality that made his performance stand out from the usual way of playing such roles. While in England he married Celia Lovsky.

In July 1934 Lorre moved to the United States when Harry Cohn of Columbia Pictures promised him some artistic freedom. After several months, however, no suitable Columbia material had appeared, and Lorre was lent to Metro-Goldwyn-Mayer (MGM) for *Mad Love* (1935). He played a brilliant but sexually unfulfilled plastic surgeon who derives pleasure from watching the onstage torture of an actress in a Grand Guignol production. Lorre, who had shaved his head for the part, made the character extremely repulsive yet gave him some humanity and pathos.

He had accepted the lead in *Mad Love* with the condition that Cohn would give him the role of Raskolnikov, another brilliant but disturbed person, in a filmed version of Dostoevski's novel *Crime and Punishment*. Lorre was happy to have the chance to appear in such a serious work, but the film, released in 1935, was only moderately successful.

The actor's hair had partially grown back by then, and he had become thin. He kept his weight low for the next two decades.

In 1936 he returned briefly to England to appear in Hitchcock's *Secret Agent*. He then came back to America and from 1937 to 1939 starred as the Japanese detective Mr. Moto in a series of movies. In his career Lorre played many different nationalities, including Arab, French, German, Hungarian, Mexican, and Russian.

In 1941 he portrayed a strange gentleman crook in *The Maltese Falcon*. A similar part was played by Sidney Greenstreet. Audiences enjoyed the contrast and interplay between the two villains—Lorre small and quiet, Greenstreet large and loud—and they appeared together again in *Casablanca* (1943), *Passage to Marseille* (1944), *The Mask of Dimitrios* (1944), *Three Strangers* (1946), and *The Verdict* (1946).

Lorre also entered the realm of the horror film. He appeared with Boris Karloff and Bela Lugosi in *You'll*

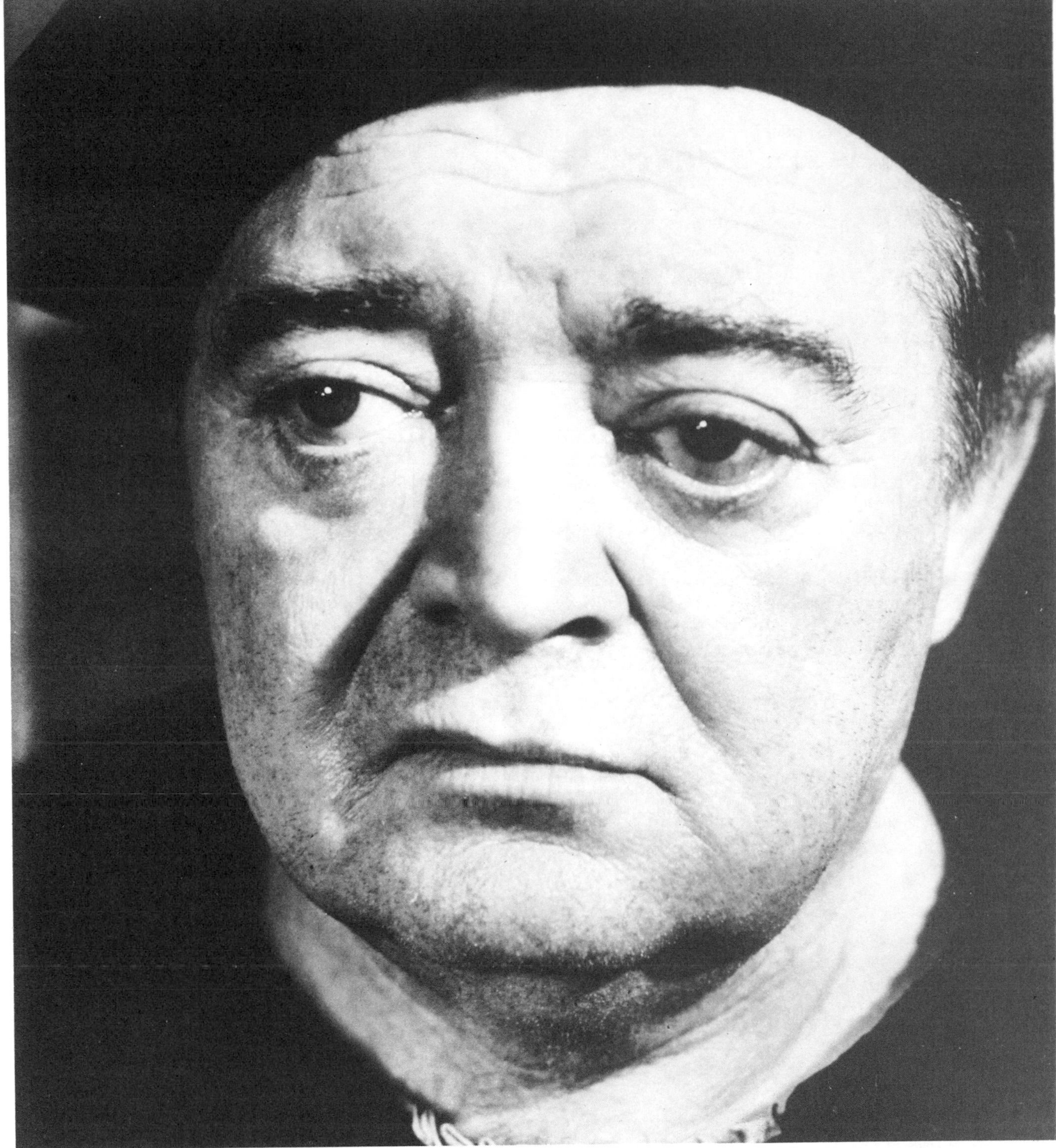

Find Out (1940) and starred in *The Face behind the Mask* (1941), in which he again displayed his gift for pathos. Later he returned to the genre in *The Beast with Five Fingers* (1946).

In 1945 Lorre divorced his first wife and married Kaaren Verne, a former actress. They broke up only a few years later.

In 1950 he met Annemarie Brenning (or Stoldt) when both were staying at a sanatorium. She soon became his secretary, and in 1953 they married. They had one child: Catherine.

Unhappy with his career in Hollywood, Lorre went to Germany, where he wrote, directed, and starred in the film *Der Verlorene* ("The Lost One," 1951). Ironically, though he had grown weary of being typecast as a neurotic killer, he decided to portray a homicidal Nazi scientist in this unsuccessful movie.

At about that point in his life he began to suffer from

high blood pressure and obesity. His facial expression seemed to portray a perpetual comical melancholy.

In 1952 Lorre returned to America. His career was now quickly fading. He played minor parts in *Twenty Thousand Leagues under the Sea* (1954), *Silk Stockings* (1957), *Voyage to the Bottom of the Sea* (1961), and other comedies and adventures. He played a caricature of his earlier serious roles in the comic-horror movies *Tales of Terror* (1962), *The Raven* (1963), and *The Comedy of Terrors* (1964).

Lorre was a unique talent in the history of films. He was capable of depicting the most evil of villains, yet he also had a genuine flair for comedy, as he displayed, for example, in *Arsenic and Old Lace* (1944). He could turn his mild manner, short stature (5′5″), large eyes, and soft nasal voice into a slithery sinister monster; yet he could also be cute and lovable. His distinct mannerisms made him one of the most widely copied subjects by comic impressionists.

In the early 1960s Lorre separated from his third wife. He died in Los Angeles, California, on March 23, 1964.

Selected performances:

Stage

Pioniere in Ingolstadt (1929)
Happy End (1929)
Dantons Tod (1929)
Frühlings Erwachen (1929)
Die Quadratur des Kreises ("Squaring the Circle," 1930)
Mann Ist Mann ("Man Is Man," 1931)
Geschichten aus dem Wiener Wald ("Tales from the Vienna Woods," 1931)

Films

M (1931)
Bomben auf Monte Carlo ("The Bombardment of Monte Carlo," 1931)
Die Koffer des Herrn O.F. ("The Trunks of Mr. O.F.," 1931)
Fünf von der Jazzband ("The Jazzband Five," 1932)
Schuss im Morgengrauen ("A Shot at Dawn," 1932)
F.P. 1 Antwortet Nicht ("F.P. 1 Doesn't Answer," 1932)
Der Weisse Dämon ("The White Demon," 1932)
Was Frauen Träumen ("What Women Dream," 1933)
Unsichtbare Gegner ("Invisible Opponent," 1933)
Der Haut en Bas ("From Top to Bottom," 1933)
The Man Who Knew Too Much (1934)
Mad Love (1935)
Crime and Punishment (1935)
Secret Agent (1936)
Crack-up (1937)
Nancy Steele Is Missing (1937)
Think Fast, Mr. Moto (1937)
Lancer Spy (1937)
Thank You, Mr. Moto (1937)
Mr. Moto's Gamble (1938)
Mr. Moto Takes a Chance (1938)
I'll Give a Million (1938)
Mysterious Mr. Moto (1938)
Mr. Moto's Last Warning (1939)
Danger Island (1939)
Mr. Moto Takes a Vacation (1939)
Strange Cargo (1940)
I Was an Adventuress (1940)
Island of Doomed Men (1940)
Stranger on the Third Floor (1940)
You'll Find Out (1940)
The Face behind the Mask (1941)
Mr. District Attorney (1941)
They Met in Bombay (1941)
The Maltese Falcon (1941)
All through the Night (1942)
Invisible Agent (1942)
The Boogie Man Will Get You (1942)
Casablanca (1943)
Background to Danger (1943)
The Constant Nymph (1943)
The Cross of Lorraine (1943)
Passage to Marseille (1944)
The Mask of Dimitrios (1944)
Arsenic and Old Lace (1944)
The Conspirators (1944)
Hollywood Canteen (1944)
Hotel Berlin (1945)
Confidential Agent (1945)
Three Strangers (1946)
Black Angel (1946)
The Chase (1946)
The Verdict (1946)
The Beast with Five Fingers (1946)
My Favorite Brunette (1947)
Casbah (1948)
Rope of Sand (1949)
Quicksand (1950)
Double Confession (1950)
Der Verlorene (1951)
Beat the Devil (1954)
Twenty Thousand Leagues under the Sea (1954)
Meet Me in Las Vegas (1956)
Congo Crossing (1956)
Around the World in Eighty Days (1956)
The Buster Keaton Story (1957)
Silk Stockings (1957)
The Story of Mankind (1957)
Hell Ship Mutiny (1957)
The Sad Sack (1957)
The Big Circus (1959)
Scent of Mystery (1960)
Voyage to the Bottom of the Sea (1961)
Tales of Terror (1962)
Five Weeks in a Balloon (1962)
The Raven (1963)
The Comedy of Terrors (1964)
Muscle Beach Party (1964)
The Patsy (1964)

Radio

Mystery in the Air (1947)
Nightmare (1953)

★★★

Paul Lukas

Suave Hungarian Leading Man

(1895-1971)

Paul Lukas was born on a railway train as it was pulling into Budapest, Hungary, on May 26, 1895. His original name was Pal Lukacs.

After attending the Hungarian equivalent of high school, he served during World War I in the Austro-Hungarian army (1913-15). He was wounded in action against the Russians in 1915.

Released from the army, Lukas studied briefly at the Royal Academy of Acting in Budapest (1915). He then began his professional acting career by working for two years (1916-18) at the opera house in the little Hungarian town of Kassa. There he sang in opera and operetta choruses and performed in plays, working his way up from small roles to such parts as Shakespeare's Shylock (in *The Merchant of Venice*) and Othello (in *Othello*). He then spent nine years (1918-27) at Budapest's Comedy Theater, where he played more than sixty different roles by a wide variety of playwrights, including Chekhov.

In 1927 the American film producers Jesse Lasky and Adolph Zukor saw Lukas on the Budapest stage and signed him to make American movies. He had already appeared in numerous European silent films; and when he moved to the United States, it was with the intention of making more silent pictures. However, soon after his arrival in Hollywood, silents were replaced by sound movies. Lukas, of course, spoke with an accent, but he quickly mastered English well enough to continue in American films. In Hollywood, studio executives convinced him to Americanize his name from Pal Lukacs to Paul Lukas.

In his early years in American movies, Lukas, because of his suave, dominating manner, was often cast as a Continental seducer, as in *The Shopworn Angel* (1929) and *Dodsworth* (1936), or as a sophisticated foreign villain, as in *The Lady Vanishes* (1938) and *Confessions of a Nazi Spy* (1939).

But Lukas was actually a fine, versatile actor. In his Broadway debut he played the tired consumptive Dr. Rank in Ibsen's *A Doll's House* (1937).

The role by which Lukas won his greatest fame was his starring performance in *Watch on the Rhine* (stage, 1941; film, 1943), as the worn-out Kurt Muller, a gentle German engineer whose work in the anti-Fascist Ger-

man underground forces him into exile in America but who finally returns to Germany to continue his fight against Nazism. Lukas imbued the part with sorrow, humility, and human compassion, yet also with a fiery, invincible spirit.

His roles as lovers, villains, and exhausted intellectuals were actually quite far removed from his true nature. Always actively athletic and energetic, he was a skilled wrestler and weight lifter in his youth. Later he turned to tennis, fencing, and horsemanship. He was also a licensed airplane pilot.

In his later films Lukas frequently played kindly old men, as in *Lord Jim* (1965). Particularly memorable was his role in Walt Disney's production of Jules Verne's *Twenty Thousand Leagues under the Sea* (1954). Lukas portrayed Professor Pierre Arronax, a specialist in sea creatures, who is captured by the misanthropic genius Captain Nemo and confined aboard the latter's submarine, the *Nautilus*. The gentle Arronax convinces Nemo to make peace with the world and to share his fantastic scientific knowledge with humankind. But Nemo is ambushed by warships, and he orders the *Nautilus*, with its scientific secrets, to make a final trip to the ocean floor. Lukas's Professor Arronax epitomized the idealistic conception of the humanitarian scientist altruistically pursuing knowledge.

Lukas was married twice. He wedded Gizella (nicknamed Daisy) Benes in 1927. She died in 1962, and in 1963 he married Anna Driesens.

Lukas himself died in Tangier, Morocco, on August 15, 1971.

Selected performances:

Stage

A Doll's House (1937)
Watch on the Rhine (1941)
Call Me Madam (1950)
Flight into Egypt (1952)
The Wayward Saint (1955)

Films

Two Lovers (1928)
Three Sinners (1928)
Loves of an Actress (1928)
The Night Watch (1928)
The Woman from Moscow (1928)
Manhattan Cocktail (1928)
The Shopworn Angel (1929)
The Wolf of Wall Street (1929)
Half Way to Heaven (1929)
Behind the Makeup (1930)
Slightly Scarlet (1930)
Young Eagles (1930)
The Benson Murder Case (1930)
The Devil's Holiday (1930)
Grumpy (1930)
Anybody's Woman (1930)
Unfaithful (1931)
City Streets (1931)
The Vice Squad (1931)
Women Love Once (1931)
The Beloved Bachelor (1931)
Strictly Dishonorable (1931)
No One Man (1932)
Tomorrow and Tomorrow (1932)
Thunder Below (1932)
A Passport to Hell (1932)
Downstairs (1932)
Rockabye (1932)
Grand Slam (1933)
Kiss before the Mirror (1933)
Sing, Sinner, Sing (1933)
Captured (1933)
The Secret of the Blue Room (1933)
Little Women (1933)
The Countess of Monte Cristo (1934)
Glamour (1934)
Affairs of a Gentleman (1934)
I Give My Love (1934)
The Fountain (1934)
The Casino Murder Case (1935)
Age of Indiscretion (1935)
The Three Musketeers (1935)
I Found Stella Parish (1935)
Dodsworth (1936)
Ladies in Love (1936)
Espionage (1937)
Dinner at the Ritz (1937)
The Lady Vanishes (1938)
Confessions of a Nazi Spy (1939)
Captain Fury (1939)
Strange Cargo (1940)
The Ghost Breakers (1940)
The Monster and the Girl (1941)
Chinese Den (1941)
They Dare Not Love (1941)
Lady in Distress (1942)
Watch on the Rhine (1943)
Hostages (1943)
Uncertain Glory (1944)
Address Unknown (1944)
Experiment Perilous (1944)
Deadline at Dawn (1946)
Temptation (1946)
Whispering City (1947)
Berlin Express (1948)
Kim (1950)
Twenty Thousand Leagues under the Sea (1954)
The Roots of Heaven (1958)
Scent of Mystery (1960)
The Four Horsemen of the Apocalypse (1962)
Tender Is the Night (1962)
Fifty-five Days at Peking (1963)
Lord Jim (1965)
Sol Madrid (1968)
The Challenge (TV, 1970)

★★

Marx Brothers

Madcap Comedy Team

Chico	Harpo	Groucho	Zeppo
(1887-1961)	(1888-1964)	(1890-1977)	(1901-1979)

All of the brothers were born in New York City, New York. However, only Groucho's and Zeppo's births were officially recorded with the city government, and for many years Groucho fibbed about his true age. (About 85 percent of the births and deaths in New York City were unrecorded by the government before 1898, by which time more stringent reporting requirements had been established.) Consequently many different birth dates for the brothers have been published. The following birth dates are based on the best recent evidence: Chico (originally Leonard), August 21, 1887; Harpo (originally Adolph, later Arthur), November 23, 1888; Groucho (originally Julius), October 2, 1890; and Zeppo (originally Herbert), February 25, 1901. Another brother, Gummo (originally Milton; born October 23, 1892, unrecorded), left the team in their early years.

Their father, Sam ("Frenchy") Marx (originally Simon Marrix), was an unsuccessful tailor who had immigrated to the United States from Alsace-Lorraine. Their mother, Minnie Marx (originally Minna Schoenberg), had come to America from Germany, where her parents had operated a traveling theatrical troupe. Her father was a magician, her mother a harpist. One of Minnie's brothers changed his name to Al Shean and became a famous American vaudeville comedian in the team Gallagher and Shean (beginning in 1910).

The older boys left school early to pursue separate careers in show business. Chico, for example, played the piano in nickelodeons, brothels, and vaudeville theaters. Harpo, whose principal musical instrument was the harp, played the piano (though he knew only two tunes) in a nickelodeon, a job he had inherited from Chico. And Groucho sang with various groups, including Gus Edwards's famous vaudeville kid act.

Then Minnie decided to form her own group of singers. It went through a couple of changes of membership before settling on Harpo, Groucho, Gummo, and Lou Levy, billed as the Four Nightingales. They toured from 1907 to 1910, and during that time they moved to Chicago, the center of the small-time vaudeville circuits that the group played.

The Four Nightingales remained basically straight singers till one memorable day in Nacogdoches, Texas. While they were performing in an outdoor theater, a mule caused a disturbance nearby. Most of the audience went out to watch the mule. When some of the people straggled back, the boys—furious at being topped by a mule—hurled insults at the audience (for example, Groucho's "Nacogdoches is full of roaches"). The audience loved the "jokes" and laughed hysterically. Thus a new phase began for the team.

Soon they developed a comedy schoolroom show called *Fun in Hi Skule,* which they used from 1910 to 1913. At first they were billed as the Three Marx Brothers, and the cast consisted of Harpo, Groucho, Gummo, and several others. Then Chico joined the act, which became the Four Marx Brothers and Company. In 1913 the show evolved into *Mr. Green's Reception,* and in 1914 into *Home Again,* which was written by Al Shean. Later in their vaudeville career they performed other skits as well.

Before 1914 the boys were still known by their original given names (though Adolph had early changed his name to Arthur). It was during a 1914 poker game in Galesburg, Illinois, that they were dubbed with the names by which they would become famous. They and their poker partner, a monologist named Art Fisher, were noting how the popular comic-strip character Sherlocko the Monk had spawned such vaudeville names as Nervo, Henpecko, and Tightwado. Fisher applied the same naming system to the Marxes. He called Leonard, known for his success in chasing pretty girls, or chicks, Chicko (the *k* was later accidentally dropped by a typesetter, and the name became Chico, though it was still pronounced to rhyme with *chick,* not *cheek*). Arthur, the harpist, became Harpo. Julius, the moody one, became Groucho. Milton, who wore gumshoes to help ward off colds, was henceforth Gummo.

During World War I Gummo was drafted into the army. He never returned to the act, choosing instead to become a businessman. His place was taken by the youngest brother, Herbert, who was named Zeppo when he joined the act.

In 1919 the Marx Brothers made it to the prestigious Palace Theater in New York City. Soon they were the biggest attraction in all of vaudeville.

Also in 1919 they performed in their first musical comedy, *The Cinderella Girl,* which lasted only three days in Battle Creek, Michigan. In 1920 or 1921 they made a silent movie, *Humor Risk*, which was so bad that they destroyed it.

But the musical revue *I'll Say She Is!* was a tremendous success. It opened in Philadelphia in the summer of 1923. After touring with the show for a year, they took it to Broadway, where it was also a hit. They followed up with two extremely successful Broadway musical comedies: *The Cocoanuts* (1925) and *Animal Crackers* (1928).

However, the Marx Brothers gained their greatest fame through movies, beginning with filmed versions of *The Cocoanuts* (1929) and *Animal Crackers* (1930). In the former the boys are involved in the Florida land boom. In *Animal Crackers* they are guests at a party where thieves covet a valuable oil painting. In one of his most memorable roles, Groucho portrayed Captain Jeffrey Spaulding, a bumbling African explorer.

Those two movies were shot on the East Coast. The Marx Brothers made the rest of their films in Hollywood. In *Monkey Business* (1931) the boys stow away on a ship, crash a party, and reluctantly catch some crooks. *Horse Feathers* (1932) is a spoof of college life, especially football. Groucho, as Professor Quincy Adams Wagstaff, played the newly appointed president of the school. In *Duck Soup* (1933) Groucho was Rufus T. Firefly, president of the mythical land of Freedonia, which wages war on its scheming neighbor Sylvania. A highlight of *Duck Soup* is the mirror scene, in which Harpo, who is being chased by Groucho, accidentally smashes a large mirror and then pretends to be Groucho's mirror image in a series of intricate and hilarious moves.

Their first five movies were wild conglomerations of pure madcap energy and anarchy. Plots were barely begun before the Marx Brothers began to destroy them by shifting attention to a series of tangential comedy routines showcasing the boys in various combinations. They were zany outsiders who thumbed their noses at the Establishment (often personified by the stately actress Margaret Dumont, their favorite comic foil).

The principal figure on the screen was Groucho, who wore an ill-fitting frock coat, a carry-over from his days as the schoolmaster in *Fun in Hi Skule* and a parody of the uniform of the society that he mocked. He also had a painted-on mustache, constantly smoked and flicked a cigar, insinuatingly twitched his eyebrows, and uttered savage wisecracks at virtually everyone and everything. Groucho sang comic songs with a unique nasal twang and outrageous, lovable mockery. In *Animal Crackers,* for example, he performed the nonsense song "Hello, I Must Be Going" and the self-descriptive "Hooray for Captain Spaulding," which became his theme song for the rest of his career.

Chico's screen humor was largely based on his use of a mock Italian accent and his misuse of the English language. In *The Cocoanuts,* for example, he confuses *viaduct* with *why a duck*. He was the "real" world's link with the silent Harpo, whom only Chico could understand. Chico, a fine instinctive pianist, provided the Marx Brothers films with many lighthearted melodious moments at the piano. He applied comedy even to his pianism, especially in his technique of "shooting the keys," that is, pointing his index finger like a pistol, using his thumb as a "trigger," and striking a key.

Harpo portrayed a totally uninhibited childlike mute. His stage character became mute when Al Shean's script for *Home Again* accidentally left Harpo with only a few lines. Shean compensated for his oversight by asking Harpo to use pantomime. Thus was created one of the world's most beloved pantomimists. His brothers frequently played straight men to his zaniness, as when Groucho, in *The Cocoanuts,* fed Harpo flowers and a telephone, and when Chico, in several films, deciphered messages that Harpo conveyed through charades. Harpo's most characteristic prop was his fright wig. In vaudeville he had used a red wig, but the red showed up too dark on the screen in *The Cocoanuts*. Consequently, from *Animal Crackers* on, he used a blond wig. In every Marx Brothers show, Harpo pulled a face called a Gookie, in which he puffed out his cheeks and crossed his widened eyes. The look was named after a New York City cigar roller named Gookie, who unintentionally made the face as he worked in a cigar store, where Harpo, as a youngster, spotted and copied the expression. He began to play the harp as a child because his maternal grandmother had bequeathed her harp to the Marx family, and Minnie was determined that one of her boys would use it. Harpo had no formal lessons, and he tuned the instrument eccentrically; yet he became a highly admired harpist, even among professional musicians. He was particularly adept at improvising on popular tunes.

Zeppo played the straight man to Groucho and generally supplied the romantic relief: he got the girl but not the gags. He also sang the romantic ballads.

After *Duck Soup* Zeppo left the team and opened what came to be one of the largest talent agencies in show business. At the same time, Gummo gave up his dress-manufacturing business to become Zeppo's partner, specifically as manager of the three remaining Marx Brothers.

The first five Marx Brothers films, made for Paramount Pictures, were dominated by the boys' comic anarchy at the expense of plot and of production values (such as direction and camera work). Their methods bordered on the surreal and appealed to a rather narrow urban audience.

Then they signed with the executive Irving Thalberg at Metro-Goldwyn-Mayer (MGM). Through his influence their next two films, at MGM, were made with firmer plots, stronger production values, and a broader audience appeal.

Marx Brothers

In *A Night at the Opera* (1935) the boys pave the way for the happiness of two young opera singers by deflating an unfair opera director and an egotistical tenor. A highlight of the film is the stateroom scene: the three Marx Brothers and a dozen other people are gradually squeezed into a tiny room; when Margaret Dumont opens the door to visit Groucho (as Otis B. Driftwood), the bodies pour out at her feet.

In *A Day at the Races* (1937) the Marx Brothers help a young woman to raise money for her sanatorium by assisting her boyfriend's horse in winning a big race. Groucho played Dr. Hugo Z. Hackenbush, a veterinarian who tries to pass himself off as a people doctor. In one scene, Chico pretends to be a tutti-frutti (in his lingo, "tutsi-frutsi") ice-cream salesman at a racetrack, while actually selling Groucho phony betting aids. In another scene, Harpo pounds a piano till it falls apart, leaving only the inside "harp," which he proceeds to play.

Thalberg died in 1936. His efforts had helped the Marx Brothers to reach the zenith of their career. But with Thalberg gone, their later movies never rose to the same plateau.

In *Room Service* (1938) they are penniless theatrical producers trying to find ways to stay in a hotel till they can find a backer. In *At the Circus* (1939) they save a circus from bankruptcy. Groucho played the shyster lawyer J. Cheever Loophole and sang the delightfully risqué "Lydia, the Tattooed Lady."

In *Go West* (1940) the boys tackle a western villain. The rousing finale is a train chase in which they literally tear their train apart to fuel the wood-burning engine. In *The Big Store* (1941) they save a department store from crooks.

After *The Big Store* the team split up for several years. But then they got together again, chiefly because Chico needed the money.

In *A Night in Casablanca* (1946) they rout Nazi refugees in a North African hotel. Their last film as a team was *Love Happy* (1950), in which they search for a stolen diamond necklace. The story was conceived by Harpo, who, for the first time, had the limelight.

All three brothers were in the movie *The Story of Mankind* (1957) but not as a team; each appeared in scenes that did not include the other two brothers. The last time that all three appeared together on a screen was in the TV play "The Incredible Jewel Robbery" (1959) on *General Electric Theater.*

However, in their late years they did remain active in separate careers. In the 1950s Chico and Harpo had a dual act in nightclubs and at county fairs. Chico's solo work included guest-starring in the TV play "Papa Romani" (1950) on *The Bigelow Theater,* hosting the TV variety series *The College Bowl* (1950-51), and playing the piano in numerous engagements. Harpo's solo work included guest-starring in a 1955 episode of the TV comedy series *I Love Lucy,* in which he and Lucy recreated the famous mirror scene from *Duck Soup;* appearing in the dramas "The Red Mill" (1958) and "Silent Panic" (1960) on TV's *The Du Pont Show;* and playing the harp in numerous engagements. He also published his autobiography, *Harpo Speaks!* (with Rowland Barber, 1961).

Groucho's fame continued to grow after the team broke up. He served as the wisecracking host of the quiz show *You Bet Your Life* on both radio (1947-51) and TV (1950-61, for which he grew a real mustache to replace the painted-on one that he had used on the stage and in movies). He also acted in several films, including *Copacabana* (1947), *A Girl in Every Port* (1952), and *Skidoo* (1968). Besides working on his own TV show, he made many guest appearances on the small screen. A longstanding fan of Gilbert and Sullivan's operettas, Groucho particularly enjoyed playing Ko-Ko, the Lord High Executioner, in *The Mikado* on TV in 1960. In 1972 he performed a one-man show at Carnegie Hall in New York City.

Groucho read voraciously and became a skilled writer. He coauthored (with Norman Krasna) the play *Time for Elizabeth* (1948) and wrote the humorous books *Beds* (1930), a history of sleeping accommodations, and *Many Happy Returns!* (1942), an indictment of the Internal Revenue Service. He also wrote the autobiographical books *Groucho and Me* (1959), *Memoirs of a Mangy Lover* (1963), *The Groucho Letters* (1967), *The Secret Word Is Groucho* (with Hector Arce, 1976), and *The Groucho Phile* (1976).

In real life Chico was the charmer of the brothers. An inveterate womanizer and gambler, he was very successful as the former, less so as the latter. In 1924 he married Betty Karp, a dancer. They had a daughter, Maxine, who wrote the book *Growing Up with Chico* (1980). That marriage ended in divorce, and in 1958 he wedded the actress Mary De Vithas (also known as Mary Dee). In 1961 Chico entered the Cedars of Lebanon Hospital in Los Angeles. Later he was released, but soon he died in his Beverly Hills home of a heart ailment on October 11, 1961.

The real-life Harpo was much like his fictional character—sweet, gentle, and puckish. In 1936 he married the actress Susan Fleming, a former *Ziegfeld Follies* showgirl. They adopted four children: William, Alexander, Minnie, and James. Harpo finally broke his professional silence in January 1963 when he announced his retirement just after giving a stage performance. The following year he underwent heart surgery at Mount Sinai Hospital in Los Angeles, where he died on September 28, 1964.

Groucho, in real life, was shy, thoughtful, and kindhearted, much in contrast with his smart-alecky fictional character. But his fame as a caustic wit in films was so great that he felt obligated to live up to his reputation in real life as well. The conflict between his natural shyness and his desire to please others by insulting them often led him to great inner turmoil.

In his late years Groucho became a cult figure among many film enthusiasts. But his own interests were wide. A literate, articulate man, he corresponded with such notables as T. S. Eliot, James Thurber, and E. B. White. He was also a liberal activist, as in his support of George McGovern for the United States presidency in 1972.

Groucho was married three times. In 1920 he married Ruth Johnson, who had been hired for the Marx Brothers vaudeville act as Zeppo's dancing partner. Groucho and Ruth had two children: Arthur and Miriam. Arthur became a prominent writer of movie and TV scripts and of biographical-autobiographical books, including *Son of Groucho* (1972).

After divorcing Ruth in 1942, Groucho married the aspiring singer-dancer Catherine (or Kay) Gorcey in 1945. She had previously been married to the actor Leo Gorcey, one of the Dead End Kids. Groucho and Kay had a daughter, Melinda, who, as a youth, performed as a singer-dancer-actress, sometimes appearing with her father, as in *The Mikado* and on *You Bet Your Life*. His second marriage ended in divorce in 1951.

Groucho wedded the former model Eden Hartford (originally Eden Higgins) in 1954. She had a bit part with him in *The Story of Mankind*. They divorced in 1969.

Shortly after that divorce he began to receive secretarial help from the aspiring actress Erin Fleming. She later became his close personal companion and business manager.

In his final years Groucho was considerably slowed down by a major heart attack and by several small strokes. His last few months of life were marred by a bitter legal battle between Erin Fleming and his son, Arthur, for the conservatorship of Groucho's considerable estate, the responsibility finally falling to Andy Marx, Arthur's son. Groucho died of pneumonitis at Cedars-Sinai Medical Center in Los Angeles on August 19, 1977.

Gummo, who had acted as Groucho's agent in the 1950s, died in Palm Springs, California, on April 21, 1977.

Zeppo, in real life, was a witty person and a shrewd businessman. He was married twice. In 1927 he wedded the actress Marion Benda (originally Marion Bimberg), with whom he had a son, Timothy, before divorcing in 1937. His second wife, Barbara, divorced Zeppo in 1973 and later married Frank Sinatra. Zeppo's last public appearance came in 1977 when he testified in favor of Groucho's companion, Erin Fleming, in the conservatorship hearing. Zeppo died of lung cancer in Palm Springs on November 30, 1979.

Selected performances:

Stage

Chico, Harpo, Groucho, Zeppo:

I'll Say She Is! (1924)
The Cocoanuts (1925)
Animal Crackers (1928)

Films

Chico, Harpo, Groucho, Zeppo:

The Cocoanuts (1929)
Animal Crackers (1930)
Monkey Business (1931)
Horse Feathers (1932)
Duck Soup (1933)

Chico, Harpo, Groucho:

A Night at the Opera (1935)
A Day at the Races (1937)
Room Service (1938)
At the Circus (1939)
Go West (1940)
The Big Store (1941)
A Night in Casablanca (1946)
Love Happy (1950)
The Story of Mankind (1957)

Groucho:

Copacabana (1947)
Mr. Music (1950)
Double Dynamite (1951)
A Girl in Every Port (1952)
Skidoo (1968)

Radio

Groucho:

You Bet Your Life (1947-51)

TV

Chico:

The College Bowl (1950-51)

Groucho:

You Bet Your Life (1950-61)

★★

Walter Matthau

Sardonic Actor

(1920-)

Walter Matthau was born in New York City, New York, on October 1, 1920. His original name was Walter Matuschanskayasky.

His father, Melas Matuschanskayasky, had been an Eastern Rite Catholic priest in czarist Russia. After leaving the priesthood, Melas met and married Rose Berolsky, a Jewess, in Lithuania and then immigrated to the United States, where the family name became Matthow. Later Walter changed the spelling to Matthau.

Melas (now Milton) left his family when Walter was three. The boy was raised by his mother in the Jewish milieu of New York City's Lower East Side of Manhattan. As a youngster he worked in the refreshment concessions at various theaters. At the age of eleven he was given a small role in a Yiddish-language play. He later performed in school plays at Seward Park High School, from which he graduated in 1939.

After working at a series of odd jobs, he enlisted in the air force in 1942. Returning to civilian life at the end of World War II, he studied acting under Erwin Piscator at the Dramatic Workshop of the New School for Social Research in New York City. During that time (1946-48) Matthau gave public performances in Dramatic Workshop productions, in summer stock, and on TV.

In 1948 he reached Broadway as an understudy for seven characters in *Anne of a Thousand Days,* playing various roles on separate occasions. Over the next few years he worked his way up till, in 1951, he earned a leading role in *Twilight Walk.* He continued to work on both Broadway and TV for several years, earning the respect of colleagues but as yet lacking public recognition.

In 1955 Matthau finally landed a role in a play that won large public favor: *Will Success Spoil Rock Hunter?* The same year saw his entry into movies, beginning with *The Kentuckian* and *The Indian Fighter,* in both of which he played a supporting role as a villain.

Matthau then played a variety of supporting roles in such films as *Bigger Than Life* (1956), *A Face in the Crowd* (1957), and *Onionhead* (1958). Real success, however, still eluded him.

He gained wide recognition for his comic portrayal of a haughty French aristocrat in the Broadway play *A Shot in the Dark* (1961). And his reputation continued to grow as a character actor in movies, including *Lonely Are the*

Brave (1962), *Ensign Pulver* (1964), and *Goodbye Charlie* (1964).

Matthau finally reached genuine stardom with his role as Oscar Madison in Neil Simon's Broadway comedy *The Odd Couple* (1965). Simon had written the work with Matthau in mind, and the character of Oscar turned out to be the major role in a top script that had always eluded the actor. Matthau readily identified with Oscar's easygoing lifestyle (though not with the character's sloppiness) and sardonic humor, a quality that has characterized much of the actor's work.

He followed with another outstanding performance, as the conniving shyster lawyer in the film comedy *The Fortune Cookie* (1966). While making that movie, Matthau had a major heart attack. He thereupon decided to limit himself principally to filmmaking, which he felt was less exhausting than stage work. (In 1976 he had heart bypass surgery to help prevent further problems.)

Matthau reprised his Oscar Madison role in the filmed version of *The Odd Couple* (1968). He solidified his star status with outstanding comic performances in *Hello, Dolly!* (1969), as a grouchy merchant who eventually mellows; *Plaza Suite* (1971), as three different characters; *Kotch* (1971), as a septuagenarian; *The Sunshine Boys* (1975), as an old vaudevillian; *The Bad News Bears* (1976), as a down-at-heel children's baseball coach; *Buddy, Buddy* (1981), as a hit man; *The Survivors* (1983), as a gas-station owner battling a right-wing military unit; and *Movers and Shakers* (1985), as a Hollywood executive trying to produce a box-office hit from a best-selling sex book.

Matthau is married to the former Carol Marcus. They met in 1955 when he was in *Will Success Spoil Rock Hunter?* and she was a stand-in for the female lead (Jayne Mansfield) in the same show. In 1959 they got married, and in that year they also appeared together in the movie *Gangster Story*. They had one child: Charles. It was Matthau's second marriage, since he had earlier been married for a time to Grace Johnson, with whom he had his children David and Jennifer. Matthau has used David and Charles, as well as Lucy Saroyan (his stepdaughter by way of Carol's earlier marriage, to the author William Saroyan), in some of his movies.

Selected performances:

Stage

The Aristocrats (1946)
Anne of a Thousand Days (1948)
The Liar (1950)
Twilight Walk (1951)
Fancy Meeting You Again (1952)
One Bright Day (1952)
The Glass Menagerie (1952)
In Any Language (1952)
The Grey-eyed People (1952)
The Ladies of the Corridor (1953)
The Wisteria Trees (1955)
Guys and Dolls (1955)
Will Success Spoil Rock Hunter? (1955)
Once More with Feeling (1958)
Once There Was a Russian (1961)
A Shot in the Dark (1961)
The Odd Couple (1965)
Juno and the Paycock (1974)

Films

The Kentuckian (1955)
The Indian Fighter (1955)
Bigger Than Life (1956)
A Face in the Crowd (1957)
Slaughter on Tenth Avenue (1957)
King Creole (1958)
Voice in the Mirror (1958)
Ride a Crooked Trail (1958)
Onionhead (1958)
Gangster Story (1959)
Strangers When We Meet (1960)
Lonely Are the Brave (1962)
Who's Got the Action? (1962)
Island of Love (1963)
Charade (1963)
Ensign Pulver (1964)
Goodbye Charlie (1964)
Fail Safe (1964)
Mirage (1965)
The Fortune Cookie (1966)
A Guide for the Married Man (1967)
The Odd Couple (1968)
The Secret Life of an American Wife (1968)
Candy (1968)
Hello, Dolly! (1969)
Cactus Flower (1969)
A New Leaf (1971)
Plaza Suite (1971)
Kotch (1971)
Pete 'n' Tillie (1972)
Charley Varrick (1973)
The Laughing Policeman (1973)
The Taking of Pelham One Two Three (1974)
Earthquake (credited as Walter Matuschanskayasky, 1974)
The Front Page (1974)
The Sunshine Boys (1975)
The Bad News Bears (1976)
Casey's Shadow (1978)
House Calls (1978)
California Suite (1978)
Little Miss Marker (1980)
Hopscotch (1980)
First Monday in October (1981)
Buddy, Buddy (1981)
I Ought to Be in Pictures (1982)
The Survivors (1983)
Movers and Shakers (1985)

TV

Tallahassee 7000 (filmed 1959, syndicated 1961)

★★

Bette Midler

Queen of Camp

(1945-)

Bette Midler was born in Honolulu, Hawaii, on December 1, 1945, not long after her parents had arrived from New Jersey. Her mother named the girl after the actress Bette Davis; but Mrs. Midler, like many other fans, mistakenly thought that Davis pronounced her first name "Bet" (instead of the correct "Bet-tē"). Thus, Bette Midler's given name has always been pronounced "Bet."

In Hawaii the Midlers were the only white people in a predominantly Oriental community. For psychological survival Bette pretended to be Portuguese because, as she later explained, "Portuguese people were accepted. Jews were not. I was an alien, a foreigner—even though I was born there."

Her sensitivity was increased by the fact that she was an overweight, plain-looking child. As she has put it, "I was an ugly, fat little Jewish girl with problems."

But she soon found an excellent way to build her self-esteem: performing. In the first grade she won a prize for singing "Silent Night, Holy Night." After that, she was featured in many school and amateur productions. All during her youth, she dreamed of becoming a professional actress. When she attended the University of Hawaii for one year, she studied drama.

In 1965 Midler got a bit part (as the seasick wife of a missionary) in the movie *Hawaii* (1966), which was being filmed on location. When the movie company traveled to Los Angeles to finish filming, she went with it.

After the movie was completed, she moved to New York City to begin a stage career. There followed a rough period of time during which she held a variety of odd jobs, including one as a go-go dancer.

In 1966 she landed a job in the chorus of the hit Broadway musical *Fiddler on the Roof*. The following February she was promoted to the role of Tzeitel, one of the show's major parts. She remained with *Fiddler on the Roof* for three years.

Midler then decided to concentrate on a singing career. After having some minor engagements in Greenwich Village, she got her big break in 1970 when she was hired as a singer at the Continental Baths, a New York City Turkish bath for male homosexuals. Her work there led to requests for her to appear on the David Frost and Johnny Carson TV shows. Soon she was in demand at leading nightclubs and theaters across the country.

She billed herself as the Divine Miss M. Her unique song stylings covered not only contemporary rock but also material from the 1940s, 1950s, and 1960s. However, her fame grew less from her singing than from her lively, sometimes bizarre, manner of presentation. She often wore odd or out-of-date clothing, proudly calling herself "the last of the truly tacky women." Her onstage costumes included one as a giant hot dog and one as a female King Kong. Midler soon came to be dubbed the Queen of Camp.

In 1971 she appeared in the rock opera *Tommy* with the Seattle Opera Company, and in 1973 she performed at the famed Palace Theater in New York City. Her New York City revue *Clams on the Half Shell* (1975) was very successful. In 1979 she starred in the bawdy one-woman Broadway show *Divine Madness*, a performance that she re-created on film in 1980.

Midler's first album was *The Divine Miss M* (1972). Later albums included *Live at Last* (1977) and *No Frills* (1983).

She has written two books. *A View from a Broad* (1980) covers her adventures when she took her act on a world tour. *The Saga of Baby Divine* (1983) is a poetic fairy tale, ostensibly for children, about living life to the fullest.

Midler never abandoned her original ambition to be an actress. She appeared in the minor film *The Divine Mr. J.* (1974), a religious satire. But her first important movie role was in *The Rose* (1979), starring as a hard-living, ill-fated rock singer.

However, Midler has also expressed a strong interest in comedy, a natural outgrowth of her humorous stage acts. She gave fine comedic performances in the movies *Jinxed* (1982), *Down and Out in Beverly Hills* (1986), and *Ruthless People* (1986).

In December 1984 Midler married Martin von Haselberg (alias Harry Kipper), a performing artist and commodities trader. They have a daughter named Sophie.

Selected performances:

Stage

Fiddler on the Roof (1966)
Salvation (1970)
Tommy (1971)
Clams on the Half Shell (1975)
Divine Madness (1979)
De Tour (1983)

Films

Hawaii (1966)
The Divine Mr. J. (1974)
The Rose (1979)
Divine Madness (1980)
Jinxed (1982)
Down and Out in Beverly Hills (1986)
Ruthless People (1986)
Outrageous Fortune (1987)

★★★

Marilyn Monroe

Sex Symbol
(1926-62)

Marilyn Monroe was born of non-Jewish parents in Los Angeles, California, on June 1, 1926. Her original name was Norma Jean Mortensen. Her mother, originally named Gladys Monroe, had been married first to a man named Baker and then to a man named Mortensen, who soon deserted her. It is believed, however, that Norma Jean's natural father was C. Stanley Gifford, a fellow employee at the studio where Gladys worked as a film technician.

Gladys came from a family with a history of mental illness, and she herself was frequently institutionalized with that problem. Her daughter, who went by the name

Norma Jean Baker in her childhood, spent her early years in a succession of foster homes and in an orphanage.

In 1942 Norma Jean dropped out of high school to marry James Dougherty, an aircraft production worker. After he entered the merchant marine for World War II service, she supported herself by working in a defense plant and by part-time modeling.

In 1946 she divorced Dougherty and began to look for a career in show business. She bleached her previously dark hair, got an agent, and changed her name to Marilyn (after the actress Marilyn Miller) Monroe (after her mother's maiden name).

She managed to get a screen test, which led to a movie contract. Her first film appearance came in *Scudda-Hoo! Scudda-Hay!* (1948), but her brief close-ups were cut and she remained in the picture only as an extra in the distance. In *Dangerous Years* (1948) her bit part was retained. Finally, in the minor musical *Ladies of the Chorus* (1949) she had one of the leading roles. During the production of *Ladies of the Chorus,* she began her first serious dramatic study, under Natasha Lytess.

There followed a year during which Monroe could get no film work. She earned her living by modeling.

Returning to movies, she made a brief, sexy appearance in the Marx Brothers film *Love Happy* (1950) and played in several minor pictures. She also had small parts in the important movies *The Asphalt Jungle* (1950) and *All about Eve* (1950), in both of which she played inexperienced young women protégées of worldly older men. She was beginning to attract attention through her sensuous presence, her wiggly walk, and her little-girl voice.

While she was filming *Clash by Night* (1952), it became nationally known that Monroe had posed for a full-length nude photograph being used on a widely distributed calendar. She and her press agents turned the discovery to their own advantage and used the publicity to increase her market value.

With *Niagara* (1953) Monroe, as an unfaithful wife, first gained serious attention from film critics; and with the comedy *Gentlemen Prefer Blondes* (1953), as a gold-digging chorus girl, she attained true movie stardom. In *How to Marry a Millionaire* (1953) she costarred with Betty Grable and Lauren Bacall as three models who share a penthouse and scheme to marry wealthy men.

In January 1954, after a well-publicized courtship, Monroe married the retired baseball player Joe DiMaggio, the great "Yankee Clipper." It was a brief and stormy marriage, ending in divorce in October of that year. The culminating factor in the breakup was Monroe's willingness to perform a particular scene for the movie *The Seven Year Itch* (1955): she stood over a sidewalk grating while an updraft billowed her skirt and exposed more of her than DiMaggio thought proper. A still of that scene was enlarged to a height of sixty feet and used to advertise the motion picture.

Meanwhile, Monroe continued to make serious efforts to improve her acting. She came to be widely recognized as a fine comedienne besides being a dumb-blonde sex symbol. Her style often involved a touch of self-satire as she played the coquette.

From 1954 on, Monroe periodically studied with Lee and Paula Strasberg at the famed Actors Studio in New York City. The Strasbergs encouraged her to attempt serious dramatic parts and to cultivate the Method technique of internalizing her roles. One of her best efforts along those lines was in *Bus Stop* (1956), in which she imbued her dumb-blonde character with a poignancy and emotional depth not apparent in her earlier work.

In June 1956 Monroe married the Jewish playwright Arthur Miller (author of *Death of a Salesman*). She converted to Judaism.

Monroe then appeared in the popular movies *The Prince and the Showgirl* (1957), *Some Like It Hot* (1959), and *Let's Make Love* (1960). Her performance in *Some Like It Hot* was an overt parody of her usual dumb-blonde screen character.

She was already having marital problems again. It seemed that she needed a man who could be a father figure by day and a lover by night. Above all, he had to devote himself entirely to her. Miller, busy with a rich career of his own to pursue, could not satisfy her.

Consequently, while filming *Let's Make Love,* she became the aggressor in a love affair with her costar, the French actor Yves Montand. He was already married to the actress Simone Signoret, and he eventually broke off his relationship with Monroe.

For several years she had been showing signs of increasing mental and emotional deterioration: insomnia, addiction to sleeping drugs, exotic behavior, frequent outbursts of temper, and reliance on psychiatric help. Her instability may have been rooted in her childhood loneliness and aggravated by pressures from studios and the press, by exploitation at the hands of close associates, by her own ambition, and by the loss of two pregnancies during her marriage to Miller.

In 1960, while filming Miller's screenplay *The Misfits* (1961), Monroe was often late or psychologically unable to function at all. Her role itself, tailored for her by her husband, was the deepest and most complex of her career. Though once again a dumb blonde, the character showed a touching vulnerability, compassion, and capacity to love. In January 1961, shortly after completing the movie, Monroe and Miller divorced.

Later that year she spent some time in a New York City mental hospital. Then she began work on the film *Something's Got to Give.* However, she was dismissed because she showed up for work only twelve days during

Marilyn Monroe

the first month of shooting. Shortly thereafter she was reinstated, but before filming could resume she was found dead at her home in the Brentwood section of Los Angeles on August 5, 1962.

An autopsy revealed a lethal amount of barbiturates in her system, and her death was officially declared a probable suicide. In recent years speculation has risen about possible complexities in Monroe's death. Some even claim that she was murdered. But in 1985 Los Angeles officials looked into the matter and decided that the case did not require reopening.

Joe DiMaggio arranged Monroe's funeral. Lee Strasberg, in his eulogy for her, captured her essence when he spoke of her "childlike naïveté which was at once so shy and yet so vibrant."

Selected performances:

Films

Scudda-Hoo! Scudda-Hay! (1948)
Dangerous Years (1948)
Ladies of the Chorus (1949)
Love Happy (1950)
A Ticket to Tomahawk (1950)
The Fireball (1950)
Right Cross (1950)
The Asphalt Jungle (1950)
All about Eve (1950)
Let's Make It Legal (1951)
Home Town Story (1951)
As Young As You Feel (1951)
Love Nest (1951)
We're Not Married (1952)
O. Henry's Full House (1952)
Clash by Night (1952)
Don't Bother to Knock (1952)
Monkey Business (1952)
Niagara (1953)
Gentlemen Prefer Blondes (1953)
How to Marry a Millionaire (1953)
River of No Return (1954)
There's No Business like Show Business (1954)
The Seven Year Itch (1955)
Bus Stop (1956)
The Prince and the Showgirl (1957)
Some Like It Hot (1959)
Let's Make Love (1960)
The Misfits (1961)

★★

Zero Mostel

Unpredictable Comic Actor

(1915-77)

Zero Mostel was born in New York City, New York, on February 28, 1915. His original name was Samuel Joel Mostel, an anglicization of his Hebrew name, Simcha Yoel Mostel.

He graduated from Seward Park High School in 1931 and from City College of the City University of New York in 1935. His B.A. degree was in art; but after finishing college, he had a series of menial jobs in factories and on docks. During that time he developed a strong interest in social causes.

Later he was hired by the federal Work Projects Administration (WPA) to teach art at various museums. Mostel, however, was a natural-born zany, and his lectures soon turned into hilarious routines. When word spread about his lectures, he began to get calls to entertain at various local functions, where he would pick up a few extra dollars.

His first formal engagement as a professional comedian was at a nightclub called Café Society Downtown, where he debuted early in 1942. He was an immediate hit. It was the club's press agent who gave Mostel the name Zero, hoping to make people say, "Here's a man who's made something of nothing." Later Mostel playfully told interviewers a number of lies about the origin of the name, such as that it was a reflection of his standing in school or of the state of his bank account.

Zero Mostel (right) and David Kolatch (left)

Within the next few months Mostel appeared on the radio series *The Chamber Music Society of Lower Basin Street;* made his Broadway debut, in *Keep 'Em Laughing;* and went to Hollywood to make his first movie, *Du Barry Was a Lady* (1943). But his work in the movie consisted only of a few of his nightclub routines, and he soon returned to New York City.

Mostel was then drafted into the army. After six months he developed an ulcer and was discharged.

In 1944 he married Kathryn (or Kate) Harkin, a dancer with the famous Rockettes at the Radio City Music Hall. They had two children: Joshua and Tobias. Joshua (or Josh) became an actor and appeared in the films *Going Home* (1971), *Harry and Tonto* (1974), and

Zero Mostel

Seventh Avenue (TV, 1977). Kate Mostel and Madeline Gilford, with some help from their husbands, Zero Mostel and Jack Gilford, wrote *170 Years of Show Business* (1978), a book about all four of their lives.

Through the rest of the 1940s and the early 1950s, Mostel's career moved slowly. He was blacklisted during much of that time for his earlier involvement with progressive social causes. His stage work during those years included roles in the comedy *Beggar's Holiday* (1946) and the drama *A Stone for Danny Fisher* (1954). He often appeared as a villain, as in the movies *Panic in the Streets* (1950) and *The Enforcer* (1951).

In 1958 he began to come out from the blacklisting shadows when he was cast as Leopold Bloom in the off-Broadway show *Ulysses in Nighttown*. Finally, in 1961, Mostel reached stardom when he played John, the clerk who turns into a wild animal, in the play *Rhinoceros*. That was followed by his memorable stage performance as Pseudolus, an ancient Roman slave conniving to gain his freedom, in the musical comedy *A Funny Thing Happened on the Way to the Forum* (1962).

Mostel reached the peak of his career when he starred in the original Broadway production of the musical *Fiddler on the Roof* (1964). In that show he created the role of Tevye, the poor Jewish milkman struggling to marry off his daughters and to uphold tradition. He repeated the role in several revivals in later years.

Mostel then began to spend more time on movies, including filmed versions of *A Funny Thing Happened on the Way to the Forum* (1966) and *Rhinoceros* (1974). In *The Producers* (1967) he played Max Bialystock, a seedy Broadway producer who devises an elaborate scheme to cheat his backers out of their money. In *The Angel Levine* (1970) he was Morris Mishkin, a Jewish tailor beset by problems. He gave a fine performance in *The Front* (1976), a re-creation of the witch-hunting McCarthy era, during which Mostel, in real life, had been victimized (blacklisted). For the animated film *Watership Down* (1978) he supplied the voice of Kehaar.

Mostel was a brilliant and unpredictable comic actor, both on and off the stage. He performed virtually anywhere he happened to be. For example, he once shaved his good friend Sam Jaffe (the great actor) in Sardi's deluxe restaurant, using as shaving cream the whipped cream off Jaffe's strawberry shortcake.

Mostel was a master of slapstick (as in *A Funny Thing Happened on the Way to the Forum*), yet he could also be a subtle and sensitive humorist (as in *Fiddler on the Roof*).

He prepared the book *Zero by Mostel* (1965), consisting mostly of photographs of him. And his *Book of Villains* (with Israel Shenker, 1976) has many photographs of him in various villainous poses.

Mostel spent the first half of 1977 touring major American cities in *Fiddler on the Roof*. In September of that year he was in Philadelphia to try out the new play *The Merchant*. He deeply believed in the play because it addressed some important aspects of anti-Semitism. While he was in Philadelphia he suddenly died of a burst aorta on September 8, 1977.

Selected performances:

Stage

Keep 'Em Laughing (1942)
Top-Notchers (1942)
Beggar's Holiday (1946)
Flight into Egypt (1952)
A Stone for Danny Fisher (1954)
Once Over Lightly (1955)
Good As Gold (1957)
Ulysses in Nighttown (1958)
Rhinoceros (1961)
A Funny Thing Happened on the Way to the Forum (1962)
Fiddler on the Roof (1964)
The Latent Heterosexual (1968)
Ulysses in Nighttown (1974)
Fiddler on the Roof (1977)

Films

Du Barry Was a Lady (1943)
Panic in the Streets (1950)
The Enforcer (1951)
Sirocco (1951)
Mr. Belvedere Rings the Bell (1951)
The Guy Who Came Back (1951)
The Model and the Marriage Broker (1952)
A Funny Thing Happened on the Way to the Forum (1966)
The Producers (1967)
Great Catherine (1968)
The Great Bank Robbery (1969)
The Angel Levine (1970)
The Hot Rock (1972)
Rhinoceros (1974)
The Front (1976)
Watership Down (1978)

Radio

The Chamber Music Society of Lower Basin Street (1942)

TV

Off the Record (1949)

★★

Paul Muni

Man of Many Faces

(1895-1967)

Paul Muni was born in Lemberg, Austria (now Lvov, the Soviet Union) on September 22, 1895. His original name was Mehilem Meyer ben Nachum Favel Weisenfreund. *Mehilem* can be translated into English as "Michael," but his parents always called him by the Austrian nickname *Muni* or its diminutive *Munya*.

His parents were itinerant players who sang, danced, and acted in European ghettos till they moved to the United States in 1901. Muni Weisenfreund himself began to perform in Yiddish theaters in 1908. Soon he developed a wide range of theatrical skills, including performing in burlesque and acting in Yiddish versions of plays by Ibsen and Strindberg.

From 1918 to 1926 he toured with the Yiddish Art Theater troupe and became one of the most highly regarded Yiddish actors in the country. He first became a major force with his performance in *Hard to Be a Jew* (1920), as Ivanov, an aristocratic young Russian Christian who trades places with a Jewish student to prove that it is not difficult to be a Jew, that discrimination does not really exist.

In 1921 Weisenfreund married the actress Bella Finkel. In 1923 he became a naturalized American citizen.

The young Yiddish star made his English-speaking debut in 1926 by playing the role of Morris Levine, the aged Orthodox Jewish father in *We Americans* on Broadway. He was Benny Horowitz, a tough just out of prison, in *Four Walls* (1927), in which his wife also acted. (She retired from the stage soon afterward.)

He went to Hollywood to make *The Valiant* (1929) and *Seven Faces* (1929), two of the earliest talkies. In his early years on the English-language stage his name was sometimes recorded as Muni Wisenfrend or Frederich Wisenfreund. In Hollywood he faced movie executives who wanted to make even more drastic changes. They suggested *Muni* as a last name, and he reluctantly accepted. Then he wanted to honor his father by taking as a first name an English translation of *Favel,* such as "Philip"; they finally settled on "Paul." From 1929 on, he used the name Paul Muni for all of his stage and film work.

Returning to Broadway, he played the gangster Saul Holland in *This One Man* (1930). His rise to great prominence in the English-language theater came as George Simon, a dynamic Jewish lawyer, in the heartwarming play *Counsellor-at-Law* (1931).

Over the next several years Muni conquered the film world as well. He had long been renowned in the Yiddish theater for his makeup and acting skills in portraying characters of widely assorted ages and physical types. Using those skills on the screen, he became the character actor par excellence.

For example, he played the lead in *Scarface* (1932), a scarred thug who turns coward when the law captures him. In *I Am a Fugitive from a Chain Gang* (1932) he was an innocent man who, after being duped into participating in a robbery and sentenced to inhuman treatment on a Southern chain gang, escapes only to find that he must resort to a life of crime to survive. In *The Good Earth* (1937) he played a Chinese farmer.

Muni remains perhaps best known for his screen portrayals of real-life people in three reverent biopics. He played the title characters in *The Story of Louis Pasteur* (1936), as the scientist fighting for sterilization of medical instruments; *The Life of Emile Zola* (1937), as the French writer crusading against the unjust imprisonment of the military officer (and Jew) Alfred Dreyfus; and *Juarez* (1939), as the famed Mexican statesman.

Muni said that he sought roles that were "vital and lifelike." For his great versatility, he was dubbed the Man of Many Faces.

His wife, being a former actress herself, regularly helped him on the set while he was making films. At the end of each scene, he would look at her for her signs of approval or disapproval.

In 1939 he returned to the stage to play in *Key Largo,* as King McCloud, a wartime deserter who attempts to atone for his faithlessness. From that point on, Muni alternated roughly equally between stage and film work.

In 1943 he participated in the Madison Square

Paul Muni

Garden pageant *We Will Never Die,* an outcry against the Nazi horrors in Europe. It consisted of three parts: "The Roll Call," a recitation of great Jewish names in the arts and sciences from ancient times to the modern era; "Jews in the War," a dramatization of the contributions of American Jewish war heroes; and "Remember Us," a presentation of reports about the slaughters in Nazi Europe.

He portrayed Joseph Elsner, Chopin's teacher, in the fictionalized biopic *A Song to Remember* (1945). In 1946 Muni played Tevya in the drama-pageant *A Flag Is Born,* which was designed to aid and explain the cause of Zionism. In 1949 he replaced Lee J. Cobb as Willy Loman in the Broadway play *Death of a Salesman.*

In 1955 Muni performed in the explosive play *Inherit the Wind,* based on the famous Scopes Monkey Trial of 1925. Eventually he took both leading parts: the agnostic Henry Drummond (in real life, Clarence Darrow), who defends a young teacher's right to teach the Darwinian theory of evolution in a high-school classroom; and the religious fanatic Matthew Harrison Brady (in real life, William Jennings Bryan), who prosecutes the young man.

In the movie *The Last Angry Man* (1959) Muni gave a

memorable performance as a rugged old doctor who has dedicated his life to helping the poverty-stricken residents of his New York City neighborhood.

Muni spent his last years living in Montecito (near Santa Barbara), California. He died at his home there on August 25, 1967.

Selected performances:

Stage

Two Corpses at Breakfast (1908)
The Gold Chain (1920)
Hard to Be a Jew (1920)
Anathema (1923)
Wolves (1924)
Sabbethai Zvi (1924)
We Americans (1926)
Four Walls (1927)
This One Man (1930)
Rock Me, Julie (1931)
Counsellor-at-Law (1931)
Key Largo (1939)
Yesterday's Magic (1942)
We Will Never Die (1943)
A Flag Is Born (1946)
They Knew What They Wanted (1949)
Death of a Salesman (1949)
Inherit the Wind (1955)
At the Grand (1958)

Films

The Valiant (1929)
Seven Faces (1929)
Scarface (1932)
I Am a Fugitive from a Chain Gang (1932)
The World Changes (1933)
Hi, Nellie! (1934)
Bordertown (1935)
Black Fury (1935)
Dr. Socrates (1935)
The Story of Louis Pasteur (1936)
The Good Earth (1937)
The Woman I Love (1937)
The Life of Emile Zola (1937)
Juarez (1939)
We Are Not Alone (1939)
Hudson's Bay (1941)
Commandos Strike at Dawn (1943)
Stage Door Canteen (1943)
A Song to Remember (1945)
Counter-Attack (1945)
Angel on My Shoulder (1946)
Stranger on the Prowl (1953)
The Last Angry Man (1959)

★★★

Leonard Nimoy

Mr. Spock

(1931-)

Leonard Nimoy was born of Russian immigrants in Boston, Massachusetts, on March 26, 1931. He played juvenile roles at the Elizabeth Peabody Playhouse in Boston. There, at the age of seventeen, he had the role of the teenager Ralphie in *Awake and Sing!,* about a matriarchal Jewish family during the Great Depression. "This role," Nimoy later explained, "the young man surrounded by a hostile and repressive environment, so touched a responsive chord that I decided to make a career of acting."

He went to Boston College on a drama scholarship but dropped out after a few months. Moving to California, he took classes at the Pasadena Playhouse and had minor roles on TV and in the films *Queen for a Day* (1951) and *Rhubarb* (1951). He was given the title role in the movie *Kid Monk Baroni* (1952), about a facially disfigured boxer from the streets of New York City. Nimoy, who had been raised in a basically Italian neighborhood in Boston, closely identified with his part as the socially outcast prizefighter.

He then returned to supporting roles, as in the movies *Old Overland Trail* (1953), where he played an

Indian, and *Them* (1954), a science-fiction classic where he had a bit part as a military paper-pusher. From 1954 to 1956 he served in the real army.

Returning to civilian life, Nimoy worked at odd jobs and resumed his apprenticeship as an actor. His first important TV role came in an episode called "His Brother's Fist" (1956) on the *West Point* series. He played an alien in the science-fiction movie *Satan's Satellites* (1958).

From 1958 to 1960 he studied acting under Jeff Corey in Hollywood. From 1960 to 1962 Nimoy assisted Corey as a teacher of acting. In 1962 Nimoy opened his own acting studio, which he ran for three years. His teaching methods were greatly influenced by Stanislavski.

During his years as a teacher, he continued to labor as a minor acting figure. He made guest appearances on TV series, such as *Dr. Kildare,* and he starred in a Hollywood stage production of *Deathwatch* (1960) and in the filmed version of the same story (1966).

Nimoy's big break came in 1966 when he was cast as Mr. Spock, the pointy-eared half human and half alien, in the TV science-fiction series *Star Trek* (1966-69). Spock was the first officer of the starship *Enterprise,* which engaged in various adventures as it traveled through space. The series developed a cult of fanatic fans called Trekkies. Nimoy himself became a popular hero as Spock.

He then had a regular role in the TV international-intrigue adventure series *Mission: Impossible* (1969-71). In the summer of 1971 he toured as Tevye in the Jewish musical *Fiddler on the Roof.* Late in 1971 he performed in a San Diego, California, production of *The Man in a Glass Booth.* In 1973 he starred as an escapee from a Nazi concentration camp in a New York City production of *Full Circle.*

From 1973 to 1975 he provided the voice of Spock for an animated *Star Trek* series. In 1976 he began to serve as host and narrator for the syndicated TV shows *The Coral Jungle,* a documentary series about the undersea world, and *In Search of . . .,* a documentary series that attempted to explain, and provide possible answers for, such mysteries as ghosts, monsters, and strange phenomena.

In the mid-1970s Nimoy became active as a writer. He published his autobiography as *I Am Not Spock* (1975). His other books focus on his poetry and photography, as in *You and I* (1973), *We Are All Children Searching for Love* (1977), and *Come Be with Me* (1979).

Nimoy also became involved with other activities, such as composing and recording songs. A committed liberal, he participated in the Vietnam antiwar movement, served as a delegate to the Democratic Central Committee in 1971 and 1972, campaigned for Eugene McCarthy for president in 1972, became a member of the American Civil Liberties Union, supported the United Farm Workers, and taught at Synanon (the controversial self-help program for former drug addicts).

Meanwhile, Nimoy was also broadening his acting range. He starred as a psychiatrist in the Broadway play *Equus* (1977) and played a similar role in a remake of the classic science-fiction movie *Invasion of the Body Snatchers* (1978). From 1978 to 1980 he gave stage performances in the one-man show *Vincent* (which he also wrote and directed), as Theo van Gogh, brother of the famed painter Vincent van Gogh. He played Golda Meir's husband, Morris Meyerson, in the movie *A Woman Called Golda* (TV, 1982).

But Nimoy's reputation still rests principally on his performances as Mr. Spock. In recent years he has played the role in a series of full-length movies: *Star Trek, the Motion Picture* (1979); *Star Trek II: The Wrath of Khan* (1982); *Star Trek III: The Search for Spock* (1984); and *Star Trek IV: The Voyage Home* (1986). He also directed the last two of those films. In 1986 he appeared in a Western Airlines commercial that alluded to his Spock role.

Nimoy met Sandi Zober when both were acting at the Pasadena Playhouse. They married in 1954 and had two children: Julie and Adam.

Selected performances:

Stage

Awake and Sing! (1948)
Stalag 17 (1951)
A Streetcar Named Desire (1955)
Cat on a Hot Tin Roof (1959)
Deathwatch (1960)
Monserrat (1963)
Irma La Douce (1965)
Fiddler on the Roof (1971)
The Man in the Glass Booth (1971)
Oliver! (1972)
Full Circle (1973)
Camelot (1973)
One Flew over the Cuckoo's Nest (1974)
The King and I (1974)
Caligula (1975)
The Fourposter (1975)
Twelfth Night (1975)
My Fair Lady (1976)
Sherlock Holmes (1976)
Equus (1977)
Vincent (1978-80)

Films

Queen for a Day (1951)
Rhubarb (1951)
Kid Monk Baroni (1952)
Old Overland Trail (1953)
Them (1954)
Satan's Satellites (1958)
The Balcony (1963)

Leonard Nimoy

Deathwatch (1966)
Valley of Mystery (1967)
Catlow (1971)
Assault on the Wayne (TV, 1971)
Baffled! (TV, 1973)
The Alpha Caper (TV, 1973)
The Missing Are Deadly (TV, 1975)
Invasion of the Body Snatchers (1978)
Star Trek, the Motion Picture (1979)
Seizure: The Story of Kathy Morris (TV, 1980)
A Woman Called Golda (TV, 1982)
Marco Polo (TV, 1982)
Star Trek II: The Wrath of Khan (1982)
Star Trek III: The Search for Spock (1984)
Star Trek IV: The Voyage Home (1986)

TV

Star Trek (1966-69)
Mission: Impossible (1969-71)
Star Trek (animated, voice only, 1973-75)
The Coral Jungle (1976)
In Search of . . . (1976-82)

★★

Lilli Palmer

Multitalented Artist

(1914-86)

Lilli Palmer was born in Posen, Germany (now Poznań, Poland), on May 24, 1914. Her original name was Maria Lilli Peiser.

She was raised in Berlin. Her mother had been an actress, and Lilli began to perform in amateur plays when she was ten. In April 1932 she graduated from high school and from drama school.

Later that year she left Berlin and joined the players at the Darmstadt State Theater, where she soon made her professional debut. In 1933, however, Hitler took over Germany and the Nazis halted her career. Moving to Paris, she literally sang for her supper at cabarets and strip joints.

Palmer then went to England, where she began to win roles in English-language movies, such as *Crime Unlimited* (1934), *Secret Agent* (1936), and *Thunder Rock* (1942). She also appeared onstage in *The Tree of Eden* (1938), *Little Ladyship* (1939), and other plays.

In 1943 Palmer married the British actor Rex Harrison. They had one child: Rex Carey Alfred Harrison, whom they always called Carey (Harrison's original surname).

In 1945 Palmer and Harrison made their first movie together: *The Rake's Progress* (released as *Notorious Gentleman* in the United States). She played an Austrian Jewess who marries, and is then swindled by, the rake. Late that year Palmer and Harrison moved to the United States.

She soon made fine impressions in the Hollywood movies *Cloak and Dagger* (1946) and *Body and Soul* (1947). In the latter film she played a sophisticated French painter who profoundly affects an American boxer (portrayed by John Garfield).

Palmer and Harrison continued to appear together on both stage and screen. They acted in the New York City productions of *Bell, Book, and Candle* (1950); *Venus Observed* (1952); and *The Love of Four Colonels* (1953). And they starred in the films *The Long Dark Hall* (1951) and *The Fourposter* (1952).

But their marriage was slowly dissolving. In 1957 they were divorced, and later that year she married the Argentine film star Carlos Thompson.

In the mid-1950s Palmer began to make French and German films in addition to British and American pictures. But only a few roles were worthy of her talents. In *The Counterfeit Traitor* (1962), set in the Hitler era, she played a German resistance fighter who is executed by a Nazi firing squad. In *The Boys from Brazil* (1978) she was the sister and helper of a Nazi-hunter (played by Laurence Olivier).

In later years Palmer turned increasingly to other artistic endeavors. She became a highly acclaimed painter, and her canvases were hung in major galleries.

Palmer also showed remarkable ability as a writer, beginning with the book *Change Lobsters—and Dance: An Autobiography* (German, 1974; English, 1975). She followed that with a series of novels, written in German and translated by Palmer or her son, Carey Harrison, into English, including *The Red Raven* (German, 1977; English, 1978) and *Night Music* (German, 1981; English, 1982).

Nevertheless, she continued to appear as an actress. She had, for example, the role of Natalya in the miniseries *Peter the Great* (TV, 1986).

Palmer died in Los Angeles, California, on January 27, 1986.

Selected performances:

Stage

Road to Gandahar (1938)
The Tree of Eden (1938)
Little Ladyship (1939)
You, of All People (1939)
Ladies into Action (1940)
No Time for Comedy (1941)
My Name is Aquilon (1949)
Caesar and Cleopatra (1949)
ANTA Album (1950)
Bell, Book, and Candle (1950)
Venus Observed (1952)
The Love of Four Colonels (1953)
A Song at Twilight (1966)
Suite in Three Keys (1966)

Films

Crime Unlimited (1934)
Secret Agent (1936)
Command Performance (1937)
A Girl Must Live (1938)
The Door with Seven Locks (1940)
Thunder Rock (1942)
The Gentle Sex (1943)
The Rake's Progress (1945, G.B.; U.S., *Notorious Gentleman*)
Cloak and Dagger (1946)
Body and Soul (1947)
My Girl Tisa (1948)
No Minor Vices (1949)
The Long Dark Hall (1951)
The Fourposter (1952)
Main Street to Broadway (1953)
But Not for Me (1959)
Modigliani of Montparnasse (1961)
The Pleasure of His Company (1961)
The Counterfeit Traitor (1962)
Miracle of the White Stallions (1963)
Adorable Julia (1964)
Torpedo Bay (1964)
The Amorous Adventures of Moll Flanders (1965)
And So to Bed (1965)
Operation Crossbow (1965)
Jack of Diamonds (1967)
Devil in Silk (1968)
The High Commissioner (1968)
Oedipus the King (1968)
Sebastian (1968)
De Sade (1969)
Hard Contract (1969)
Hauser's Memory (TV, 1970)
The House That Screamed (1971)
Murders in the Rue Morgue (1972)
The Boys from Brazil (1978)
The Holcroft Covenant (1985)
Peter the Great (TV, 1986)

TV

The Lilli Palmer Show (1951)
Lilli Palmer Theater (1956)
The Zoo Gang (1975)

★★★

Nehemiah Persoff

Powerful Supporting Actor

(1920-)

Nehemiah Persoff was born in Jerusalem, Palestine (now Israel), on August 14, 1920. He immigrated to the United States in 1929.

Persoff studied at the Hebrew Technical Institute in New York City (1934-37), worked as an electric-motor repairman in the signal department of the New York City subway system (1939-41), and served in the army (1942-45).

Returning to civilian life in New York City, he decided to become an actor. He studied under Stella Adler, Elia Kazan, Lee Strasberg, and others. Since 1948 he has been a member of the Actors Studio.

His first stage performance came as Candy, the lame cleaning man, in *Of Mice and Men* (1947) at a summer production in Haverhill, Massachusetts. Later that year he made his New York City debut by appearing in *Galileo*. Over the next several years he continued to perform regularly as a character actor on the New York City stage, as in *Richard III* (1949), *Peter Pan* (1950), and *Peer Gynt* (1951).

In 1952 Persoff returned to Israel, and in Tel Aviv he played Tom in *The Glass Menagerie*. He also appeared there in *Volpone*.

In 1953 he was in New York City again to act in the play *Camino Real*. Over the next couple of years he performed in *Golden Boy* (1954) and several other stage works.

An important step in Persoff's career was his move into TV during the 1950s. He had a supporting role in the original TV version of the play "Marty" (1953) on the *Philco Television Playhouse*, portrayed Pablo in "For Whom the Bell Tolls" (1958) on *Playhouse Ninety*, and appeared in many other plays on anthology series during TV's Golden Age.

For many years Persoff has been one of the busiest guest performers on American TV drama and comedy series. His credits include such wide-ranging material as the mystery of *Alfred Hitchcock Presents*, the comedy of *Barney Miller*, the slapstick of *Gilligan's Island*, the crime drama of *Hawaii Five-O*, the medical drama of *Marcus Welby*, and the western adventure of *Rawhide*. In 1986 he appeared in an episode of the fantasy series *Highway to Heaven*.

He has also been active as a powerful supporting actor in numerous films. In his early movies he frequently portrayed heavies, as in his gangster roles in *The Harder They Fall* (1956), *Al Capone* (1959), and *Some Like It Hot* (1959). In *Fate Is the Hunter* (1964) he played an airline executive scheming for a promotion.

Persoff occasionally returned to the stage, as in *Rosebloom* (1970). He made a strong impression in the one-man show *Aleichem Sholem—Sholem Aleichem* (1971). And he played Rabbi Azrielke in *The Dybbuk* (1975).

His later films included *Mafia* (1969), *Red Sky at Morning* (1971), *Psychic Killer* (1976), *Ziegfeld: The Man and His Women* (TV, 1978), and *Condominium* (TV, 1980). In *Sadat* (TV, 1983) he played Leonid Brezhnev, head of the Soviet Union. In *Yentl* (1983) he was the title character's father.

Persoff married Thia Persov in 1951. They had four children: Jeffrey, Dan, Perry, and Dahlia.

He has explained the source of his energy and determination as follows: "I suspect that one of the most powerful forces shaping my life when I was growing up in the U.S.A. was that German with the small mustache who questioned the right of my people (and therefore me) to live. He put the burden of proof on me, personally. I was then determined to develop whatever talent I had to prove worthy of the gift of life. The habit of work remained with me in later years."

Selected performances:

Stage

Of Mice and Men (1947)
The Male Animal (1947)
The Devil's Disciple (1947)
Hay Fever (1947)
Galileo (1947)
Sundown Beach (1948)
Richard III (1949)
Montserrat (1949)
Peter Pan (1950)
King Lear (1950)
Peer Gynt (1951)
The Glass Menagerie (1952)

Volpone (1952)
Camino Real (1953)
Detective Story (1953)
The Road to Rome (1953)
Mademoiselle Colombe (1954)
Golden Boy (1954)
Reclining Figure (1954)
Tiger at the Gates (1955)
Only in America (1959)
Rosebloom (1970)
Aleichem Sholem—Sholem Aleichem (1971)
The Dybbuk (1975)

Films

A Double Life (1947)
The Naked City (1948)
On the Waterfront (1954)
The Harder They Fall (1956)
The Wild Party (1956)
The Wrong Man (1956)
Men in War (1957)
This Angry Age (1958)
The Badlanders (1958)
Never Steal Anything Small (1959)
Green Mansions (1959)
Al Capone (1959)
Some Like It Hot (1959)
The Big Show (1961)
The Comancheros (1961)
The Hook (1963)
Fate Is the Hunter (1964)
A Global Affair (1964)
The Greatest Story Ever Told (1965)
The Money Jungle (1968)
The Dangerous Days of Kiowa Jones (TV, 1966)
Escape to Mindanao (TV, 1968)
Panic in the City (1968)
The Power (1968)
The Girl Who Knew Too Much (1969)
Mafia (1969)
The People Next Door (1970)
Cutter's Trail (TV, 1970)
Red Sky at Morning (1971)
Lieutenant Schuster's Wife (TV, 1972)
The Sex Symbol (TV, 1974)
The Stranger Within (TV, 1974)
Eric (TV, 1975)
Francis Gary Powers: The True Story of the U-2 Spy Incident (TV, 1976)
Psychic Killer (1976)
Voyage of the Damned (1976)
Killing Stone (TV, 1978)
Ziegfeld: The Man and His Women (TV, 1978)
The Word (TV, 1978)
The Rebels (TV, 1979)
The French Atlantic Affair (TV, 1979)
F.D.R.: The Last Year (TV, 1980)
The Henderson Monster (TV, 1980)
Turnover Smith (TV, 1980)
Condominium (TV, 1980)
Sadat (TV, 1983)
Yentl (1983)

★★★

Molly Picon

The Yiddish Helen Hayes

(1898-)

Molly Picon was born in New York City, New York, in 1898. When she was about three years old, she moved with her parents to Philadelphia.

At the age of five, billed as Baby Margaret, she began to win money for her singing and dancing at amateur contests. She also performed in early movie theaters, known as nickelodeons.

In 1904 Picon joined Michael Thomashefsky's Yiddish repertory company in Philadelphia, where she played juvenile roles for the next three years. Afterward she appeared in plays at the Arch Street theater in the same city (1908-1912) and then performed in cabaret (1912-15). She left William Penn High School after her second year so that she would have time to earn more money on the stage.

During 1918-19 she toured in a vaudeville act called

The Four Seasons. That work took her to Boston, where she was hired in 1919 by Jacob Kalich, head of a Yiddish repertory company. At that time Picon was largely ignorant of Jewish culture. Kalich, a highly literate man, taught her.

Later in 1919 Picon and Kalich, whom she nicknamed Yonkel, were married. In 1920 she delivered a stillborn baby girl. A pelvic problem prevented her from ever having children, but later they took youngsters into their home as part of the Foster Parents' Plan for War Children.

Picon rapidly became a major Yiddish star, especially in comic roles. She performed with her husband's troupe at the Boston Grand Opera House (1919-20) and then toured with the company in Europe (1920-22). Returning to the United States, she settled in New York City and appeared in such shows as *Yankele* (1923), *Shmendrik* (1924), *Rabbi's Melody* (1926), and *Hello, Molly!* (1928). With her husband she toured Europe, the Near East, South Africa, and Argentina in the early 1930s. She then returned to work in New York City.

With the decline of the Yiddish theater, Picon turned increasingly to Broadway, debuting there as Becky Felderman in *Morning Star* (1940). Then came World War II, during which she toured American military camps. In 1946 she and her husband entertained Holocaust survivors in European displaced-persons camps.

After the war she continued to work in a variety of stage formats, both Yiddish and English. Perhaps the highlight of her stage career came with her role as Clara Weiss, an American widow looking for a husband in Israel, in the musical *Milk and Honey*. She starred in the play on Broadway in 1961-62 and then toured the United States with the show in 1963-64.

Picon also played a Jewish widow, Mrs. Jacoby, in *A Majority of One* (1960, 1965, 1966). She appeared in the revue *How to Be a Jewish Mother* (1967); played Dolly Levi in *Hello, Dolly!* (1971); and gave a one-woman show in Yiddish, *Hello, Molly!* (1979).

Because of her small size (only 5′ tall) but large talent, Picon has been called the Bean-sized Bernhardt and, more appropriately, the Yiddish Helen Hayes.

She has frequently appeared on TV. In 1949 she hosted *The Molly Picon Show,* a variety program.

Her film career began with two Yiddish musical-comedy pictures made in Poland: *Yiddle mit'n fiddle* (1936, released in America in early 1937 with English subtitles as *Yiddle with His Fiddle*) and *Mamale* (1938, released in America in 1938 with English subtitles as *Little Mother*). It was much later before she finally began to make English-language movies, beginning with the comedy *Come Blow Your Horn* (1963), in which she played the Jewish mother of two fast-living sons. In the filmed version of the Jewish musical *Fiddler on the Roof* (1971) she played Yente the matchmaker; her husband, Yonkel, also had a role in that film. In *For Pete's Sake* (1974) she was a motherly madam. She also appeared in *Murder on Flight 502* (TV, 1975) and *Cannonball Run II* (1984).

Picon wrote her family biography in the book *So Laugh a Little* (1962), while she presented her autobiography in *Molly!* (with Jean Bergantini Grillo, 1980).

In March 1985 she received one of the first ten Goldie Awards ever presented by the Congress for Jewish Culture (the awards are so named because they are statuettes of Abraham Goldfaden, father of the Yiddish theater). The honor was bestowed on Picon for her lifetime of contributions to the Jewish performing arts.

Selected performances:

Stage

Gabriel; The Silver King; Sappho; Uncle Tom's Cabin; Shulamite (1904-1907)
Girl of the Golden West; God of Revenge; Medea; King Lear; The Kreutzer Sonata (1908-1912)
Broadway Jones (1915)
Bunty Pulls the Strings (1915)
The Four Seasons (1918)
Yankele (1923)
Zipke (1924)
Shmendrik (1924)
Gypsy Girl (1925)
Molly Dolly (1926)
Rabbi's Melody (1926)
Little Devil (1926)
Kid Mother (1927)
Little Czar (1927)
Raizelle (1927)
Mazel brocke (1928)
Hello, Molly! (1928)
Girl of Yesterday (1931)
Love Thief (1931)
Kale loift (1936)
Morning Star (1940)
Oy is dus a leben (1942)
For Heaven's Sake (1948)
Sadie Is a Lady (1949)
Abi gezunt (1950)
Mazel tov Molly (1950)
Take It Easy (1950)
Make Momma Happy (1953)
Farblonjet Honeymoon (1956)
The Kosher Woman (1959)
A Majority of One (1960)
Milk and Honey (1961)
Dear Me, the Sky Is Falling (1965)
Madame Mousse (1965)
The Rubaiyat of Howard Klein (1967)
How to Be a Jewish Mother (1967)
Paris Is Out! (1970)
The Front Page (1970)
Hello, Dolly! (1971)
How Do You Live with Love? (1975)
Something Old, Something New (1977; also in retitled version, *Second Time Around,* 1978)
Hello, Molly! (1979)

Films

Yiddle mit'n fiddle (1936, Pol. in Yid.; U.S., *Yiddle with His Fiddle*)
Mamale (1938, Pol. in Yid.; U.S., *Little Mother)*
Come Blow Your Horn (1963)
Fiddler on the Roof (1971)
For Pete's Sake (1974)
Murder on Flight 502 (TV, 1975)
Cannonball Run II (1984)

TV

The Molly Picon Show (1949)

★★

Luise Rainer

Poignantly Winsome Actress

(1910-)

Luise Rainer was born in Vienna, Austria, on January 12, 1910 (some sources give 1909 or 1912). At the age of sixteen she began to appear on the Viennese stage under the famed producer-director Max Reinhardt.

In the early 1930s she made a few films in Austria and Germany. A talent scout for the American film company Metro-Goldwyn-Mayer (MGM) discovered her in Vienna and signed her to a Hollywood movie contract.

Her big break came when Myrna Loy walked out on the filming of *Escapade*. Rainer replaced Loy in the picture, which was released in 1935.

She reached major stardom with her next movie, *The Great Ziegfeld* (1936). Playing the actress Anna Held, the unhappy first wife of the impresario Florenz Ziegfeld, Rainer made a lasting impression. Perhaps the most memorable moment in the film occurs when Anna calls her ex-husband on the telephone to congratulate him on his forthcoming marriage (to the actress Billie Burke, played by Myrna Loy) and emotionally begins, "Hello, Flo?—Yes, this is Anna."

Rainer's next performance, as a passive but strong Chinese peasant-wife in *The Good Earth* (1937), was also well received.

But her next five films did not fare well. The best of the lot was *The Great Waltz* (1938), in which she played Poldi Vogelhuber in an apocryphal story of the Viennese waltz composer Johann Strauss II.

Rainer's petite size, wide soulful eyes, and poignant winsomeness were attractive to audiences. But her accent made her difficult to cast, and many felt that she was too quick to tears and emotional excesses.

After *Dramatic School* (1938) she left movies for several years, during which she appeared on the New York City stage in a few plays, notably *Saint Joan* (1940).

In 1937 she married the playwright Clifford Odets. But they soon developed marital problems, and they divorced a few years later.

Rainer returned to movies one last time, in *Hostages* (1943), after which she permanently retired from films. She had had one of the most notable, but also one of the briefest, careers of any major movie actress.

In the mid-1940s she married the American publisher Robert Knittel, moved with him to London, and had a daughter, Franceska.

Rainer later made only rare appearances on TV and in stage plays, as in the New York City production of *The Lady from the Sea* (1950).

Her principal activity in recent years has been painting, for which she has shown a great gift. A one-person exhibition of her paintings was held at the Patrick Seale Gallery in London in 1978.

Rainer has also taken up recitation. She recited Tennyson's narrative poem *Enoch Arden,* with background music by Richard Strauss, during tours of the United States in 1981-82 and 1983.

Selected performances:

Stage

Behold the Bride (1939)
Saint Joan (1940)
A Kiss for Cinderella (1942)
The Lady from the Sea (1950)

Films

Escapade (1935)
The Great Ziegfeld (1936)
The Good Earth (1937)
The Emperor's Candlesticks (1937)
Big City (1937)
The Toy Wife (1938)
The Great Waltz (1938)
Dramatic School (1938)
Hostages (1943)

★★★

Tony Randall

Supreme Light-Comedy Actor

(1920-)

Tony Randall was born in Tulsa, Oklahoma, on February 26, 1920. His original name was Leonard Rosenberg.

He tried out for, but failed to get roles in, plays at Central High School in Tulsa. Later, after studying speech and drama for one year at Northwestern University, he went to the Neighborhood Playhouse School of the Theater in New York City, where he was coached by Sanford Meisner in acting and Martha Graham in movement.

In the summer of 1939, as Anthony Randall, he made his first stage appearances by acting in productions at the Upper Ferndale Country Club. His New York City debut came in 1941 when he played a Chinese in *The Circle of Chalk* at the Dramatic Workshop of the New School for Social Research. He then acted in other plays, such as *The Corn Is Green* (1942).

In 1942 Randall married Florence Mitchell, whom he had met when both were students at Northwestern. He then spent four years (1942-46) in the army.

Returning to civilian life, Randall began to develop a reputation as a character actor through his appearances on radio soap operas, such as *Life's True Story*. He was a regular on the radio adventure series *I Love a Mystery* (1949-52).

Meanwhile, he also resumed his stage career. He toured in *The Barretts of Wimpole Street* (1947), playing the stuttering brother. In 1947 he made his Broadway debut by appearing as Scarus in Shakespeare's *Antony and Cleopatra*. In *To Tell You the Truth* (1948) he played Adam in a sex comedy about the Garden of Eden. In 1949 he had the role of the Major Domo in *Caesar and Cleopatra*.

Throughout the 1950s Randall continued to show a wide range of theatrical skills on Broadway. Shortening his stage name to Tony Randall, he played a drunken movie star in *Oh, Men! Oh, Women!* (1954), a satire on psychoanalysis. In *Inherit the Wind* (1955) he was the sarcastic newsman E. K. Hornbeck. And in the musical comedy *Oh, Captain!* (1958) he displayed his singing and dancing talents.

However, it was television that brought Randall to national renown. As Harvey Weskitt, the swaggering but ineffectual high-school English teacher in the comedy series *Mr. Peepers* (1952-55), Randall developed his basic acting persona for the years to come. Frequently playing an intelligent but frustrated and lonely bumbler, Randall has come to be regarded by many critics as the supreme light-comedy actor of his time.

His movie debut was in the filmed version of *Oh, Men! Oh, Women!* (1957), not in his stage role but as a patient in love with his analyst's fiancée. Then, in *Will Success Spoil Rock Hunter?* (1957), he had the title role as a sheepish advertising man. There followed a series of impeccably constructed performances in *Pillow Talk* (1959), *Send Me No Flowers* (1964), and other film comedies.

The single role by which Randall is most widely known is that of Felix Unger in the TV comedy series based on Neil Simon's play *The Odd Couple.* Though Randall was not in the original Broadway cast or in the movie version, he did tour in the show before it ran as a TV series from 1970 to 1975. Unger is an obsessively neat perfectionist who constantly irritates his sloppy, generally easygoing roommate, Oscar Madison (played by Jack Klugman).

Randall later starred in two more TV comedy series. In *The Tony Randall Show* (1976-78) he played the widower and father Judge Walter Franklin. In *Love, Sidney* (1981-82) he had the title role as a lonely middle-aged bachelor who shares his Manhattan apartment on a platonic basis with a young woman and her daughter.

Randall has also continued to make films, including *Kate Bliss and the Ticker Tape Kid* (TV, 1978), *Foolin' Around* (1980), and *Sidney Shorr: A Girl's Best Friend* (TV, 1981; which led to the TV series *Love, Sidney*). In *Off Sides* (TV, made 1980, telecast 1984) he portrayed a bearded guru who coaches a hippie football team.

Randall is also busy outside the sphere of acting. He is an avid classical-music, especially opera, buff and frequently appears at concerts and operas as a commentator or supporter. For example, he has often participated in the "Opera Quiz" segments aired during intermissions of live Metropolitan Opera broadcasts. And on December 31, 1984, he served champagne to the members of the New York Philharmonic during the *Live from Lincoln Center* telecast.

In 1984 Randall participated in a New York City radio program commemorating the anniversary of the atomic bombing of Hiroshima. He has been especially active in the movement to free Soviet Jews and has lent his name to many public rallies in their behalf.

Selected performances:

Stage

The Circle of Chalk (1941)
Candida (1941)
The Corn Is Green (1942)
The Barretts of Wimpole Street (1947)
Antony and Cleopatra (1947)
To Tell You the Truth (1948)
Caesar and Cleopatra (1949)
Oh, Men! Oh, Women! (1954)
Inherit the Wind (1955)
Oh, Captain! (1958)
Arms and the Man (1960)
Goodbye Again (1961)
UTBU (1966)
The Odd Couple (1970, 1976)
The Music Man (1978)

Films

Oh, Men! Oh, Women! (1957)
Will Success Spoil Rock Hunter? (1957)
No Down Payment (1957)
The Mating Game (1959)
Pillow Talk (1959)
The Adventures of Huckleberry Finn (1960)
Let's Make Love (1960)
Lover Come Back (1961)
Boys' Night Out (1962)
Island of Love (1963)
The Brass Bottle (1964)
Robin and the Seven Hoods (1964)
Send Me No Flowers (1964)
Seven Faces of Dr. Lao (1964)
Fluffy (1965)
The Alphabet Murders (1966)
Bang! Bang! You're Dead! (1966)
Hello Down There (1969)
Kate Bliss and the Ticker Tape Kid (TV, 1978)
Scavenger Hunt (1979)
Foolin' Around (1980)
Sidney Shorr: A Girl's Best Friend (TV, 1981)
Off Sides (TV, 1984)
Hitler's SS: Portrait in Evil (1985)
My Little Pony, the Movie (1986)
Sunday Drive (TV, 1986)

Radio

I Love a Mystery (1949-52)

TV

Mr. Peepers (1952-55)
The Odd Couple (1970-75)
The Tony Randall Show (1976-78)
Love, Sidney (1981-82)

★★

Don Rickles

Insult Comedian

(1926-)

Don(ald) Rickles was born in New York City, New York, on May 8, 1926. He has long been one of America's leading stand-up comedians, working at major nightclubs and hotels in New York City, Miami, Las Vegas, and elsewhere. The basis of his humor is insult, and he has been labeled the Merchant of Venom.

But Rickles is also a dependable character actor. He is, in fact, a graduate of the American Academy of Dramatic Arts. His first important dramatic role was in "A Note of Fear" (1955) on the TV anthology series *Stage Seven*. During his early years he also had roles in the film dramas *Run Silent, Run Deep* (1958) and *The Rat Race* (1960), and in the film comedies *Bikini Beach* (1964) and *Enter Laughing* (1967).

Besides appearing as a guest comedian on most of the major talk and variety shows on TV, he has starred in his own series. *The Don Rickles Show* of 1968-69 was a part-game, part-variety program that he hosted. In 1972 *The Don Rickles Show* was a situation-comedy series with him as an advertising executive. More successful was *C.P.O. Sharkey* (1976-78), a situation comedy in which he starred as Chief Petty Officer Otto Sharkey, a navy drill instructor.

In the early 1980s he had a small role in the movie *For the Love of It* (TV, 1980) and gave a fine seriocomic performance in an episode of the TV series *Archie Bunker's Place*. In 1984 he cohosted the TV comedy series *Foul-ups, Bleeps, and Blunders*.

Rickles married Barbara Sklar, a secretary, in 1965. They had two children: Mindy and Lawrence.

Selected performances:

Stage

The Odd Couple (1967)

Films

Run Silent, Run Deep (1958)
The Rat Race (1960)
X: The Man with X-Ray Eyes (1963)
Bikini Beach (1964)
Muscle Beach Party (1964)
Beach Blanket Bingo (1965)
Enter Laughing (1967)
The Money Jungle (1968)
Where It's At (1969)
Kelly's Heroes (1970)
For the Love of It (TV, 1980)

TV

The Don Rickles Show (1968-69)
The Don Rickles Show (1972)
C.P.O. Sharkey (1976-78)
Foul-ups, Bleeps, and Blunders (1984)

★★★

Edward G. Robinson

Filmdom's Preeminent Tough Guy

(1893-1973)

Edward G. Robinson was born in Bucharest, Romania, on December 12, 1893. His original name was Emanuel Goldenberg.

Because the Romanian government was engaged in the systematic persecution of Jews, the Goldenbergs left Romania and moved to the United States in 1902. Young Emanuel attended New York City's Townsend Harris High School and the City College of the City University of New York. He dropped out of college after his sophomore year so that he could study acting at the American Academy of Dramatic Arts in New York City.

While he was at the academy, he was urged to change his name because it was too long, too foreign, and (he suspected) too Jewish. He selected Edward (after the current king of England) Robinson (after a character in an English comedy). However, he retained G. for Goldenberg as a middle initial. "Deep down in my deepest heart," he later wrote in his autobiography, *All My Yesterdays* (with Leonard Spigelgass, 1973), "I am, and have always been, Emanuel Goldenberg."

In 1913, soon after leaving the academy, he joined an Albany, New York, stock company, with which he made his professional acting debut, in *Paid in Full.* The play was staged in Binghamton, New York. Returning to New York City, he began to make a name for himself by performing three different roles in *Under Fire* (1915). For the next decade he served as a reliable supporting player in numerous stage productions.

In 1926 he married the actress Gladys Lloyd, with whom he had appeared in *Henry Behave* (1926). They had one child: Edward G. Robinson, Jr. (always referred to as Manny).

The big break in Robinson's career came in 1927 when he was given the leading role, that of the gangster Nick Scarsi, in *The Racket.*

Robinson was not interested in making movies, but economic pressures finally induced him to give in to the lure of Hollywood contracts. After appearing in several minor films, he rose to stardom with his brilliant portrayal of the title character, a ruthless mobster, in *Little Caesar* (1931). There followed a number of other racketeer or tough-guy roles in films throughout the 1930s, including *The Little Giant* (1933), *Barbary Coast* (1935), and *The Last Gangster* (1937). He soon became filmdom's preeminent performer of such roles.

In the early 1930s he began to experience marital troubles, apparently because Gladys wanted to go back to work as an actress. Robinson helped her to get roles in his movies *Smart Money* (1931), *Five Star Final* (1931), *The Hatchet Man* (1932), and *Two Seconds* (1932). The tensions between them eased, at least temporarily.

Meanwhile, Robinson was gradually being allowed to show the wide range of his acting ability. He displayed his flair for comedy in *The Whole Town's Talking* (1935) and *A Slight Case of Murder* (1938). He created deeply moving biographical portrayals in *Dr. Ehrlich's Magic Bullet* (1940), about a scientist trying to find a cure for venereal disease, and *A Dispatch from Reuters* (1940), about the founder of a news service. In *Brother Orchid* (1940) he took a gangster character and, by the end of the picture, convincingly turned him into a monk.

Robinson's versatility reflected his general intelligence and cultivation. He read voraciously and omnivorously, spoke numerous languages (and read Hebrew), built a remarkable art collection, painted some fine pictures himself, and loved great music (his favorite composer being Beethoven).

In the 1940s he continued to give memorable film performances. In *The Sea Wolf* (1941) he portrayed the maniacal captain of a ship. In *The Stranger* (1946) he hunted Nazi war criminals. Guilt haunted him in several movies: in *Scarlet Street* (1946), as a milquetoast who is driven to murder and who lets another man be executed for the crime; in *The Red House* (1947), as a man who loses his mind because of the horrible secret that he keeps about the red house, where he committed double murder; and in *All My Sons* (1948), as a manufacturer who sold defective airplane parts to the government during World War II and who finally kills himself when he learns that his treachery indirectly caused the death of his own son. In *Key Largo* (1948) he returned to a gangster character.

In 1943 Robinson was one of the stars featured in Ben Hecht's pageant *We Will Never Die,* which was a reaction to the growing reports of the Nazi horrors in Europe. The program comprised three parts: "The Roll Call," a recitation of great Jewish names in the arts and sciences from ancient times to the modern era; "Jews in the War," a dramatization of the contributions of American Jewish war heroes; and "Remember Us," a presentation of reports about the slaughters in Nazi Europe.

Through the years, Robinson had closely identified himself with many social and political causes promoting peace, democracy, and the betterment of minorities. But by the late 1940s the Communist witch-hunt in America had reached full swing, and Robinson, because of his fame, was one of the principal targets. At his own request he testified before the House Committee on Un-American Activities in 1947, 1950, and 1952. Nevertheless, he was blacklisted as a Communist sympathizer by major producers from the late 1940s through the mid-1950s.

But Robinson fought back, taking whatever films he could get and going back to the stage in *Darkness at Noon* (1951) and *Middle of the Night* (1956). Finally the famed producer-director Cecil B. DeMille returned Robinson to major films by giving him a central role in the biblical epic *The Ten Commandments* (1956).

The mid-1950s also saw the final deterioration of his marriage to Gladys, who had threatened divorce many times and had been in and out of mental hospitals for many years. In 1956 he divorced her, and while making the property settlement he had to give up his art collection.

In 1958 he married Jane Bodenheimer Adler, director of a firm through which the first Mrs. Robinson had purchased clothes for many years. With Jane he finally found the love and peace that had always been missing from his life. She was highly knowledgeable about painting, and she helped him to build another picture collection.

At an age when most actors retire, Robinson kept working and showing no loss of energy or skills. From 1954 to 1971 he guest-starred in numerous TV series, including *For the Defense* (1954), *Playhouse Ninety* (1958), *General Electric Theater* (1961), and *Night Gallery* (1971). Among his later movies were *A Hole in the Head* (1959), *The Prize* (1964), *The Cincinnati Kid* (1965), *Mackenna's Gold* (1969), and *Song of Norway* (1970).

His portrayals of elderly men were dignified and richly evocative, such as his part as the witness to a crime that no one believes really happened in *The Old Man Who Cried Wolf!* (TV, 1970). In *Soylent Green* (1973) he had his final movie role, as Sol(omon) Roth, a serene philosopher who, in the horribly deprived New York City of 2022, gives up his life to prove that a new kind of food (soylent green) is made of human flesh.

In his last years Robinson fought off several health problems. He had a heart attack in Africa while filming *A Boy Ten Feet Tall* (1965). In 1966 he had a near-fatal auto accident. In 1970 it was discovered that he had cancer of the bladder. After many sessions of cobalt treatment, he seemed to have made a remarkable recovery. But cancer finally claimed him in Los Angeles, California, on January 26, 1973.

Selected performances:

Stage

Paid in Full (1913)
Under Fire (1915)
Under Sentence (1916)
The Pawn (1917)
The Little Teacher (1918)
First Is Last (1919)
Night Lodging (1919)
Poldekin (1920)
Samson and Delilah (1920)
The Idle Inn (1921)
The Deluge (1922)
Banco (1922)
Peer Gynt (1923)
The Adding Machine (1923)
Launzi (1923)
A Royal Fandango (1923)
The Firebrand (1924)
Androcles and the Lion (1925)
The Man of Destiny (1925)
The Goat Song (1926)
The Chief Thing (1926)
Henry Behave (1926)
Juarez and Maximilian (1926)
Ned McCobb's Daughter (1926)
The Brothers Karamazov (1927)
Right You Are If You Think You Are (1927)
The Racket (1927)
A Man with Red Hair (1928)
Kibitzer (1929)
Mr. Samuel (1930)
Darkness at Noon (1951)
Middle of the Night (1956)

Films

The Bright Shawl (1923)
The Hole in the Wall (1929)
Night Ride (1929)
A Lady to Love (1930)
Outside the Law (1930)
East Is West (1930)
The Widow from Chicago (1930)
Little Caesar (1931)
Smart Money (1931)
Five Star Final (1931)
The Hatchet Man (1932)
Two Seconds (1932)
Tiger Shark (1932)
Silver Dollar (1932)
The Little Giant (1933)
I Loved a Woman (1933)
Dark Hazard (1934)
The Man with Two Faces (1934)
The Whole Town's Talking (1935)
Barbary Coast (1935)

Edward G. Robinson

Bullets or Ballots (1936)
Thunder in the City (1937)
Kid Galahad (1937)
The Last Gangster (1937)
A Slight Case of Murder (1938)
The Amazing Dr. Clitterhouse (1938)
I Am the Law (1938)
Confessions of a Nazi Spy (1939)
Blackmail (1939)
Dr. Ehrlich's Magic Bullet (1940)
Brother Orchid (1940)
A Dispatch from Reuters (1940)
The Sea Wolf (1941)
Manpower (1941)
Unholy Partners (1941)
Larceny, Inc. (1942)
Tales of Manhattan (1942)
Destroyer (1943)
Flesh and Fantasy (1943)
Tampico (1944)
Mr. Winkle Goes to War (1944)
Double Indemnity (1944)
The Woman in the Window (1945)
Our Vines Have Tender Grapes (1945)
Scarlet Street (1946)
Journey Together (1946)
The Stranger (1946)
The Red House (1947)
All My Sons (1948)
Key Largo (1948)
Night Has a Thousand Eyes (1948)
House of Strangers (1949)
It's a Great Feeling (1949)
My Daughter Joy (1950)
Actors and Sin (1952)
Vice Squad (1953)
Big Leaguer (1953)
The Glass Web (1953)
Black Tuesday (1954)
The Violent Men (1955)
Tight Spot (1955)
A Bullet for Joey (1955)
Illegal (1955)
Hell on Frisco Bay (1956)
Nightmare (1956)
The Ten Commandments (1956)
A Hole in the Head (1959)
Pepe (1960)
My Geisha (1961)
Two Weeks in Another Town (1962)
The Prize (1964)
Good Neighbor Sam (1964)
Robin and the Seven Hoods (1964)
The Outrage (1964)
Cheyenne Autumn (1964)
A Boy Ten Feet Tall (1965)
The Cincinnati Kid (1965)
The Biggest Bundle of Them All (1968)
Operation St. Peter's (1968)
Never a Dull Moment (1968)
Mackenna's Gold (1969)
Song of Norway (1970)
The Old Man Who Cried Wolf! (TV, 1970)
Soylent Green (1973)

★★★

Jill St. John

Beautiful Leading Lady

(1940-)

Jill St. John was born in Los Angeles, California, on August 19, 1940. Her original name was Jill Oppenheim.

She began to act professionally when she was only six years old. Her radio work included many episodes of the series *One Man's Family*, and she made her TV debut in a 1948 production of *A Christmas Carol*. By the time she was sixteen she had performed on radio over a thousand times and on TV at least fifty times.

In 1957 she married the millionaire Neil Durbin. They divorced in 1959, and the following year she married another wealthy man, Lance Reventlow. That marriage dissolved in 1963. In 1967 she wedded the entertainer Jack Jones, whom she divorced in 1969.

Meanwhile, St. John had begun her film career, debuting in *Summer Love* (1958). She also appeared in *The Roman Spring of Mrs. Stone* (1961), *Tender Is the Night* (1962), *Come Blow Your Horn* (1963), *The Oscar* (1966), and other movies.

St. John had been educated at the University of California in Los Angeles (UCLA), and the American diplomat Henry Kissinger once referred to her as "one of the brightest women I have ever met." Yet her physical beauty was so striking that for years she was consistently cast in roles that merely exploited her sexuality. Perhaps the clearest example of that aspect of her career was seen in her role as the sexy Tiffany Case in the James Bond spy picture *Diamonds Are Forever* (1971).

More recently, however, she has finally been able to break away from sexist stereotypes. A notable example was her role as the tough warden of a women's prison in *The Concrete Jungle* (1982). In the 1983-84 TV season she appeared in *Emerald Point, N.A.S.*

St. John now spends much of her time at her Aspen, Colorado, home, where she runs a sweater business. The main man in her life is the actor Robert Wagner.

Selected performances:

Films

Summer Love (1958)
The Remarkable Mr. Pennypacker (1959)
Holiday for Lovers (1959)
The Lost World (1960)
The Roman Spring of Mrs. Stone (1961)
Tender Is the Night (1962)
Come Blow Your Horn (1963)
Who's Been Sleeping in My Bed? (1963)
Who's Minding the Store? (1963)
Honeymoon Hotel (1964)
The Liquidator (1966)
The Oscar (1966)
Fame Is the Name of the Game (TV, 1966)
How I Spent My Summer Vacation (TV, 1967)
Banning (1967)
Eight on the Lam (1967)
The King's Pirate (1967)
Tony Rome (1967)
The Spy Killer (TV, 1969)
Foreign Exchange (TV, 1970)
Diamonds Are Forever (1971)
Sitting Target (1972)
Brenda Starr (TV, 1976)
Telethon (TV, 1977)
Hart to Hart (TV, 1979)
Rooster (TV, 1982)
The Concrete Jungle (1982)

TV

Emerald Point, N.A.S. (1983-84)

★★★

Joseph Schildkraut

First Actor to Play Otto Frank

(1896-1964)

Joseph Schildkraut was born in Vienna, Austria, on March 22, 1896. From an early age he traveled widely with his father, Rudolf Schildkraut, an internationally famous actor.

Joseph's first interest was music. He studied violin and piano at the Imperial Academy of Music in Berlin, from which he graduated with honors at the youthful age of fifteen in 1911.

Later that year he moved to the United States, his father having been engaged to act in German (and later Yiddish) plays in New York City. Joseph, against his father's wishes, decided to become an actor. He studied at the American Academy of Dramatic Arts, where his classmates included Paul Muni, William Powell, and Edward G. Robinson. Shortly after graduating from the academy in 1913, young Schildkraut made his professional debut, touring as the juvenile lead in *The Romantics*.

Later that year he returned with his parents to

JS-8-1137

Europe and settled in Berlin. There he was cast with his father in *The Prodigal Son* (1913). Soon he began to study with Albert Bassermann, the single greatest influence on Schildkraut as an actor.

Still an Austrian citizen (he became a naturalized American citizen in 1938), Schildkraut was inducted into the Austrian army for World War I service (1914-16). In 1918 he hit his full stride as an actor by appearing in three consecutive hits in Vienna: *Jeremiah, The Coral,* and *Shadow Dance.*

In 1920 Schildkraut returned to New York City, where he was soon chosen to play the title role, a carnival barker, in *Liliom* (1921). The play was a tremendous success, and it shot the young actor to stardom. With his new status he was asked to play his first important part in a movie (having earlier made a few minor film appearances), the D. W. Griffith production *Orphans of the Storm* (1921).

Meanwhile, he continued to appear in *Liliom.* In 1922, during its long run, he married the young actress Elise Bartlett. They divorced in 1931.

Soon after finishing *Liliom,* Schildkraut starred in two other important stage roles: the title part in *Peer Gynt* (1923) and the roguish artist-lover Benvenuto Cellini in *The Firebrand* (1924). In the late 1920s he made movies in Hollywood, including *The King of Kings* (1927), in which he acted with his father, *Tenth Avenue* (1928), and *Show Boat* (1929).

In the early 1930s Schildkraut went to England to do film work. While in London he met Marie McKay, whom he married in Vienna in 1932.

In Vienna, Schildkraut intended to accept a stage engagement. However, the anti-Semitism in the city had become so great that he decided to return to New York City.

In the early 1930s he appeared on the American stage in *Camille* (1932), *Alice in Wonderland* (1932), *Between Two Worlds* (1934), and other plays. He also returned to Hollywood to make numerous films, including *Viva Villa!* (1934), *The Crusades* (1935), *Souls at Sea* (1937), *The Three Musketeers* (1939), and *The Shop around the Corner* (1940). For his portrayal of Captain Dreyfus in *The Life of Emile Zola* (1937), Schildkraut won international acclaim.

Returning to the stage, he played in *Clash by Night* (1941), *Uncle Harry* (1942), and *The Cherry Orchard* (1944). In the late 1940s, while under contract with Republic Pictures, he was cast in a number of undistinguished films.

In 1951 he appeared on Broadway in *The Green Bay Tree,* and in 1953 he played in the New York City Center's production of Shakespeare's *Love's Labour's Lost.* Unable to find significant film roles, Schildkraut began to work heavily in a new medium—television. From 1949 to 1955 he appeared in over eighty-five live TV shows, some of them for *Joseph Schildkraut Presents* (1953-54), an anthology series of dramas that he hosted.

In October 1955 he returned to the stage and created a memorable characterization as Otto Frank in *The Diary of Anne Frank,* the true story of the young Jewish girl who, with family and friends, fled Hitler's Nazi Germany and hid in an Amsterdam attic till she was arrested and later killed in a concentration camp. Schildkraut himself regarded his work in that play as the high point of his career and life. In his autobiography, *My Father and I* (as told to Leo Lania, 1959), he explained that he had never before "felt such an intimate relationship with a play, never such an identification with a part."

Anne Frank's diary wrote the epitaph to the one-hundred-year history of the "emancipated" Germanized Jew. Rudolf Schildkraut had been a symbol of that era: the Jew who proudly thought of himself as a German, who assimilated German culture, and who in turn enriched the arts for all German people. Joseph Schildkraut, through his simple, humble, dignified portrayal of Otto Frank (Anne's father), paid homage not only to the Franks but also to his own father, who, after arriving in America, finally came to realize that, in Joseph's words, "his soul and heartbeat were Jewish," not German.

Schildkraut re-created the role in the filmed version of *The Diary of Anne Frank* (1959). In 1962 his wife, Marie, died, and in 1963 he married the young actress Leonora Rogers. His last performance came as Nicodemus in the movie *The Greatest Story Ever Told* (1965). He died in New York City on January 21, 1964.

Schildkraut had appeared in several dozen plays, over sixty films, and nearly one hundred TV productions. His acting range was extremely wide, from a romantic lead to virtually any kind of a supporting-character role. His hallmark was economy of gesture.

Schildkraut's heart was in the theater, which, like his father, he viewed as a "moral institution." Art, he said, should "plant in the hearts and minds of the bewildered and frustrated the seeds of understanding, hope, goodness, and humanity."

Selected performances:

Stage

The Romantics (1913)
The Prodigal Son (1913)
Jeremiah (1918)
The Coral (1918)
Shadow Dance (1918)
Pagans (1921)
Liliom (1921)
Peer Gynt (1923)
The Firebrand (1924)
An American Tragedy (1932)
Camille (1932)
Dear Jane (1932)

Alice in Wonderland (1932)
Between Two Worlds (1934)
Tomorrow's a Holiday! (1935)
Clash by Night (1941)
Uncle Harry (1942)
The Cherry Orchard (1944)
The Green Bay Tree (1951)
Love's Labour's Lost (1953)
The Diary of Anne Frank (1955)

Films

Orphans of the Storm (1921)
Dust of Desire (1923)
The Song of Love (1924)
The Road to Yesterday (1925)
Young April (1926)
The King of Kings (1927)
The Heart Thief (1927)
His Dog (1927)
The Forbidden Woman (1927)
Tenth Avenue (1928)
The Blue Danube (1928)
Show Boat (1929)
The Mississippi Gambler (1929)
Cock o' the Walk (1930)
Carnival (1931)
Blue Danube (new version, 1932)
Viva Villa! (1934)
Sisters under the Skin (1934)
Cleopatra (1934)
The Crusades (1935)
The Garden of Allah (1936)
Slave Ship (1937)
Souls at Sea (1937)
The Life of Emile Zola (1937)
Lancer Spy (1937)
The Baroness and the Butler (1938)
Marie Antoinette (1938)
Suez (1938)
Idiot's Delight (1939)
The Three Musketeers (1939)
Mr. Moto Takes a Vacation (1939)
The Man in the Iron Mask (1939)
Lady of the Tropics (1939)
The Rains Came (1939)
Pack Up Your Troubles (1939)
The Shop around the Corner (1940)
Phantom Raiders (1940)
Rangers of Fortune (1940)
Meet the Wildcat (1940)
The Parson of Panamint (1941)
The Cheaters (1945)
Monsieur Beaucaire (1946)
The Plainsman and the Lady (1946)
Northwest Outpost (1947)
Old Los Angeles (1948)
The Diary of Anne Frank (1959)
King of the Roaring Twenties (1961)
The Greatest Story Ever Told (1965)

TV

Joseph Schildkraut Presents (1953-54)

★★

George Segal

The Jewish Cary Grant

(1934-)

George Segal was born in New York City, New York, on February 13, 1934. While growing up in Great Neck, on Long Island, he regularly entertained children with magic tricks at parties. After attending George School, a privately run Quaker institution in Pennsylvania, he enrolled at Haverford College and then transferred to Columbia University, where he received a B.A. degree in 1955.

After working at a series of menial theater-related jobs, such as cleaning and ushering, Segal began to have opportunities to appear onstage. He had, for example, a small part in a Broadway revival of Eugene O'Neill's *The Iceman Cometh* in 1956.

In that year he also married Marion Sobol, a former TV story editor. They had two children: Elizabeth and Patty.

Following service in the army (1956-57), Segal returned to the stage and continued to perform without

George Segal

any spectacular results. He appeared in *Antony and Cleopatra* (1959), *Gideon* (1961), and a variety of other plays. Then, after a couple of minor roles in movies, including *The Young Doctors* (1961), he finally began to receive serious attention as an actor when he played the brother in Broadway's *Rattle of a Simple Man* (1963).

Segal became a major star with his performance in the film *King Rat* (1965). He had the leading role as a conniving American corporal who breeds rats and sells their flesh as game meat to his deceived fellow inmates at a prisoner-of-war camp during World War II. He also made a powerful impression in *Ship of Fools* (1965), which explores relationships among a shipload of Jews and non-Jews on a German passenger vessel in 1933.

He quickly followed with a series of strong performances. He was highly praised for his portrayal of Biff, Willy Loman's son, in the 1966 TV production of *Death of a Salesman*. In the movie *Who's Afraid of Virginia Woolf?* (1966) he played a young teacher caught up in a vicious battle between an older colleague and the latter's wife. In *Bye Bye Braverman* (1968), a comic story about New York City Jewish intellectuals, he had the lead. In *No Way to Treat a Lady* (1968), as a police detective hunting a serial killer, Segal combined serious and humorous elements in his character.

Indeed, through the years he has shown that he can play intensely serious roles and light comic-romantic leads with equal skill. The detective story *Trackdown: Finding the Goodbar Killer* (TV, 1983) and the psychological thriller *The Cold Room* (TV, 1984) exemplified his more serious personae. *The Owl and the Pussycat* (1970), on the other hand, showed his comedy skills. His light, sophisticated performance in *A Touch of Class* (1973) has been favorably compared with the work of Cary Grant. On a less subtle level there was his title role in *The Zany Adventures of Robin Hood* (TV, 1984), a broad spoof of the old Sherwood Forest legend. In the wild satirical comedy *Many Happy Returns* (TV, 1986) he played a man who is victimized by, and then wages war on, the Internal Revenue Service.

Though he has worked fairly steadily throughout his career, Segal spent many years in a drug-induced mental fog. He began to use drugs in the 1960s, but his work was most seriously affected from the mid-1970s to the early 1980s, particularly by cocaine. Finally he kicked the habit cold turkey by spending two weeks in a Palm Springs, California, motel room, where he was aided by Linda Rogoff, whom he married in 1983.

Regardless of the type of role he plays, Segal approaches it with wit and intelligence. The more complex the character, the better he likes it, his forte being thought rather than action.

Selected performances:

Stage

The Iceman Cometh (1956)
Don Juan (1956)
Antony and Cleopatra (1959)
Our Town (1959)
Leave It to Jane (1959)
Gideon (1961)
Rattle of a Simple Man (1963)
The Knack (1964)
Requiem for a Heavyweight (1985)

Films

The Young Doctors (1961)
Act One (1963)
Invitation to a Gunfighter (1964)
The New Interns (1964)
King Rat (1965)
Ship of Fools (1965)
Lost Command (1966)
The Quiller Memorandum (1966)
Who's Afraid of Virginia Woolf? (1966)
The St. Valentine's Day Massacre (1967)
Bye Bye Braverman (1968)
No Way to Treat a Lady (1968)
The Bridge at Remagen (1969)
The Girl Who Couldn't Say No (1969)
The Southern Star (1969)
Loving (1970)
The Owl and the Pussycat (1970)
Where's Poppa? (1970)
Born to Win (1971)
The Hot Rock (1972)
Blume in Love (1973)
A Touch of Class (1973)
The Terminal Man (1974)
California Split (1974)
Russian Roulette (1975)
The Black Bird (1975)
The Duchess and the Dirtwater Fox (1976)
Fun with Dick and Jane (1977)
Rollercoaster (1977)
Who Is Killing the Great Chefs of Europe? (1978)
Lost and Found (1979)
The Last Married Couple in America (1980)
Carbon Copy (1981)
The Deadly Game (TV, 1982)
Trackdown: Finding the Goodbar Killer (TV, 1983)
The Cold Room (TV, 1984)
The Zany Adventures of Robin Hood (TV, 1984)
Not My Kid (TV, 1985)
Stick (1985)
Many Happy Returns (TV, 1986)

TV

Take Five (1987)

★★

Peter Sellers

Comic Genius

(1925-80)

Peter Sellers was born of a Protestant father and Jewish mother in the Southsea district of Portsmouth, England, on September 8, 1925. His father, Bill Sellers, was a pianist, while his mother, Peg Sellers (née Marks), was part of a family theatrical touring company created by her mother. Bill met Peg when he was asked to join the troupe.

Peter Sellers began his own attempt at a show-business career in 1941 when he teamed up with a friend, Derek Altman, to form a song-and-joke act. Soon he took up the drums and played with various groups, including his father's touring band that entertained wartime troops and munition workers. Sellers himself served in the Royal Air Force (RAF) from 1943 to 1946.

Returning to civilian life, Sellers had a liaison with a woman whom he later called Sky Blue. The union produced a daughter, who was immediately put into the adoption system. He never saw the child.

Meanwhile, his attempts to rekindle his drumming career met with little success. He worked up a variety act—jokes, comic impersonations, and a little drumming and ukelele playing—and began to appear in music halls.

In 1948 Sellers telephoned a producer and impersonated the voices of two radio stars (Kenneth Horne and Richard Murdoch). Impressed, the producer hired him for some radio appearances. Sellers was an immediate hit, and he soon found himself inundated with offers for radio and concert engagements.

In 1949 he and a few friends, calling themselves Goons, made a recording of a comedy act and sent it to some radio officials. Two years later the recording finally led to the Goons' own radio series, called *Crazy People*. In 1952 the program became known as *The Goon Show*. One of England's most popular radio programs, the zany, anarchic, surrealistic *Goon Show* lasted till January 1960 and made Sellers famous.

Meanwhile, he also made his first ventures into movies. He began with a spinoff of the Goon characters in *Penny Points to Paradise* (1951), appeared as one of the eccentric robbers in the classic *The Ladykillers* (1956), and made a good impression as the comical elderly movie projectionist in *The Smallest Show on Earth* (1957). But the first film that really showed what he could do was *The Naked Truth* (1958), in which Sellers played several different roles: a hypocritical Scottish quizmaster, an aging bureaucrat, a sportsman, and a genial policeman.

In 1958 he starred in the stage satire *Brouhaha* as the sultan of a small Persian Gulf state. But Sellers's temperament was unsuited for the legitimate theater. Unable to sustain his interest in a single part for a long period of time, he kept changing his character and causing problems for the other performers. He left the show in February 1959 and never took another stage role.

His comic genius found its natural medium in films. In *The Mouse That Roared* (1959), set in a mythical European duchy, Sellers played three parts: the wily prime minister, the aged Grand Duchess Gloriana, and the shy, love-struck commander-in-chief of the army. In *I'm All Right, Jack* (1959), a brilliant satire of British management and labor practices, he played Fred Kite, the pompous, pathetically ignorant union leader.

At about that time Sellers began to develop a personal characteristic that lasted for the rest of his life: while he was making a film, he tended to be overtaken in real life by the character that he was playing. For example, in a rare noncomedic role, he played a vicious stolen-car dealer in *Never Let Go* (1960); and for many hours after work each day, he continued to act boorishly and to shout at people in the thug's rasping voice.

Sellers's first American movie was *Lolita* (1962). After that, he periodically alternated his filmmaking between American and British companies, often with international casts and locations.

His first internationally flavored movie was *The Pink Panther* (1964), filmed in Rome with French (Capucine), Italian (Claudia Cardinale), American (Robert Wagner), and British (Sellers and David Niven) stars. In *The Pink Panther* Sellers created one of the most universally popular characters of the modern cinema: the bumbling French detective Inspector Jacques Clouseau.

The part was originally slated for Peter Ustinov, who reportedly withdrew out of disappointment that Ava Gardner was not cast opposite him. Sellers got his basic idea for Inspector Clouseau from a box of Captain Webb matches. The label on the box pictured Captain Webb, the first man to swim across the English Channel to France. He had a big mustache and a facial expression

that Sellers associated with the ostentatious virility affected by some Frenchmen. At that moment, the actor decided to give the foolish Clouseau a big mustache and a great dignity, feeling that "a forgivable vanity would humanize him and make him kind of touching." Sellers also invented Clouseau's strange French accent, while the film's director, Blake Edwards, suggested the character's physical clumsiness, which would make his dignity even funnier.

Sellers played Clouseau again in *A Shot in the Dark* (1964), *The Return of the Pink Panther* (1975), *The Pink Panther Strikes Again* (1976), and *Revenge of the Pink Panther* (1978).

One of Sellers's most memorable achievements came in *Dr. Strangelove; or, How I Learned to Stop Worrying and Love the Bomb* (1964). He played three roles: the liberal-humanist president of the United States, the captive English RAF captain, and the mad German nuclear scientist Dr. Strangelove, whose right arm uncontrollably reasserts its inbred violence (attempting to strangle himself) and Fascism (giving the Nazi salute).

On a lighter note were his roles in the comedies *The World of Henry Orient* (1964), as a lecherous and lousy concert pianist; *What's New, Pussycat?* (1965), as a nutty psychiatrist; *The Wrong Box* (1966), as the disreputable Dr. Pratt; *I Love You, Alice B. Toklas* (1968), as a Jewish lawyer who becomes a hippie; *There's a Girl in My Soup* (1971), as an aging playboy; *Murder by Death* (1976), as the Chinese sleuth Sidney Wang; and *The Prisoner of Zenda* (1979), as both the cockney hansom cabdriver and the monarch of a mythical kingdom.

Sellers's greatest role was as Chauncey Gardiner (or Chance the gardener) in *Being There* (1979), an allegory of American society's worship of the appearance of things rather than their substance. Chance has spent his entire life inside the home and walled garden of the millionaire whose plants he tends. All he knows of life comes from what he has seen of it on TV. When the millionaire dies, Chance is turned out into the world. Through other people's illusions about him, he comes to be seriously thought of as a candidate for the presidency of the United States.

Sellers's work in *Being There* shows his artistry at its peak. The role of Chance required a naïve character who had been tranquilized against the harsh realities of the world and benumbed into a permanent passivity by his overexposure to the slick packaging of TV. In creating the part, Sellers felt that the key was the voice, which he eventually derived as an offshoot of the childlike, innocent voice of Sellers's favorite comedian—Stan Laurel. Then came the leisurely walk and the rest of the passionless character.

In real life Sellers was an ardent romantic, falling in love easily and frequently. In 1951 he married the aspiring actress Anne Hayes. They had two children: Michael and Sarah. In 1963 he divorced Anne, and in 1964 he wedded the actress Britt Ekland, with whom he had his daughter Victoria. Sellers and Ekland appeared together in *After the Fox* (1966) and *The Bobo* (1967) before divorcing in 1968. Michael, with Sarah and Victoria, wrote the book *P.S. I Love You: An Intimate Portrait of Peter Sellers* (1981).

From 1970 to 1974 Sellers was married to the socialite Miranda Quarry. Through the years, however, he had had romances with many others, including Sophia Loren, who appeared with him in *The Millionairess* (1960), and Liza Minnelli, who costarred with him in *Soft Beds and Hard Battles* (1974).

His final and greatest love was for the actress Lynne Frederick, whom he married in 1977. She helped him through the illnesses of his last years and served (at his pleading) as a buffer in his dealings with other people. She appeared with him in *The Prisoner of Zenda.*

Sellers's last role was in *The Fiendish Plot of Dr. Fu Manchu* (1980). He was preparing to do another Inspector Clouseau movie, *The Romance of the Pink Panther,* when he died of a long-standing heart ailment (he had had attacks in 1964, 1977, and 1979) in London, England, on July 24, 1980.

In 1982 the movie *Trail of the Pink Panther* was created from outtakes and previously unused sequences originally filmed for earlier comedies in the Pink Panther series.

Selected performances:

Stage

Brouhaha (1958)

Films

Penny Points to Paradise (1951)
Down among the Z Men (1952)
Orders Are Orders (1954)
John and Julie (1955)
The Ladykillers (1956)
The Smallest Show on Earth (1957)
The Naked Truth (1958, G.B.; U.S., *Your Past Is Showing*)
Up the Creek (1958)
Tom Thumb (1958)
Carlton-Browne of the F.O. (1959, G.B.; U.S., *Man in a Cocked Hat*)
The Mouse That Roared (1959)
I'm All Right, Jack (1959)
Two-Way Stretch (1960)
The Battle of the Sexes (1960)
Never Let Go (1960)
The Millionairess (1960)
Mr. Topaze (1961)
Only Two Can Play (1962)
The Waltz of the Toreadors (1962)
Lolita (1962)
The Dock Brief (1962)
The Wrong Arm of the Law (1963)
Heavens Above (1963)
The Pink Panther (1964)
Dr. Strangelove; or, How I Learned to Stop Worrying and Love the Bomb (1964)
The World of Henry Orient (1964)
A Shot in the Dark (1964)
What's New, Pussycat? (1965)
The Wrong Box (1966)
After the Fox (1966)
Casino Royale (1967)
Woman Times Seven (1967)
The Bobo (1967)
The Party (1968)
I Love You, Alice B. Toklas (1968)
The Magic Christian (1970)
Hoffman (1970)
There's a Girl in My Soup (1971)
Alice's Adventures in Wonderland (1972)
Where Does It Hurt? (1972)
Soft Beds and Hard Battles (1974, G.B.; U.S., *Undercovers Hero*)
The Optimists of Nine Elms (1974)
The Great McGonagall (1975)
The Return of the Pink Panther (1975)
Murder by Death (1976)
The Pink Panther Strikes Again (1976)
Revenge of the Pink Panther (1978)
The Prisoner of Zenda (1979)
Being There (1979)
The Fiendish Plot of Dr. Fu Manchu (1980)
Trail of the Pink Panther (1982)

Radio

The Goon Show (as *Crazy People,* 1951-52; as *The Goon Show,* 1952-60)

★★★

William Shatner

Captain Kirk

(1931-)

William Shatner was born in Montreal, Canada, on March 22, 1931. He developed an early interest in acting when, as a small child in a summer-camp play, he had a profoundly moving experience while portraying a Jewish boy in Europe during the Nazi era.

After graduating from McGill University (B.A., 1952), Shatner performed onstage in a Montreal playhouse during the summers of 1952 and 1953. In the winters of 1952-53 and 1953-54 he played juvenile roles with the Canadian Repertory Theater in Ottawa. He then performed at the Stratford Shakespeare Festival in Ontario (1954-56), again frequently in juvenile roles.

Moving to New York City, Shatner made his Broadway debut in *Tamburlaine the Great* (1956) and played Robert Lomax in the very successful play *The World of Suzie Wong* (1958). He also began to appear in films. In *The Brothers Karamazov* (1958) he played the youngest brother. In *The Explosive Generation* (1961) he starred as a teacher trying to implement sex education in a high school. In *The Intruder* (1962) he starred as a violent bigot. And in *Judgment at Nuremberg* (1961), as a military officer, and *The Outrage* (1964), as a preacher, he gave strong performances in supporting roles.

From his earliest days in the United States, Shatner appeared on TV. His work in anthology series during the medium's Golden Age included performances in "All Summer Long" (1956) on *Goodyear Playhouse,* "Oedipus Rex" (1957) on *Omnibus,* and "Walk with a Stranger" (1958) on *The U.S. Steel Hour.* He also made guest appearances on *Alfred Hitchcock Presents* (1957, 1960), *Twilight Zone* (1960, 1963), and *Dr. Kildare* (1961, 1966). In the short-lived series *For the People* (1965) he had a regular role as an assistant district attorney.

By the mid-1960s Shatner could be seen as one of the most talented actors of his generation, but one who had never had the right role to give him true stardom.

That role finally came in 1966 when he became Captain Kirk in the TV science-fiction adventure series *Star Trek.* Kirk commanded the starship *Enterprise,* which was commissioned by the United Federation of Planets to seek out new life and new civilizations. The show ran for only three seasons (1966-69), but it has remained extremely popular in syndication ever since then. Its fanatic followers are known as Trekkies.

His later TV work included a powerful performance in "The Andersonville Trial" (1970) on *Hollywood Television Theater* and guest appearances on *Mission: Impossible* (1971), *Hawaii Five-O* (1972), and other series. From 1973 to 1975 he supplied Kirk's voice for an animated version of *Star Trek* on TV. From 1982 to 1986 he starred in the title role of the TV police-drama series *T. J. Hooker.*

Most of his films since 1970 have been made-for-TV movies, including *Owen Marshall, Counselor at Law* (TV, 1971); *The Bastard* (TV, 1978); and *The Babysitter* (TV, 1980).

However, he has also continued to appear in theater movies. For example, in *The Kidnapping of the President* (1980) he starred as the chief of the Secret Service.

His Captain Kirk persona continues to be a major factor in his career. Shatner played the character again in the theater movies *Star Trek, the Motion Picture* (1979); *Star Trek II: The Wrath of Khan* (1982); *Star Trek III: The Search for Spock* (1984); and *Star Trek IV: The Voyage Home* (1986). In 1986 he appeared in a Western Airlines TV commercial that alluded to his identification as Captain Kirk.

Shatner wedded the actress Gloria Rand in 1956. They had three daughters: Leslie, Liz, and Melanie. That marriage ended in divorce in 1969. In 1973 he married Marcy Lafferty.

Selected performances:

Stage

Tom Sawyer (1952)
Measure for Measure (1954)
The Taming of the Shrew (1954)
Oedipus Rex (1954)
Julius Caesar (1955)
The Merchant of Venice (1955)
King Oedipus (1955)
The Merry Wives of Windsor (1956)
Henry V (1956)
Tamburlaine the Great (1956)
The World of Suzie Wong (1958)
A Shot in the Dark (1961)
The Tender Trap (1970)

William Shatner

Remote Asylum (1971)
Tricks of the Trade (1977)

Films

The Brothers Karamazov (1958)
The Explosive Generation (1961)
Judgment at Nuremberg (1961)
The Intruder (1962)
The Outrage (1964)
Sole Survivor (TV, 1970)
Vanished (TV, 1971)
Owen Marshall, Counselor at Law (TV, 1971)
The People (TV, 1972)
The Hound of the Baskervilles (TV, 1972)
Incident on a Dark Street (TV, 1973)
Go Ask Alice (TV, 1973)
The Horror at 37,000 Feet (TV, 1973)
Pioneer Woman (TV, 1973)
Indict and Convict (TV, 1974)
Pray for the Wildcats (TV, 1974)
The Barbary Coast (TV, 1975)
The Devil's Rain (1975)
Perilous Voyage (TV, 1976)
Testimony of Two Men (TV, 1977)
The Bastard (TV, 1978)
Little Women (TV, 1978)
Crash (TV, 1978)
Disaster on the Coastline (TV, 1979)
Star Trek, the Motion Picture (1979)
The Kidnapping of the President (1980)
The Babysitter (TV, 1980)
Airplane II: The Sequel (1982)
Visiting Hours (1982)
Star Trek II: The Wrath of Khan (1982)
Star Trek III: The Search for Spock (1984)
Secrets of a Married Man (TV, 1984)
Star Trek IV: The Voyage Home (1986)

TV

For the People (1965)
Star Trek (1966-69)
Star Trek (animated, voice only, 1973-75)
Inner Space (1974)
Barbary Coast (1975-76)
T. J. Hooker (1982-86)

★★

Norma Shearer

Early Product of the Star System

(1902-1983)

Norma Shearer was born of non-Jewish parents in Westmount, a suburb of Montreal, Canada, on August 15, 1902. (The date is so recorded on her birth certificate, though during her lifetime the day was usually given as August 10, with the year listed as early as 1900 and as late as 1904.)

In 1920 she moved with her mother and sister, Athole, to New York City. There the girls began to get jobs as extras in silent movies. Athole soon dropped out of the business (though she later married the film director Howard Hawks). Norma continued her extra work and did some modeling.

Her first important role was in *The Stealers* (1920), where she received fourth billing for her performance as the wholesome daughter of a minister. She had her first feminine lead in *The Man Who Paid* (1922), a melodrama set in the Canadian Northwest.

After making several more movies in the East, she was signed by the producer Irving Thalberg to work for the Mayer Company in Hollywood (though in her early years in California she was occasionally lent to other studios). Shearer began in minor films. Having never formally studied acting, she learned her craft simply by doing it. In 1924 Mayer became part of Metro-Goldwyn-Mayer (MGM), Shearer's professional home for the rest of her career.

She began to blossom as an actress in *The Snob* (1924), in which she played a young woman who marries a snobbish professor. In *He Who Gets Slapped* (1924) she was a bareback rider in a circus.

At that point Thalberg, one of the originators of the Hollywood star system (his other stars including Lon Chaney, Sr., and Greta Garbo), began to expand Shearer's appeal by casting her in comedy roles. Her first such role was in *Excuse Me* (1925), as a young woman who, with her fiancé, encounters many trials and tribulations while trying to locate a minister to perform a marriage ceremony. The romantic comedy-drama *A Slave of Fashion* (1925) was the first movie to show her in a glamorous wardrobe, for which she later came to be famous, both in her pictures and in her real life.

The year 1927 was a major turning point in Shearer's career and life. Her performance in *The Demi-Bride* (1927), a French farce, helped to make her one of the most popular comediennes of her time.

Meanwhile, her professional association with Thalberg had developed into a close personal relationship as well, and in September 1927 they were married. Thalberg came from an Orthodox Jewish family, and when Shearer visited his parents, as she later reported, she "found peace and contentment in their religion. I wanted peace and contentment in our marriage. I decided I had no particular religious convictions—that I could find it in the Jewish faith. I loved Irving so much that I wanted our children brought up in the same way he had been." Thus, she converted to Judaism. They had two children: Irving and Katherine.

Thalberg again began to expand Shearer's range and to change her image by placing her in prestige pictures. She was cast, for example, in the silent-movie version of the famed operetta *The Student Prince* (1927), in which she displayed an appealing tender fragility.

At about that time sound entered filmmaking. Douglas Shearer, Norma's brother, became the head sound engineer at MGM, a post that he held for thirty-nine years.

Norma Shearer became one of the few silent-screen stars to successfully make the transition to sound pictures. Her first speaking role was as the title character in *The Trial of Mary Dugan* (1929). In an emotional yet restrained performance that surprised many observers in its effectiveness, she played an ex-showgirl accused of murdering her lover.

In *The Divorcée* (1930) she played a free-spirited woman involved with her ex-husband's best friend. It was one of Shearer's few roles in which she strayed from conventional virtue.

She was best known for her genteel roles, as in the romantic tearjerker *Smilin' Through* (1932). Also in 1932 she appeared in the filmed version of Eugene O'Neill's celebrated play *Strange Interlude* and became a naturalized American citizen.

There followed two more prestige films. In *The Barretts of Wimpole Street* (1934) she played the poetess Elizabeth Barrett, an invalid whose life is dominated by her father till she meets, and falls in love with, the poet Robert Browning. Shearer then played Juliet in *Romeo and Juliet* (1937).

Thalberg died in 1936 at the age of only thirty-seven. Shearer considered retiring, but after a period of rest she returned to play the lead in *Marie Antoinette* (1938). In *The Women* (1939) she again played a genteel role, as a woman whose marriage is failing because of the interference of a hussy.

Shearer was offered the part of the selfish, unscrupulous Scarlett O'Hara in *Gone with the Wind* (1939). In fact, she accepted the role till she began to receive letters from her fans, urging her not to take the part. The role was eventually given to Vivien Leigh.

Shearer's last movie was *Her Cardboard Lover*. In the same year that the film was released, 1942, she married the skier Martin Arrouge (in a Christian ceremony), who was fourteen years her junior. She then retired.

Shearer's great asset was not acting skill but personality—her star quality. She had charm, poise, elegance, and—when given free rein—wit and spirit.

After retiring, Shearer continued to stay in touch with the movie industry. In the mid-1940s she discovered Janet Leigh. In 1956 she met Robert J. Evans, a young New York clothing manufacturer; noticing his resemblance to her first husband, she was instrumental in getting Evans the role of Thalberg in the Lon Chaney biopic *Man of a Thousand Faces* (1957).

In 1980 Shearer, ill and for the previous several years a virtual recluse, entered the Motion Picture and Television Country House and Hospital in Woodland Hills, California. She died there on June 12, 1983.

Selected performances:

Films

The Stealers (1920)
The Man Who Paid (1922)
The Bootleggers (1922)
Channing of the Northwest (1922)
A Clouded Name (1923)
Man and Wife (1923)
The Devil's Partner (1923)
Pleasure Mad (1923)
The Wanters (1923)
Lucretia Lombard (1923)
The Trail of the Law (1924)
The Wolf Man (1924)
Broadway after Dark (1924)
Broken Barriers (1924)
Married Flirts (1924)
Empty Hands (1924)
The Snob (1924)
He Who Gets Slapped (1924)
Excuse Me (1925)
Lady of the Night (1925)

Norma Shearer

Waking Up the Town (1925)
A Slave of Fashion (1925)
Pretty Ladies (1925)
The Tower of Lies (1925)
His Secretary (1925)
The Devil's Circus (1926)
The Waning Sex (1926)
Upstage (1926)
The Demi-Bride (1927)
After Midnight (1927)
The Student Prince (1927)
The Latest from Paris (1928)
The Actress (1928)
A Lady of Chance (1928)
The Trial of Mary Dugan (1929)
The Last of Mrs. Cheyney (1929)
The Hollywood Revue (1929)
Their Own Desire (1929)
The Divorcée (1930)
Let Us Be Gay (1930)
Strangers May Kiss (1931)
A Free Soul (1931)
Private Lives (1931)
Strange Interlude (1932)
Smilin' Through (1932)
Riptide (1934)
The Barretts of Wimpole Street (1934)
Romeo and Juliet (1937)
Marie Antoinette (1938)
Idiot's Delight (1939)
The Women (1939)
Escape (1940)
We Were Dancing (1942)
Her Cardboard Lover (1942)

★★

Dinah Shore

Popular TV Personality

(1917-)

Dinah Shore was born in Winchester, Tennessee, on March 1, 1917. Her original name was Frances Rose Shore.

When she was eighteen months old, she was stricken with poliomyelitis, which caused a paralysis in her right leg and foot. She went through six years of rigid physical therapy, and her mother encouraged her to participate in ballet and in vigorous outdoor exercise. The illness made the girl shy yet ambitious to prove her worth despite her infirmity. Besides excelling in many sports, she sang, danced, and showed off to get attention. Even before she could talk plainly, she had performed in public by singing to the customers in her father's department store.

The Shores were the only Jewish family in Winchester, and they had to face the usual anti-Semitic prejudices of the time and place. Little Frances Shore once saw a Ku Klux Klan parade going down a street, the Klansmen hiding behind hoods and sheets. She began to realize that she, as a "different" person, had to work harder than others for success. That feeling was underscored then and later by her sensitivity about her illness and about what she regarded as her physical unattractiveness at the time.

At six she moved with her family to Nashville. Her mother, Anna, who was an aspiring opera singer, encouraged Frances to sing, though the child's devotion to popular music was contrary to Anna's classical tastes. Frances took ukulele lessons and accompanied herself on that instrument while she sang everywhere she went, including the public swimming pool, where she serenaded the lifeguards.

At Hume-Fogg High School in Nashville, she participated in cheerleading, drama, and singing (in a Gilbert and Sullivan operetta). She graduated as the Best All-around Girl of her class.

On the advice of her family (except her mother, who had died when Frances was in high school), young Shore enrolled at Vanderbilt University as a sociology major. However, she continued her interest in music, singing at school assemblies and in student musicals.

In her sophomore year at Vanderbilt, she won a job singing on a local radio show called *Rhythm and Romance,* billing herself as Fannye Rose Shore. The theme song of the show was "Dinah," which she sang not in the usual fast tempo but in a slow, personal manner. Radio was a perfect medium for Shore, who could sing her heart out without worrying about her physical imperfections. While experimenting with different distances from, and qualities conveyed over, the microphone, she became one of the pioneers in modern microphone techniques.

After graduating from college in 1938, Shore moved to New York City. She began to sing at WNEW, a local radio station. With her were the young unknowns Dennis Day, Frankie Laine, and Frank Sinatra, with the last of whom Shore had a sometimes bitter rivalry. From her first appearance at WNEW, she called herself Dinah Shore because she had sung "Dinah" at her audition and the people at the station had referred to her as "the 'Dinah' girl." (In 1944 she changed her legal first name from Frances to Dinah.)

In 1939 she was given her own radio series, *The Dinah Shore Show,* which ran for the next three years at fifteen minutes per program. But she first began to earn a national following when she spent two months on the radio show *The Chamber Music Society of Lower Basin Street* in 1940.

She left that series for an even better position: a regular spot on Eddie Cantor's weekly radio show *Time to Smile,* which shot her to stardom and lasting fame. Cantor taught Shore to relax and enjoy singing, which in turn brought more enjoyment vicariously to the audience.

She rapidly became the top female blues singer in the country and the undisputed queen of the juke boxes. Among her early recording hits were "Yes, My Darling Daughter" (1940), "Memphis Blues" (1940), "Jim" (1941), "Body and Soul" (1941), and "Blues in the Night" (1942).

In 1942 her radio series, *The Dinah Shore Show,* was lengthened from fifteen to thirty minutes per program. The show continued to run for another five years.

In the summer of 1943 she hosted *Paul Whiteman Presents,* yet another radio show. During World War II she became a favorite with troops, for whom she traveled many thousands of miles to entertain at camps and hospitals.

In the early 1940s she was signed by Warner Bros. to begin her movie career. First, however, the studio com-

LOW
CLEAR
HOT
RAIN

pletely remade her appearance. Her black hair was bleached honey-blonde. She had plastic surgery to shorten and reconstruct her nose. Massive dental work was done. And the studio's makeup department did the rest.

Soon after that, in 1943, she married the actor George Montgomery. They both had all-American images, and both lived quieter lives than most of the Hollywood elite. Theirs was called "Hollywood's most successful marriage." They had one child of their own (Melissa) and adopted another (John, known as Jody). After the birth of her daughter, in 1948, Shore had no desire to return to work, but Montgomery prodded her into picking up her career again.

Shore made her film debut in *Thank Your Lucky Stars* (1943). She also appeared in *Up in Arms* (1944), *Follow the Boys* (1944), *Belle of the Yukon* (1945), *Till the Clouds Roll By* (1946), and *Aaron Slick from Punkin Crick* (1952). Her voice was featured in two Disney feature-length animated films: *Make Mine Music* (1946) and *Fun and Fancy Free* (1947).

But Shore was never comfortable or particularly successful in movies, largely because of the poor roles that she was given. Meanwhile, however, she continued to sparkle on radio and in recordings. After the war, she performed on her own radio show and on other broadcasts. Among her recording hits were "Shoofly Pie and Apple Pan Dowdy" (1946), "Buttons and Bows" (1948), "Dear Hearts and Gentle People" (1949), "Whatever Lola Wants" (1955), "Love and Marriage" (1955), "Chantez-Chantez" (1957), and "Fascination" (1957).

Her career found its culminating point with the rise of television. She hosted her own musical-variety series, known successively as *The Dinah Shore Chevy Show* (1951-56) and *The Dinah Shore Show* (1956-62).

While her career was skyrocketing in the 1950s, Montgomery's was plummeting. In 1958 he, too, entered TV, in a series called *Cimarron City*. Shore allowed him to tout the series on her own show, but *Cimarron City* failed anyway. The different states of their respective careers caused tension in the family. Shore and Montgomery drifted apart for a few more years and then divorced in 1962.

In 1963 she married Maurice Smith, a building contractor whom she had met as a tennis partner in Palm Springs, California. They divorced the following year.

Having left her TV series in 1962, she spent the rest of the 1960s performing at benefits, in nightclubs, and on TV specials. Then she returned to TV on a regular basis, with a variety-talk series entitled *Dinah's Place* (1970-74).

On one of her TV shows in 1971 she met the actor Burt Reynolds. They soon developed one of the most talked-about love affairs in entertainment history. The alliance ended in 1975.

In the late 1970s Shore returned to films. In *Oh, God!* (1977) she appeared as herself, hosting her TV show. In *Death on the Freeway* (TV, 1979) she gave a straight dramatic performance.

Recently she has hosted a TV talk show known successively as *Dinah!* (1974), *Dinah* (1975-79), and *Dinah and Friends* (since 1979).

She also hosts her own annual golf tournament in California. Since 1984 it has been the richest tournament on the ladies' professional tour.

In 1986 she was seen in TV commercials for Glendale Federal Savings and Oreo cookies. In 1987 she sang with a jazz group on a tour of the United States and Japan.

Selected performances:

Films

Thank Your Lucky Stars (1943)
Up in Arms (1944)
Follow the Boys (1944)
Belle of the Yukon (1945)
Till the Clouds Roll By (1946)
Make Mine Music (1946)
Fun and Fancy Free (1947)
Aaron Slick from Punkin Crick (1952)
Oh, God! (1977)
Death on the Freeway (TV, 1979)

Radio

The Dinah Shore Show (1939-47)
The Chamber Music Society of Lower Basin Street (1940)
Time to Smile (or *The Eddie Cantor Show,* 1940-43, 1948)
Paul Whiteman Presents (1943)
Call for Music (1948)

TV

The Dinah Shore Chevy Show (1951-56)
The Dinah Shore Show (1956-62)
Dinah's Place (1970-74)
Dinah! (1974)
Dinah (1975-79)
Dinah and Friends (1979-)

★★★

Sylvia Sidney

Fragile Heroine of 1930s Films

(1910-)

Sylvia Sidney was born in New York City, New York, on August 8, 1910. Her original name was Sophia Kosow.

She studied acting at the Theater Guild School, where she starred in the title role of the school's graduation play, *Prunella* (1926). Soon she made her professional debut by appearing in *The Challenge of Youth* (1926) in Washington, D.C. In early 1927 she gave her first Broadway performance, succeeding Grace Durkin as Anita in *The Squall*. Over the next few years she was busy in a number of New York City stage productions.

Sidney made her film debut with an appearance in *Thru Different Eyes* (1929). During the 1930s she gained considerable fame as a sweet, fragile slum girl in such films as *Street Scene* (1931) and *Dead End* (1937).

Tiring of being typecast in movies, Sidney began to spend more time on the stage again. She toured as Eliza in *Pygmalion* in 1938 and had the role of Stella Goodman in a New York City production of *The Gentle People* in 1939. In 1943 she appeared in the Ben Hecht and Kurt Weill Jewish pageant *We Will Never Die,* staged at Madison Square Garden. Also in the 1940s she performed onstage in *Jane Eyre* (1943), *The Two Mrs. Carrolls* (1949), and other plays.

In 1958-59 Sidney toured the United States in the title role of *Auntie Mame*. She portrayed Mrs. Kolowitz in *Enter Laughing* (1963) and showed her ability in eighteenth-century classics by playing Mrs. Malaprop in Sheridan's *The Rivals* (1965) and Mrs. Hardcastle in Goldsmith's *She Stoops to Conquer* (1968). Later she appeared in the comedy *Arsenic and Old Lace* (1974).

Meanwhile, in the 1950s Sidney began to make guest appearances on TV programs. Eventually she acted in *The Defenders; My Three Sons; Playhouse Ninety; Trapper John, M.D.;* and many other TV series. In 1963 she performed in the Yom Kippur special *In the Last Place.*

After reaching middle age, Sidney found new interest in motion pictures as an older character actress. In *Behind the High Wall* (1956) she played a wife torn between her sense of right and her loyalty to her husband, a prison warden who allows an innocent man to be convicted of murder.

She won high praise for her portrayal of the impatient

mother in *Summer Wishes, Winter Dreams* (1973). In *Raid on Entebbe* (TV, 1977), based on a true story, she played Dora Bloch, one of a planeload of people kidnapped by terrorists and imprisoned at the Entebbe Airport in Uganda. In *Siege* (TV, 1978) she was a senior citizen terrorized by young hoodlums. In *Damien: Omen II* (1978) she was the first to sense something evil in young Damien.

Even after turning seventy, Sidney remained active. She appeared, for example, in the plays *Vieux Carré* (1981) and *Sabrina Fair* (1981), and in the movies *The Shadow Box* (TV, 1980) and *Finnegan Begin Again* (TV, 1985). In 1986 she had a regular role in the sentimental TV series *Morningstar/Eveningstar,* which focused on the continuing usefulness of the elderly.

One of her favorite activities outside acting is needlepoint. She has published two books on that subject (1968, 1975).

Sidney's first marriage, from 1935 to 1936, was to the well-known publisher Bennett Cerf. In 1938 she married the actor Luther Adler, with whom she had a son, Jacob. That marriage ended in the late 1940s, and soon afterward she wedded Carlton Alsop. They were divorced in the early 1950s.

Selected performances:

Stage

Prunella (1926)
The Challenge of Youth (1926)
The Squall (1927)
Crime (1927)
Mirrors (1928)
The Breaks (1928)
Gods of the Lightning (1928)
Nice Women (1929)
Cross Roads (1929)
Many a Slip (1930)
Bad Girl (1930)
To Quito and Back (1937)
Pygmalion (1938)
The Gentle People (1939)
Accent on Youth (1941)
Angel Street (1942)
Pygmalion (1942)
Jane Eyre (1943)
We Will Never Die (1943)
Joan of Lorraine (1947)
Kind Lady (1948)
O Mistress Mine (1948)
The Two Mrs. Carrolls (1949)
Goodbye, My Fancy (1950)
The Fourposter (1952)
A Very Special Baby (1956)
Auntie Mame (1958)
The Dark at the Top of the Stairs (1960)
Enter Laughing (1963)
All My Pretty Little Ones (1964)
Damn You, Scarlett O'Hara (1964)
The Rivals (1965)
The Little Foxes (1966)
She Stoops to Conquer (1968)
Come Blow Your Horn (1968)
Cabaret (1970)
Butterflies Are Free (1972)
Suddenly Last Summer (1973)
A Family and a Fortune (1974)
Arsenic and Old Lace (1974)
Me Jack, You Jill (1976)
Vieux Carré (1981)
Sabrina Fair (1981)
Morning at Seven (1981)

Films

Thru Different Eyes (1929)
City Streets (1931)
Confessions of a Co-ed (1931)
An American Tragedy (1931)
Street Scene (1931)
Merrily We Go to Hell (1932)
Madame Butterfly (1932)
Pick Up (1933)
Jennie Gerhardt (1933)
Good Dame (1934)
Thirty Day Princess (1934)
Behold My Wife (1935)
Accent on Youth (1935)
Mary Burns, Fugitive (1935)
The Trail of the Lonesome Pine (1936)
Fury (1936)
You Only Live Once (1937)
The Woman Alone (1937)
Dead End (1937)
You and Me (1938)
One Third of a Nation (1939)
The Wagons Roll at Night (1941)
Blood on the Sun (1945)
The Searching Wind (1946)
Mr. Ace (1946)
Love from a Stranger (1947)
Les Misérables (1952)
Violent Saturday (1955)
Behind the High Wall (1956)
Do Not Fold, Spindle, or Mutilate (TV, 1971)
Summer Wishes, Winter Dreams (1973)
The Secret Night Caller (TV, 1975)
Winner Take All (TV, 1975)
Death at Love House (TV, 1976)
Raid on Entebbe (TV, 1977)
Snowbeast (TV, 1977)
I Never Promised You a Rose Garden (1977)
Damien: Omen II (1978)
Siege (TV, 1978)
The Gossip Columnist (TV, 1980)
F.D.R.: The Last Year (TV, 1980)
The Shadow Box (TV, 1980)
A Small Killing (TV, 1981)
Having It All (TV, 1982)
Order of Death (1983)
Finnegan Begin Again (TV, 1985)
Pals (TV, 1987)

TV

Morningstar/Eveningstar (1986)

★★★

Phil Silvers

Hilarious Manipulator

(1911-85)

Phil Silvers was born of Russian immigrants in New York City, New York, on May 11, 1911. (The year is so given in his autobiography, though many sources continue to list 1912.) His original name was Philip Silver. He added an *s* to his surname because several other performers named Silvers had already become successful in show business, such as Lou Silvers (Al Jolson's conductor) and Sid Silvers (Phil Baker's heckler).

Before he had reached the age of five, he was already singing at family weddings and bar mitzvahs. Soon, however, he was initiated into the violent street life of his native Brownsville section of Brooklyn. When he was eight, he sang at a stag coming-out-of-jail party for a local hoodlum named Little Doggie; in the middle of the number, a man was shot to death at the boy's feet. Young Silvers himself became a gang member and committed petty crimes.

But he turned his life around through show business. At a Brooklyn silent-movie house, the Supreme Theater, he got a job singing for the audience whenever the film broke, which happened quite often. His pay was simply free admission.

He began to frequent Brooklyn's Bushwick Theater, where he could study the routines of vaudeville stars, such as Sophie Tucker. With material that he learned at the Bushwick, Silvers sang one night at a sleazy beer hall and then a number of times at variety shows performed by children.

In 1923, while singing for a group of his friends on the beach at Coney Island, he was spotted by the great entertainer Gus Edwards. Known as the Star Maker, Edwards had for years staged a series of popular vaudeville revues featuring children. He discovered Eddie Cantor, George Jessel, and many other youngsters who later became show-business superstars.

At the age of twelve Silvers hit the big time by appearing with Edwards's troupe at the famed Palace Theater in New York City. Silvers went on to perform in Edwards's acts in several other cities. But within a few months the boy's voice began to change, and he was out of work.

By then he had already dropped out of high school, and his immediate future looked bleak. In desperation, he convinced his parents that he needed to have his tonsils removed, secretly hoping that the operation would restore his pure child's voice. It did not.

When he was fourteen, however, he got a job playing a juvenile in a comedy routine with the experienced vaudevillians Joe Morris and Flo Campbell. Silvers stayed with the act for six years.

After a brief time spent in more vaudeville work and on the borscht circuit, Silvers entered burlesque and performed in obscurity there for seven years (1932-39). One of his early burlesque partners was Jack Albertson, who later became a renowned straight actor.

In 1939 Silvers was asked to play a small role in the Broadway musical comedy *Yokel Boy*. One of the leading members of the cast was Jack Pearl, a once-popular Dutch-dialect comedian. When Pearl left the show at an early stage, Silvers replaced him. Pearl's role as a Dutch-dialect film director was rewritten to make Silvers a sharp Hollywood press agent who speaks New Yorkese. The role thus created, Punko Parks, became the prototype for the kind of comic character that Silvers played to perfection many times during the rest of his career: the aggressive, smiling manipulator.

Later that year he was signed to make Hollywood films. At first, however, the movie people did not know what to do with him. Silvers miserably failed his initial screen test when he was miscast as an English vicar for the film *Pride and Prejudice*. He had a funny bit part in *Babes in Arms*, but it was cut out. Meanwhile, he performed in a nightclub act with Rags Ragland, with whom he had worked in burlesque.

Silvers finally began to land appropriate comedy roles in films, including *Tom, Dick, and Harry* (1941); *My Gal Sal* (1942); *Cover Girl* (1944); and *Four Jills in a Jeep* (1944).

Something for the Boys (1944) brought a special bonus. A bit part in the movie was played by Jo-Carroll Dennison, who was Miss America of 1942. Silvers began to court her. Her patron, an elderly state senator in her native Texas, offered to set up an annuity of $100,000 for her if she did not marry "that Jew." Refusing the offer, she married Silvers in 1945.

In the late 1940s he worked principally in nightclubs. He did, however, perform in the Broadway musical *High Button Shoes* (1947).

During those years, he traveled a great deal. Jo-Carroll, childless, increasingly felt left out of his life. They separated amicably and divorced in 1950.

Phil Silvers

In 1951 he made a tremendous impression in the Broadway musical comedy *Top Banana* as Jerry Biffle, a burlesque comic whose whole life centers on getting laughs at any cost. Silvers modeled his performance of the role after the real-life comedian Milton Berle.

During the 1950s Silvers's fame shot to its peak through the medium of television. He had already had some experience in TV by hosting the variety series *Welcome Aboard* (1948) and *The Arrow Show* (1948-49). But he hit pay dirt with *You'll Never Get Rich* (1955-59) in his role as Master Sergeant Ernie Bilko, the manipulator par excellence. By the end of its four-season run, the comedy series had become known as *The Phil Silvers Show;* and it was later syndicated as *Sergeant Bilko.*

Soon after beginning *You'll Never Get Rich,* he met Evelyn Patrick, another beauty-contest winner (Miss Florida). Evelyn also worked on TV, notably as the Revlon girl on the quiz show *The $64,000 Question.* In 1956 they were married. They had five children, all daughters: Tracey, Nancey, Cathy, Candy, and Laury. Ten years later, however, this marriage, too, ended in divorce.

In the 1960s he had another TV series: *The New Phil Silvers Show* (1963-64), in which he played the factory foreman and con artist Harry Grafton. He also performed in the stage musical *Do Re Mi* (1960) and appeared in a number of movies, including *It's a Mad, Mad, Mad, Mad World* (1963) and *A Guide for the Married Man* (1967).

He was offered the lead in the Broadway musical *A Funny Thing Happened on the Way to the Forum* (1962), based on ancient Roman comedies by Plautus. But Silvers, feeling that the work was "too artsy," avoided the project. Later, however, he changed his mind and played the secondary role of Lycus, the procurer, in the filmed version (1966). In a 1972 stage revival of the play, he took the starring role of Pseudolus, the conniving slave.

An admitted neurotic and a compulsive gambler, Silvers went through many years of torment both professionally (worrying about his performances) and personally (losing his wives). Eventually, relying on his work and on his daughters and friends, he developed the confidence and courage to face life afresh. "I've gone back to people—I don't see how I can withdraw into my cocoon again," he wrote in his autobiography, *This Laugh Is on Me: The Phil Silvers Story* (with Robert Saffron, 1973).

In 1974 he suffered a stroke, and for a time he had to reduce his activities. Among his later performances were roles in the movies *Won Ton Ton, the Dog Who Saved Hollywood* (1976); *The Cheap Detective* (1978); and *Goldie and the Boxer* (TV, 1979).

Silvers died at his apartment in the Century City section of Los Angeles on November 1, 1985. Milton Berle delivered the eulogy.

Selected performances:

Stage

Yokel Boy (1939)
High Button Shoes (1947)
Top Banana (1951)
Do Re Mi (1960)
A Funny Thing Happened on the Way to the Forum (1972)

Films

Tom, Dick, and Harry (1941)
You're in the Army Now (1941)
All through the Night (1942)
Roxie Hart (1942)
My Gal Sal (1942)
Just off Broadway (1942)
Footlight Serenade (1942)
Coney Island (1943)
A Lady Takes a Chance (1943)
Cover Girl (1944)
Four Jills in a Jeep (1944)
Take It or Leave It (1944)
Something for the Boys (1944)
A Thousand and One Nights (1945)
Don Juan Quilligan (1945)
If I'm Lucky (1946)
Summer Stock (1950)
Top Banana (1954)
Lucky Me (1954)
Forty Pounds of Trouble (1963)
It's a Mad, Mad, Mad, Mad World (1963)
A Funny Thing Happened on the Way to the Forum (1966)
A Guide for the Married Man (1967)
Follow That Camel (1967)
Buona Sera, Mrs. Campbell (1969)
The Boatniks (1970)
The Strongest Man in the World (1975)
Won Ton Ton, the Dog Who Saved Hollywood (1976)
The Night They Took Miss Beautiful (TV, 1977)
The Cheap Detective (1978)
Goldie and the Boxer (TV, 1979)

TV

Welcome Aboard (1948)
The Arrow Show (1948-49)
You'll Never Get Rich (or *The Phil Silvers Show,* 1955-59; syndicated as *Sergeant Bilko*)
The New Phil Silvers Show (1963-64)

★★

Rod Steiger

Burly Character Actor

(1925-)

Rod(ney) Steiger was born in Westhampton, New York, on April 14, 1925. His parents had worked as a song-and-dance team. They divorced when Rod was about one year old. His mother, Lorraine Steiger (née Driver), later remarried, and the boy was raised as a Lutheran.

His boyhood friends nicknamed him Rodney the Rock because of his physical strength. He acted in elementary-school plays. Later he briefly attended high school in Newark, New Jersey. But he left school, lied about his age, and enlisted in the navy, where he saw World War II action as a torpedoman on a destroyer in the South Pacific. He participated in operations at Iwo Jima and elsewhere.

After four years in the navy, Steiger returned to Newark and got a civil-service job at the Veteran's Administration. He joined the Civil Service Little Theater group, which he enjoyed so much that he decided to become a professional actor.

Taking advantage of the GI bill that offered ex-servicemen financial assistance for education, Steiger went to New York City, where he studied for two years at the New School for Social Research. Later he studied elsewhere, including the famed Actors Studio.

In 1947 he made his professional stage debut with a bit part in the road company of *The Trial of Mary Dugan.* After some other stage work, he made his Broadway debut by appearing in *Night Music* (1951), where the twenty-six-year-old was highly praised for his performance as a detective of fifty-five.

However, his principal activity during the late 1940s and early 1950s was on TV. Between 1948 and 1953 he appeared in about 250 live TV productions. They were climaxed by his performance in the title role of "Marty" (1953) on the *Philco Television Playhouse,* as a lonely, plain-looking man who unexpectedly finds true love.

Among his later TV work was a fine performance as the crippled scientific genius Charles Steinmetz in "The Lonely Wizard" (1957) on the *Schlitz Playhouse of Stars.* His later stage work included his role as the bandit in the Broadway production of *Rashomon* (1959).

But the focus of Steiger's career since the mid-1950s has been movies. His film debut came with a minor role in *Teresa* (1951). Then, in *On the Waterfront* (1954), he gave a memorable performance as a young gangster who draws his brother (played by Marlon Brando) into the rackets and then, to save him, gives up his own life.

A burly, heavy-jowled man, Steiger was not going to play romantic leading men in films. Throughout his movie career most of his best roles have tended to be villains who, on closer examination, turn out to be social misfits with deep underlying insecurities. Steiger has brought his characters to life through an intelligent, unabashed use of Method acting, a dramatic technique by which an actor seeks close personal identification with the character being portrayed.

In the Rodgers and Hammerstein musical *Oklahoma!* (1955) Steiger acted, sang, and danced in the role of the neurotic Jud. Then he played a ruthless film producer in *The Big Knife* (1955), a rough prosecutor in *The Court-martial of Billy Mitchell* (1955), an Iago-like troublemaking ranchhand in *Jubal* (1956), and an unscrupulous boxing promoter in *The Harder They Fall* (1956). He portrayed the title role, a gangster, in *Al Capone* (1959).

In the 1960s Steiger's reputation continued to grow. He played an opportunist in *Doctor Zhivago* (1965) and an effeminate embalmer in *The Loved One* (1965). In *The Pawnbroker* (1965) he gave one of his finest performances, as a Jew warped into misanthropy by his experiences in a Nazi concentration camp. He played a bigoted Southern police chief in *In the Heat of the Night* (1967); a psychotic serial killer in *No Way to Treat a Lady* (1968); and a lonely, sadistic, latent homosexual in *The Sergeant* (1968).

In the 1970s Steiger faced a downswing in his life and career. He experienced mental depression and a serious heart operation. His roles, mostly in second-rate movies, did not compare with the meaty parts that he had had in previous years. Among the highlights, however, were his portrayals of Napoleon in *Waterloo* (1971), of W. C. Fields in *W. C. Fields and Me* (1976), and of a priest in *The Amityville Horror* (1979).

Steiger's later performances included his work as Benito Mussolini in *Lion of the Desert* (1981), as a Hasidic father in *The Chosen* (1982), and as the explorer

Robert E. Peary in *Cook and Peary: The Race to the Pole* (TV, 1983). He portrayed a member of Mossad, Israel's intelligence agency, in *Sword of Gideon* (TV, 1986), a story about an Israeli antiterrorist squad formed after the murders of Israeli athletes at the Munich Olympics in 1972.

Steiger has had three marriages, all unsuccessful. In 1952 he married the actress Sally Gracie, with whom he had worked in New York City. Separating after only a few months, they later divorced. In 1959 he married the actress Claire Bloom. They sometimes acted together, as in the movie *Three into Two Won't Go* (1969). Steiger and Bloom had one child, Anna, before divorcing in 1969. He wedded Sherry Nelson in 1973. But that marriage, too, failed, ending in divorce in 1979.

Selected performances:

Stage

Stevedore (1949)
John Brown (1950)
Night Music (1951)
Seagulls over Sorrento (1952)
Rashomon (1959)
Moby Dick (1962)

Films

Teresa (1951)
On the Waterfront (1954)
Oklahoma! (1955)
The Big Knife (1955)
The Court-martial of Billy Mitchell (1955)
Jubal (1956)
The Harder They Fall (1956)
Back from Eternity (1956)
Run of the Arrow (1957)
Across the Bridge (1957)
The Unholy Wife (1958)
Cry Terror (1958)
Al Capone (1959)
Seven Thieves (1960)
The Mark (1961)
Convicts Four (1962)
The Longest Day (1962)
13 West Street (1962)
The World in My Pocket (1962)
Doctor Zhivago (1965)
The Loved One (1965)
The Pawnbroker (1965)
Time of Indifference (1965)
The Girl and the General (1967)
In the Heat of the Night (1967)
And There Came a Man (1968)
No Way to Treat a Lady (1968)
The Sergeant (1968)
The Illustrated Man (1969)
Three into Two Won't Go (1969)
Waterloo (1971)
Happy Birthday, Wanda June (1971)
Hennessy (1975)
W. C. Fields and Me (1976)
Dirty Hands (1976)
Jesus of Nazareth (TV, 1977)
F.I.S.T. (1978)
The Amityville Horror (1979)
Love and Bullets (1979)
Klondike Fever (1980)
Lion of the Desert (1981)
Cattle Annie and Little Britches (1981)
The Chosen (1982)
Lucky Star (1982)
Cook and Peary: The Race to the Pole (TV, 1983)
The Naked Face (1984)
Sword of Gideon (TV, 1986)
The Kindred (1987)

★★★

Susan Strasberg

First Actress to Play Anne Frank

(1938-)

Susan Strasberg was born in New York City, New York, on May 22, 1938. She was raised in a theatrical milieu. Her father was the great director and teacher Lee Strasberg, later the artistic director of the famed Actors Studio. Her mother was the actress and acting coach Paula Strasberg (née Miller).

Susan made her stage debut when she was only fifteen, in an off-Broadway production of *Maya* (1953), playing the small role of Fifine, a young, innocent waif destined to become a streetwalker. She then appeared in the TV plays "The Duchess and the Smugs" (1953) on the *Omnibus* series and "Catch a Falling Star" (1953) on *Goodyear Playhouse*. In 1954 she played Juliet in "Romeo and Juliet" for *Kraft Television Theater*.

At that time she was still a student at the High School of Performing Arts in New York City. Later she also studied at the Actors Studio. Her private coach for some time to come would be her mother.

In 1954 Susan appeared as a regular in the TV series *The Marriage*. There followed many other TV guest assignments.

Her film debut came in *The Cobweb* (1955), in which she played a hypersensitive, paranoid teenager. Then, in *Picnic* (1955), she made an outstanding impression in her sensitive portrayal of the outsider Millie Owens, a rebellious girl struggling to emerge from tomboyishness into maturity.

The highlight of young Strasberg's early career was her Broadway performance in the original production of *The Diary of Anne Frank* (1955). Portraying the title role of the real-life girl who had hidden in an Amsterdam attic for two years till she was captured and killed by Nazis, Strasberg became, at seventeen, the youngest actress ever to star on Broadway.

During the next decade she continued to perform on the stage, on TV, and in films. Her stage work included *Time Remembered* (1957) and *The Lady of the Camellias* (1963). For TV she made guest appearances on *Dr. Kildare* (1963) and other series. Among her movies were *Stage Struck* (1958), *Hemingway's Adventures of a Young Man* (1962), and *Disorder* (1964).

But Strasberg's career had clearly slowed down. As she later explained in her strikingly honest autobiography, *Bittersweet* (1980), she had become "trapped in a welter of guilt, self-pity, fear, and doubt." She seemed to be running away from the success that she had earned perhaps too early and too easily.

Strasberg was led to near disaster by many elements in her life. She had an ambivalent relationship with her father, whose preoccupation with his students left him little time for her. She faced years of hostility from her mother, who tried to fulfill her own acting ambitions through her daughter. Susan also suffered from her feelings of rivalry with her surrogate sister Marilyn Monroe, whom the elder Strasbergs befriended and coached. In addition, young Strasberg was scarred by a reckless love affair with the married actor Richard Burton, with whom she had appeared in *Time Remembered.* In 1965 she wedded the actor Christopher (real name, William Frank) Jones, with whom she had a short, stormy marriage.

In the late 1960s Strasberg's emotional and psychological decline reached its nadir. Her mother died. Her brother, John, nearly killed himself while on an LSD trip. Her husband beat her and led her into the use of drugs, including LSD. And her daughter, Jennifer, was born with a seriously defective heart. Strasberg tormented herself wondering if Jenny's condition had been caused by the parents' use of drugs.

But with great courage and determination, Strasberg pulled her life together. She ended the marriage with Jones. She provided the love and strength to help her child through corrective heart surgery. And, aided by psychotherapy, she resolved her identity crisis, finally coming out from the shadows of her parents to genuinely perceive herself as an individual.

Strasberg kept working. Even in the unhappy late 1960s and early 1970s she appeared in the movies *The Trip* (1967); *Chubasco* (with Christopher Jones, 1968); *Marcus Welby, M.D.* (TV, 1969); *Frankenstein* (TV, 1973); and others. She also guest-starred on TV programs and had a regular role on the series *Toma* (1973-74).

In recent years she has shown a mature command of her craft in various outlets. She played Sarah Levy in *The Immigrants* (TV, 1978) and Ida Cohen in *Beggarman, Thief* (TV, 1979). In 1982-83 she toured Ohio and Florida in the one-woman show *A Woman's Rites.* In 1986 she appeared in the theatrical release *The Delta Force.*

Selected performances:

Stage

Maya (1953)
The Diary of Anne Frank (1955)
Time Remembered (1957)
Shadow of a Gunman (1958)
The Time of Your Life (1958)
Caesar and Cleopatra (1959)
The Lady of the Camellias (1963)
A Woman's Rites (1982-83)

Films

The Cobweb (1955)
Picnic (1955)
Stage Struck (1958)
Kapo (1960)
Scream of Fear (1961)
Hemingway's Adventures of a Young Man (1962)
Disorder (1964)
McGuire, Go Home! (1966)
The Trip (1967)
The Brotherhood (1968)
Chubasco (1968)
The Name of the Game Is Kill! (1968)
Psych-out (1968)
Marcus Welby, M.D. (TV, 1969)
Hauser's Memory (TV, 1970)
Mr. and Mrs. Bo Jo Jones (TV, 1971)
Frankenstein (TV, 1973)
Toma (TV, 1973)
SST—Death Flight (TV, 1977)
Rollercoaster (1977)
The Manitou (1978)
The Immigrants (TV, 1978)
Beggarman, Thief (TV, 1979)
In Praise of Older Women (1979)
Mazes and Monsters (TV, 1982)
The Delta Force (1986)

TV

The Marriage (1954)
Toma (1973-74)

★★★

Barbra Streisand

Electric Entertainer

(1942-)

Barbra Streisand was born in New York City, New York, on April 24, 1942. Her original name was Barbara Joan Streisand.

The death of her father, when she was only fifteen months old, had an extremely important effect on the formation of her personality. She felt deprived yet special: "It's like someone being blind; they hear better. With me, I felt more, I sensed more—I wanted more."

She was also self-conscious about being awkward and not particularly attractive. She had few close friends. While growing up in Brooklyn, she had a tense relationship with her stepfather, who married into the household when she was seven and who left at about the time that she started high school. And her practical mother had little sympathy for the girl's restless nature and impractical dreams of future glory in show business.

To escape her unhappy life, young Streisand spent as much time as possible in the local movie theater. Sometimes she hid under her seat or in the ladies' room to avoid being shooed out with the other children after each Saturday matinee. She watched the pictures over and over again and dreamed of becoming an actress.

In her early teens she plunged into the world of real acting by going to the Malden Bridge Playhouse in upstate New York to try out for work in summer stock. She managed to appear onstage a few times.

After her Malden Bridge experiences, she was totally committed to a career in show business. Eager to get her career under way, she studied extra hard to graduate six months early, in January 1959, from Erasmus Hall High School. Streisand soon moved from Brooklyn to Manhattan, where she enrolled in acting classes and went to theater auditions, without much success.

Some of her friends heard her sing and encouraged her to concentrate on a vocal career. Thus, she entered, as a singer, a talent contest held at the Lion, a Greenwich Village nightclub. She won the contest and earned a short-term job at the club. It was during that time, June 1960, that she decided to drop the middle *a* from her first name.

Streisand then became a regular performer at the Bon Soir nightclub. While working at the Lion and the Bon Soir, she began to conceive of singing as a form of acting. That insight led her to select unusual or seldom-heard songs and to perform them with unique interpretations that displayed an incredible range and depth of emotion. One of her selections was a song from a Disney cartoon of the 1930s: "Who's Afraid of the Big Bad Wolf?" Usually performed as a light and playful ditty, the song was transformed by Streisand into a surrealistic yet childlike lament. Her performances at the Bon Soir made a tremendous impact on audiences, and her stint there has become legendary.

In 1961 Streisand's star began to rise. She became a regular guest on *PM East,* Mike Wallace's late-night TV show. She also performed in the off-Broadway revue *Another Evening with Harry Stoones* and moved up from the Bon Soir to the Blue Angel nightclub.

In late 1961 came the major breakthrough in her career: she landed her first significant role in a Broadway play. The show, which opened in New York City in March 1962, was a musical entitled *I Can Get It for You Wholesale.* Streisand's acting (a comedic part as a shy secretary) and singing (especially her self-revealing solo, "Miss Marmelstein") stole the show.

The male lead in *I Can Get It for You Wholesale* was Elliott Gould, who later became a well-known dramatic actor. Streisand and Gould married in 1963, had one child (Jason), and then, after a long separation, divorced in 1971.

After her success in *I Can Get It for You Wholesale,* Streisand got calls to work for major nightclubs and TV shows. A memorable and truly historic TV program resulted from Streisand's appearance on one of Judy Garland's TV shows in 1963, during which the two stars sang together and praised each other's gifts. In May 1963 Streisand was invited to the White House to sing for President Kennedy.

In 1963 she also issued her first album: *The Barbra Streisand Album.* Her later albums in the 1960s included two more *Barbra Streisand* sets (1963, 1964), *People* (1965), *Color Me Barbra* (1966), and *What about Today* (1967).

Streisand's most famous performance undoubtedly remains her role as the legendary entertainer Fanny Brice in *Funny Girl,* a Broadway musical of 1964. In 1968

she reprised her performance in the filmed version of the show. Her sensitive portrayal of the tragedienne behind Brice's mask of comedy and her rendition of the song "People" were electric. That same quality of intense excitement has characterized most of her work, both as singer and as actress, throughout her career.

During the next decade, Streisand appeared in the movie musicals *Hello, Dolly!* (1969); *On a Clear Day You Can See Forever* (1970); *Funny Lady* (1975, a sequel to *Funny Girl*); and *A Star Is Born* (1976). Her nonmusical pictures included *The Owl and the Pussycat* (1970), *Up the Sandbox* (1972), *The Way We Were* (1973), and *The Main Event* (1979).

During the early 1970s Streisand began to broaden the stylistic range of her singing. Formerly, concentrating on a nonrock ballad style and singing standards and special material, she had succeeded Judy Garland as the queen of theatrical and torch songs. Now, however, she expanded her repertory and stylistic versatility to include various kinds of rock and soft-rock songs along with her previous material. Her album *Stoney End* (1971) was the first to show her new style. *The Way We Were* (1974) contains rock and nonrock ballads. *Lazy Afternoon* (1975) reverts to her prerock manner, while *Streisand Superman* (1977) is one of her most thoroughly contemporary pop-rock albums. However, she rightly remains principally identified with the artistically rich and musically sophisticated genre of theatrical songs, as she stunningly proved in *The Broadway Album* (1985).

Streisand spent much of her time during the late 1970s and early 1980s on the movie *Yentl* (1983). Based on a short story (whose movie rights she purchased in 1968) by Isaac Bashevis Singer, the film is set in a turn-of-the-century Polish ghetto and focuses on a young woman, Yentl (played by Streisand), who masquerades as a male so that she can study to become a rabbi. When she falls in love with a young man, she cannot reveal her feelings without exposing her true identity. Thus, she expresses her deepest emotions only to herself, by singing dramatic songs as interior monologues. Besides starring and singing in *Yentl,* Streisand coscripted, produced, and directed the movie—an unprecedented accomplishment for a woman in the history of major motion pictures.

Yentl was a very deep personal experience for Streisand. She has said, "I made the commitment to *Yentl* when I read the first four words of the story, 'After her father's death . . .' " Those four words brought back memories of the death of Streisand's own father, Emanuel Streisand, who held a Ph.D. in education and who taught English, history, and psychology at a Brooklyn high school. Because she had had an unhappy relationship with her stepfather, Streisand developed through the years an obsession with putting her real father back into her life.

In the movie, Yentl's father secretly teaches her the Talmud, a study traditionally forbidden to women. When her father dies, she disguises herself as a man so that she can continue her studies in honor of her father. Streisand saw her own father in Yentl's, since both men were intellectual and religious Jews. She also saw herself in Yentl, since each had lost her father, had tried to keep him spiritually involved in her life, and had become enmeshed in a battle with the male establishment while trying to find her own identity. Streisand made the film as a memorial to her father: "*Yentl* gave me the chance to create the father I never had."

While researching for *Yentl,* Streisand sought the advice of rabbis. The rabbi of a Venice, California, synagogue refused her offer of payment for his help, but he said that he would be glad to teach her son, Jason Emanuel (named after her father) Gould, for his bar mitzvah. In gratitude, she has given much financial support to the Pacific Jewish Center's new day school, which became the Emanuel Streisand School.

In preparation for *Yentl,* Streisand studied Hebrew and the Talmud (studies that also made her feel closer to her devout father). During the same period, she donated a large sum to an institute for Jewish intellectual research and, in 1981, gave $500,000 to the cardiology department at the University of California in Los Angeles (UCLA), which thereupon established a cardiology chair in Emanuel Streisand's name.

Since breaking up with Gould, Streisand has been romantically linked with many well-known personalities. In the early 1970s her escorts included Pierre Trudeau (the prime minister of Canada) and Ryan O'Neal (the rising young actor). She then lived for nearly ten years with Jon Peters, a hairdresser who became a film producer. Now separated from Peters, Streisand has recently dated such prominent men as the actor Richard Gere and the film director George Lucas.

Selected performances:

Stage

Another Evening with Harry Stoones (1961)
I Can Get It for You Wholesale (1962)
Funny Girl (1964)

Films

Funny Girl (1968)
Hello, Dolly! (1969)
On a Clear Day You Can See Forever (1970)
The Owl and the Pussycat (1970)
What's Up, Doc? (1972)
Up the Sandbox (1972)
The Way We Were (1973)
For Pete's Sake (1974)
Funny Lady (1975)
A Star Is Born (1976)
The Main Event (1979)
All Night Long (1981)
Yentl (1983)

★★

Elizabeth Taylor

Last of the Studio Stars

(1932-)

Elizabeth Taylor was born of non-Jewish parents in London, England, on February 27, 1932. Her parents, Francis and Sara Taylor, both American nationals, were in England to run an art gallery for Francis's multimillionaire uncle. In 1939, to avoid the growing World War II hostilities in Europe, the family returned to the United States and settled in Los Angeles, California, where Francis opened his own art gallery.

Elizabeth's star-struck mother enrolled the girl in a dancing class with the daughters of many movie executives. Soon Elizabeth was offered screen tests, not only by the parents of a child in the dancing class but also by a patron in Francis's art gallery. The auditions soon led to a contract with Universal Pictures, and Elizabeth's career became the passion of Sara's life.

After playing a small role in Universal's *There's One Born Every Minute* (1942), young Taylor moved to Metro-Goldwyn-Mayer (MGM), where she remained for many years (though her services were occasionally lent to other studios). She became totally immersed in being a movie star. Her formal education consisted only of the inadequate tutoring that she received in the little schoolhouse set up for movie youngsters at the MGM studio. She was, however, able to write and sell a book called *Nibbles and Me* (1945), about her pet chipmunk.

After a few minor appearances, notably in *Jane Eyre* (1944), Taylor came to prominence with a leading role opposite Mickey Rooney in *National Velvet* (1944). In her next film, *Courage of Lassie* (1946), she received top billing for the first time. Following that was *Cynthia* (1947), again in the lead.

But for the next few years she was cast in secondary roles as a pretty but sometimes spoiled teenager, as in *Little Women* (1949). Her first adult role was as the screen wife of Robert Taylor (no relation) in the forgettable film *The Conspirator* (1950). She played Spencer Tracy's daughter in the popular movie *Father of the Bride* (1950).

She first began to understand moviemaking as an art when she made *A Place in the Sun* (1951) with George Stevens (the director) and Montgomery Clift (her costar). But she continued to get shallow roles till she was cast as an Easterner fighting Texas primitivism in *Giant* (1956), costarring Rock Hudson and James Dean. In that film Taylor had to age thirty years, from young bride to grandmother. Then, in *Raintree County* (1957), again with Clift, she played a young woman who becomes mentally ill. In the filmed version of Tennessee Williams's play *Cat on a Hot Tin Roof* (1958), she played a seductive wife trying to get her homosexual husband to impregnate her. In Williams's gothic horror story *Suddenly Last Summer* (1959), she played a young woman who becomes hysterical and incoherent after witnessing the murder and cannibalistic devouring of her homosexual cousin. In *Butterfield 8* (1960) she played a prostitute.

By then she had reached the top of her profession, becoming the last of the glamorous studio-cultivated stars. She was America's biggest box-office attraction and the highest-paid actress in the world. Her acting ability was (and continues to be) disparaged by some. But her screen presence, her ability to make the screen sizzle, was undeniable.

Among her most important films in the 1960s were *Cleopatra* (1963), in the title role; *Who's Afraid of Virginia Woolf?* (1966), as the drunken, venomous wife of a college professor; and Shakespeare's *The Taming of the Shrew* (1967), as Katherina.

In the 1970s memorable roles were harder for her to come by. She played four parts in *The Blue Bird* (1976), the first Soviet-American coproduction in film history. In the filmed version of Steven Sondheim's musical *A Little Night Music* (1977), Taylor identified closely with her role as the aging actress.

Throughout her career, Taylor has had probably the most widely publicized personal life in Hollywood history. She gave her own version of her life in the book *Elizabeth Taylor* (1964). Her extravagances (particularly her love of diamonds), her recurring weight problems, and her numerous bouts with a variety of accidents and illnesses have been followed by the press for years.

Taylor's ailments have included back problems, bursitis, ulcers, amoebic dysentery, and acute bronchitis. In 1961 a case of pneumonia almost killed her, and once she nearly choked to death on a chicken bone. She has had over thirty operations.

Most dramatic of all have been her innumerable love affairs and her seven (to date) marriages. Taylor's first marriage, in 1950, was to Conrad Nicholson (known as Nicky) Hilton, Jr., heir to the Hilton Hotel corporation.

MGM purposely released *Father of the Bride* (in which she played the bride) just one month after the wedding ceremony to capitalize on the attending publicity. But within a year the marriage broke up.

In 1952 she wedded the British matinee idol Michael Wilding. They had two sons, Christopher and Michael, before separating in 1956 and divorcing in 1957.

Also in 1957 Taylor married Mike Todd (originally Avrom Hirsch Goldbogen), producer of Broadway shows and the movie *Around the World in Eighty Days* (1956). They had one daughter, Elizabeth (or Liza), before he died in a plane crash in 1958. While married to Todd, who was a Jew, Taylor wanted to convert to his faith. But he convinced her that such an important step should be preceded by lengthy consideration.

After his death, she was comforted by one of his best friends, the singer Eddie Fisher, also a Jew. The comfort soon turned into a romance, though he was already married to the actress Debbie Reynolds. The triangle made headlines for weeks, most Americans regarding Reynolds as an innocent victim and Taylor as a home wrecker. During that period, in 1959, Taylor formally converted to the Jewish faith, adopting the name Elisheba Rachel. Capitalizing on the scandal, MGM released *Cat on a Hot Tin Roof,* featuring Taylor as a seductress, at the height of the public interest in the affair.

Shortly afterward, in 1959, she married Fisher, who had obtained a divorce from Reynolds. Taylor and Fisher adopted a German daughter: Maria. Through Taylor's insistence, studio executives allowed Fisher an important role in *Butterfield 8.*

In the early 1960s she began a widely publicized romance with Richard Burton, her costar (as Mark Antony) in *Cleopatra.* In 1964, immediately after divorcing Fisher, she married Burton, who legally adopted Maria. They had a stormy ten-year marriage, during which they made numerous movies together, including *The V.I.P.s* (1963), *The Sandpiper* (1965), *Who's Afraid of Virginia Woolf?, The Taming of the Shrew, Doctor Faustus* (1967), *Hammersmith Is Out* (1972), and *Divorce His/Divorce Hers* (TV, 1973). In 1974 they divorced. The following year they remarried, but in 1976 they split up again.

In that same year, 1976, over one hundred Jewish airplane passengers were being held hostage at the Entebbe Airport in Uganda. Taylor privately communicated to Israeli officials that she would be willing to go to Uganda to negotiate with the hijackers and even to offer herself as a hostage for the release of the others. However, on July 4, 1976, Israeli commandos stormed the airport and rescued the hostages. Taylor later had a role in a filmed story of the episode, entitled *Victory at Entebbe* (TV, 1976), in which she played an Israeli who pleads with her government to negotiate with the terrorists, her daughter being one of the hostages.

Through the years, Taylor has supported many Jewish and Israeli causes. As a result, her films have been banned in some Arab countries.

Taylor's seventh marriage came late in 1976. Her new husband was John Warner, who was elected to the United States Senate as a Republican from Virginia in 1978. Since their divorce in 1982, Taylor has dated many men and has formed and broken at least two marriage engagements.

In January 1983 she was slightly injured in an auto accident in Tel Aviv. While in Israel on a private tour, she visited Prime Minister Menachem Begin.

In April 1983 Taylor and Burton reunited, at least professionally, to appear onstage in the Broadway play *Private Lives.* She missed a number of performances, reportedly because of bronchitis and laryngitis.

In December of that year Taylor entered the Betty Ford Center in California to cure herself of addictions to alcohol, sleeping pills, and painkillers. She checked out in January 1984.

In 1985 she became instrumental in raising funds for fighting the deadly disease Acquired Immune Deficiency Syndrome (AIDS). At that time, her good friend Rock Hudson was dying of that disease.

Taylor's work in the 1980s has included narrating the Holocaust documentary *Genocide* (1982) and making guest appearances on TV programs, such as the series *General Hospital* and *Hotel.* In the movie *Malice in Wonderland* (TV, 1985) she portrayed the gossip columnist Louella Parsons. In *There Must Be a Pony* (TV, 1986) she was a fading movie queen trying to stage a comeback.

Selected performances:

Stage

The Little Foxes (1981)
Private Lives (1983)

Films

There's One Born Every Minute (1942)
Lassie Come Home (1943)
Jane Eyre (1944)
The White Cliffs of Dover (1944)
National Velvet (1944)
Courage of Lassie (1946)
Cynthia (1947)
Life with Father (1947)
A Date with Judy (1948)
Julia Misbehaves (1948)
Little Women (1949)
The Conspirator (1950)
The Big Hangover (1950)
Father of the Bride (1950)
Father's Little Dividend (1951)
A Place in the Sun (1951)
Callaway Went Thataway (1951)

Elizabeth Taylor

Love Is Better Than Ever (1952)
Ivanhoe (1952)
The Girl Who Had Everything (1953)
Rhapsody (1954)
Elephant Walk (1954)
Beau Brummell (1954)
The Last Time I Saw Paris (1954)
Giant (1956)
Raintree County (1957)
Cat on a Hot Tin Roof (1958)
Suddenly Last Summer (1959)
Butterfield 8 (1960)
Cleopatra (1963)
The V.I.P.s (1963)
The Sandpiper (1965)
Who's Afraid of Virginia Woolf? (1966)
The Taming of the Shrew (1967)
Doctor Faustus (1967)
Reflections in a Golden Eye (1967)
The Comedians (1967)
Boom! (1968)
Secret Ceremony (1968)
The Only Game in Town (1970)
Under Milk Wood (1972)
Z and Co. (1972, G.B.; U.S., *X Y and Zee*)
Hammersmith Is Out (1972)
Divorce His/Divorce Hers (TV, 1973)
Night Watch (1973)
Ash Wednesday (1973)
The Blue Bird (1976)
Victory at Entebbe (TV, 1976)
A Little Night Music (1977)
Winter Kills (1979)
The Mirror Crack'd (1980)
Genocide (narrator, 1982)
Between Friends (TV, 1983)
North and South (TV, 1985)
Malice in Wonderland (TV, 1985)
There Must Be a Pony (TV, 1986)
Poker Alice (TV, 1987)

★★

Sophie Tucker

Last of the Red-hot Mamas

(1884-1966)

Sophie Tucker was born somewhere in Russia on January 13, 1884. Her mother was en route to the United States when she gave birth to Sophie. The family's name at that time was Kalish. Earlier, however, Sophie's father had run away from his military service and had fled to the United States. Along the way, he made friends with an Italian, Charles Abuza. When Abuza died, Kalish, in fear of being caught by the Russian police, took the dead man's name and papers. Arriving in Boston, he got a job and sent for his pregnant wife. Thus, when the baby girl reached America, she became Sophie, or Sophia (originally Sonia), Abuza.

In 1892 the Abuzas moved from Boston to Hartford, Connecticut, where they opened a restaurant. Sophie hated working in the restaurant. But one day she began to sing popular songs to help bring in customers. Theater people who frequented the restaurant inspired and encouraged Sophie to enter show business.

She began to appear in local amateur shows. At first, however, she was shy because of her bulk (145 pounds at the age of thirteen), and she restricted herself to playing the piano accompaniment (with one finger) for the singing of her younger sister, Anna. "Gradually," Sophie later wrote in her autobiography, *Some of These Days* (1945), "at the concerts I began to hear calls for 'the fat girl.' . . . Then I would jump up from the piano stool, forgetting all about my size, and work to get all the laughs I could get." She concluded that "maybe in show business size didn't matter if you could sing and could make people laugh."

Sophie begged her parents to let her leave town so that she could begin a career in show business, but they refused. After graduating from high school, she stayed with the restaurant till 1903, when she married Louis Tuck, a local beer-wagon driver. Louis, however, could not support Sophie and their son, Bert, and the Tucks soon separated.

In 1906, not long after her separation from Tuck,

Sophie left her son to be raised by her family, with her financial support, while she went to New York City to enter show business under the name Sophie Tucker. She found jobs scarce and often had to literally sing for her supper at restaurants.

Late in 1906 she entered an amateur show, and when the manager saw her he told an associate, according to Tucker's autobiography, "This one's so big and ugly the crowd out front will razz her. Better get some cork and black her up." At that time the use of blackface was still common among white entertainers, but it was usually a matter of choice. Tucker, already insecure about her own appearance, was led to believe that she needed blackface as a disguise. Though she hated blackface, she put it on for her performance in the amateur show, where her robust singing style was very successful.

In December 1906 Tucker made her professional New York City debut, again in blackface, at the Music Hall. She played in various vaudeville theaters for the next couple of years, and in 1908 she joined a traveling burlesque show. One day the luggage with her makeup failed to arrive, and she had to perform without blackface. Initially worried, she soon discovered to her pleasant surprise that the audience loved her just as she was. She never used blackface again.

In 1909 she was signed to appear on Broadway in Florenz Ziegfeld's annual *Follies.* But the female stars of the revue became jealous of her talent, and she was fired before she could appear during the show's New York City run.

Returning to vaudeville, Tucker soon became a major star, specializing in belting out ragtime songs. She also developed a distinctive stage personality in which her large dimensions became an asset, as in her humorous double-entendre singing of the song "Nobody Loves a Fat Girl, but Oh, How a Fat Girl Can Love."

In 1911 Tucker appeared in two musical comedies in Chicago, and while she was there she introduced "Some of These Days," which became her trademark song. In 1914 she appeared at the Palace Theater in New York City, the most prestigious house in vaudeville.

Also in 1914 she married her pianist, Frank Westphal, in Chicago. However, the marriage soon began to fail. After setting Frank up in a garage business, Sophie went on with her career alone. They were divorced in 1919.

During World War I the fashion in popular music changed from ragtime to jazz. Tucker organized her own little band, called the Five Kings of Syncopation, and billed herself as the Queen of Jazz.

After her father's death in 1915, Tucker suddenly began to incorporate sad, sentimental ballads into her performances. She also began to dramatize songs by introducing them with skits and monologues that intensified the emotional impact. By 1920 she had polished her act into its final form: a booming voice, a dramatic and emotional presentation, a suggestive kind of humor, and a repertory of songs ranging from lively jazz to tear-jerking ballads.

In December 1916 Tucker, with the Five Kings of Syncopation, opened at Reisenweber's New York City restaurant, where the group stayed for five years. During that time she also appeared elsewhere, as in the Broadway show *Hello, Alexander* (1919).

In 1922, shortly after Tucker and her jazz group broke up, she made the first of many tours in England, where she immediately became a huge success and where she remained extremely popular throughout the rest of her career. While she was there, she appeared in the London stage production of *Round in Fifty* (1922). But her proudest moment during her first trip to England was when London's Jewish population gave her a tremendous reception at the Rivoli Theater in Whitechapel.

Back in the United States, she made a two-year vaudeville tour. In 1925 she introduced "My Yiddishe Momme" (or "My Yiddisha Mama"), which became one of the songs with which she was most closely identified.

In 1928, at the Palace Theater, Tucker introduced the song "I'm the Last of the Red-hot Mamas." From that time forward she was billed as the Last of the Red-hot Mamas.

Also in 1928 she married Al Lackey, a fan who had become her personal manager. It was another short-lived marriage, and they were divorced in 1933.

Though successful in England, Tucker had difficulty on the Continent because of the language barrier. But her rendition of "My Yiddishe Momme" became very popular in Vienna, and she was invited to broadcast the song over the Berlin radio in 1931. However, after Hitler came to power, her existing records were smashed and further sales of her recordings were banned.

In the early 1930s, when American vaudeville was rapidly dying out, Tucker successfully made the transition to nightclubs, where she remained a headliner for the rest of her life.

She also worked in other major forums for variety stars, including the Broadway shows *Leave It to Me* (1938) and *High Kickers* (1941), in the latter of which she portrayed herself.

Her energetic performances enlivened the film musicals *Honky Tonk* (1929), *Broadway Melody of 1938* (1937), and *Follow the Boys* (1944). In 1937 she took acting lessons from Laura Hope Crews and performed a nonmusical character-acting role in the movie *Thoroughbreds Don't Cry* (1937).

Tucker also made numerous guest appearances on radio. Later she was a hit on TV, notably on Ed Sullivan's variety show.

But Tucker always preferred live theater to films, radio, and TV. "I couldn't even say 'hell' or 'damn,' " she complained about radio, "and nothing, honey, is more expressive than the way I say 'hell' or 'damn.' "

In England, however, music halls continued the tradition of uninhibited live variety shows, and Tucker performed there frequently. Her 1934 tour of England was climaxed by her command performance for King George V.

By the late 1930s Tucker was already being referred to as an American "institution." Particularly with her explosive live performances, she maintained her popularity for over fifty years.

Tucker's personal life, however, was troubled by the fact that though she always wanted to be home with her family, her career often required her to travel. In marriage, she had to face the inner conflict of simultaneously wanting a strong man and wanting independence. She became the provider and leader in each of her three marriages.

Tucker was a giving person, being involved with much fund raising and philanthropy. In 1945 she established the Sophie Tucker Foundation, and ten years later she endowed a chair in the theater arts at Brandeis University. Also an activist, she helped to organize the American Federation of Actors (later absorbed into the American Guild of Variety Artists, a division of Actors' Equity), which elected her president in 1938.

Even late in life Tucker held her audiences. In the 1950s she appealed to the new generation with her self-effacing humor: "I'm the 3-D Mama with the Big Wide Screen." In 1962 she gave another command performance in London. In 1963 she was the subject of the Broadway musical play *Sophie*.

In late 1965, at nearly eighty-two years of age, she made a successful appearance in the Latin Quarter of New York City. Tucker died a few months later in the same city on February 9, 1966.

Selected performances:

Stage

Merry Mary (1911)
Louisiana Lou (1911)
Hello, Alexander (1919)
Tick-Tack-Toe (1920)
Round in Fifty (1922)
Earl Carroll Vanities of 1924 (1924)
Gay Paree (1927)
Follow a Star (1930)
Leave It to Me (1938)
High Kickers (1941)

Films

Honky Tonk (1929)
Broadway Melody of 1938 (1937)
Thoroughbreds Don't Cry (1937)
Follow the Boys (1944)
Sensations of 1945 (1944)

★★★

Erich von Stroheim

The Man You Love to Hate

(1885-1957)

Erich von Stroheim was born in Vienna, Austria, on September 22, 1885. As an adult he asserted that his original name was Erich Oswald Hans Carl Maria Stroheim von Nordenwald and that his parents were members of the Catholic aristocracy in Austria. But shortly after his death, research uncovered what appears to be his birth certificate, which states that his parents were Jewish and that his real name was Erich Oswald Stroheim.

Details about his early years in Europe are in doubt, many of his own claims later proving to be false. He did, however, arrive in the United States in November 1909.

Settling at first in New York City, von Stroheim took odd jobs for the next few years. In 1912 a job as a traveling salesman took him to San Francisco, where he married Margaret Knox in 1913. She helped him perfect his English and collaborated with him in writing stories and plays. They were divorced in 1914.

Continuing with odd jobs, he went to Lake Tahoe and then to Los Angeles. From a group of extras, he was selected by the producer-director D. W. Griffith to play the small part of a black Confederate soldier in *The Birth of a Nation* (1915). Von Stroheim soon went on to perform as a bit player and assistant director in other pictures, such as Griffith's *Intolerance* (1916).

In 1917 he married May Jones, a theatrical costume designer. They had one son: Erich. Later that year they were divorced. In 1919 he married Valerie Germonprez, with whom he had his son Josef.

During that time von Stroheim appeared in many films, usually typecast as the brutal Prussian soldier and advertised as "the man you love to hate." He continued to play principally villainous roles throughout the rest of his career.

His first step into the limelight came with *Blind Husbands* (1919), which he wrote, directed, and starred in. The film shows an Austrian lieutenant (von Stroheim) attempting to seduce the wife of an American doctor.

Von Stroheim then coauthored and directed, but did not appear in, *The Devil's Passkey* (1920). In *Foolish Wives* (1922), which he directed, he played a ruthless seducer preying on wealthy, idle women. It was banned in some American cities.

Von Stroheim next wrote and began to direct *Merry-Go-Round,* a story of prewar Vienna. But the costs of the filming became so great that Irving Thalberg, the young production chief at Universal, fired von Stroheim. The film was completed in 1923 by Rupert Julian, who, in fact, followed his predecessor's shooting script.

Moving over to the Goldwyn Studio (soon to become Metro-Goldwyn-Mayer, or MGM), von Stroheim prepared an adaptation of Frank Norris's novel *McTeague* and filmed it as *Greed.* Intent on making the movie a naturalistic epic, he shot it on locations in San Francisco, Oakland, and the Mojave Desert. The result was a forty-two reel picture that ran for nine hours. He suggested that it be released in two or three sections. The studio, rejecting that plan, slashed the film down to ten reels and released it in 1924. *Greed* is now regarded as a masterpiece.

He then directed his own adaptation of Franz Lehár's operetta *The Merry Widow* (1925). It was a tremendous success, and in 1926 American critics voted von Stroheim the best director of the year. Also in 1926 he became a naturalized American citizen.

Leaving MGM, he made his next film for an independent producer, Pat Powers. Von Stroheim wrote, directed, and starred in the picture, entitled *The Wedding March,* another drama of pre-World War I Vienna. The lush production was becoming enormously long, and the producer stopped the filming before completion. The footage was divided by others into two movies: *The Wedding March* (1928) and *Honeymoon* (unreleased in the United States, though later shown in Europe and South America).

In 1928 Joseph P. Kennedy, the Boston financier (and father of the later president John F. Kennedy) who had become involved in films, engaged von Stroheim to write and direct a movie starring Gloria Swanson. In the film, *Queen Kelly,* von Stroheim deliberately restored episodes that had been eliminated from the script at the urging of the Hays censorship office. He also made *Queen Kelly* as a silent film even though talkies had already been firmly established. Those factors caused Kennedy and Swanson to halt the production before it was finished. Swanson later released the first half of the film abroad.

Erich von Stroheim

The last, and only sound, movie that von Stroheim directed was *Walking down Broadway*. But his 1933 work was judged unmarketable by Fox studio officials and was never released, though a few scenes were incorporated into *Hello, Sister* (1933).

Von Stroheim was one of the great creative directors in the history of the cinema, a master of realism and surrealism. Sergei Eisenstein called him "The Director." But because of his extravagances and his independence, producers gave up on him.

Rejected as a director, von Stroheim returned to acting. He played a schizophrenic music-hall ventriloquist in *The Great Gabbo* (1929), a treacherous German diplomat in *Friends and Lovers* (1931), a fanatically realistic movie director in *The Lost Squadron* (1932), and a sadistic writer in *As You Desire Me* (1932).

Soon, however, he was reduced to roles in minor films. In 1934 he became a wardrobe consultant at MGM. The following year he went bankrupt and joined the MGM story department, where he worked on several scripts. During that time he also wrote a successful novel, *Paprika* (1935).

In 1936 he was invited to Paris, where he appeared in a number of popular films. Most notable was his role as the disabled aristocratic German military officer in *La grande illusion* (1937, released in America as *Grand Illusion* in 1938).

The outbreak of World War II in Europe caused von Stroheim to return to Hollywood, where his stock had risen because of his success in France. He appeared in many films during the war, including *I Was an Adventuress* (1940) and *So Ends Our Night* (1941). His finest performance during that time was as the German general Rommel in *Five Graves to Cairo* (1943). In *The North Star* (1943) he had the role of a cold-blooded Nazi doctor who performs fiendish medical experiments on prisoners of war. In *The Great Flamarion* (1945) von Stroheim played a trick-shot artist who falls in love with the wife of his assistant and then, during a performance, "accidentally" kills the man.

He also made a rare venture into stage work. From early 1941 to late 1942 he toured in the comedy *Arsenic and Old Lace*. He then replaced Boris Karloff in the Broadway production of the play.

In 1945 von Stroheim returned to France. He made several films there, including *La danse de mort* ("The Dance of Death," 1947).

His last appearance in an American film came in *Sunset Boulevard* (1950). He portrayed a director who has become the butler of a former movie queen (played by Gloria Swanson).

In the early 1950s von Stroheim acted in French films, notably *Napoléon* (1954), in which he portrayed Beethoven. He also devoted much time to writing scenarios (still hoping to have a chance to direct again) and novels, including *Les feux de Saint-Jean* ("The Fires of Saint Joan"; volume 1, 1951; volume 2, 1954). He was preparing to write his memoirs when he died in Maurepas, Seine-et-Oise, France, on May 12, 1957.

Selected performances:

Stage

Arsenic and Old Lace (1941)

Films

The Birth of a Nation (1915)
Ghosts (1915)
Old Heidelberg (1915)
The Social Secretary (1916)
Intolerance (1916)
His Picture in the Papers (1916)
Panathea (1917)
Sylvia of the Secret Service (1917)
For France (1917)
The Unbeliever (1918)
The Hun Within (1918)
In Again, Out Again (1918)
Hearts of the World (1918)
The Heart of Humanity (1918)
Blind Husbands (1919)
Foolish Wives (1922)
The Wedding March (1928)
The Great Gabbo (1929)
Three Faces East (1930)
Friends and Lovers (1931)
The Lost Squadron (1932)
As You Desire Me (1932)
Crimson Romance (1934)
Fugitive Road (1934)
The Crime of Dr. Crespi (1935)
Marthe Richard, au service de la France ("Martha Richard, in the Service of France," 1936)
La grande illusion (1937)
Ultimatum (1938)
Tempête sur Paris (1939, Fr.; U.S., *Thunder over Paris*)
I Was an Adventuress (1940)
So Ends Our Night (1941)
Five Graves to Cairo (1943)
The North Star (1943)
The Lady and the Monster (1944)
Storm over Lisbon (1944)
The Great Flamarion (1945)
The Mask of Dijon (1946)
La danse de mort (1947)
Portrait d'un assassin ("Portrait of an Assassin," 1949)
Sunset Boulevard (1950)
Napoléon (1954, Fr.)

★★★

Eli Wallach

Master of Method Acting

(1915-)

Eli Wallach was born in New York City, New York, on December 7, 1915. He grew up in a predominantly Italian neighborhood in Brooklyn, where he acted in plays at school. At a local boys' club he portrayed the Old Man in *Fiat Lux* (1930).

After graduating from Erasmus Hall High School (1932), he attended the University of Texas (B.A., 1936), where he had the title role in *Liliom* (1936). He then majored in education at the City College of the City University of New York (M.S., 1938).

Deciding against a career in education, Wallach studied acting under Sanford Meisner at the Neighborhood Playhouse School of the Theater in New York City. His studies were interrupted by World War II, during which he served in the army medical corps (1941-45).

Returning to civilian life, Wallach began to appear onstage, making his Broadway debut as the Crew Chief in *Skydrift* (1945). In 1946 he played Cromwell in *Henry VIII* and the coward in *Androcles and the Lion.*

In 1947 Wallach became a charter member of the Actors Studio in New York City. There, under Lee Strasberg, he became a master of Method acting, a dramatic technique by which an actor seeks close personal identification with the character being portrayed.

In 1948 Wallach married the actress Anne Jackson, whom he had met when they were doing off-Broadway work together. They had three children: Peter, Roberta, and Katherine.

Meanwhile, though working fairly steadily, Wallach was unsatisfied with the progress of his career. He even put in an application to become a postman.

Then, in early 1949, the producer Joshua Logan asked him to replace Ted Kazanoff as Stefanowski in the fabulously successful Broadway production of *Mister Roberts.* That role finally gave Wallach the showcase necessary for advancing his career.

In 1951 his performance as Mangiacavallo, the passionate truck driver in Tennessee Williams's *The Rose Tattoo,* won him wide critical acclaim. He then turned down the juicy role of Maggio (eventually played by Frank Sinatra) in the film *From Here to Eternity* so that he could appear in Williams's next play, *Camino Real* (1953). Though the play itself did not fare well, Wallach's performance as Kilroy was hailed by critics.

Since then Wallach has appeared in many plays, frequently with his wife. They acted together in *Major Barbara* (1956); *Rhinoceros* (1961); *The Typists* and *The Tiger* (as a double bill, 1963); *Luv* (1964); *The Waltz of the Toreadors* (1973); *the Diary of Anne Frank* (1978), with their two daughters; *Twice around the Park* (1982); *The Nest of the Wood Grouse* (1984); and others.

Wallach's film debut came in *Baby Doll* (1956), as the sly and terrifying seducer. He has since played a wide variety of leading and supporting roles, both villainous and sympathetic, in a number of movies, including *The Misfits* (1961), *Lord Jim* (1965), *The Tiger Makes Out* (1967), *Cinderella Liberty* (1973), and *Skokie* (TV, 1981).

In *The Wall* (TV, 1982) he participated in a dramatization of the Warsaw Jews' desperate attempt to defend themselves against the Nazis in April 1943. In *Sam's Son* (1984), written and directed as an autobiographical essay by Michael Landon, Wallach sensitively conveyed the humiliations and hopes of Sam, the hero's father. Anne Jackson appeared in the movie as Sam's wife.

Wallach has made TV commercials and appeared on many TV programs. Throughout the 1985-86 season he gave masterful performances as Vincent Danzig, head of a Mafia family, in *Our Family Honor.* He also guest-starred in a 1986 episode of *Highway to Heaven.*

Wallach is widely regarded as a consummate craftsman and is renowned for the passion that he puts into his performances.

Selected performances:

Stage

Fiat Lux (1930)
Liliom (1936)
The Bo Tree (1939)
Skydrift (1945)
Henry VIII (1946)
Androcles and the Lion (1946)
Yellow Jack (1947)
Alice in Wonderland (1947)
Antony and Cleopatra (1947)
Mister Roberts (1949)
The Lady from the Sea (1950)
The Rose Tattoo (1951)
Camino Real (1953)
The Scarecrow (1953)

Mademoiselle Colombe (1954)
The Teahouse of the August Moon (1954)
Major Barbara (1956)
The Chairs (1958)
The Cold Wind and the Warm (1958)
Rhinoceros (1961)
Brecht on Brecht (1961)
The Typists (1963)
The Tiger (1963)
Luv (1964)
Staircase (1968)
Promenade, All! (1971)
The Waltz of the Toreadors (1973)
Saturday, Sunday, Monday (1974)
Absent Friends (1977)
The Diary of Anne Frank (1978)
Every Good Boy Deserves Favour (1979)
Twice around the Park (1982)
The Nest of the Wood Grouse (1984)

Films

Baby Doll (1956)
Seven Thieves (1960)
The Magnificent Seven (1960)
The Misfits (1961)
Hemingway's Adventures of a Young Man (1962)
Act One (1963)
How the West Was Won (1963)
The Victors (1963)
Kisses for My President (1964)
The Moon-Spinners (1964)
Genghis Khan (1965)
Lord Jim (1965)
How to Steal a Million (1966)
The Poppy Is Also a Flower (1966)
The Good, the Bad, and the Ugly (1967)
The Tiger Makes Out (1967)
How to Save a Marriage—and Ruin Your Life (1968)
A Lovely Way to Die (1968)
New York City—the Most (1968)
Ace High (1969)
The Brain (1969)
Mackenna's Gold (1969)
The Angel Levine (1970)
The People Next Door (1970)
Zigzag (1970)
Cinderella Liberty (1973)
A Cold Night's Death (TV, 1973)
Indict and Convict (TV, 1974)
Crazy Joe (1974)
Nasty Habits (1977)
The Domino Principle (1977)
The Deep (1977)
Seventh Avenue (TV, 1977)
The Pirate (TV, 1978)
Girlfriends (1978)
Movie Movie (1978)
The Adventures of Gerard (1978)
Circle of Iron (1979)
Firepower (1979)
Winter Kills (1979)
The Hunter (1980)
Fugitive Family (TV, 1980)
The Pride of Jesse Hallam (TV, 1981)
Skokie (TV, 1981)
The Wall (TV, 1982)
The Executioner's Song (TV, 1982)
Anatomy of an Illness (TV, 1984)
Sam's Son (1984)
Murder: By Reason of Insanity (TV, 1985)
Christopher Columbus (TV, 1985)
Tough Guys (1986)
Something in Common (TV, 1986)

TV

Our Family Honor (1985-86)

★★

Jesse White

Comedy Character Actor

(1919-)

Jesse White was born in Buffalo, New York, on January 3, 1919. His original name was Jesse Weidenfeld.

He moved with his family to Akron, Ohio, as a youngster. There he made his stage debut, as the Court Jester, in *Mary of Scotland* (1934) and graduated from high school (1936).

After working at odd jobs and breaking into small-time show business, White had his first big chance when he toured as a Nazi soldier in *The Moon Is Down* in 1942. Also in 1942 he married Cecelia Kahn, with whom he had two daughters: Carole and Janet.

Then, in New York City, White played a vacuum-cleaner salesman in *Sons and Soldiers* (1943). Over the next few years he appeared in numerous plays. One highlight was his performance as Duane Wilson, the mental-hospital attendant, in the comedy-fantasy *Harvey* (1944). Another was his role as Harry Brock (succeeding Paul Douglas) in the comedy *Born Yesterday* (1949).

White also began to make guest appearances on TV during its early years. He acted, for example, on the *Chevrolet Theater* (1945) and the *Ford Theater* (1947).

His movie debut came when he repeated his role for the filmed version of *Harvey* (1950). White quickly became a staple character actor in movies, such as *Bedtime for Bonzo* (1951), *Death of a Salesman* (1951), *Million Dollar Mermaid* (1952), *The Bad Seed* (1956), and *Marjorie Morningstar* (1958).

He also became a familiar figure on TV as a regular on the comedy series *Private Secretary* (1953-57, syndicated as *Susie*), *Make Room for Daddy* (or *The Danny Thomas Show,* 1954-57), and *The Ann Sothern Show* (1959-61). Later he frequently appeared as a guest performer on many shows.

White was a dependable actor in either drama or comedy. But his most characteristic role was as a comically nervous, cigar-chewing heavy.

After moving to films and TV, White continued to return occasionally to the stage, as in *Will Success Spoil Rock Hunter?* (1956), *Guys and Dolls* (1959), and *Show Boat* (1963). He replaced John McGiver as the mayor in *The Front Page* in 1969, and he revived Wilson in *Harvey* in 1970 and 1971.

His later movies included *It's a Mad, Mad, Mad, Mad World* (1963); *Pajama Party* (1964); *The Reluctant Astronaut* (1967); and *The Cat from Outer Space* (1978).

Since 1967 White has been the TV spokesman for Maytag Company. Many young people know him principally as the "lonely" Maytag repairman in TV commercials, the sales ploy being that Maytag appliances are so reliable that no one ever goes to him for help.

"At age seven," White has said, "I knew what I wanted in life—to bring a little laughter and joy to the world. I've been blessed twice—to be able to do the thing I know and do best and to make a decent and respectable living at it. I have had a good life in show business and feel sorry for people who are not in it."

Selected performances:

Stage

Mary of Scotland (1934)
The Moon Is Down (1942)
Sons and Soldiers (1943)
My Dear Public (1943)
Unexpected Honeymoon (1943)
Mrs. Kimball Presents (1944)
Helen Goes to Troy (1944)
Harvey (1944)
The Cradle Will Rock (1947)
A Month in the Country (1948)
Red Gloves (1948)
Goodnight Ladies (1949)
Born Yesterday (1949)
Will Success Spoil Rock Hunter? (1956)
A Hole in the Head (1957)
Guys and Dolls (1959)
Kiss Me, Kate (1960)
Show Boat (1963)
Stubborn Ernie (1964)
Kiss Me, Kate (1965)
Kelly (1965)
The Front Page (1969)
Harvey (1970, 1971)

Films

Harvey (1950)
Bedtime for Bonzo (1951)
Francis Goes to the Races (1951)

Jesse White

Callaway Went Thataway (1951)
Death of a Salesman (1951)
The Girl in White (1952)
Million Dollar Mermaid (1952)
Forever Female (1954)
Hell's Half Acre (1954)
Witness to Murder (1954)
Not as a Stranger (1955)
The Come On (1956)
Back from Eternity (1956)
The Bad Seed (1956)
Designing Woman (1957)
Marjorie Morningstar (1958)
The Rise and Fall of Legs Diamond (1960)
The Big Night (1960)
A Fever in the Blood (1961)
On the Double (1961)
The Right Approach (1961)
Tomboy and the Champ (1961)
It's Only Money (1962)
Sail a Crooked Ship (1962)
It's a Mad, Mad, Mad, Mad World (1963)
The Yellow Canary (1963)
A House Is Not a Home (1964)
Looking for Love (1964)
Pajama Party (1964)
Dear Brigitte (1965)
The Ghost in the Invisible Bikini (1966)
The Reluctant Astronaut (1967)
The Spirit Is Willing (1967)
Bless the Beasts and Children (1971)
New Girl in Town (1977)
The Cat from Outer Space (1978)

TV

Private Secretary (1953-57, syndicated as *Susie*)
Make Room for Daddy (or *The Danny Thomas Show*, 1954-57)
The Ann Sothern Show (1959-61)
Devlin (animated, voice only, 1974-76)

★★

Gene Wilder

Deadpan Comic Actor

(1935-)

Gene Wilder was born in Milwaukee, Wisconsin, on June 11, 1935. His original name was Jerome Silberman.

When he was six years old, his mother had a heart attack that left her a partial invalid. He used to cheer her up by improvising comedy skits, thus developing an early awareness of the coexistence of laughter and pain.

His parents sent him to the Black Fox Military Institute in Los Angeles. "I was the only Jew in school," he later said, "and I got either beaten up or insulted every day." He soon returned to his native city, where he began acting lessons in 1947 and made his first stage appearance, as Balthazar in *Romeo and Juliet* at the Milwaukee Playhouse, in 1948.

After graduating from Washington High School in 1951, he enrolled at the University of Iowa. While he was there, he acted in student plays and worked in summer stock. He graduated with a B.A. degree in 1955.

Then, at the Old Vic Theater School in Bristol, England (1955-56), he studied voice, judo, fencing, and gymnastics. However, he left when he reached the acting class.

Returning to America, he was drafted for two years of service in the army (1956-58), where he was assigned to the Valley Forge Hospital in Pennsylvania. He requested duty in the neuropsychiatric ward because he felt that the experience would be helpful in his acting studies. On weekends he went to drama classes at the Herbert Berghof Studio in New York City.

In 1961 he joined the Actors Studio, where he began to study with the famed Lee Strasberg. That same year saw his off-Broadway debut, in the comedy *Roots,* and his first Broadway role, as the confused valet in *The Complaisant Lover.* By then he had changed his name to Gene Wilder.

While playing in *Mother Courage and Her Children* (1963), Wilder met Mel Brooks, who called for the show's star, Anne Bancroft, every evening. Brooks promised to give the young actor a role in a movie someday.

Wilder honed his dramatic and comedic skills in several more plays. One of them was *One Flew over the Cuckoo's Nest* (1963), which was set in a mental hospital, giving him a chance to draw on his experiences in the neuropsychiatric ward at Valley Forge Hospital.

During the early 1960s he also made some guest appearances on TV series, such as *The Defenders.* On the *Eternal Light* series, he acted in "Home for Passover" (1966).

Wilder's film debut came in *Bonnie and Clyde* (1967), in which he played a neurotic undertaker kidnapped by a gang of outlaws. Then Brooks, keeping his promise, gave Wilder an important role in Brooks's first film, *The Producers* (1967); Wilder portrayed the neurotic accountant Leo Bloom, who is drawn into a wild scheme by a crooked producer (played by Zero Mostel). There followed several movies in which Wilder's comic acting far outshone the scripts, as in *Start the Revolution without Me* (1970) and *Willy Wonka and the Chocolate Factory* (1971).

But when he turned once again to Brooks's films, comic magic resulted. For example, in *Blazing Saddles* (1974), a spoof of Hollywood westerns, Wilder portrayed a brazen alcoholic gunslinger. In *Young Frankenstein* (1974), a gothic-horror parody whose script he cowrote with Brooks, Wilder played the title role, a brain surgeon who tries to live down the scandal of his infamous ancestor but who finally succumbs to the temptation to follow in his forebear's footsteps.

Encouraged by his successful collaboration on *Young Frankenstein,* Wilder began to write, direct, and star in his own movies. Following Brooks's lead, he constructed spoofs of well-known film genres. First was *The Adventure of Sherlock Holmes' Smarter Brother* (1975), a parody of the Holmes detective movies. *The World's Greatest Lover* (1977), which he also produced, was a takeoff on the Rudolph Valentino romantic films of the 1920s. In *Skippy* (1981) Wilder spoofed sex comedies, the hero (Wilder) going so far as to sign himself into a mental hospital to overcome a sex problem.

Among the other movies he appeared in were *The Frisco Kid* (1979), a comedy about an Orthodox rabbi (Wilder) traveling from Poland to San Francisco in 1850; *Stir Crazy* (1980); *Hanky Panky* (1982); *The Woman in Red* (1984); and *Haunted Honeymoon* (1986).

Wilder, perhaps reflecting his early experiences in

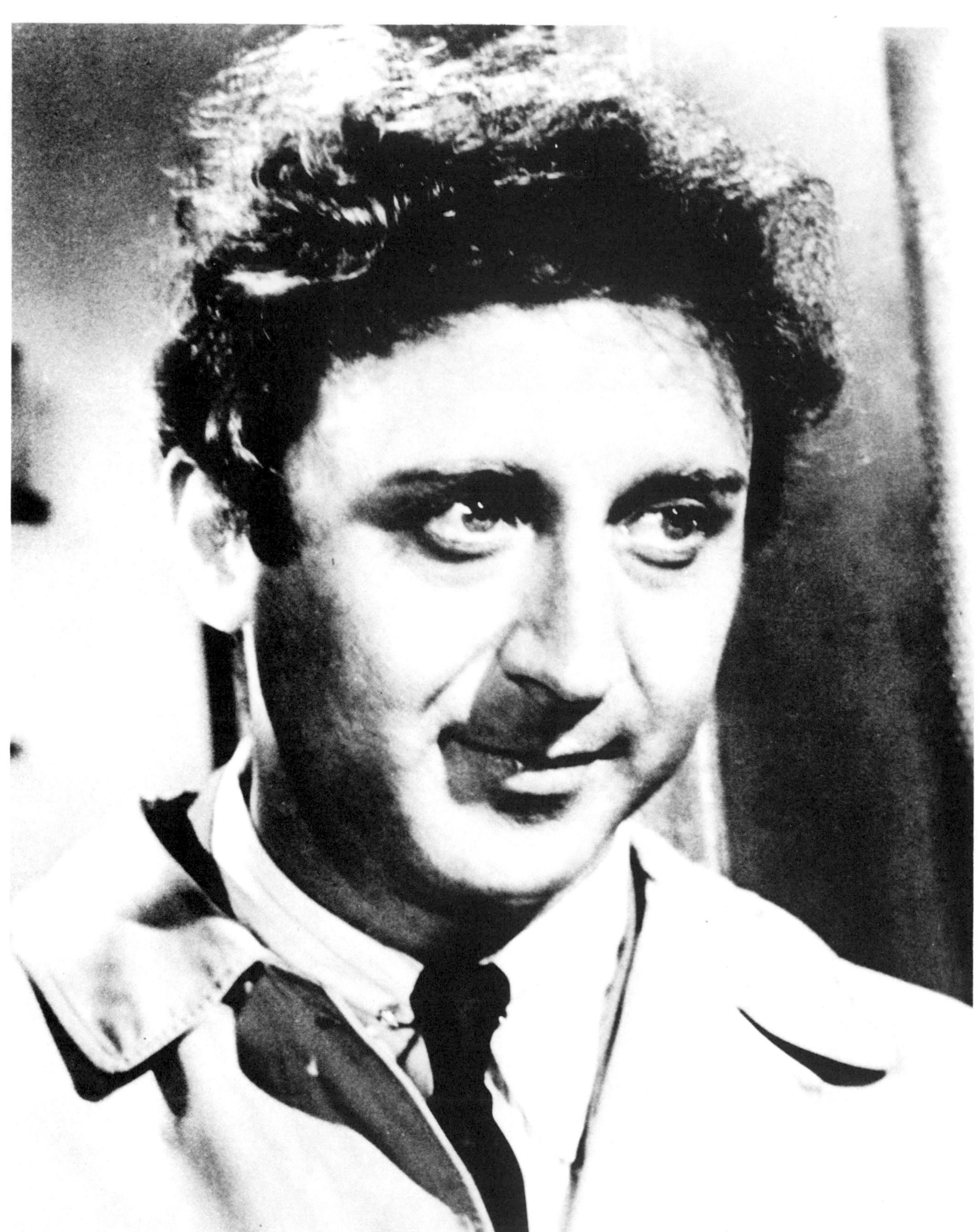

Gene Wilder

creating comedy for his stricken mother, likes to draw humor from characters who are essentially sad. His fame rests largely on the wild contrast between his bland expression and his madcap behavior. That contrast reflects the real man: "My quiet exterior used to be a mask for hysteria," he has said. "After seven years of analysis, it just became a habit."

Wilder has been married three times. In 1960 he wedded the actress Mary Mercier, who appeared with him in *Roots*. After divorcing her he married Mary Joan Schutz in 1967; he also adopted her daughter, Katharine, from a previous marriage. Wilder's second marriage also ended in divorce. In September 1984 he married the actress Gilda Radner, who had appeared with him in *Hanky Panky* and *The Woman in Red*.

Selected performances:

Stage

Roots (1961)
The Complaisant Lover (1961)
Mother Courage and Her Children (1963)
One Flew over the Cuckoo's Nest (1963)
Dynamite Tonight (1964)
The White House (1964)

Films

Bonnie and Clyde (1967)
The Producers (1967)
Quackser Fortune Has a Cousin in the Bronx (1970)
Start the Revolution without Me (1970)
Willy Wonka and the Chocolate Factory (1971)
Thursday's Game (TV, 1974)
Rhinoceros (1974)
Blazing Saddles (1974)
The Little Prince (1974)
Young Frankenstein (1974)
The Adventure of Sherlock Holmes' Smarter Brother (1975)
Silver Streak (1976)
The World's Greatest Lover (1977)
The Frisco Kid (1979)
Stir Crazy (1980)
Skippy (1981)
Hanky Panky (1982)
The Woman in Red (1984)
Haunted Honeymoon (1986)

★★★

Debra Winger

Intense Young Actress

(1955-)

Debra Winger was born in Cleveland, Ohio, on May 16, 1955. Her full name was Mary Debra Winger. As a small child she moved with her parents to Van Nuys, California.

After graduating from high school in 1971, Winger briefly visited Europe and then went to Israel to live and work on a kibbutz. She also applied for Israeli citizenship. But after three months of rigorous military training with the Israeli army, she changed her mind.

Returning to the United States, Winger studied sociology and criminology at California State University in Northridge. However, while working in her spare time at Magic Mountain amusement park, she was thrown from a moving truck. As a result she developed a cerebral hemorrhage that almost killed her, and for several months she was partly paralyzed and was blind in one eye.

That experience gave Winger a new perspective on life, and she decided to pursue the potentially deep experiences of an acting career. Therefore, one year short of graduation, she dropped out of college and began a three-year period of drama study with the actor Michael V. Gazzo. During that time she also acted in some repertory theater in the San Fernando Valley.

Soon Winger began to appear on TV. She made commercials for McDonald's hamburgers, Metropolitan

Debra Winger

Life Insurance, and other companies. She made good impressions in guest roles on TV series, such as *Wonder Woman*. And she was in the movie *Special Olympics* (TV, 1978).

Winger's first theater-film role was a small part in *Thank God It's Friday* (1978). But she first attracted major attention with her small role as Melanie, an American student in Paris, in the comedy *French Postcards* (1979).

Winger became a full-fledged star with her performance as the female lead, the tough but sweet Sissy, in the blue-collar romantic melodrama *Urban Cowboy* (1980). She prepared for her part with a vigorous exercise routine so that she could ride a mechanical bucking bull in a bar.

Winger soon followed with several films that established her as one of the major film talents of her generation. In *Cannery Row* (1982) she played a reluctant bordello girl. In *An Officer and a Gentleman* (1982) she was a sexy but sensitive Polish-American paper-mill worker. In *Terms of Endearment* (1983) she portrayed an ill-starred daughter caught in a volatile relationship with her overly possessive mother. In *Mike's Murder* (1984) she played a young woman drawn into the sleazy world of the Los Angeles drug culture. In *Legal Eagles* (1986) she extended her range by giving an excellent performance as a young attorney.

Unlike many actresses of her generation, who quickly rise to TV stardom on the basis of publicity and physical beauty and then lack the motivation to develop the big talents to go with their big names, Winger has risen solely through her genuine gift for bringing passion and intensity to her performances.

Her most noticeable physical characteristic is her gravelly voice, which can be strangely touching. In the movie *E.T.* (1982) her voice was one of two that were electronically mixed to create the sound of the extraterrestrial creature.

Winger has been romantically linked with several men, including Robert Kerrey, Nebraska's bachelor governor.

Selected performances:

Films

Special Olympics (TV, 1978)
Thank God It's Friday (1978)
French Postcards (1979)
Urban Cowboy (1980)
Cannery Row (1982)
An Officer and a Gentleman (1982)
Terms of Endearment (1983)
Mike's Murder (1984)
Legal Eagles (1986)
Black Widow (1987)

★★

Henry Winkler

Fonzie

(1945-)

Henry Winkler was born in New York City, New York, on October 30, 1945. His parents had grown up and married in Germany, moved to Amsterdam in 1938, and immigrated to the United States in 1939. Many of their relatives who stayed in Germany perished in Nazi concentration camps.

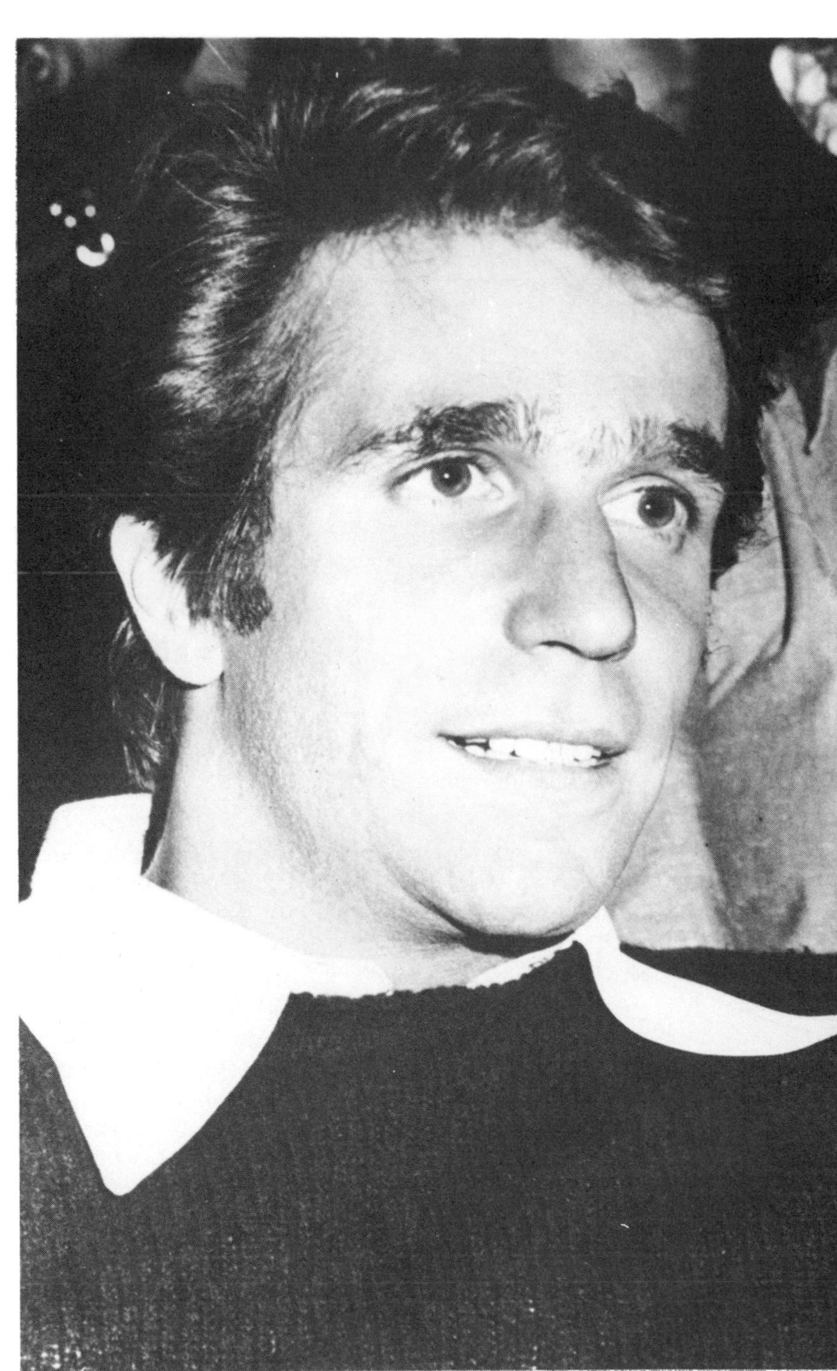

While growing up in New York City, Winkler appeared in many school dramatic productions. After graduating from McBurney, a private boys' school in Manhattan, he attended Emerson College (1963-67) in Boston. There he performed onstage in theater productions for both Emerson and nearby Harvard.

Having earned his B.A. degree at Emerson, Winkler went to Yale for postgraduate study. While at the Yale School of Drama (1967-70), he became one of the founders of the New Haven Free Theater (1968). He graduated from Yale with an M.F.A. in 1970 and then spent one year (1970-71) with the Yale Repertory Theater.

Moving to New York City, Winkler did some TV commercials and performed in a revue called *Off the Wall* (1972). Late in 1972 his career took a major step forward when he won a role in the movie *The Lords of Flatbush,* a lighthearted story of leather-jacket teenagers in 1957. The picture was filmed in New York City and released in 1974.

By the time the movie hit the theaters, he had already moved to Hollywood and established himself on TV. After making good comedic impressions with guest performances on Mary Tyler Moore's show and then on Bob Newhart's, Winkler won a leading role in a new TV series, *Happy Days* (1974-84), a nostalgic look at high-school life in late-1950s Milwaukee, Wisconsin. In that series he created one of the most popular characters in TV history, Arthur ("Fonzie" or "the Fonz") Fonzarelli, the respected know-it-all high-school dropout who works as an auto mechanic and dominates everyone around him; yet when the chips are down, he continually shows an underlying softheartedness.

Winkler has had difficulty finding roles of sufficient force to help the public see him as more than just Fonzie. But he is a solidly trained actor who has performed well in a variety of films, including the drama *Heroes* (1977), as a demented Vietnam veteran; the comedy *The One and Only* (1978), as a wound-be actor who tries to win stardom by wrestling on TV; the sentimental drama *An American Christmas Carol* (TV, 1979), as a Scrooge-like character in Depression-era New Hampshire; and the comedy *Night Shift* (1982), as a milquetoast morgue supervisor who becomes a pimp.

In 1978 Winkler married Stacey Weitzman. They had a daughter: Zoe.

A man of great personal depth and integrity, Winkler has used his Fonzie-based fame as a means to do good. He has been chairman of the Toys for Tots and honorary chairman of the Epilepsy Foundation. He wrote the book *The Other Side of Henry Winkler: My Story* (1976), in which his intelligence and good nature shine.

In recent years he has turned increasingly to producing. He served, for example, as coexecutive producer of the movies *Starflight: The Plane That Couldn't Land* (TV, 1983) and *When Your Lover Leaves* (TV, 1983).

Selected performances:

Stage

The Bacchae (1969)
Don Juan (1970)
Three Philip Roth Stories (1970)
Cops and Horrors (1970)
The Revenger's Tragedy (1970)
Off the Wall (1972)

Films

The Lords of Flatbush (1974)
Katherine (TV, 1975)
Heroes (1977)
The One and Only (1978)
An American Christmas Carol (TV, 1979)
Night Shift (1982)

TV

Happy Days (1974-84)

★★

Shelley Winters

Young Innocent and Mature Meanie

(1922-)

Shelley Winters was born in Saint Louis, Missouri, on August 18, 1922. Her original name was Shirley Schrift. Her mother had sung at the Saint Louis Municipal Opera, and Shirley developed an early interest in show business.

As a small child she moved with her parents to the borough of Brooklyn in New York City. In her early teens she entered a number of beauty contests, winning some. She also participated in many theatrical productions at school and elsewhere. In her senior year at Thomas Jefferson High School, she sang in the school's production of Gilbert and Sullivan's operetta *The Mikado*.

A few months before she would have graduated from high school, she dropped out and began to work as a model in New York City's garment district. Then she studied at the New Theater School and performed in a variety of show-business jobs, including some work on the borscht circuit.

By then, still in her teens, she had adopted the stage name Shelley (the name of her favorite poet) Winter (her mother's maiden name). Later, in Hollywood, her studio added an s to make her last name Winters.

In 1941 she began to appear on the New York City stage. But the first job to give her important exposure was a part in the operetta *Rosalinda* on Broadway in 1942.

Also in 1942 she married Mack Mayer, a textile salesman. They divorced in 1948.

Her work in *Rosalinda* was followed by the role of Ado Annie Carney (alternating with two other actresses) in the original Broadway run of the Rodgers and Hammerstein musical *Oklahoma!* (1943).

Soon she was signed to a Hollywood movie contract. After a few minor film appearances, she made a vivid impression in *A Double Life* (1948), as a waitress strangled by a deranged actor (played by Ronald Colman).

Her best early roles were in a similar vein, that is, a young, innocent woman victimized by her own vulnerability. In *He Ran All the Way* (1951), for example, her character becomes romantically involved with a doomed criminal (played by John Garfield). In *A Place in the Sun* (1951) she was a factory worker who becomes pregnant by her boy friend (played by Montgomery Clift), is deserted by him, and then tries so hard to pressure him into marriage that he drowns her (or allows her to drown) because of his love for a beautiful girl (played by Elizabeth Taylor). In *The Night of the Hunter* (1955) her character is murdered again, in a particularly gruesome manner.

In 1952 Winters married the Italian actor Vittorio Gassman. It was a stormy, sometimes violent, marriage. They had one child, Vittoria, before divorcing in 1954.

In the mid-1950s Winters took some time away from films to work on the stage. She appeared, for example, in *Girls of Summer* (1956).

During that time, in 1957, she married the Italian-American actor Anthony Franciosa. They divorced in 1960.

Returning to movies in the late 1950s, she developed a completely different image—plump, matronly, sometimes rowdy, and often downright evil. Her first of these "mature" roles was in *The Diary of Anne Frank* (1959), as the most self-centered of the Jews hiding in an Amsterdam attic during the period of Nazi control in Europe.

In *A Patch of Blue* (1965) she played a bitchy whore who is the mother of a blind girl, whom the mother wants to turn into a prostitute. In *Bloody Mama* (1970) she was the matriarch of a gang of violent hoods. Winters portrayed mentally unbalanced women in the horror tales *What's the Matter with Helen?* (1971) and *Who Slew Auntie Roo?* (1972). In *The Devil's Daughter* (TV, 1973) she was Satan's vessel. And she made an effectively revolting hag in *The Magician of Lublin* (1979).

Nevertheless, she remains capable of a wide range of roles. She played Minnie Marx, the Marx Brothers' mother, in the Broadway musical *Minnie's Boys* (1970). Winters appeared in the comedy film *Over the Brooklyn Bridge* (1984), and in *Alice in Wonderland* (TV, 1985) she portrayed the Dodo Bird.

She has also turned to writing. Her stage work *One Night Stands of a Noisy Passenger* (consisting of three short plays) began a New York City run near the end of December 1970. In 1980 she came out with her widely publicized and highly controversial autobiography of her early years, *Shelley: Also Known as Shirley,* in which she tells about her romances with Marlon Brando, Errol Flynn, Burt Lancaster, and many others. Since then she has been a frequent guest on TV talk shows.

Selected performances:

Stage

Meet the People (1941)
The Night before Christmas (1941)
Rosalinda (1942)
Oklahoma! (1943)
The Merry Widow (1946)
Born Yesterday (1950)
A Streetcar Named Desire (1952)
A Hatful of Rain (1955)
Girls of Summer (1956)
A Piece of Blue Sky (1959)
Two for the Seesaw (1960)
The Country Girl (1961)
A View from the Bridge (1961)
The Night of the Iguana (1961)
Cages (1963)
Under the Weather (1966)
Minnie's Boys (1970)
The Effect of Gamma Rays on Man-in-the-Moon Marigolds (1973)
Kennedy's Children (1976)

Films

Knickerbocker Holiday (1944)
A Double Life (1948)
Larceny (1948)
Cry of the City (1948)
Take One False Step (1949)
The Great Gatsby (1949)
Johnny Stool Pigeon (1949)
South Sea Sinner (1950)
Winchester '73 (1950)
Frenchie (1951)
He Ran All the Way (1951)
A Place in the Sun (1951)
Behave Yourself! (1951)
Phone Call from a Stranger (1952)
Meet Danny Wilson (1952)
Untamed Frontier (1952)
My Man and I (1952)
Saskatchewan (1954)
Executive Suite (1954)
Playgirl (1954)
Mambo (1955)
I Am a Camera (1955)
The Night of the Hunter (1955)
The Big Knife (1955)
I Died a Thousand Times (1955)
The Treasure of Pancho Villa (1955)
Cash on Delivery (1956)
The Diary of Anne Frank (1959)
Odds against Tomorrow (1959)
Let No Man Write My Epitaph (1960)
The Young Savages (1961)
The Chapman Report (1962)
Lolita (1962)
The Balcony (1963)
Wives and Lovers (1963)
A House Is Not a Home (1964)
The Greatest Story Ever Told (1965)

Shelley Winters

A Patch of Blue (1965)
Time of Indifference (1965)
Alfie (1966)
Harper (1966)
Enter Laughing (1967)
The Scalphunters (1968)
Wild in the Streets (1968)
Buona Sera, Mrs. Campbell (1969)
The Mad Room (1969)
Bloody Mama (1970)
Flap (1970)
How Do I Love Thee? (1970)
What's the Matter with Helen? (1971)
Revenge (TV, 1971)
A Death of Innocence (TV, 1971)
The Adventures of Nick Carter (TV, 1972)
Who Slew Auntie Roo? (1972)
The Poseidon Adventure (1972)
Blume in Love (1973)
Cleopatra Jones (1973)
The Devil's Daughter (TV, 1973)
Big Rose (TV, 1974)
The Sex Symbol (TV, 1974)
Next Stop, Greenwich Village (1976)
The Tenant (1976)
Diamonds (1976)
The Three Sisters (1977)
Tentacles (1977)
Pete's Dragon (1977)
King of the Gypsies (1978)
The Initiation of Sarah (TV, 1978)
Elvis (TV, 1979)
The French Atlantic Affair (TV, 1979)
City on Fire (1979)
The Magician of Lublin (1979)
S.O.B. (1981)
Over the Brooklyn Bridge (1984)
Alice in Wonderland (TV, 1985)
Déjà Vu (1985)
The Delta Force (1986)

★★

Joseph Wiseman

Dr. No

(1918-)

Joseph Wiseman was born in Montreal, Canada, on May 15, 1918. As a child he moved to New York City, where he graduated from John Adams High School (1935) in the Ozone Park district and then briefly attended the City College of the City University of New York.

He began his professional acting career by appearing in three stage productions in Saugerties, New York, during the summer of 1936. His New York City debut came when he played a Union soldier in *Abe Lincoln in Illinois* (1938).

Over the next decade Wiseman developed a fine reputation as a character actor on the stage. Among the plays that he appeared in were *The Three Sisters* (1939), *Journey to Jerusalem* (1940), *Antony and Cleopatra* (1947), and *Detective Story* (1949).

In 1943 Wiseman married Nell Kinard, with whom he had a son and a daughter. That marriage ended in divorce, and he later wedded Pearl Lang.

Wiseman made his film debut with a role as a moody Italian unionist in *With These Hands* (1950). He then made a strong impression by repeating his role as a tough criminal in the filmed version of *Detective Story* (1951).

Because of his gaunt, severe appearance, he was frequently cast as a sinister villain in movies. In *Viva Zapata!* (1952), for example, he played a ruthless manipulator in revolutionary Mexico. And in the James Bond spy thriller *Dr. No* (1963), Wiseman had the title role as a mad scientist.

Meanwhile, he also began to appear on TV. He acted in "Darkness at Noon" (1955) on *Producers' Showcase* and in many other plays telecast on anthology series during TV's Golden Age. During the 1950s he frequently performed on TV's *Frontiers of Faith;* and later he made memorable guest appearances on drama series, such as *The Untouchables* (1965) and *Twilight Zone* (1966).

Wiseman also continued to work on the stage, where he was allowed a wide range of roles. For example, he played the gentle Mr. Frank in *The Diary of Anne Frank* (1958). Wiseman portrayed the saintly Thomas Beckett in *Murder in the Cathedral* (1966), the Rabbi in *The Madness of God* (1974), and the evil Tadeus in *The Golem* (1984).

In the movie *The Apprenticeship of Duddy Kravitz* (1974) Wiseman had the role of Uncle Benjy, a rich Jewish socialist. In *Buck Rogers* (1979) he was Draco, the tyrannical king of Draconia. Among his other films were *The Valachi Papers* (1972), *Masada* (TV, 1981), and *Rage of Angels* (TV, 1983).

Selected performances:

Stage

The Milky Way (1936)
Abe Lincoln in Illinois (1938)
The Three Sisters (1939)
The Grass Is Always Greener (1939)
Journey to Jerusalem (1940)
Candle in the Wind (1941)
The Three Sisters (1942)
The Barber Had Two Sons (1943)
Storm Operation (1944)
Joan of Lorraine (1946)
Antony and Cleopatra (1947)
Detective Story (1949)
That Lady (1949)
King Lear (1950)
Golden Boy (1952)
The Lark (1955)
Susan and the Stranger (1956)
The Duchess of Malfi (1957)
The Diary of Anne Frank (1958)
The Queen and the Rebels (1959)
Turn On the Night (1961)
Naked (1963)
Marco Millions (1964)
Incident at Vichy (1964)
Murder in the Cathedral (1966)
In the Matter of J. Robert Oppenheimer (1968)
Uncle Vanya (1969)
The Madness of God (1974)
Balyasnikov (1977)
The Lesson (1978)
The Golem (1984)

Films

With These Hands (1950)
Detective Story (1951)
Viva Zapata! (1952)
Les Misérables (1952)
The Silver Chalice (1954)
The Prodigal (1955)
Three Brave Men (1957)
The Garment Jungle (1957)
The Unforgiven (1960)
The Happy Thieves (1961)
Dr. No (1963)
The Outsider (TV, 1967)
Bye Bye Braverman (1968)
The Counterfeit Killer (1968)
The Night They Raided Minsky's (1968)
Stiletto (1969)
The Mask of Sheba (TV, 1970)
Lawman (1971)
The Valachi Papers (1972)
Pursuit (TV, 1972)
Men of the Dragon (TV, 1974)
QB VII (TV, 1974)
The Apprenticeship of Duddy Kravitz (1974)
Murder at the World Series (TV, 1977)
The Betsy (1978)
Buck Rogers (1979)
Masada (TV, 1981)
Rage of Angels (TV, 1983)
Seize the Day (TV, 1986)

Joseph Wiseman

★★★

Ed Wynn

Perfect Fool

(1886-1966)

Ed Wynn was born in Philadelphia, Pennsylvania, on November 9, 1886. His original name was Isaiah Edwin Leopold.

His father, a moderately prosperous manufacturer and retailer of women's hats, had come from Bohemia, while his mother had been born of Sephardic Jews in Turkey. As soon as the boy could walk, he was putting on ladies' hats and drawing laughs from his father's customers.

Young Leopold desperately wanted to become a professional comedian, but his parents objected. Hence, in the summer of 1902, at the age of fifteen, he ran away from home and joined a repertory company as a backstage helper and occasional onstage player. Soon, however, the company went bankrupt in New England and he returned home.

After selling hats for a while, he ran away again. To avoid embarrassing his father, he formed a stage name by splitting the two syllables of his middle name: Edwin became Ed Wynn.

In 1903 he began his long, successful vaudeville career. For a while he teamed up with Jack Lewis, billing themselves as Win and Lose. However, Wynn worked principally on his own as one of the top vaudeville comedians of his time.

In 1910 he made his Broadway debut in the short-lived musical *The Deacon and the Lady*. But it was through the *Ziegfeld Follies of 1914* that Wynn became a Broadway star. In the 1915 edition of the *Follies*, Wynn was in the show with W. C. Fields. During the latter's famous pool-table act, the audience kept laughing at the wrong times. At last Fields discovered Wynn under the table—comically catching flies. The two great comedians did not speak to each other for several years, but peace was eventually restored.

Wynn went on to perform in many Broadway shows, including *Ed Wynn Carnival* (1920); *The Perfect Fool* (1921); *The Laugh Parade* (1931); and *Laugh, Town, Laugh* (1942). His most successful creation was the character known as the Perfect Fool, by which epithet he billed himself and became famous. He also wrote a book called *Philosophy of a Fool* (1933).

Besides clowning in his Broadway and vaudeville shows, he often had a hand in producing, directing, writing books and lyrics, and composing music for them. As a performer, he had many trademarks: zany hats, misfit clothes, oversized shoes, lisping, fluttering hands, squeaky giggling, and preposterous inventions (including an eleven-foot pole for people who would not touch him with a ten-foot pole). He also loved puns; for example, in *Boys and Girls Together* (1940) he played a showboat impresario who said, "I bred my cast upon the waters." His celebrated exit line was "I'll be back in a flash with more trash."

Wynn was the first performer to broadcast a full-length comedy show to a radio audience, performing *The Perfect Fool* on an East Coast station in 1922. In his first radio series, *The Fire Chief* (1932-35), he introduced the technique of combining his comedy with the sponsor's commercial messages. He also starred in *Happy Land* (1944-45), as King Bubbles, ruler of a mythical kingdom of happiness. His shows were popular, but Wynn was essentially a visual comedian, working in costume even for his radio broadcasts.

The arrival of television in the late 1940s gave him a much more appropriate medium. He hosted the independent variety program *The Ed Wynn Show* (1949-50) and then a similarly titled program (1950-51) on a rotating basis with other shows as part of the *Four-Star Revue* series.

However, by the mid-1950s his brand of vaudeville humor had become dated. He feared that his career was over.

Then, in 1956, Wynn surprised everyone and opened a whole new facet to his career when he performed a straight dramatic role in the movie *The Great Man*, in which he gave a prolonged monologue on the phoniness of the "great" man. However, by the time *The Great Man* was released in early 1957, he had already performed a larger and more important dramatic role in Rod Serling's TV play "Requiem for a Heavyweight" (1956) on the *Playhouse Ninety* anthology series. It was a live telecast (a frightening prospect even for experienced dramatic actors), but Wynn, playing the faithful trainer of a broken-down boxer, came through beautifully.

In the 1958-59 TV season he starred in *The Ed Wynn*

Ed Wynn (right) and Keenan Wynn (left)

Show, a situation comedy with him as a widower and retired businessman.

During the rest of his career, he concentrated on being a film actor, in both dramatic and comedic roles. Among his serious parts were roles in *The Diary of Anne Frank* (1959), as one of the Jews hiding from the Nazis, and *The Greatest Story Ever Told* (1965), as Old Aram, a blind man whose sight is restored. On the light side, he played a fairy godfather in *Cinderfella* (1960) and numerous roles in Disney pictures, such as the fire chief in *The Absentminded* [spelled *AbsentMinded* on the screen] *Professor* (1961), the toymaker in *Babes in Toyland* (1961), Uncle Albert (who floats to the ceiling whenever he laughs—and he cannot stop laughing!) in *Mary Poppins* (1964), and Rufus (the 1,100-year-old gnome king) in *The Gnome-Mobile* (1967).

Wynn was married three times. In 1914 he wedded the actress Hilda Keenan, daughter of the Irish-American actor Frank Keenan. She was a staunch Catholic. Their son, Keenan, became a well-known character actor and performed with his father a number of times, as in *The Great Man,* "Requiem for a Heavyweight," and *The Absentminded Professor.*

In 1937 Wynn divorced Hilda and married Frieda Mierse, a showgirl. That marriage ended in divorce in 1939.

His final marriage, to Dorothy Nesbitt, began in 1946. It was dissolved in 1955.

Wynn died in Beverly Hills, California, on June 19, 1966.

Selected performances:

Stage

The Deacon and the Lady (1910)
Ziegfeld Follies of 1914 (1914)
Ziegfeld Follies of 1915 (1915)
The Passing Show of 1916 (1916)
Doing Our Bit (1917)
Over the Top (1918)
Sometime (1918)
Ed Wynn Carnival (1920)
The Perfect Fool (1921)
The Grab Bag (1924)
Manhattan Mary (1927)
Simple Simon (1930)
The Laugh Parade (1931)
Hooray for What! (1937)
Boys and Girls Together (1940)
Laugh, Town, Laugh (1942)
Big Time (1948)

Films

Rubber Heels (1927)
Follow the Leader (1930)
The Chief (1933)
Stage Door Canteen (1943)
The Great Man (1957)
Marjorie Morningstar (1958)
The Diary of Anne Frank (1959)
Cinderfella (1960)
The Absentminded Professor (1961)
Babes in Toyland (1961)
Son of Flubber (1963)
Sound of Laughter (1963)
Mary Poppins (1964)
The Patsy (1964)
Dear Brigitte (1965)
The Greatest Story Ever Told (1965)
That Darn Cat (1965)
Those Calloways (1965)
The Daydreamer (1966)
The Gnome-Mobile (1967)

Radio

The Fire Chief (1932-35)
Happy Island (1944-45)

TV

The Ed Wynn Show (1949-50)
The Ed Wynn Show (1950-51, part of *Four-Star Revue*)
The Ed Wynn Show (1958-59)

THUMBNAIL SKETCHES

★★★

A

ADAMS, JOEY (originally JOSEPH ABRAMOWITZ; born January 6, 1911, in New York City, New York). Comedian. After becoming a leading vaudeville and nightclub entertainer, he turned his attention to writing humorous books.

ADLER, CELIA (born 1890; died January 31, 1979, in New York City, New York). Yiddish stage actress. Daughter of Jacob Adler and half sister of Frances, Jay, Luther, and Stella Adler. Celia was often referred to as the First Lady of the Yiddish Theater.

ADLER, FRANCES (born 1891 in New York City, New York; died December 13, 1964, in New York City, New York). Yiddish stage actress. Daughter of Jacob and Sarah Adler; sister of Jay, Luther, and Stella Adler; and half sister of Celia Adler.

ADLER, JACOB P(AVLOVITCH) (born February 12, 1855, in Odessa, the Ukraine [now in the Soviet Union]; died April 1, 1926, in New York City, New York). Yiddish stage actor. He began his stage career in Russia and then immigrated to the United States in 1887. Striving toward lofty artistic goals rather than quick commercial success, he became the preeminent figure in the American Yiddish theater. His Yiddish performances as Shylock in Shakespeare's *The Merchant of Venice* were so impressive that he was engaged to appear in Broadway productions of the play in 1903 and 1905, speaking the part in Yiddish while the other players used English. Adler's three marriages produced many children who became well-known actors and actresses. With his first wife, the stage actress Sophia Oberlander, Adler had his son Abram. With his second wife, the stage actress Dinah Shtettin, Adler had his daughter Celia. With his third wife, the stage actress Sarah Heine (née Levitzky), Adler had seven children, including Frances, Jay, Julia, Luther, and Stella.

ADLER, JAY (born 1896; died September 24, 1978, in Woodland Hills, California). Character actor. Son of Jacob and Sarah Adler; brother of Frances, Luther, and Stella Adler; and half brother of Celia Adler. Jay began on the stage, but soon he turned to films, such as *The Juggler* (1953), *Lust for Life* (1956), and *The Family Jewels* (1965).

ADLER, SARAH (originally SARAH LEVITZKY; born 1858 in Odessa, the Ukraine [now in the Soviet Union]; died April 28, 1953, in New York City, New York). Yiddish stage actress. Wife of Jacob Adler and mother of Frances, Jay, Luther, and Stella Adler. Sarah joined a Yiddish acting troupe in Russia and married its manager, Maurice Heine. In 1884 she immigrated to the United States and began to work in the American Yiddish theater. In 1890 she divorced Heine to marry Jacob Adler. She appeared in hundreds of plays, and her performances as Katusha Maslova in Tolstoy's *Resurrection* established her as the greatest Yiddish actress of her time.

ADLER, STELLA (born February 10, 1902, in New York City, New York). Stage actress. Daughter of Jacob and Sarah Adler; sister of Frances, Jay, and Luther Adler; and half sister of Celia Adler. Stella began in her father's Yiddish theater troupe and later alternated between Yiddish and English plays. A highlight of her Broadway work was her performance as Bessie Berger, the harassed matriarch of a financially troubled Jewish family, in *Awake and Sing!* (1935). Billed as Stella Ardler, she made her film debut in *Love on Toast* (1938). Under her real name she appeared in the movies *Shadow of the Thin Man* (1941) and *My Girl Tisa* (1948). Since 1961 she has concentrated on teaching.

AIMÉE, ANOUK (originally FRANÇOISE DREYFUS; later FRANÇOISE SORYA, after her mother's name, Geneviève Sorya [née Durand]; born April 27, 1932, in Paris, France). Leading lady of films in various languages, notably as a nymphomaniac in *La dolce vita* ("The Sweet Life," 1960), a prostitute in *Lola* (1961), and a lover in *Un homme et une femme* ("A Man and a Woman," 1966).

ALCALAY, MOSCU (born September 10, 1931, in Bucharest, Romania). He began his stage career in Bucharest and then moved to Israel in 1962. A mainstay at the Habimah Theater, he has also performed with the Cameri company.

ALITURUS (or ALITYROS; flourished in the first century). Roman actor. A special favorite of the emperor Nero.

ALLEN, MARTY (born March 23, 1922, in Pittsburgh, Pennsylvania). Comedian and comedy character actor with a mournful nasal voice, a mass of black hair, and large frightened eyes. He worked in a comedy duo with Steve Rossi for several years till they amicably broke up in 1968. Allen then worked solo in nightclubs and on TV game shows till 1983, when he and Rossi reunited. Allen's film appearances included a role in *Murder Can Hurt You!* (TV, 1980).

★★

AMSTERDAM, MOREY (born December 14, 1914, in Chicago, Illinois). Comedian and character actor. He was a panelist on the TV game show *Stop Me If You've Heard This One,* the first series to be telecast with a live studio audience (beginning locally in Los Angeles in 1945; network, 1948-49). Then he hosted his own variety series, *The Morey Amsterdam Show* (network, 1948-50; later New York City only). Amsterdam is best remembered, however, for his role as the wisecracker on the situation-comedy series *The Dick Van Dyke Show* (1961-66). He also appeared in some movies, including *Beach Party* (1963) and *Sooner or Later* (TV, 1979).

ASHEROFF, MISHA (or MISHA ASHEROV; born March 28, 1924, in Samarkand, the Soviet Union). At the age of ten he moved to Palestine, where he became an important actor with the Habimah Theater. He won the Habimah Prize in 1957 and the Kinor David in 1968. Asheroff has also worked in Israeli film productions and coproductions, including *Raq lo b'shabbat* (1965; U.S., *Impossible on Saturday)* and *Shlosha yamim ve yeled* (1966; U.S., *Not Mine to Love* or *Three Days and a Child).*

B

BALIN, INA (originally INA ROSENBERG; born November 12, 1937, in New York City, New York). Leading lady. She appeared on the New York City stage in *Compulsion* (1957) and *A Majority of One* (1959); in the films *The Patsy* (1964), *The Don Is Dead* (1973), and *The Comeback Trail* (1982); and on TV as a guest star in *Barnaby Jones, Bonanza, Run for Your Life,* and other series.

BANNER, JOHN (born January 28, 1910, in Stanislau, Poland [now Ivano-Frankovsk, the Soviet Union]; died January 28, 1973, in Vienna, Austria). He worked on European stages before arriving in the United States in 1938. Often playing fiery Europeans, Banner became a reliable character actor in English-language movies, such as *The Fallen Sparrow* (1943), *The Juggler* (1953), and *Operation Eichmann* (1961). He gained his greatest fame as the bumbling Sergeant Hans Schultz in the TV comedy series *Hogan's Heroes* (1965-71).

BAR, SHIMON (born October 26, 1927, in Romania). Actor and singer permanently associated with Tel Aviv's Cameri Theater.

BAUR, HARRY (born 1881 in Paris, France; died April 1943 in Paris, France). Known in France as the King of the Character Actors. Baur made a lasting impression as a withdrawn father in *Poil de carotte* (literally, "Carrot Hair"; idiomatically, "The Redhead" or "Carrot Top"; 1932). He played Jean Valjean in *Les misérables* ("The Miserable Ones," 1933), Porfiry in *Crime et châtiment* ("Crime and Punishment," 1935), and Rasputin in *La tragédie impériale* ("The Imperial Tragedy," 1938). Among his other films, many of them costume dramas, were *Le golem* ("The Golem," 1936) and *Mollenard* (1938). In May 1942 he was arrested by the Gestapo in Berlin, charged with forging a certificate of Aryan ancestry. He was tortured for several months. Shortly after his release he died in Paris.

BAYES, NORA (originally DORA GOLDBERG; born about 1880, perhaps in Milwaukee, Wisconsin; died March 19, 1928, in New York City, New York). Singing actress. She was one of the most popular vaudeville and musical-comedy stars of the period 1900-1925. In 1907 Bayes starred in the very first edition of Ziegfeld's *Follies.* She helped Jack Norworth (her husband) to compose the melody for the song "Shine On, Harvest Moon" (lyrics, Norworth), which she introduced in the *Follies of 1908* and which became her trademark.

BECKER, ISRAEL (born June 13, 1917, in Białystok, Poland). In his youth he performed with Jewish theater troupes all over Poland. Since 1948 he has been an actor-director with the Habimah Theater in Israel.

BEN-AMI, JACOB (originally JACOB SHTCHIRIN; born November 23, 1890, in Minsk, Russia; died July 22, 1977, in New York City, New York). Stage actor. In his early twenties he immigrated to the United States, where he alternated between Yiddish-language and English-language plays. One critic called Ben-Ami "the knight of the Yiddish intelligentsia." In a rare film appearance, he gave an outstanding performance in the leading role of the Yiddish movie (with English subtitles) *The Wandering Jew* (1933). His most popular English-language stage success was as the grandfather in *The Tenth Man* (1959).

BEREGI, OSCAR (or OSZKAR BEREGI; born 1875 in Hungary; died October 18, 1965, in Los Angeles, California). Stage actor, famous in Hungary for his Shakespearean roles. Later in his career he moved to the United States and appeared in some films. Oscar Beregi, Jr., his son, acted in many movies, including *Young Frankenstein* (1974).

BERG, GERTRUDE (originally GERTRUDE EDELSTEIN; born October 3, 1899, in New York City, New York; died September 14, 1966, in New York City, New York). Character actress. She acquired her new surname by marrying Lewis Berg. Gertrude Berg won fame principally by playing a single character, the lovable Jewish housewife Molly Goldberg. The part originated on the radio series *The Rise of the Goldbergs,* later called simply *The Goldbergs* (1929-34, 1937-45, 1949-50), often referred to as the earliest soap opera. Berg also appeared as Molly in the Broadway play *Me and Molly* (1948), in the TV series *The Goldbergs* (1949-55), and in the movie *Molly* (1951). Later Berg was praised for her performance as a middle-aged Jewish woman who finds romance with a Japanese man in the play *A Majority of One* (1959).

BERGNER, ELISABETH (born August 22, 1900, in Vienna, Austria; died May 12, 1986, in London, England). Leading lady of fragile beauty and sensitive acting. After attaining success in German-language stage and film productions, she moved to England in the early 1930s, later working in the United States as well. Her stage performances were highlighted by her role as Sally, whose husband tries to poison her, in *The Two Mrs. Carrolls* (1943) and by her title role in *The Duchess of Malfi* (1946). Bergner's most memorable film performances were in *Catherine the Great* (1934) and *Escape Me Never* (1935). Her later appearances included a part in the movie *Cry of the Banshee* (1970).

BERLINGER, WARREN (born August 31, 1937, in New York City, New York). Chubby character actor, often, especially in his youth, as an innocent. He began his New York City stage career as a juvenile, in *Annie Get Your Gun* (1946). His later performances included roles in the stage work *Blue Denim* (1958), the TV comedy series *The Joey Bishop Show* (1961-62), and the films *Teenage Rebel* (1956), *Blue Denim* (1959), *Thunder Alley* (1967), *The Magician of Lublin* (1979), and *The Other Woman* (TV, 1983).

BERMAN, SHELLEY (originally SHELDON BERMAN; born February 3, 1926, in Chicago, Illinois). Comedian and character actor. A popular performer in nightclubs, he also became the first comedian to appear at Carnegie Hall. Berman acted in several films, including *The Best Man* (1964) and *Divorce American Style* (1967). Onstage he portrayed Oscar Madison in *The Odd Couple* (1966), the biblical Noah in *Two by Two* (1972), Meyer Rothschild in *The Rothschilds* (1973), and other roles.

BERNARDI, HERSCHEL (born October 30, 1923 in New York City, New York; died May 9, 1986, in Los Angeles,

Herschel Bernardi

California). Character actor. As a child he was a star in the New York City Yiddish theater and appeared in the Yiddish film *Green Fields* (1937). Later he played in a production of *The World of Sholom Aleichem* (1953), made his Broadway debut by appearing in *Bajour* (1964), starred as Tevye in *Fiddler on the Roof* (1965, 1981), and had the title role in *Zorba* (1968). On TV he played Lieutenant Jacoby in the popular crime-drama series *Peter Gunn* (1958-61) and the title character in the comedy series *Arnie* (1970-72). He also worked on famous TV commercials, lending his voice to the Charlie the Tuna ads and providing the Jolly Green Giant's deep, reverberating "Ho-ho-ho!" His films included *Irma La Douce* (1963) and *The Front* (1976).

BERNHARDT, SARAH (born October 22 or 23, 1844, in Paris, France; died March 26, 1923, in Paris, France). Leading lady, known as the Divine Sarah. Accounts of her birth date and original name vary because she was the illegitimate offspring of a Jewish courtesan and a non-Jewish man named Bernard or Bernhardt, and her birth certificate was not made out till she was eleven years old. Different sources record her original given name(s) as Rosine, Henriette Rosine, Sarah-Marie-Henriette, and variants of those possibilities. Touring frequently and performing mostly French plays and Shakespeare, she dominated world stages for nearly sixty years. She was renowned for her acting prowess, emotional range, perfect diction, clear voice (like a "golden bell"), and flair for self-publicity (some dubbed her Sarah Barnum). Bernhardt was the first great actress to appear in films, such as *La dame aux camélias* ("The Lady of the Camellias," 1912) and *Jeanne Doré* (1917). She also recorded some dramatic recitations. In 1905 she injured her right leg, and in 1914 it was amputated; using an artificial leg, she continued to act for the rest of her life.

BERNSTEIN-COHEN, MIRIAM (born December 14, 1895, in Kishinev, Russia). Daughter of the renowned Russian Zionist leader Jacob Bernstein-Kogan (or Cohen). She earned a medical degree in Russia and served in the Red Army. From 1917 to 1921 she acted on the Russian stage. In 1921 she moved to Palestine and became one of the pioneers in the Hebrew theater there. She appeared with many companies, including the Habimah and the Cameri. In 1969 Bernstein-Cohen won the Tel Aviv Municipal Prize for her work in *Harp of David*. She earned international acclaim for her outstanding performance in the Israeli film *Neither by Day nor by Night* (1972). In 1975 she won the Israel Prize for her lifetime achievements.

BERTONOFF, YEHOSHUA (born 1879 in Russia; died 1971 in Israel). He performed in Russian and Yiddish plays before moving to Palestine in 1927. Later he became one of the Habimah Theater's most popular actors, especially as folk and patriarchal types, as in *Tevye the Milkman* (1943). Deborah Bertonoff, his daughter, became an important nationalistic dancer.

BISHOP, JOEY (originally JOSEPH ABRAHAM GOTTLIEB; born February 3, 1918, in New York City, New York). Comedian and character actor. He worked as a comedian in nightclubs and on TV, and he starred in the TV series *The Joey Bishop Show* (situation comedy, 1961-65; variety, 1967-69). Bishop had roles in several films, including *The Naked and the Dead* (1958), *Sergeants Three* (1962), and *The Delta Force* (1986).

BLANC, MEL(VIN) (born May 30, 1908, in San Francisco, California). The voice of cartoon characters Bugs Bunny, Daffy Duck, Porky Pig, Tweety Pie (the canary), Sylvester (the cat), Woody Woodpecker, Yosemite Sam, and many others.

BOCHNER, LLOYD (born July 29, 1924, in Canada). He appeared in New York City productions of Shakespeare plays in the 1950s; had a role in the TV series *Hong Kong* (1960-61); and acted in the movies *Drums of Africa* (1963), *The Man in the Glass Booth* (1975), *The Golden Gate Murders* (TV, 1979), *The Lonely Lady* (1983), and many others. He is a frequent guest star on TV drama series.

BOND, STEVE (originally SHLOMO GOLDBERG; born 1953 in Haifa, Israel). Leading man. He arrived in the United States when he was twelve. His recent rise to fame has come through his role as Jimmy Lee Holt in the daytime TV serial *General Hospital*.

BORGE, VICTOR (originally BORGE ROSENBAUM; born January 3, 1909, in Copenhagen, Denmark). Comedian. Originally a concert pianist (1922-34), he combined his musical ability and his unique brand of sophisticated humor to become one of the most popular performers in Denmark. In 1940 he fled Nazi Europe and immigrated to the United States, where he has entertained on radio, in nightclubs, in theaters, and on TV specials. From 1953 to 1956 he starred on Broadway in the one-man show *Comedy in Music*.

BOSLEY, TOM (originally THOMAS BOSLEY; born October 1, 1927, in Chicago, Illinois). Character actor. After years of struggling, he won critical acclaim for his Broadway performance as New York City's Mayor La Guardia in *Fiorello!* (1959). When other good stage roles were not forthcoming, he turned to theater films, such as *Love with the Proper Stranger* (1963) and *The World of Henry Orient* (1964). He also appeared in many made-for-TV movies, including *Who Is the Black Dahlia?* (TV, 1975), *The Bastard* (TV, 1978), and *The Jesse Owens Story* (TV, 1984). However, his greatest popular success came in his role as Howard Cunningham in the TV comedy series *Happy Days* (1974-84). Since 1984 he has played Amos in the TV crime-drama series *Murder, She Wrote*.

BRAND, OSCAR (born February 7, 1920, in Winnipeg, Canada). Folksinger and TV-radio personality. He has hosted many TV and radio shows in Canada and the United States, notably the New York City radio program *Folksong Festival* (since 1945).

BRENNER, DAVID (born February 4, 1945, in Philadelphia, Pennsylvania). Comedian. One of the most successful

★★★

humorists of his generation. He has frequently guest-hosted the TV talk-variety program *The Tonight Show*. In 1986 he began to host his own late-night series, *Nightlife*.

BROOKS, GERALDINE (originally GERALDINE STROOCK; born October 29, 1925, in New York City, New York; died June 19, 1977, in Riverhead, New York). Intense leading lady. She made her biggest impact in a few 1940s movies, including *Possessed* (1947) and *The Reckless Moment* (1949). In her later years she frequently guest-starred in TV series, such as *Ben Casey* and *The Fugitive*.

BROTHERS, JOYCE (originally JOYCE BAUER; born 1928 in New York City, New York). TV and radio personality. In 1949 she married Milton Brothers, an internist. In 1955 she first gained public attention when she won the grand prize on the TV game show *The $64,000 Question;* her subject was boxing. Later Brothers, a popular psychologist, hosted several TV talk-show series and appeared as a guest on many others.

BROWN, GEORGIA (originally LILLIAN CLAIRE LAIZER GETEL KLOT; born October 21, 1933, in London, England). Singer-actress. She appeared in the stage musicals *The Threepenny Opera* (London, 1956; New York City, 1957) and *Oliver!* (London, 1960; New York City, 1963). Among her films were *The Fixer* (1968) and *The Bawdy Adventures of Tom Jones* (1976).

BRUCE, LENNY (originally LEONARD ALFRED SCHNEIDER; born October 13, 1926, in Mineola, New York; died August 3, 1966, in Los Angeles, California). Comedian. Working mostly in nightclubs, he focused on social commentary and became controversial for overdosing his audiences with obscenities. Ultimately he killed himself with a drug overdose.

BULOFF, JOSEPH (born December 6, 1899 [some sources give 1907], in Vilnius, Lithuania [now in the Soviet Union]; died February 27, 1985, in New York City, New York). Character actor. He performed with a Yiddish theater troupe in Europe (1918-28) and then immigrated to the United States to join the Yiddish Art Theater. Buloff eventually produced, directed, and acted in hundreds of plays in several languages—including English, Russian, and Yiddish—in North and South America, Europe, and Israel. His first widespread fame resulted from his performance as the peddler in the original Broadway production of *Oklahoma!* (1943). During the 1960s and 1970s he was a mainstay in the imperiled Yiddish theater. In Broadway's *The Price* (1979) he displayed a rich comic flair. He also appeared in movies, such as *Somebody up There Likes Me* (1956) and *Running Out* (TV, 1983).

BURSTEIN, MICHAEL (or MORDECAI BURSTEIN; born 1945 in New York City, New York). He moved to Israel in 1954 with his parents, the entertainers Pesach and Lillian Burstein. Michael appeared many times onstage with his parents in their hit musical comedy *The Megilla*. He went on to become a popular Israeli singer and performer in plays and movies, starring, for example, in the Israeli musical-comedy film *Shnei Kuni Lemel* (1965; U.S., *The Flying Matchmaker)*.

BURSTEIN, PESACH (born 1897 in Warsaw, Poland; died April 6, 1986, in New York City, New York). He joined a wandering Yiddish troupe when he was just a boy. In 1924 he was engaged by Thomashefsky's Yiddish company in New York City. There he met the Yiddish actress Lillian Lux, whom he married in 1940 and with whom he organized a theatrical company in Brooklyn. In 1954 they moved to Israel. The Bursteins were especially successful with their performances of the musical comedy *The Megilla,* in which they were joined by their son, Michael. Pesach appeared in the Israeli musical-comedy film *Shnei Kuni Lemel* (1965; U.S., *The Flying Matchmaker)*. He issued about three hundred recordings, which made him one of the most famous and beloved personalities in the Yiddish-speaking world. In 1985 he was among the first ten recipients of the Goldie Awards, bestowed by the Congress of Jewish Culture to individuals for their lifetime achievements. In Burstein's later years he lived in both New York City and Tel Aviv.

C

CARLISLE, KITTY (originally CATHERINE CONN; also known by her mother's surname, HOLZMAN; born September 3, 1914 or 1915, in New Orleans, Louisiana). Singing actress and TV personality. In the 1930s she performed in musicals and operettas on the New York City stage, such as *White Horse Inn* (1936), and appeared in a few movies, notably the Marx Brothers gem *A Night at the Opera* (1935). She scored her biggest acting success by playing the mother who admits to premarital sex in the stage comedy *Anniversary Waltz* (1954). A few years later she began a twenty-year run as a panelist on the TV game show *To Tell the Truth*.

CAROLY, FELIX (born March 3, 1933, in Iași, Romania). He was active in the Romanian classical theater. In Israel he has worked as a stage actor and director. Caroly has also appeared as a pantomimist on Israeli TV.

CARTER, JACK (original surname, CHAKRIN; born June 24, 1923, in New York City, New York). Comedian and character actor. A successful stand-up comedian on TV and in nightclubs, he is also a fine actor in both dramatic and comedic roles. His films included *The Horizontal Lieutenant* (1962), *The Family Rico* (TV, 1972), and *History of the World, Part I* (1981).

CLARY, ROBERT (original surname, WIDERMAN; born March 1, 1926, in Paris, France). Character actor. He appeared on the New York City stage, as in *New Faces of 1952* (1952), and in films, including *The Hindenburg* (1975). But he is probably best known as Corporal Louis LeBeau, a French prisoner, in the TV comedy series *Hogan's Heroes* (1965-71). Clary is a volunteer in an outreach program of the Simon Wiesenthal Center, teaching high-school students about the Nazi extermination of European Jewry.

COHEN, MYRON (born 1902 in Grodno, Russian-ruled Poland [now Grodno, the Soviet Union]; died March 10, 1986, in Nyack, New York). Comedian. Brought to the United States when he was a child, Cohen later worked for many years as a textile salesman in New York City, where he told jokes to amuse his customers. Though he had no foreign accent in his ordinary speech, he told his stories with imitations of the eastern European dialects of his colleagues in the garment district. In his forties he finally became a professional comedian, usually working in a Yiddish dialect but sometimes in Irish or Italian. When other dialect comedians went out of favor, Cohen maintained his popularity because of his low-key manner, his inoffensive material, and his unique delivery of universal appeal.

COREY, IRWIN ("PROFESSOR") (born January 29, 1912, in New York City, New York). Comedian famous for his double-talk. Wearing an overlarge frock coat and a mop of flying hair, he gives "lectures" that turn into social and political satire.

CROSBY, NORM (born September 15, 1927, in Boston, Massachusetts). Comedian. Besides appearing regularly in theaters, nightclubs, and concert halls, he has frequently worked on TV. His style is based on the use of malapropisms, such as *puberty* for *poverty* in the line "President Johnson declared war on puberty."

CRYSTAL, BILLY (originally WILLIAM CRYSTAL; born March 14, 1947, in Long Beach, New York). Comedian and actor. He has been a stand-up comedian since 1975. From 1977 to 1981 he was a regular member of the cast in the TV comedy series *Soap*. He has frequently appeared in the TV variety series *Saturday Night Live,* where his imitation of the actor Fernando Lamas saying "You look maaaaaavelous" created a new catchphrase. Crystal also came out with the comedy album *Mahvelous* (1985). He appeared in the films *Rabbit Test* (1978), *Enola Gay* (TV, 1980), and *Running Scared* (1986).

DALE, CHARLIE. *See* SMITH AND DALE.

DAMON, STUART (originally STUART ZONIS; born February 5, 1937, in New York City, New York). Leading man. He appeared on Broadway in *From A to Z* (1960), *The Boys from Syracuse* (1963), and *Do I Hear a Waltz?* (1965). His other work included the TV series *The Adventurer* (1972) and the film *Fantasies* (TV, 1982).

DANA, BILL (originally WILLIAM SZATHMARY; born October 5, 1924, in Quincy, Massachusetts). Comedian and character actor. He is best known for his portrayal of the comical character José Jiménez on TV in the late 1950s and early 1960s, especially on Steve Allen's variety show and Danny Thomas's comedy series. Dana continued the character in his own comedy series, *The Bill Dana Show* (1963-65). In 1970 pressure from Latin-Americans caused him to drop José. Later he played a variety of roles on TV and in movies, such as *The Snoop Sisters* (TV, 1972) and *The Nude Bomb* (1980).

DARVAS, LILI (born April 10, 1902, in Budapest, Hungary; died July 22, 1974, in New York City, New York). Leading lady. She was a major figure on the European stage from the early 1920s till 1938, when she moved to the United States and began a long, active career in the theater and on TV. Darvas appeared in a handful of movies, notably as the dying mother in the Hungarian film *Szerelem* ("Love," 1971).

DONATH, LUDWIG (born March 6, 1900, in Vienna, Austria; died September 29, 1967, in New York City, New York). He appeared onstage in major European cities before moving to the United States in the 1930s. His American stage performances included *The Dybbuk* (1954). He became a fine character actor in American films. In *The Strange Death of Adolf Hitler* (1943) he played a dual role, as Hitler and as Hitler's double, Franz Huber. Donath portrayed Al Jolson's father, a cantor, in *The Jolson Story* (1946) and *Jolson Sings Again* (1949). His other films included *Sirocco* (1951) and *Torn Curtain* (1966).

DYLAN, BOB (originally ROBERT ALLEN ZIMMERMAN; born May 24, 1941, in Duluth, Minnesota). The popular singer played a dramatic role in the movie *Pat Garrett and Billy the Kid* (1973), as a retarded hanger-on to Billy.

Bob Dylan

★★★

E

EDELMAN, HERB(ERT) (born November 5, 1933, in New York City, New York). Bald, lanky character actor, usually in comic roles. He made his New York City stage debut in *Barefoot in the Park* (1963). Among his films were *The Odd Couple* (1968), *The Front Page* (1974), *On the Right Track* (1981), and *Cracking Up* (1983, originally released as *Smorgasbord).* He is a frequent guest star on TV.

EPSTEIN, ALVIN (born May 14, 1925, in New York City, New York). Stage actor and mime. He was a resident member of the Habimah Theater in Tel Aviv (1953-55). In New York City and elsewhere in the United States, he has appeared in many plays, including *Waiting for Godot* (1956), *The Passion of Josef D.* (1964), and *The Possessed* (1974).

F

FELDSHUH, TOVAH (born December 27, 1952, in New York City, New York). Leading lady. She made her Broadway debut by performing in the musical *Cyrano de Bergerac* (1973). Later she starred in *Yentl* (1974) and other stage works. Her films included *Holocaust* (TV, 1978); *Beggerman, Thief* (TV, 1979); and *Daniel* (1983).

FIELDS, LEW. *See* WEBER AND FIELDS.

FIELDS, TOTIE (originally SOPHIE FELDMAN; born May 7, 1930, in Hartford, Connecticut; died August 2, 1978, in Las Vegas, Nevada). Comedienne. Performing in nightclubs and on TV, she had the gift of being able to laugh at herself.

FIERSTEIN, HARVEY (born June 6, 1954, in New York City, New York). Actor and playwright. He gained renown by writing and starring in the seriocomic play *Torch Song Trilogy* (1981), which explores the homosexual experience in universal terms.

FINKEL, SHIMON (born December 8, 1905, in Grodno, Russian-ruled Poland [now Grodno, the Soviet Union]). He began to appear on the Polish stage when he was a boy. Later he joined a Yiddish troupe. In 1922 he went to Berlin, and in 1924 he settled in Palestine. A few years later he joined the Habimah Theater. Finkel became one of the company's most important figures, starring in many productions, such as *Hamlet* (1946, winning the Jewish Agency Prize), *Peer Gynt* (1952), *King Lear* (1957, Tel Aviv Prize), and *Touch of the Poet* (1960, Gnessin Prize). He also served as the Habimah's artistic director during 1961-62 and 1970-75. In 1969 he was awarded the Israel Prize for his lifetime accomplishments. In 1980 he directed and acted in a highly acclaimed production of *Between Two Worlds* (a musical adaptation of *The Dybbuk),* which opened New York City's Yiddish National Theater. Finkel has published many books about the Israeli theater, including *Onstage and Backstage* (1968), *Margin of the Bill* (1976), *Chana Rovina* (1978), and *Sparks* (1985).

FISHER, EDDIE (originally EDWIN FISHER; born August 10, 1928, in Philadelphia, Pennsylvania). The popular singer acted in a few movies, including *Bundle of Joy* (1956) and *Butterfield 8* (1960).

FLANAGAN, BUD (originally CHAIM REEVEN WEINTROP; anglicized on birth certificate as ROBERT WINTHROP; born October 14, 1896, in London, England; died October 20, 1968, in London, England). Comedian. He chose his stage name as an act of revenge against a sergeant-major named Flanagan who had made the aspiring comedian's life miserable in the artillery during World War I. In 1926 Flanagan teamed up with Chesney Allen, and they became immensely successful music-hall performers, Allen's patient dignity contrasting with Flanagan's hilarious roguery. In many of their shows they worked as part of a group known as the Crazy Gang, of which the undisputed leader was Flanagan. Flanagan and Allen also appeared in movies, such as *Underneath the Arches* (1937) and *Here Comes the Sun* (1945). In 1945 Allen retired and Flanagan went on alone, working in his last Crazy Gang show in 1959.

FOSTER, PHIL (originally FIVEL FELDMAN; born March 29, 1914, in New York City, New York; died July 8, 1985, in Rancho Mirage, California). Comedian and actor. Though he began as a stand-up comedian, he gained his greatest fame as the gruff but kindhearted Frank DeFazio in the TV comedy series *Laverne and Shirley* (1976-83).

FRYE, DAVID (originally DAVID SHAPIRO; born 1934 in New York City, New York). Impressionist and comedian. For a brief period in the 1970s he was at the top of his profession. He was best known for his impersonations of politicians, especially Richard Nixon, with whom Frye felt an empathy because, according to the comedian, both men were neurotic. In his nightclub work today he does William F. Buckley, Billy Graham, and other personalities.

FUNT, ALLEN (born September 16, 1914, in New York City, New York). TV personality. In 1947 he created a radio program called *Candid Microphone.* Soon he took it to TV under the title *Candid Camera,* a very popular series that he hosted off and on in various formats for many years.

★★★★★★★★★★★★★★★★★★★★★★

Shimon Finkel

G

GABEL, MARTIN (born June 19, 1912, in Philadelphia, Pennsylvania; died May 22, 1986, in New York City, New York). Character actor. His stage appearances included roles in *Dead End* (1935); *Will Success Spoil Rock Hunter?* (1955); and *Big Fish, Little Fish* (1961). Among his films were *M* (1951); *Marnie* (1964); *The Front Page* (1974), as Dr. Eggelhofer; and *The First Deadly Sin* (1980). He often appeared with his wife, Arlene Francis, on TV's *What's My Line?*

GAON, YEHORAM. Popular actor and singer. Best known in the West for his role in the Israeli fact-based film *Operation Thunderbolt* (1977), as the colonel who was killed while leading his men in the July 4, 1976, rescue of Jewish hostages at the Entebbe Airport in Uganda.

GARFUNKEL, ART(HUR) (born November 5, 1941, in New York City, New York). The popular singer has also appeared as an actor, as in the films *Catch-22* (1970), *Carnal Knowledge* (1971), and *Bad Timing: A Sensual Obsession* (1980).

GELLER, URI (born December 20, 1946, in Tel Aviv, Palestine [now Israel]). Entertainer. Performing in many parts of the world, he does some acts involving clairvoyance and telepathy. But his celebrity rests principally on his claim to having psychokinesis, or the power of mind over matter.

GETTY, ESTELLE (originally ESTELLE SCHER; married Arthur Gettleman; born July 1923 in New York City, New York). Character actress. In her youth she worked as an actress in the Yiddish theater and as a stand-up comedienne on the borscht circuit. After leaving the theater and spending many years as a housewife and mother, she gradually returned to the stage, notably as the Jewish mother in the off-off-Broadway play *Torch Song Trilogy* (1981). Since 1985 she has played the role of Sophia in the popular TV comedy series *The Golden Girls,* for which Getty uses makeup to age herself twenty years.

GNESSIN, MENAHEM (born 1882 in Russia; died 1952 in Israel). He moved from the Ukraine to Palestine in 1903. In 1907 he founded the Amateur Dramatic Arts Company for producing plays in Hebrew. In 1912 he returned to Russia and, in Moscow, helped Nahum Zemach to organize a group that became a forerunner of the Habimah Theater, which Zemach created there in 1917. Gnessin worked on his own in various cities till 1928, when he joined the Habimah in Palestine. He became one of the company's most important actors.

GOLDSTEIN, JENNIE (born 1897 in New York City, New York; died February 9, 1960, in New York City, New York). Stage actress. At the age of six she began in the Yiddish theater, where she eventually became the leading tragedienne of her time. Later she added English-language plays to her repertory, including *Camino Real* (1953).

GOODMAN, BENNY (originally BENJAMIN GOODMAN; born May 30, 1909, in Chicago, Illinois; died June 13, 1986, in New York City, New York). The popular clarinetist and bandleader had fairly extended acting roles in a few movies, including *A Song Is Born* (1948).

Benny Goodman

★★

GRAHAM, VIRGINIA (originally VIRGINIA KOMISS; born July 4, 1912, in Chicago, Illinois). TV and radio personality. She hosted the TV talk show *Girl Talk* (1962-69) and the TV talk-variety series *The Virginia Graham Show* (1970-72).

GREENE, SHECKY (originally SHELDON GREENFIELD; born April 8, 1926, in Chicago, Illinois). Comedian and character actor. He has performed in nightclubs since 1947 and on TV since 1953. His films included *Splash* (1984).

H

HAAS, HUGO (born February 19, 1903, in Brno, Moravia [now in Czechoslovakia]; died December 1, 1968, in Vienna, Austria). Character actor. He appeared in Czech films from the mid-1920s till the late 1930s, when he immigrated to the United States. His early American movies included *A Bell for Adano* (1945) and *Casbah* (1948). Later he wrote, directed, and starred in low-budget melodramas, such as *Lizzie* (1957).

HALL, MONTY (original surname, HALPARIN; born August 25, 1925, in Winnipeg, Canada). Host of TV's *Let's Make a Deal* (1963-76).

HANRAY, LAWRENCE (born May 16, 1874, in London, England; died November 28, 1947). Character actor. His stage work was highlighted by his performances in Galsworthy plays. Hanray's films included *The Private Life of Henry VIII* (1933), *The Scarlet Pimpernel* (1935), and *Mine Own Executioner* (1947).

HARAREET, HAYA (or HAYA HARARIT; born 1931 in Haifa, Palestine [now Israel]). She worked onstage at the Cameri Theater and appeared in Israel's first important feature film, *Hill 24 Doesn't Answer* (1955). In 1959 she won international stardom with her performance in the American epic *Ben-Hur*. Later she starred in a number of European and American movies, including *The Secret Partner* (1961) and *The Interns* (1962).

HELD, ANNA (born probably March 18, 1865, in Warsaw, Poland; died August 12, 1918, in New York City, New York). Singing actress, known for her coquettish manner. She claimed to have been born a Catholic in Paris, France; her death record stated her year of birth as 1877, while obituaries listed the year as 1873. But much evidence indicates that she came from Jewish parents, and according to the Institute for Jewish Research she was born in Warsaw in 1865. Held began her career by performing in the Yiddish theater in London. Later she became one of London's top music-hall comediennes. In the late 1890s she was hired by the American impresario Florenz Ziegfeld, and she moved to the United States. She married Ziegfeld and performed in American musical comedies. Held and Ziegfeld separated in 1908 and divorced in 1913. In her late years she performed in vaudeville.

HILL, STEVEN (originally SOLOMON BERG; born 1924 in Seattle, Washington). Character actor. His stage work included *A Flag Is Born* (1946) and *Mister Roberts* (1948). Among his films were *A Child Is Waiting* (1963) and *Rich and Famous* (1981).

HIRSCH, JUDD (born March 15, 1935, in New York City, New York). Leading man. He has appeared in many New York City plays and in some films, such as *Ordinary People* (1980). But he is best known as Alex Rieger, a career cab-driver, in the TV comedy series *Taxi* (1978-83).

HIRSCH, ROBERT PAUL (born July 26, 1925, in L'Isle-Adam, France). Character actor. He distinguished himself for many years as a comic actor and mime onstage in Paris at the Comédie-Française. Hirsch also appeared in some movies, notably the French-Israeli fantasy released in Paris as *Pas question le samedi* (1965; Israeli title, *Raq lo b'shabbat;* American title, *Impossible on Saturday);* Hirsch played eight roles in the film.

I

INGELS, MARTY (original surname, INGERMAN; born March 9, 1936, in New York City, New York). Comedian and character actor. He was Arch Fenster in the TV comedy series *I'm Dickens—He's Fenster* (1962-63), and he had roles in the movies *The Ladies' Man* (1961) and *If It's Tuesday, This Must Be Belgium* (1969). Later he quit performing to become a theatrical agent and producer.

★★★★★★★★★★★★★★★★★★★★★★★

★★

Haya Harareet

★★★

J

JACOBI, LOU(IS) (born December 28, 1913, in Toronto, Canada). Character actor. He was on the stage in Toronto and London before making his Broadway debut, as Mr. Van Daan in *The Diary of Anne Frank* (1955), a role that he repeated in the filmed version of the story (1959). His other movies included *Irma La Douce* (1963), *Cotton Comes to Harlem* (1970), *Lucky Star* (1982), and *Isaac Littlefeathers* (1984). He is an expert performer of comic roles, as he amply proved when he guest-starred in a couple of hilarious episodes of the TV series *Too Close for Comfort* and in several shows on the *Barney Miller* series.

JAFFE, CARL (born 1902 in Germany; died April 12, 1974, in London, England). Aristocratic-looking character actor. He fled Hitler's Germany and later appeared in many British and American films, including *The Life and Death of Colonel Blimp* (1943) and *The Roman Spring of Mrs. Stone* (1961).

JAMES, HARRY (born March 15, 1916, in Albany, Georgia; died July 5, 1983, in Las Vegas, Nevada). The popular trumpeter and bandleader had fairly extended acting roles in several movies, including *If I'm Lucky* (1946).

Harry James

JAMES, SID(NEY) (born May 8, 1913, in Johannesburg, South Africa; died April 26, 1976, in Sunderland, England). Crumple-faced comedy character actor. In 1946 he settled in England, where he worked extensively on TV. He also appeared in many British films, including *The Lavender Hill Mob* (1951). James was featured in most of the Carry On series of movies, such as *Carry On, Constable* (1961); *Carry On, Cabby* (1967); and *Carry On, Matron* (1972).

JESSEL, GEORGE (born April 3, 1898, in New York City, New York; died May 24, 1981, in Los Angeles, California). Entertainer. He was a child singer in vaudeville, where he performed as one of Gus Edwards's famous troupe of juveniles. His later stage career was highlighted by his starring role in the original Broadway production of *The Jazz Singer* (1925). He also acted in silent movies, including *The Other Man's Wife* (1919). But after making the mistake of turning down the filmed version of *The Jazz Singer,* he had only a sporadic career as an actor, including appearances in the films *Four Jills in a Jeep* (1944) and *The Busy Body* (1967). He also worked as a producer. But his fame in his late years rested on his melodramatic speeches at funerals, banquets, and fund-raising affairs for Israel and other causes. Jessel came to be known as the Toastmaster General of the United States.

K

KALICH, BERTHA (surname also spelled KALISH or KALISCH; born May 17 [sometimes given as September 8], 1874 [sometimes given as 1872], in Lemberg, Galicia [now Lvov, the Soviet Union]; died April 18, 1939, in New York City, New York). Stage actress. She began her career in Europe and then, in 1894, immigrated to the United States, where she became a leading lady in the Yiddish theater and later in English-language Broadway plays as well. Kalich was at her best in highly emotional plays, such as *The East Side Ghetto.* Her greatest role was as the Jewess whose marriage to a Russian nobleman leads to tragedy in *The Kreutzer Sonata* (Yiddish, 1902; English, 1906).

KAMEN, MILT (born March 5, 1921, in Hurleyville, New York; died February 24, 1977, in Beverly Hills, California). Comedian and character actor. He worked as a stand-up comedian in nightclubs; appeared on TV game and variety programs, such as *To Tell the Truth* and *The Tonight Show;* and acted on the stage, as in *The Passion of Josef D.* (1964), and in films, including *W. C. Fields and Me* (1976).

KAMINSKA, IDA (born September 4, 1899, in Odessa, the Ukraine [now in the Soviet Union]; died May 21, 1980, in New York City, New York). Character actress. From the late 1940s till the late 1960s she directed the Jewish State Theater of Poland. She won international fame as the aged Jewish shopkeeper facing deportation in the Czech film *Obchod na korze* (1965; released in the United States as *The Shop on Main Street,* also known as *The Shop on High Street*). In the late 1960s she immigrated to the United States. Kaminska was widely known as the Queen of the Yiddish Theater.

KAPLAN, GABE (full name, GABRIEL KAPLAN; born March 31, 1945, in New York City, New York). Originally a nightclub comedian, Kaplan recorded the comedy album *Holes and Mellow Rolls* (1974). He reached stardom as Gabe Kotter on the TV comedy series *Welcome Back, Kotter* (1975-79). His few movies included *Fast Break* (1979).

KAPLAN, MARVIN (born January 24, 1924 or 1927, in New York City, New York). Comedy character actor of owlish appearance. His films included *The Reformer and the Redhead* (1950), *Angels in the Outfield* (1951), *Wake Me When It's Over* (1960), *The Nutty Professor* (1963), and *The Great Race* (1965). On TV he was in the comedy series *Meet Millie* (1952-56); and in the late 1970s and early 1980s he played Henry, the telephone repairman, in the comedy series *Alice.*

KATCH, KURT (originally ISSER KAC; born January 28, 1896, in Grodno, Russian-ruled Poland [now Grodno, the Soviet Union]; died August 14, 1958, in Los Angeles, California). Bald character actor. He settled in Hollywood in the early 1940s. His films included *Watch on the Rhine* (1943), *The Mask of Dimitrios* (1944), and *Song of Love* (1947).

KATZ, MICKEY (originally MEYER MYRON KATZ; born June 15, 1909, in Cleveland, Ohio; died April 30, 1985, in Los Angeles, California). Comedian and musician. Father of entertainer Joel Grey. For many years Katz toured and starred in an English-Yiddish stage revue called *Borscht Capades,* which he coproduced.

KAYE, STUBBY (born November 11, 1918, in New York City, New York). Chubby comic actor and singer. He began as a vaudeville comedian and later became successful on Broadway as Nicely-Nicely Johnson in *Guys and Dolls* (1950) and as Marryin' Sam in *Li'l Abner* (1956). Kaye also appeared in the filmed versions of those musical plays (1955 and 1959 respectively). He had regular roles in the TV comedy series *Love and Marriage* (1959-60) and *My Sister Eileen* (1960-61). Other works in which he appeared included the play *The Ritz* (1975) and the movies *Forty Pounds of Trouble* (1963), *Cat Ballou* (1965), *Goldie and the Boxer Go to Hollywood* (TV, 1981), and *Ellis Island* (TV, 1984).

KEITEL, HARVEY (born May 13, 1939, 1941, or 1947, in New York City, New York). Character actor. He worked briefly on Broadway before turning to motion pictures. His film roles have tended to be seedy streetwise characters: in *Mean Streets* (1973) he was a petty hood, in *Taxi Driver*

(1976) a pimp, in *The Border* (1982) an unscrupulous guard, and in *Order of Death* (1983) a cop on the take.

KESSLER, DAVID (born probably 1859 in Kishinev, Russia; died May 14, 1920, in New York City, New York). Yiddish stage actor.

KING, ALAN (originally IRWIN ALAN KNIBERG; born December 26, 1927, in New York City, New York). Comedian and character actor. Working with a cigar in hand, he has become a top nightclub and TV comedian, sometimes called "an aggressive Jack Benny." He gently lampoons just about everyone and everything. King has acted in stage plays, such as *Applause* (1970), and in movies, including *Hit the Deck* (1955), *Bye Bye Braverman* (1968), and *I, the Jury* (1982).

KLATZKIN, RAPHAEL (or RAPHAEL KLATSCHKIN; born January 15, 1906, in Russia). He has been a member of the Habimah Theater since 1928. Klatzkin was a cofounder of Hakumkum, Israel's first satirical theater. He played Reb Kalman, the matchmaker, in the Israeli musical-comedy film *Shnei Kuni Lemel* (1965; U.S., *The Flying Matchmaker).*

KLEIN, ROBERT (born February 8, 1942, in New York City, New York). Comedian and character actor. As a stand-up comedian, he has performed on TV and in theaters. He has also acted on Broadway, as in *The Apple Tree* (1966), and in movies, such as *Your Place or Mine* (TV, 1983).

KOSSOFF, DAVID (born November 24, 1919, in London, England). Character actor. He appeared onstage in *The World of Sholom Aleichem* (1955), *Come Blow Your Horn* (1962), and other plays. His films included *A Kid for Two Farthings* (1956), *The Bespoke Overcoat* (1956), *Freud* (1962), and *The Private Life of Sherlock Holmes* (1970). Since 1970 he has performed a solo stage act called *As According to Kossoff.*

KRUSCHEN, JACK (born March 20, 1922, in Winnipeg, Canada). Character actor, often in comedies. He was one of the earliest performers on TV, appearing on an experimental Los Angeles station in 1939. His stage work included *I Can Get It for You Wholesale* (1962). Among his many films were *The War of the Worlds* (1953), *Money from Home* (1954), *The Apartment* (1960), *The Unsinkable Molly Brown* (1964), *Sunburn* (1979), and *Dark Mirrors* (TV, 1984).

LANCET-FRYE, BATIA (born 1922 in Hungary). When she was two years old, she was taken to Palestine. In the mid-1940s she helped to found the Cameri Theater, of which she has been a permanent member ever since. She was named Actress of the Year (1956-57) for her title role in Lorca's *Yerma.* In 1959 she won the Klausner Prize for her performance as Eliza Gant in *Look Homeward, Angel.* Lancet-Frye has also appeared in Israeli films.

LEDERER, FRANCIS (originally FRANTISEK LEDERER; born November 6, 1906, in Prague, Bohemia [now in Czechoslovakia]). Leading man. After getting stage and screen experience in Europe, he settled in the United States in the early 1930s. His stage roles included Joe Bonaparte in *Golden Boy* (1937) and Mr. Frank in *The Diary of Anne Frank* (1958). His films were highlighted by *Confessions of a Nazi Spy* (1939).

LEE, MICHELE (originally MICHELE LEE DUSICK; born June 24, 1942, in Los Angeles, California). Leading lady. She appeared onstage in *How to Succeed in Business without Really Trying* (1961) and later repeated her performance for the filmed version (1967). Her other movies included *The Comic* (1969), *Bud and Lou* (TV, 1978), and *A Letter to Three Wives* (TV, 1985). Since the mid-1980s she has been a regular on the TV series *Knots Landing.*

LEE, PINKY (originally PINCUS LEFF; born 1916 in Saint Paul, Minnesota). Comedian. A wild sight-gag performer, Lee began in vaudeville. But he reached the peak of his popularity by cohosting the TV variety show *Those Two* (1951-53) and especially by hosting the children's TV series *The Pinky Lee Show* (1954-56).

LENYA, LOTTE (originally KAROLINE BLAMAUER; born October 18, 1898, in Vienna, Austria; died November 27, 1981, in New York City, New York). Known principally for her performances in the stage musicals of her first husband, Kurt Weill. She also worked as a straight dramatic actress, notably as a cynical procuress in the film *The Roman Spring of Mrs. Stone* (1961).

LEONARD, JACK E. (originally LEONARD LEBITSKY; born April 24, 1911, in Chicago, Illinois; died May 10, 1973, in New York City, New York). Comedian, known as Fat Jack. A predecessor of Don Rickles as an insult comedian, he worked in nightclubs and on TV. Leonard appeared in a few movies, including *The Disorderly Orderly* (1964) and *The Fat Spy* (1966).

LEONARD, SHELDON (originally SHELDON BERSHAD; born February 22, 1907, in New York City, New York). Character actor. He acted on Broadway during the 1930s and then moved to Hollywood, where he frequently played comic gangsters. His films included *Another Thin Man*

(1939); *Lucky Jordan* (1943); *It's a Wonderful Life* (1946); *Stop, You're Killing Me* (1952); *Guys and Dolls* (1955); and *Pocketful of Miracles* (1961). He had a regular role on the TV comedy series *The Danny Thomas Show* (1957-64). Leonard turned increasingly to TV producing and directing, though he occasionally returned to the front of the cameras, as in the movie *The Islander* (TV, 1978).

LEONTOVICH, EUGENIE (born March 21, 1900, in Moscow, Russia). Character actress. She appeared on the Moscow stage till the 1917 Revolution, after which she stayed in Paris and other European cities, finally settling in the United States in 1922. She acted in some films, including *Four Sons* (1940) and *The Rains of Ranchipur* (1955). But her principal work was on the stage, notably as the Dowager Empress in *Anastasia* (1954). Her other stage roles included Sarah Bernhardt in *Fires of Spring* (1929), Mrs. Pepys in *And So to Bed* (1945), and the title part in *Anna K* (1972).

LEVANT, OSCAR (born December 27, 1906, in Pittsburgh, Pennsylvania; died August 14, 1972, in Beverly Hills, California). Pianist who appeared as a wisecracking supporting actor in several films, including *Rhythm on the River* (1940), *Rhapsody in Blue* (1945), *Humoresque* (1946), and *An American in Paris* (1951). In the 1950s he was a panelist on many TV shows, where he displayed his cynicism and neuroses.

LEVENSON, SAM(UEL) (born December 28, 1911, in New York City, New York; died August 27, 1980, in New York City, New York). Comedian. In his nightclub and TV monologues, he stressed the happy side of being poor in the old days. For many years he was a witty panelist on TV game shows, such as *To Tell the Truth.*

LEWIS, SHARI (originally SHARI HURWITZ; born January 17, 1934, in New York City, New York). Puppeteer and ventriloquist. She has hosted several TV series, gaining national prominence with *The Shari Lewis Show* (1960-63), on which she entertained children with her puppets Charlie Horse, Hush Puppy, and Lamb Chop.

LEWIS, TED (originally THEODORE LEOPOLD FRIEDMAN; born June 6, 1891, in Circleville, Ohio; died August 25, 1971, in New York City, New York). Entertainer, clarinetist, and bandleader. Working in burlesque, vaudeville, and nightclubs, he became famous for his vocal renditions of the song "Me and My Shadow" and for his expression "Is everybody happy?" He also appeared in a few movies, including *Is Everybody Happy?* (1929) and *Follow the Boys* (1944).

LIGHT, JUDITH (born February 9, 1949, in Trenton, New Jersey). Leading lady. She played Karen in the daytime TV serial *One Life to Live* (1977-82). Currently she has the role of Angela in the TV comedy series *Who's the Boss?*

LINDER, MAX (originally GABRIEL-MAXIMILIEN LEUVIELLE; born 1883 in Cavenne, Bordeaux, France; died November 1, 1925, in Paris, France). Comic actor. He was a major star of French silent films and became the first movie figure of truly international stature, influencing Chaplin and others. Linder also made a few Hollywood films, including *The Three Must-Get-Theres* (1922). He and his wife committed double suicide by taking drugs and slashing their wrists.

LION, LEON M. (born March 12, 1879, in London, England; died March 28, 1947, in Brighton, England). Stage actor. He was well known for his performances in Galsworthy plays.

LOEB, PHILIP (born 1894 in Philadelphia, Pennsylvania; died September 1, 1955, in New York City, New York). Comedy character actor. He appeared in many plays on the New York City stage before winning fame as Molly's husband, Jake, in the radio and TV comedy series *The Goldbergs* in the late 1940s and early 1950s. His movies included *Room Service* (1938) and *Molly* (1951). Blacklisted during the McCarthy-era witch-hunts, Loeb committed suicide through an overdose of sedatives.

LOUISE, TINA (originally TINA BLACKER; born February 11, 1934 or 1937, in New York City, New York). Leading lady. She is best known for her role as Ginger Grant, the beautiful movie actress, on the TV comedy series *Gilligan's Island* (1964-67). But she also appeared in many films, including *God's Little Acre* (1958), *Armored Command* (1961), *For Those Who Think Young* (1964), and *Advice to the Lovelorn* (TV, 1981).

MANILOW, BARRY (born June 17, 1946, in New York City, New York). The popular singer made his acting debut with the leading role in the movie musical *Copacabana* (TV, 1985).

MANN, HANK (originally DAVID LIEBERMANN; born 1887 in New York City, New York; died November 25, 1971, in South Pasadena, California). Large-sized supporting actor in silent movies. One of the original Keystone Kops, he also played in many Chaplin films, notably *City Lights* (1931) and *Modern Times* (1936). His few talkies included Chaplin's *The Great Dictator* (1940).

MANNHEIM, LUCIE (born April 30, 1895, near Berlin, Germany; died July 28, 1978, in Braunlage, West Germany). Character actress. Before the rise of Nazism, she was a major stage figure in Berlin, one of her best roles being Nora in Ibsen's *A Doll's House.* Later she worked in England and America. She played the mysterious victim in Hitchcock's classic film *The Thirty-nine Steps* (1935). Her other movies

Barry Manilow

included *So Little Time* (1953) and *Bunny Lake Is Missing* (1965).

MARCEAU, MARCEL (original surname, MANGEL; born March 22, 1923, in Strasbourg, France). The world's greatest mime, particularly beloved for his character Bip, the sad, white-faced clown he created in 1947. Marceau has played in dozens of countries, language being no barrier for the enjoyment of his silent skits. Among his short pantomimes, which run the gamut from playfulness to profundity, are *Bip at a Society Party, Bip Hunts Butterfly, The Cage,* and *The Creation of the World.* His full-length "mimodramas" include *The Overcoat,* which was filmed (1951), as were several of his other works.

MARCH, HAL (originally HAROLD MENDELSON; born April 22, 1920, in San Francisco, California; died January 19, 1970, in Los Angeles, California). Comedy character actor. He won his greatest fame as host of *The $64,000 Question* (1955-58), the first prime-time big-money TV game show. But he also appeared on the stage, as in *Come Blow Your Horn* (1961), and in some films, such as *My Sister Eileen* (1955) and *Send Me No Flowers* (1964).

MARGALIT, MEIR (born 1906 in Ostrołęka, Poland). In 1921 he immigrated to Palestine, where he joined the Gedud ha-Avodah drama circle. Later he became one of the original members of the Ohel Theater, where he had a long career as a leading actor. Among his greatest successes was *Ha-ketubbah* ("The Marriage Contract," 1961). Margalit starred as Noah Simchon in the Israeli domestic-comedy film *Mishpachat Simchon* (1964; U.S., *The Simchon Family*).

MARGOLIN, JANET (born 1943 in New York City, New York). Dark-haired, attractive leading lady. She successfully played a mentally disturbed girl on the New York City stage in *Daughter of Silence* (1961). As a result, she was hired to play the schizophrenic female lead in the movie *David and Lisa* (1962). Margolin later spent much of her time guest-starring on TV series. She also appeared in the Woody Allen films *Take the Money and Run* (1969) and *Annie Hall* (1977), and she starred in the movie *The Plutonium Incident* (TV, 1980).

MARTIN, ROSS (originally MARTIN ROSENBLATT; born March 22, 1920, in Gródek, Poland [now Gorodok, the Soviet Union]; died July 3, 1981, near San Diego, California). Character actor. He came to America when he was a baby. Martin was best known for his role as an underground intelligence agent in the TV adventure series *The Wild, Wild West* (1965-69). His films included *The Great Race* (1965) and *I Married Wyatt Earp* (TV, 1983). Martin was a master of disguise.

MARTIN, TONY (originally ALVIN MORRIS; born December 25, 1913, in Oakland, California). The popular singer acted in many musical films, including *Ali Baba Goes to Town* (1937), *The Big Store* (1941), *Till the Clouds Roll By* (1946), and *Casbah* (1948).

★★★

MASON, JACKIE (originally YACOV MOSHE MAZA; born June 9, 1930, in Sheboygan, Wisconsin). Comedian and comedy character actor. He hit the big time on Ed Sullivan's TV variety show and for a brief time in the early 1960s was near the top of his field. Mason has appeared in some movies, including *The Jerk* (1979).

MAY, ELAINE (originally ELAINE BERLIN; born April 21, 1932, in Philadelphia, Pennsylvania). Comedienne and character actress. As a teenager she married and divorced Marvin May, whose surname she kept for professional use. In the late 1950s she and Mike Nichols performed prepared and improvised comedy skits in nightclubs and on TV. Later, on her own, she distinguished herself as an actress in several movies, including *Luv* (1967) and *A New Leaf* (1971). She costarred with Nichols in a stage production of the powerful drama *Who's Afraid of Virginia Woolf?* (1980). May is also active as a writer and director.

MENKEN, ADAH ISAACS (originally ADAH BERTHA THEODORE; born 1835 in Chartrain [now Milneburg], near New Orleans, Louisiana; died August 10, 1868, in Paris, France). Leading lady. Her origins are shrouded in mystery. Apparently she was raised as a Catholic, but she converted to Judaism in 1857, having married a Jew named (Alexander) Isaac Menken in 1856. Later she divorced him, but she lived the rest of her life, and was buried, as a Jew. For her stage name, she blended her and her husband's names: Adah Isaacs (adding an *s* for euphony) Menken. After struggling as an actress for a few years, she discovered the title role in *Mazeppa,* a noble Tartar youth in a melodrama based on Byron's poem. Menken first played the role in 1861, thereafter appearing in little else. But with just that one role she became famous in America and in Europe. She shocked Victorian Age audiences with a costume that exposed her thighs. And at the climax of the play, she absolutely astounded them by appearing stripped (actually wearing flesh-colored tights and a small loin cloth), being strapped to a horse, and being sent on a wild ride into the hills. Menken was popularly referred to as the Naked Lady.

MERON, HANNA (or CHANNA MARRON; original surname, MAIERZAK; born November 22, 1923, in Berlin, Germany). She appeared as a child actress on the German stage and in the Fritz Lang classic film *M* (1931). In 1933 she moved to Palestine. From 1940 to 1945 she served in the British armed forces. In the mid-1940s she joined the newly founded Cameri Theater, and in the following years she was a major factor in some of its greatest successes. She had a special flair for modern sophisticated comedy, though she also excelled in dramatic roles, such as the lead in Ibsen's *Hedda Gabler.* In 1970 Meron lost a leg as a result of an Arab terrorist attack on Israeli airplane passengers in Munich. After she recovered, she resumed her stage career in Israel.

MICHAELI, ELISHEVA (born in Tel Aviv). Actress who has worked with the Ohel, the Haifa, and the Habimah theaters. She appeared in the Israeli domestic-comedy film *Mishpachat Simchon* (1964; U.S., *The Simchon Family*).

MIKHOELS, SOLOMON (originally SOLOMON VOVSI; born 1890 in Dvinsk, Russia [now Daugavpils, the Soviet Union]; died January 13, 1948, in Minsk, the Soviet Union). Yiddish stage actor. One of the original members of the State Jewish Theater in Moscow, he gained prominence with his performance in Aleichem's *Agents* (1921). After several years as the company's leading actor, he took over its directorship in 1928. He was especially renowned for his tragic and tragicomic roles, one of his most acclaimed achievements being his interpretation of the title role in a Yiddish version of Shakespeare's *King Lear* (1935). After World War II, when Jewish refugees were trying to settle or resettle in the Soviet Union, Mikhoels served as their spokesman with Soviet authorities. He was brutally murdered by the Soviet secret police, who, with the personal aid of Stalin, covered up the deed to look like an auto accident. Mikhoels's death was the first step in Stalin's attempt to liquidate all Jewish intellectuals and cultural institutions in the Soviet Union. In 1962 a Tel Aviv square was named after Mikhoels.

MILLER, MARTIN (originally RUDOLPH MULLER; born 1899 in Kremsier, Moravia [now Kroměříž, Czechoslovakia]; died August 26, 1969, in Austria). Character actor. He worked principally in Vienna and Berlin till moving to London in the late 1930s, sometimes appearing in the United States as well. Miller acted in some stage works, but he won international recognition through such films as *Exodus* (1960), *The Phantom of the Opera* (1962), and *The Pink Panther* (1964). He was noted for his portrayals of elderly Jews.

MIROSLAVA (full name, MIROSLAVA STERN; born February 26, 1926, in Prague, Czechoslovakia; died March 10, 1955, in Mexico City, Mexico). Popular leading lady in Mexico from the mid-1940s till her death, of suicide by poisoning. She also made a few English-language films, notably *The Brave Bulls* (1951).

MOGULESKO, SIGMUND (originally ZELIG MOGULESKO; born December 16, 1858, in Kaloraush, Bessarabia [now in the Soviet Union]; died February 4, 1914, in New York City, New York). Yiddish stage actor. In 1886 he settled in New York City, where he became the premier Yiddish comedian of his time.

MOODY, RON (originally RONALD MOODNICK; born January 8, 1924, in Hornsey, London, England). Versatile character comedian. He won his reputation mainly through his fantastic characters and disguises, notably as Fagin in the musical *Oliver!* on both stage (1960) and screen (1968). His other films included the Mel Brooks comedy *The Twelve Chairs* (1970) and the black comedy *Wrong Is Right* (1982).

MORRIS, HOWARD (born September 4, 1919, in New York City, New York). Comedy character actor. He was a regular on the TV variety series *Your Show of Shows* (1950-54) and *Caesar's Hour* (1954-57) and on the TV situation-comedy series *The Andy Griffith Show* (1960-68). His films included *The Nutty Professor* (1963), *Don't Drink the*

Water (1969), *Splash* (1984), and *Return to Mayberry* (TV, 1986). Morris is also a director.

MOSCOVITCH, MAURICE (original surname, MAASKOFF or MASSKOFF; born November 23, 1871, in Odessa, the Ukraine [now in the Soviet Union]; died June 18, 1940, in Los Angeles, California). Character actor. In 1893 he arrived in the United States, where he appeared in Yiddish and English plays. His films included *Winterset* (1936) and *The Great Dictator* (1940).

MUNSHIN, JULES (born February 22, 1915, in New York City, New York; died February 19, 1970, in New York City, New York). Rubber-limbed musical-comedy performer. His stage work included *Call Me Mister* (1946). Among his films were *Easter Parade* (1948), *On the Town* (1949), and *Silk Stockings* (1957).

MURRAY, JAN (originally MURRAY JANOFSKY; born October 4, 1917, in New York City, New York). Comedian and character actor. He is an excellent nightclub performer, though he is best known as host of several TV game shows. Murray had roles in *The Busy Body* (1967); *Which Way to the Front?* (1970); *History of the World, Part I* (1981); and other films.

MYERSON, BESS (born July 16, 1924, in New York City, New York). TV personality. Miss America of 1945, Myerson later became a fixture on TV, where she helped to host the game show *The Big Payoff* (1951-59), served as a panelist on *I've Got a Secret* (1958-68), and appeared on other programs. In 1983 she became cultural-affairs commissioner of New York City.

N

NAZIMOVA (full name, ALLA NAZIMOVA; original surname, LEVENTON; in her early years, in Russia, she used the surname ALEXANDROVNA; later, in America, NAZIMOVA; during her lifetime, many sources gave her family name as NAZIMOFF; born June 4, 1878 [sometimes given as 1879], in Yalta, Crimea, Russia; died July 13, 1945, in Los Angeles, California). Dark-featured, intense leading lady. She performed on the Russian stage till czarist censors prohibited her from doing the Zionist play *The Chosen People.* Leaving Russia, she acted in that work in Berlin and London before settling in the United States, where she debuted by giving a New York City performance, in Russian, as Lia in *The Chosen People.* Beginning in 1906 she acted in English-language plays or translations of plays, most effectively in those of Ibsen. She was highly praised for her creation of the role of Christine Mannon, the murderous wife, in the original production of O'Neill's *Mourning Becomes Electra* (1931). Nazimova also starred in silent movies, including *War Brides* (1916), *Camille* (1921), and *A Doll's House* (1922). Later she became an effective motion-picture character actress, especially as an aging Polish countess in *In Our Time* (1944). Her other late films included *Escape* (1940), *Blood and Sand* (1941), and *The Bridge of San Luis Rey* (1944).

NEILSON, JULIA (born June 12, 1868, in London, England; died May 27, 1957, in London, England). Stage actress. Daughter of a Jewish mother and non-Jewish father. She was a famous leading lady in London and on tours during the period 1900-1929, especially in romantic costume comedies.

NEWMAN, BARRY (born November 7, 1938, in Boston, Massachusetts). Leading man. He starred in the title role of the TV crime-drama series *Petrocelli* (1974-76). His films included *Pretty Boy Floyd* (1960), *Vanishing Point* (1971), *Second Sight: A Love Story* (TV, 1984), and *My Two Loves* (TV, 1986).

NEWMAN, PHYLLIS (born March 19, 1935, in Jersey City, New Jersey). Actress and TV personality. She performed in the New York City stage revue *I Feel Wonderful* (1954) and the movie *Picnic* (1956). Beginning in the late 1950s she earned her greatest fame for her appearances on TV game and talk shows. She also continued to act, as in the stage work *The Prisoner of Second Avenue* (1971) and the film *To Find a Man* (1972).

NICHOLS, MIKE (originally MICHAEL IGOR PESCHKOWSKY; born November 6, 1931, in Berlin, Germany). Comedian and character actor. In his youth he and Elaine May performed prepared and improvised comedy skits in nightclubs, on TV, and in the Broadway show *An Evening with Mike Nichols and Elaine May* (1960). Later he became a successful film director. In 1980 he and May reunited to star in a stage production of the explosive drama *Who's Afraid of Virginia Woolf?*

P

PARKS, LARRY (originally SAMUEL LAWRENCE KLAUSMAN PARKS; born December 13, 1914, in Olathe, Kansas; died April 13, 1975, in Studio City, California). Light leading man. After several years in B movies, he suddenly shot to stardom with his portrayal of Al Jolson in *The Jolson Story* (1946) and *Jolson Sings Again* (1949). His career was ruined in 1951 when he admitted before the House Un-American

To David
"Mendel"
It was wonderful
appearing with you
Lehitraot
Jan Peerce

Jan Peerce

Activities Committee that he had been a member of the Communist party from 1941 to 1945. After that, he did a small amount of nightclub and theater work; appeared in a few movies, such as *Freud* (1962); and then entered the real-estate business.

PEERCE, JAN (originally JACOB PINCUS PERELMUTH; born June 3, 1904, in New York City, New York; died December 15, 1984, in New Rochelle, New York). Great opera tenor who sang in several films and had a straight dramatic role in the movie *Goodbye, Columbus* (1969).

PELEG, ALEXANDER (born May 25, 1938, in Bucharest, Romania). He moved to Israel in 1952 and has been a member of the Habimah Theater since 1963. Among the plays in which he has made excellent impressions are Kafka's *The Castle* and Albee's *Who's Afraid of Virginia Woolf?* He has also performed the one-man shows *A Way of Life* and *Flowers for a White Mouse.*

PETERS, ROBERTA (originally ROBERTA PETERMAN; born May 4, 1930, in New York City, New York). Great opera soprano who had an important acting role in the movie *Tonight We Sing* (1953).

PICHEL, IRVING (born June 24, 1891, in Pittsburgh, Pennsylvania; died July 13, 1954, in Los Angeles, California). Character actor. He appeared in *An American Tragedy* (1931), *Oliver Twist* (1933), *Juarez* (1939), *Martin Luther* (1953), and many other films. Pichel was also an important movie director. He was blacklisted for a time during the McCarthy era.

PORAT, ORNA (original surname, PLACEK; born June 6, 1924, in Cologne, Germany). She has long been associated with Israel's Cameri Theater. In 1965 she cofounded the Cameri Children's Theater, of which she became the director. In 1970 she became the artistic director of the Theater for Youth and Children. Porat has performed onstage in Europe and Israel. She is well known for her performances of classics by Euripides, Shakespeare, and George Bernard Shaw. In the mid-1980s she gave a strong performance in the Israeli film *When Night Falls.*

PREMINGER, OTTO (born December 5, 1906, in Vienna, Austria; died April 23, 1986, in New York City, New York). A major film director, he also acted in a few movies, notably as the German commandant of a World War II prisoner-of-war camp in *Stalag 17* (1953).

Roberta Peters

R

RACHEL (originally ELISABETH FELIX; born February 28, 1821, in Mumpf, Switzerland; died January 3, 1858, in Le Cannet, France). Leading lady. A world-famous star at the Comédie-Française in Paris, she played tragic roles in plays by Racine, Corneille, and others. In 1855 she made an American tour.

★★★

REEVE, ADA (born March 3, 1874, in London, England; died September 25, 1966, in London, England). Character actress. She was a popular music-hall and musical-comedy performer in the late 1800s and early 1900s. Later she acted in plays, such as *The Shop at Sly Corner* (1945), and in some movies, including *They Came to a City* (1944) and *The Passionate Stranger* (1957, G.B.; U.S., *A Novel Affair).* At the age of ninety she was still appearing on TV.

REINER, CARL (born March 20, 1922, in New York City, New York). Comedy actor. He played roles on the TV variety series *Your Show of Shows* (1950-54) and *Caesar's Hour* (1954-57) and on the TV comedy series *The Dick Van Dyke Show* (1961-66). His films included *It's a Mad, Mad, Mad, Mad World* (1963); *The Russians Are Coming, the Russians Are Coming* (1966); *The End* (1978); *Skokie* (TV, 1981); and *Dead Men Don't Wear Plaid* (1982). For many years he has also been active as a writer, producer, and director. He is the father of the comedy actor Rob(ert) Reiner, who played Mike ("Meathead") Stivic on the TV comedy series *All in the Family* (1971-78).

RITZ BROTHERS. Family of comedians consisting of AL (originally ALFRED; born August 27, 1901, in Newark, New Jersey; died December 22, 1965, in New Orleans, Louisiana), JIM (originally SAMUEL; born October 22, 1904, in Newark, New Jersey; died November 17, 1985, in Los Angeles, California), and HARRY (born 1906 or 1908 in Newark, New Jersey; died March 29, 1986, in San Diego, California). Their original surname was JOACHIM. They took their zany slapstick humor to vaudeville and then appeared in a number of movies in the late 1930s and early 1940s, including *On the Avenue* (1937), *The Goldwyn Follies* (1938), *The Three Musketeers* (1939), and *Behind the Eight Ball* (1942). Later they played nightclubs and TV till Al's death, after which Jim and Harry semiretired. They made a cameo appearance in the film *Won Ton Ton, the Dog Who Saved Hollywood* (1976), and Harry had a small part in *Silent Movie* (1976). Harry, the team's leader, greatly influenced other comedians: he encouraged Milton Berle's wearing of dresses on TV, he introduced the scat singing later emulated by Danny Kaye, and he employed some mannerisms that were adopted by Jerry Lewis.

RIVERS, JOAN (originally JOAN MOLINSKY; born June 8, 1933 [some sources give 1935 or 1937], in New York City, New York). Comedienne. A brash nightclub performer, she made her TV debut in 1965 on *The Tonight Show,* which she frequently guest-hosted from 1983 to 1986. In 1986 she took over her own TV late-night talk show on the new Fox Broadcasting Company network.

ROSENBLOOM, MAXIE ("SLAPSIE MAXIE") (born September 6, 1904, in New York City, New York; died March 6, 1976, in South Pasadena, California). Comedy character actor. An ex-boxer, he appeared in many films, often as a gangster or a punch-drunk fighter. His movies included *Nothing Sacred* (1937), *Louisiana Purchase* (1941), *Hollywood or Bust* (1956), and *Cottonpickin' Chickenpickers* (1967).

ROTH, LILLIAN (father's original surname, Rutstein; born December 13, 1910, in Boston, Massachusetts; died May 12, 1980, in New York City, New York). Singing actress. She entered show business when she was a small child; and soon she became a major star on Broadway, as in the 1928 and 1931 editions of the *Earl Carroll Vanities,* and in movies, such as *The Love Parade* (1929), *Animal Crackers* (1930), *Madam Satan* (1930), and *Take a Chance* (1933). But then her career collapsed for nearly two decades as she struggled against alcoholism and mental illness. In her book *I'll Cry Tomorrow* (with Mike Connolly and Gerold Frank, 1954), she movingly told the story of her return to a healthy life and an active career. The book was turned into a powerful 1955 movie. In 1958 she came out with another autobiographical book, *Beyond My Worth.* Among her later performances were a Broadway appearance in *I Can Get It for You Wholesale* (1962) and a small but effective role as a lonely Jewish widow in the movie *Boardwalk* (1979).

ROVINA, HANNA (born 1888 in Minsk, Russia; died 1980 in Israel). In 1917 she helped Nahum Zemach to found the Habimah Theater in Moscow. The company's first great success was the Hebrew version of Ansky's *The Dybbuk* (1922), in which she starred as Leah, a role that she subsequently played many times. Another important role in her career was that of the mother of the Messiah in *The Eternal Jew* (from 1925 on). She and the company appeared in Palestine in 1928 and then, after a European tour, permanently settled in the Holy Land in 1931. Possessing great beauty and dignity, Rovina made an excellent classical heroine, as in Euripides' *Medea.* Later in her career she turned to mature motherly roles, as in Brecht's *Mother Courage.*

SAHL, MORT(ON) (born May 11, 1927, in Montreal, Canada). Comedian and character actor. As a sardonic political-satire comedian, he peaked in popularity in the early 1960s. He also acted in several films, including *All the Young Men* (1960) and *Inside the Third Reich* (TV, 1982).

SALES, SOUPY (originally MILTON SUPMAN; born January 8, 1926, in Franklinton, near Wake Forest, North Carolina). Comedian and comedy character actor. He acquired his nickname, Soupy, from his childhood playmates who punned it from his family name, Supman. For a brief time early in his career he used the surname Hines (from which came the erroneous story that his nickname was derived by punning *Hines* with *Heinz*, the name of a well-known food-processing company). Sales hosted many local and national youth-oriented shows featuring jokes, puppets (including White Fang and Black Tooth), and pies in the face. He had local shows in Detroit (1953), Los Angeles (late 1950s), and New York City (1964); later his work was syndicated. But he reached the peak of his popularity when *The Soupy Sales Show* was nationally telecast from 1959 to 1962. Sales acted in a few movies, including *Birds Do It* (1966).

SATZ, LUDWIG (born 1891 in Lemberg, Galicia [now Lvov, the Soviet Union]; died August 31, 1944, in New York City, New York). Yiddish comedian. He appeared in the first Yiddish film made with sound: *His Wife's Lover* (1932).

SCHILDKRAUT, RUDOLF (born 1865 in Constantinople [now İstanbul], Turkey; died July 15, 1930, in Los Angeles, California). Leading man. Father of the actor Joseph Schildkraut. Rudolf had major stage careers in both Germany and the United States, performing in German, English, and Yiddish. He won fame for his Shakespearean roles of Shylock and King Lear. Schildkraut also acted in some silent films, such as *Proud Heart* (1925) and *Christina* (1929).

SCHLAMME, MARTHA (originally MARTHA HAFTEL; born about 1925 in Vienna, Austria; died October 6, 1985, in Jamestown, New York). Singing actress. Her first marriage was to a man named Hans Schlamme, whose surname she kept for professional use even after their union ended in annulment. In her concert appearances, she sang Jewish and other folksongs. She also acted in plays by Shakespeare and Sholom Aleichem. Schlamme made her Broadway debut in the musical *Fiddler on the Roof* (1968).

SCHREIBER, AVERY (born April 9, 1935, in Chicago, Illinois). Comedian and comedy character actor. Early in his career he worked with Jack Burns. Schreiber had a role on the TV comedy series *My Mother the Car* (1965-66), cohosted the TV variety series *The Burns and Schreiber Comedy Hour* (1973), appeared regularly on the TV variety series *Sha Na Na* (1977-78), and performed as a guest on many other TV shows, particularly in skits featuring him as a New York City cabdriver. Schreiber also had roles in several movies, including *Don't Drink the Water* (1969), *The Last Remake of Beau Geste* (1977), and *Silent Scream* (1980).

SCHWARTZ, MAURICE (originally AVROM MOISHE SCHWARTZ; born June 15, 1889, in Sudilkov, the Ukraine [now in the Soviet Union]; died May 10, 1960, in Tel Aviv, Israel). Yiddish stage actor. In the early 1900s he immigrated to the United States, where he directed and acted in over 150 plays in his own Yiddish Art Theater. Among his most admired performances were those as Shylock in Shakespeare's *The Merchant of Venice* and the title role, as an aging Hasidic rabbi, in *Yoshe Kalb*. Some of his stage performances were filmed for limited circulation. He also appeared in Hollywood's *Salome* (1953). Schwartz died while on tour in Israel.

SEGAL, SHMUEL (born 1924 in Poland). At the age of ten he moved to Palestine. With Shmuel Rodensky he formed a famous artistic partnership known as the Shmuliks. Segal has also given one-man performances on both the stage and the radio, and he has issued recordings in Hebrew and Yiddish.

SHAW, ARTIE (originally ABRAHAM ISAAC ARSHAWSKY; born May 23, 1910, in New York City, New York). Jazz clarinetist and bandleader who acted in a couple of movies, notably *Second Chorus* (1940).

Artie Shaw

★★★

SHAWN, DICK (originally RICHARD SCHULEFAND; born December 1, 1929, in Buffalo, New York; died April 17, 1987, in San Diego, California). Comedian and character actor. He had roles in many stage works, such as *I'm Solomon* (1968) and *The World of Sholom Aleichem* (1976). His films included *Wake Me When It's Over* (1960); *It's a Mad, Mad, Mad, Mad World* (1963); *The Producers* (1967); *Fast Friends* (TV, 1979); and *Angel* (1984).

SHEAN, AL (original surname, SCHOENBERG or SCHÖNBERG; born May 12, 1868, in Dornum, Germany; died August 12, 1949, in New York City, New York). Comedian and character actor. He and Ed(ward) Gallagher formed one of vaudeville's most popular comedy teams (1910-12, 1920-25). In 1921 they first performed their famous song "Mr. Gallagher and Mr. Shean." Shean also worked on his own in vaudeville and in Broadway musical comedies. Later in his career he played character roles in films, such as *San Francisco* (1936), *The Prisoner of Zenda* (1937), and *Atlantic City* (1944). He was an uncle of the Marx Brothers comedy team, their mother, Minnie, being Shean's sister.

SHERMAN, ALLAN (originally ALLAN COPELON; born November 30, 1924, in Chicago, Illinois; died November 20, 1973, in Los Angeles, California). Comedian. After beginning as a writer, he turned performer and issued the album *My Son, the Folksinger* (1962), a folksong travesty in Jewish style. Perhaps his greatest success came with his rendition of the song "Hello, Muddah; Hello Fadduh" (in his album *My Son, the Nut,* 1963), in which Sherman applied comical lyrics to a melody called "Dance of the Hours" from Ponchielli's 1876 opera *La Gioconda.*

SHUSTER, FRANK. *See* WAYNE AND SHUSTER.

SIDNEY, GEORGE (originally SAMMY GREENFIELD; born March 18, 1876, in New York City, New York; died April 29, 1945, in Los Angeles, California). One of America's leading vaudeville comedians. Later he became a fine comic actor in films, particularly as Abe Potash in *Potash and Perlmutter* (1923) and as Jacob Cohen in *The Cohens and the Kellys* (1926). Both films generated sequels starring Sidney, such as *In Hollywood with Potash and Perlmutter* (1924) and *The Cohens and the Kellys in Trouble* (1933).

SIMON, PAUL (born October 13, 1941, in Newark, New Jersey). The popular singer played a small nonsinging role in Woody Allen's film *Annie Hall* (1977) and starred in his own *One-Trick Pony* (1980).

SKULNIK, MENASHA (born May 15, 1892, in Warsaw, Poland; died June 4, 1970, in New York City, New York). Comedian. After working on the European Yiddish stage, he immigrated to the United States and performed as a leading member of the Yiddish Art Theater (1930-50). His English-language work included roles in the TV series *Menasha the Magnificent* (1950) and *The Goldbergs* (1953). He also performed on Broadway, notably as Noah in *The Flowering Peach* (1954). Skulnik was a sad-looking comedian, famous for his ludicrous shrugs.

SMITH AND DALE. Comedy team consisting of JOE SMITH (originally JOSEPH SULTZER; born February 16, 1884, in New York City, New York; died February 22, 1981, in Englewood, New Jersey) and CHARLIE DALE (originally CHARLES MARKS; born September 6, 1881, in New York City, New York; died November 16, 1971, in Teaneck, New Jersey). Famous in vaudeville, they also appeared in some movies, including *Manhattan Parade* (1931) and *Two Tickets to Broadway* (1951). Smith got the punch lines, while Dale was the deadpan straight man.

STANG, ARNOLD (born September 28, 1925, in Chelsea, Massachusetts). Comedy character actor, known for his hilariously weak chin. In the 1950s he was a mainstay on Milton Berle's TV variety shows. Stang also appeared regularly on the TV comedy series *The Goldbergs* (1954-55) and occasionally on the TV comedy series *December Bride* (1954-59). His films included *The Man with the Golden Arm* (1955), *The Wonderful World of the Brothers Grimm* (1962), *Hercules in New York* (1970), and *Raggedy Ann and Andy* (1977).

STEINBERG, DAVID (born August 9, 1942, in Winnipeg, Canada). Comedian and character actor. An excellent stand-up comedian, he has performed on many top TV talk and variety shows. He acted in the films *The End* (1978) and *Something Short of Paradise* (1979). Steinberg has recently turned to movie direction as well.

STERN, ISAAC (born July 21, 1920, in Kremenets, the Soviet Union). Great concert violinist who acted the role of Eugène Ysaÿe in the movie *Tonight We Sing* (1953).

STEWART, ELAINE (originally ELSY STEINBERG; born May 31, 1929, in Montclair, New Jersey). Beautiful leading lady and supporting actress. Her films included *The Bad and the Beautiful* (1952), *Brigadoon* (1954), *The Tattered Dress* (1957), and *The Rise and Fall of Legs Diamond* (1960).

STORCH, LARRY (originally LAWRENCE STORCH; born January 8, 1923, in New York City, New York). Comedy character actor. He began as a nightclub comedian and impressionist and then appeared in a few Broadway productions in the 1950s. He is best known, however, for his work on TV, especially in the comedy series *F Troop* (1965-67). His films included *Captain Newman, M.D.* (1963); *The Great Race* (1965); and *The Adventures of Huckleberry Finn* (TV, 1981).

STRASBERG, LEE (born November 17, 1901, in Budanov, Austria-Hungary [now in the Soviet Union]; died February 17, 1982, in New York City, New York). Character actor, as in the films *The Godfather, Part II* (1974) and *Skokie* (TV, 1981). Better known as artistic director of the Actors Studio in New York City (1948-82), where his pupils included Marlon Brando, Julie Harris, and many other major acting talents.

STRAUSS, PETER (born February 20, 1947, in Croton-on-Hudson, New York). Leading man. He is best known for his

★★★

Paul Simon (left) and Art Garfunkel (right)

T

Isaac Stern

appearances in TV movies and miniseries, such as *Attack on Terror: The FBI versus the Ku Klux Klan* (TV, 1975); *Rich Man, Poor Man* (TV, 1976); *Masada* (TV, 1981); *Heart of Steel* (TV, 1983); *Kane and Abel* (TV, 1985); and *Under Siege* (TV, 1986).

STRAUSS, ROBERT (full name, HENRY ROBERT STRAUSS; born November 8, 1913, in New York City, New York; died February 20, 1975, in New York City, New York). Character actor, often as comic heavies. His stage work included *Detective Story* (1949). He is best remembered for his role as Animal in the movie *Stalag 17* (1953). Among his other films were *Sailor Beware* (1952), *The Seven Year Itch* (1955), and *The Family Jewels* (1965).

SUSSKIND, DAVID (born December 19, 1920, in New York City, New York; found dead February 22, 1987, in New York City, New York). Host of a provocative TV talk show from 1958 to 1986, originally called *Open End*, later *The David Susskind Show*. Also an important producer.

TAYLOR, KENT (originally LOUIS WEISS; born May 11, 1907, in Nashua, Iowa; died April 11, 1987, in Los Angeles, California). Suave leading man. Among his best pictures were *Death Takes a Holiday* (1934), *Ramona* (1936), *I'm Still Alive* (1940), and *Playgirl* (1954). He also appeared on TV, notably in the title role of the popular mystery series *Boston Blackie* (1951-53). His later movies were low-budget horror pictures, such as *The Crawling Hand* (1963), and melodramas, including *Hell's Bloody Devils* (1970), in which he played a neo-Nazi leader.

TAYLOR, RENEE (original surname, WEXLER; born March 19, 1945, in New York City, New York). Actress and playwright. She has appeared in stage works, such as *The Rehearsal* (1952) and *The Third Ear* (1964), and in movies, including *The Errand Boy* (1961) and *The Producers* (1967). Taylor frequently coauthors and costars with her husband, Joseph Bologna, as in the films *Made for Each Other* (1971) and *Woman of the Year* (TV, 1976).

TEOMI, ODED (born 1937 in Tel Aviv, Palestine [now Israel]). He has acted onstage at Israel's principal theaters, including the Ohel, the Zavit, the Cameri, and the Habimah. Among his many Israeli films was *Hem hayu eser* (1960; U.S., *They Were Ten*).

THOMASHEFSKY, BORIS (born May 12, 1868, in Kiev, the Ukraine [now in the Soviet Union]; died July 9, 1939, in New York City, New York). Actor, playwright, producer, and impresario. In 1881 he immigrated to the United States. With his first wife, Bessie Kaufman, he became one of the founders of the American Yiddish theater. He reverently staged Yiddish versions of classics, such as Shakespeare and Goethe. However, possessing a flamboyant personality, he preferred to play in farce, musical comedy, and light romantic works. His second wife, Rebecca Zuckerberg, was, like Bessie, an actress.

THREE STOOGES. Comedy team initially consisting of MOE HOWARD (originally MOSES HORWITZ; born June 19, 1897, in New York City, New York; died May 4, 1975, in Los Angeles, California), his brother SHEMP HOWARD (originally SAMUEL HORWITZ; born March 17, 1900, in New York City, New York; died November 22, 1955, in Los Angeles, California), and LARRY FINE (originally LOUIS FINEBURG; born October 5, 1911, in Philadelphia, Pennsylvania; died January 24, 1975, in Woodland Hills, California). They worked in vaudeville with Ted Healy in an act called Ted Healy and His Stooges. In 1930 they began their film career with Healy. But soon they broke away to make short movies on their own. In the early 1930s Shemp left the team, and he was replaced by his brother CURLY HOWARD (originally JEROME LESTER HORWITZ; born 1906 in New York City, New York; died January 19, 1952, in San Gabriel, Califor-

★★

Three Stooges: Larry (left), Moe (center), and Curly (right)

★★

nia). While Shemp was on his own, he appeared in many films, notably the W. C. Fields comedy classic *The Bank Dick* (1940). When Curly retired in 1947 because of ill health, Shemp returned to the team. After Shemp's death in 1955, he was replaced by others for the last decade of the team's existence. Making numerous short films and a few features, the Three Stooges became world famous for their slapstick clowning in the old burlesque-vaudeville tradition.

TOMACK, SID(NEY) (born 1907 in New York City, New York; died November 12, 1962, in Palm Springs, California). Character actor with a rich Brooklyn accent. Tomack appeared in many movies, including *A Double Life* (1948), *Force of Evil* (1948), and *Sail a Crooked Ship* (1962). He was a familiar face on early TV series, playing Jim Gillis, Riley's neighbor, in the first version of *The Life of Riley* (1949-50); Al, the con man, in *My Friend Irma* (1952-53); and Knobby Walsh, the boxing manager, in *The Joe Palooka Story* (syndicated 1954).

TOPOL (full name, CHAIM [or HAIM] TOPOL; born September 9, 1935, in Tel Aviv, Palestine [now Israel]). He gained his first acting experience when he performed onstage with the Israeli army entertainment unit in the 1950s. Later he acted in plays at the Haifa Municipal Theater. He also began to appear in Israeli movies, including *Sallah Shabati* (1964; U.S., *Sallah*). Soon he was invited to participate in British and American films, such as *Cast a Giant Shadow* (1966), *Before Winter Comes* (1969), *Fiddler on the Roof* (1971), *Flash Gordon* (1980), and *The Winds of War* (TV, 1983). In the mid-1980s he starred in the Israeli movie *Roman be'hemschechim* (U.S., *Serial*).

Topol

V

VIGODA, ABE (born February 24, 1921, in New York City, New York). Character actor. He is best known as Sergeant Phil Fish in the TV comedy series *Barney Miller* (1975-77), a role that he continued in his own series, *Fish* (1977-78). Vigoda labored for many years as a fairly obscure stage figure, appearing in New York City productions of *Richard II* (1961), *The Man in the Glass Booth* (1968), and other plays. He first attracted major attention with his role as a loyal but dull-witted gangster in the movie *The Godfather* (1972). His other films included *The Cheap Detective* (1978) and *Gridlock* (TV, 1980). In 1986 he appeared in a New York City revival of the classic comedy *Arsenic and Old Lace*.

VOSKOVEC, GEORGE (original first name, JIŘÍ; born June 19, 1905, in Sázava, Bohemia [now in Czechoslovakia]; died July 1, 1981, in Pearblossom, California). Excellent character actor. He won immense fame in Czechoslovakia as part of the comedy team Voskovec and (Jan) Werich, performing satiric revues and plays aimed at Hitler and Nazism. In 1939 the Nazi onslaught forced him out of his homeland, and he moved to the United States. After World War II he returned to Czechoslovakia, where he proceeded to aim his satire at the new regime—the Communists. Again he was expelled from his native land, finally settling permanently in America in the early 1950s. Voskovec turned to straight dramatic acting and became one of the best character actors of his time on both stage and screen. He was especially fond of Chekhov and Shakespeare, making his New York City debut in the latter's romantic drama *The Tempest* (1945). Voskovec played Mr. Frank in a London production of *The Diary of Anne Frank* (1956). His other stage work included *The Love of Four Colonels* (1953), *Brecht on Brecht* (1961), and *Cabaret* (1968). Among his films were *The World Is Ours* (1939), *Twelve Angry Men* (1957), *The Spy Who Came In from the Cold* (1965), *The Iceman Cometh* (1973), and *Barbarosa* (1982).

★★

W

WALBROOK, ANTON (originally ADOLF ANTON WILHELM WOHLBRÜCK; born November 19, 1900, in Vienna, Austria; died August 9, 1967, in Munich, West Germany). Elegant leading man. Descended from a long line of circus clowns, he broke family tradition by entering the legitimate German-language theater. He was also a popular romantic star in German-language movies, such as *Maskerade* ("Masquerade," 1934). In the late 1930s he moved to England, where he appeared onstage in *Design for Living* (1939), *Watch on the Rhine* (1942), and other plays, including the musical *Call Me Madam* (1953). But he won his greatest distinction for a variety of roles in a number of well-known movies, such as *Victoria the Great* (1937), as the misunderstood Prince Albert; *Dangerous Moonlight* (1941, G.B.; U.S., *Suicide Squadron),* as a romantic flyer-pianist playing the *Warsaw Concerto; The Life and Death of Colonel Blimp* (1943), as a "good German"; *The Red Shoes* (1948), as a sinister ballet impresario; *Wien tanzt* (1951, Austria; U.S., *Vienna Waltzes),* as the composer Johann Strauss, Sr.; and *I Accuse!* (1958), as Major Esterhazy, the spy whose acts brought about the persecution of the Jewish officer Alfred Dreyfus.

WARFIELD, DAVID (originally DAVID WOLLFELD; born November 28, 1866, in San Francisco, California; died June 27, 1951, in New York City, New York). Stage actor. While playing only a handful of roles over and over again, he came to be regarded as the greatest American actor of the first quarter of the twentieth century. In the 1890s he played comic Jewish characters in burlesque theaters. He was raised to national celebrity when, at the turn of the century, the famed producer David Belasco signed him to play Simon Levi, a Lower East Side peddler, in *The Auctioneer.* Perhaps Warfield's greatest role was as Anton von Barwig, who searches for his long-lost daughter, in *The Music Master.* That play and Warfield's other principal vehicles were produced by Belasco.

WAYNE AND SHUSTER. Comedy team consisting of JOHNNY WAYNE (original surname, WEINGARTEN; born 1918 in Toronto, Canada) and FRANK SHUSTER (born 1916 in Toronto, Canada). Working on radio and TV, they became perhaps the only performers of international fame based almost solely in Canada.

WEBER AND FIELDS. Comedy team consisting of JOE WEBER (full name, JOSEPH MORRIS WEBER; born August 11, 1867, in New York City, New York; died May 10, 1942, in Los Angeles, California) and LEW FIELDS (originally LEWIS MAURICE SCHANFIELD; born January 1, 1867, in New York City, New York; died July 20, 1941, in Los Angeles, California). They teamed up as children and developed a German-Yiddish dialect act. At the turn of the century they were top burlesque comedians. They also appeared in vaudeville, musical comedies, and movies, including *Friendly Enemies* (1925).

Y

YADIN, YOSEPH (or JOSEPH/YOSEF/YOSSI YADIN; original surname, SUKENIK; born June 7, 1920, in Jerusalem, Palestine [now Israel]). He was a cofounder of the Cameri Theater, where he had leading roles in many plays, such as *Kasablan* and *Of Mice and Men.* Yadin appeared in Israel's first important feature film, *Hill 24 Doesn't Answer* (1955). He also acted in the European movies *Four in a Jeep* (1951) and *Stop Train 349* (1964), the Canadian picture *Lies My Father Told Me* (1975), and other films.

YOUNGMAN, HENNY (originally HENRY YOUNGMAN; born January 12, 1906, in Liverpool, England). Comedian and character actor. Born in England while his American-citizen parents were there on an extended honeymoon, he grew up in Brooklyn. He is a popular nightclub, TV, and banquet performer noted for his one-liners, such as "Take my wife—please!" Youngman made the comedy recording *Take My Album—Please* (1978). His films included *Silent Movie* (1976) and *History of the World, Part I* (1981).

Z

ZIMBALIST, EFREM, JR. (born November 30, 1918, in New York City, New York). Leading man. He won his greatest fame by starring in the TV detective series *77 Sunset Strip* (1958-64) and the TV crime-drama series *The F.B.I.* (1965-74). His stage work included *Hedda Gabler* (1948). Among his films were *The Chapman Report* (1962), *Airport 1975* (1974), and *Shooting Stars* (TV, 1983). He is the son of the violinist Efrem Zimbalist, Sr., and the singer Alma Gluck.

★★

Index

★★★

★★★

★★

About the Author

Darryl Lyman coedited *Fifty Golden Years of Oscar* (1979), the official history of the Academy of Motion Picture Arts and Sciences. He is coauthor (with Marjorie D. Lewis) of the college textbook *Essential English* (1981) and the author of *The Animal Things We Say* (1983) and *Great Jews in Music* (1986). His shorter works have appeared in such periodicals as *Newsday* and *Jack and Jill.*

★★